DISCOVERY OF PSYCHOANALYSIS

The Politics of Hysteria

William J. McGrath

Freud's Discovery of Psychoanalysis traces the historical roots of an idea that has had an incalculable impact on twentieth-century thought and culture by examining the interplay of Freud's inner life—his phantasies and dreams—with the world around him.

In this accomplished biographical interpretation, William J. McGrath looks at the development of Freud's thought in relation to the times in which he lived. Drawing on new documentary evidence, he traces Freud's intellectual evolution from childhood to the period at the turn of the century when he laid down the theoretical foundations of psychoanalysis in *The Interpretation of Dreams*. McGrath paints a compelling psychological portrait of Freud against the backdrop of fin-de-siècle Vienna, showing how the accelerating disintegration of the Habsburg empire and the rise of virulent nationalism and anti-Semitism interacted with religious traditions, scientific advances, and philosophical and literary currents to shape Freud's ideas. In a close and cogent reinterpretation of Freud's childhood phantasies, adolescent aspirations, and adult dreams, McGrath seeks to show that Freud's lifelong preoccupation with contemporary political and cultural developments played an important role in his major theoretical breakthroughs, in particular the abandonment of the seduction theory for a view in which the power of phantasy was central.

(continued on back flap)

FREUD'S DISCOVERY OF PSYCHOANALYSIS

By the same author:

Dionysian Art and Populist Politics in Austria

· William J. McGrath ·

FREUD'S DISCOVERY OF PSYCHOANALYSIS

THE POLITICS OF HYSTERIA

Cornell University Press | ITHACA AND LONDON

First published 1986 by Cornell University Press.

Library of Congress Cataloging-in-Publication Data

McGrath, William J., 1937–
Freud's discovery of psychoanalysis.

Bibliography: p. 322
Includes index.
1. Psychoanalysis—History. 2. Freud, Sigmund, 1856–1939. 3. Psychoanalysts—Austria—Biography. I. Freud, Sigmund, 1856–1939. II. Title. [DNLM: 1. Psychoanalysis—biography. 2. Psychoanalysis—history. WZ 100 M478f]
BF173.F85M226 1986 150.19'52 85-47704
ISBN 0-8014-1770-8 (alk. paper)

Printed in the United States of America

The paper in this book is acid-free and meets the guidelines for permanence and durability of the Committee on Production Guidelines for Book Longevity of the Council on Library Resources.

For Stephanie, Jennifer, and Katherine

Contents

Acknowledgments

My work on this book has received support from a wide variety of sources. A summer stipend from the National Endowment for the Humanities facilitated the early stages of research and formulation by making it possible for me to locate and make use of important documentary materials bearing on Freud's travels and his early years in Vienna. A subsequent leave made possible by the University of Rochester and a fellowship for independent study and research from the National Endowment for the Humanities allowed me to carry out additional research in Europe and provided the free time necessary to complete much of the writing.

Among the many scholars to whom I am indebted, I am particularly grateful to Carl Schorske. We began our work on the historical significance of Freud's dreams in common, and his insight, encouragement, and criticism have been of the greatest importance to my understanding of the relationship between Freud's thought and its historical context. In pursuing the psychohistorical aspect of my subject I have profited greatly from the writings and the advice of Peter Loewenberg, whose pioneering essays have explored the creative process at work in many of the central personalities of Freud's time. My consideration of religious influences on Freud's development has been most generously assisted by my colleague Abraham J. Karp, who shared with me his vast knowledge of Jewish religion and culture. Klemens von Klemperer has helped me not only with his detailed knowledge of Austrian politics and institutions but also with warm encouragement of my earliest attempts to formulate this project. My conversations with Dennis Klein and Ian Dowbiggin, drawing on their work on the history of psychoanalysis and psychiatry, have enriched my understanding of the cultural and scientific context of Freud's thought.

My work on Freud's Gymnasium and university years has profited considerably from my ability to draw on heretofore neglected or unavailable documentary materials. I am indebted to the late Anna Freud for her support and assistance in helping me obtain access to Freud's Gymnasium records, and I am particularly grateful to Peter Swales for his extraordinary generosity in making available to me a wide range of important materials that he had unearthed.

Attempting to trace the history of Freud's discoveries has made it necessary for me to study the theoretical structure and assumptions of psychoanalysis while also attempting to grasp its essential meaning from within. I owe F. Gordon Pleune the greatest possible debt of gratitude for his help in this process of objective and subjective education. Without his instruction, advice, and criticism this book could never have been written. I also thank the members of the Psycho-Dynamic Study Group for the help they gave individually and collectively to my attempts at understanding the relationship between history and psychoanalysis.

Over the years that I worked on this project I found that being able to discuss it with my close friends proved to be of the greatest importance, and I thank them for their support and indulgence. Dick Kaeuper's psychological sensitivity and keen-sighted realism have helped me over many a hurdle along the way. My discussions with Ed Berenson and Tom Cole provided valuable assistance on particular points of interpretation as well as on general historical perspective. On the various research trips required by my project I enjoyed the material and intellectual hospitality of Marilyn Sargent and Gene Taback in California as well as that of Micki Somerman and Philip Zawa in Chicago. I also owe particular thanks to Russell O'Geen for the many ways in which he has been helpful to me. Through my friendship with him and our many conversations I have learned much of value to my understanding of psychological development.

The encouragement of my wife, Stephanie Frontz, has been an invaluable support to my work. I profited not only from her willingness to understand my deep preoccupation with it but also from her efforts to divert me from it at appropriate moments. Her sympathy, patience, and vitality have provided the reinforcement necessary to complete this complex intellectual and emotional undertaking.

I am deeply grateful to Jean DeGroat for the many hours she has labored over the manuscript of this book. From the initial task of deciphering my barely legible handwriting to the final stage of the fully processed word, her careful attention has played a vital role. Finally, I would like to express my appreciation to Kay Scheuer for the skill and sensitivity she brought to the editing of the manuscript.

Copyright material has been reproduced with the permission of the firms and institutions indicated, to which I am grateful:

From *The Interpretation of Dreams,* by Sigmund Freud, translated and edited by James Strachey. Published in the United States by Basic Books, Inc., by arrangement with George Allen & Unwin Ltd and The Hogarth Press, Ltd. Reprinted by permission of Basic Books, Inc., Publishers, and by permission of George Allen & Unwin Ltd.

From *The Robbers* by Friedrich Schiller, from Schiller: *The Robbers* and *Wallenstein,* translated by F. J. Lamport (Penguin Classics, 1979). Copyright © F. J. Lamport, 1979. Reprinted by permission of Penguin Books Ltd.

From Goethe, *Faust:* Part Two, translated by Philip Wayne (Penguin Classics, 1959). Copyright © the Estate of Philip Wayne, 1959. Reprinted by permission of Penguin Books Ltd.

From "Mahler and Freud: The Dream of the Stately House," by William J. McGrath, from *Beiträge '79–81 der Österreichischen Gesellschaft für Musik, Gustav Mahler Kolloquium 1979,* edited by Rudolf Klein (Kassel: Bärenreiter-Verlag, 1981). Reprinted by permission of Bärenreiter-Verlag.

From "Freud as Hannibal: The Politics of the Brother Band," by William J. McGrath, *Central European History,* 7 (March 1974). Reprinted by permission of Emory University.

Excerpts from Freud's unpublished letters to Eduard Silberstein. Printed by permission of Sigmund Freud Copyrights Ltd., Colchester, England.

WILLIAM J. MCGRATH

Rochester, New York

FREUD'S DISCOVERY OF PSYCHOANALYSIS

Introduction

In May 1899, when Sigmund Freud decided to resume his long-postponed effort to complete *The Interpretation of Dreams,* he wrote to his friend Wilhelm Fliess: "So the dream [book] will be. That this Austria is supposed to perish in the next two weeks made my decision easier. Why should the dream [book] perish with it?"[1] Even though his ironic estimate of Austria's durability was not borne out, Freud's sense of impending political disintegration was well founded. The bitter divisions over language, nationality, and class that beset the Habsburg Empire seemed to threaten its existence repeatedly in the closing years of the nineteenth century, when Freud was engaged in what proved to be his most important scientific project. His comment, setting the writing of his book against the background of these destructive forces, hints at an important truth about the relationship between his work and the times in which he lived. It points to the underlying role of political pressures in propelling him toward a discovery of the greatest significance to twentieth-century culture.

By describing Freud's accomplishment as a discovery rather than as theory or invention, I express my own conviction that his work represents a fundamentally important advance in the understanding of human nature. At the same time my subtitle, "the politics of hysteria," indicates a complementary belief that his ideas were profoundly influenced by the political conditions of his day. Taking

[1] Sigmund Freud, *The Complete Letters of Sigmund Freud to Wilhelm Fliess, 1887–1904* (hereafter *Complete Letters*), trans. and ed. Jeffrey Moussaieff Masson (Cambridge: The Belknap Press of Harvard University Press, 1985), p. 353. The first bracketed word is the editor's; for the sake of clarity I have repeated it. Freud often referred to his dream book simply as *der Traum* (the dream).

the word "politics" in its broadest, classical sense—meaning the affairs of the city and thus by extension of the outer world in general—I have given it great prominence in this book. Although the popular notion of scientific discovery is often that of a lonely scientist working in isolation from any influences which might perturb his search for pure truth, Freud himself seems to have seen his work in a different light. As he observed in an 1897 letter to Fliess, "one always remains a child of his age, even in what one deems one's very own."[2] My emphasis on the role of politics in Freud's life should thus be seen as an attempt to show how certain historical influences helped give rise to his scientific discoveries.

In exploring the historical origins of Freud's creativity I have focused on the interplay between his inner world of dreams and phantasies and the outer influences of family situation, religious tradition, educational background, and socio-political environment. Because dreams and phantasies have a multitemporal nature, subjecting them to historical analysis requires many forward and backward glances, but I have used the evidence that they offer to trace a carefully chronological line of development from Freud's childhood, adolescence, and student days through his early professional life to the period from 1897 to 1900 when he wrote *The Interpretation of Dreams,* the book that established the intellectual foundations of psychoanalysis. Freud developed and explained his method of dream interpretation primarily with dreams of his own which occurred during these years, dreams which had served as the primary vehicle for his self-analysis, and in recounting and analyzing them he has left historians an extremely rare and valuable body of evidence for studying the emergence of a fundamentally important scientific theory. To the extent that they bear on his work these dreams offer evidence of both the conscious and unconscious components of his creativity.

Although dreams exhibit a wealth of detail contributed by the events of the day (the day residue), they also reveal recurrent patterns reflecting underlying emotional and intellectual problems, and these two dimensions of dream life point the investigation of Freud's mental processes in two different directions. On the one hand, tracing out the particular sources of the day residue and setting them in their original context, makes it possible to discover what current events had the power to evoke significant unconscious responses. These contemporary associations connect Freud's thought with its immediate historical context and relate it to the political

[2] Ibid., p. 277.

world which engaged him so powerfully during much of his life. On the other hand, detecting recurrent patterns and the ongoing emotional and intellectual problems lying behind them opens up an inner dimension of his mental life. These patterns illuminate the various wishes—often rooted in early childhood phantasies—which give form and significance to the day residue. Close examination of the interaction between these inner and outer dimensions of his dream life during the period of intense emotional difficulty following his father's death in 1896 thus helps to separate out the various personal, professional, and political ingredients of his creative scientific work.

Whether or not Freud's work was actually scientific has been much debated. Although it has been argued with some justice that his followers and translators exaggerated the scientific quality of his thought and language,[3] it seems evident that they did so in part because Freud himself strongly insisted that he was a scientist. Those who have argued that he was not have sometimes done so out of a basic disagreement about what "scientific" means, a disagreement reinforced by the fact that the English word has a substantially narrower meaning than its German equivalent, *wissenschaftlich.* Beyond the problem of translation, however, is the more substantial issue involved in the nature of Freud's evidence. The combination of using the subjective evidence of his own dreams with what some regard as an equally subjective mode of analysis has led various critics to conclude that Freud's work violates the objective standards demanded of scientific inquiry.

Although this question permits of no easy resolution, the history of Freud's intellectual development, particularly during his years as a student at the University of Vienna, casts new light on it. His letters of that time to his friend Eduard Silberstein, which were largely inaccessible to previous biographers, prove beyond any question that he approached psychological investigation from a highly sophisticated background in the philosophy of science, gained primarily through his work with Professor Franz Brentano. Freud admired Brentano's attempt to carry over the methods and standards of the natural sciences into the study of human psychology and, followed his lead in developing a dualistic approach to understanding mental processes. This approach sought to combine physiological and anatomical evidence with that gleaned from the investigating scientist's perceptions of his own inner psychological processes. Brentano believed that it was foolish to reject the insight

[3] See Bruno Bettelheim, *Freud and Man's Soul* (New York: Knopf, 1983).

offered by inner perception because of its subjectivity and argued that it was far better to develop rigorous scientific standards for the use of such subjective evidence. Freud took up Brentano's dualistic approach and focused it on an essentially monistic conception of mental activity. He believed that the physiological processes in the brain and the psychological processes of the mind were not parallel and causally linked but, rather, were identical. They were one and the same thing apprehended by the scientist in two different ways: through external observation in the natural sciences and through inner perception in psychological investigation. Freud did not come to psychology through biology or to biology through psychology; he was firmly committed to both avenues of investigation from a very early stage in his intellectual development. During the early years of his scientific career, he pursued both biological and psychological research, and even after he achieved a breakthrough in the psychological investigation of dreams, he continued to hope for biological evidence to support his findings. This was one factor in his close intellectual alliance with Wilhelm Fliess, who he hoped would provide the biological corollary to his psychological theory. In Freud's scientific framework there was room for a psychoanalytic explanation of mental disorder and a biochemical explanation of the same disorder to coexist without conflict.

Freud well understood the perils of a one-sided attempt to grasp the nature of mental activity, and he sought to avoid them through his dualistic approach. His determination to regard his work as science went well beyond a desire to secure the validation and prestige accorded to science by the value structure of his time. It rested on a broad but rigorous conception of science grounded in a careful consideration of the philosophical issues underlying his view. Even if a better understanding of Freud's intellectual development cannot fully resolve the debate over the scientific character of his work, it may offer a useful moral. In approaching the supreme puzzle involved in the workings of human intelligence, scientists are in somewhat the same position as the seven blind men who must describe an elephant using only their sense of touch. Rather than choose between those who feel the trunk and say an elephant is like a snake and those who grasp the tail and say an elephant resembles a rope, one might better assume that each may have hold of part of the truth.

Anyone who attempts to illuminate so complex and subtle an issue as the sources of Freud's creative work should acknowledge at the outset the necessarily incremental, fragmentary, and pluralistic nature of such an effort. My research has drawn on that of many previous Freud scholars, and subsequent scholars will certainly fill out and correct elements of the picture I have drawn. An awareness of this has conditioned my attitude toward the existing literature on Freud, particularly that part of it involving the reinterpretation of his dreams. The historical reinterpretation of a dream is much like solving a crossword puzzle. The clues are ambiguous, and the solution is apparent only when the letters form words which resolve the ambiguity and interlock horizontally and vertically. In my house crossword puzzles are passed around among members of the family with each of us calling on our particular expertise to add what we can, and each of us freely correcting the mistakes of the previous puzzle worker. In these situations it is always advantageous to be the last (or latest) to work on the puzzle, and I feel a debt of gratitude to such scholars as Leslie Adams, Max Schur, Carl Schorske, and most particularly Alexander Grinstein for leading the way to an understanding of Freud's dreams.[4] I feel that gratitude even when I depart from their interpretations, and for that reason I have drawn from their work what seemed both plausible and relevant to mine, while avoiding unnecessary disagreement over what was not. I have only disputed different positions when they seemed directly contradictory to mine.

The status of Freud's intellectual legacy remains deeply controversial even now, a century after he began his professional career. The pioneering work of Ernest Jones has codified the highly favorable view of Freud developed by psychoanalytic scholars and has provided an abundance of important material bearing particularly on his middle and later years, when Jones was in close contact with him.[5] Despite its apparent wealth of detail, however, Jones's biography reveals little about Freud's early years—a particularly striking fact in view of the analytic emphasis on early childhood experiences. The often adulatory view of Freud developed by Jones and the psychoanalytic school has recently come under sharp attack from various scholars who on the basis of new evidence have questioned Freud's scientific objectivity, his originality, his honesty,

[4] Leslie Adams, "A New Look at Freud's Dream: 'The Breakfast Ship,' " *American Journal of Psychiatry*, 110, no. 5 (1953). This dream interpretation is a pioneering piece of scholarship for those interested in understanding the relationship of Freud's dreams to the political world around him. Max Schur, *Freud: Living and Dying* (New York: International Universities Press, 1972); Carl Schorske, *Fin-de-Siècle Vienna: Politics and Culture* (New York: Knopf, 1980); Alexander Grinstein, *On Sigmund Freud's Dreams*, 2d ed. (Detroit: Wayne State University Press, 1980).

[5] Ernest Jones, *The Life and Work of Sigmund Freud*, 3 vols. (New York: Basic Books, 1953–57).

his devotion to his patients, his faithfulness to his wife, and the validity of his theoretical assumptions. Jeffrey Masson has used previously unpublished passages from the Fliess correspondence to argue that Freud abandoned his seduction theory for intellectually disreputable reasons. Frank Sulloway has challenged the originality of Freud's ideas and argued that much of his reputation rests on myths consciously cultivated by the psychoanalytic movement. Peter Swales has questioned Freud's honesty and pointed to evidence of an affair with his sister-in-law as an illustration of his duplicitous character. Max Schur, although personally devoted to Freud, has cited previously unpublished passages from Freud's letters that raise doubts about his treatment of patients.[6] Since all these issues involve matters of great complexity, the reader seeking simple answers will not find them here or elsewhere, but some of them can at least be clarified. The new documentary evidence brought to light in recent years offers an opportunity to move beyond the disputes between Freud's ardent admirers and his determined detractors by placing his life and work more firmly in its historical context.

With all that has been written about Freud, the historical task of understanding the relationship between the culture and time in which he lived and the creative process leading to his discoveries remains to be accomplished. Sulloway has provided an extremely useful historical service by examining Freud's thought in the context of the scientific, particularly the biological and psychological, theories of the time, but he neglects the larger historical framework. Other recent books by Alexander Grinstein, Max Schur, and Didier Anzieu provide valuable perspectives on Freud's psychological development and its bearing on his ideas, but their focus does not move far beyond Freud the individual.[7] Carl Schorske's approach to Freud, which strongly influenced my own, has yielded rich insights into the relationship of Freud's mature thought to the historical forces at work in *fin-de-siècle* Vienna, but Schorske has not attempted to extend that approach to his early life or to follow his intellectual development from youth to maturity.

[6] Jeffrey Moussaieff Masson, *The Assault on Truth: Freud's Suppression of the Seduction Theory* (New York: Farrar, Straus & Giroux, 1983); Frank Sulloway, *Freud, Biologist of the Mind* (New York: Basic Books, 1979); Peter J. Swales, "Freud, Minna Bernays and the Conquest of Rome," *The New American Review* 1 (Spring/Summer 1982); Max Schur, "Some Additional 'Day Residues' of the Specimen Dream of Psychoanalysis," Mark Kanzer and Jules Glenn, eds. *Freud and His Self Analysis* (New York: Jason Aronson, 1979); hereafter, Kanzer and Glenn, *Freud.*

[7] Didier Anzieu, *L'auto-analyse de Freud et la découverte de la psychanalyse,* 2 vols. (Paris: Presses Universitaires de France, 1975).

When Freud's work is viewed in the context of his time, it is striking how many other creative thinkers of *fin-de-siècle* Vienna displayed a deep and sensitive understanding of inner psychological reality. In some way conditions seemed to foster such an interest. In considering how Freud's particular concern with psychological issues developed, one needs to distinguish among various ways in which the outer political world proved important to his life and work. First of all, during his early life it helped shape central elements of his value system and personality. Then, as Freud developed into an adolescent, politics took on deep emotional importance because of its ability to represent symbolically a whole range of emotional issues and conflicts rooted in his early family life. His early phantasy identifications reveal an intermingling of the familial and the political within the context of his Jewish identity. His admiration for the biblical figures of Joseph and Moses expressed contrasting ideas of political behavior which reflected the different alternatives posed by his relationships to his family and his time. Joseph, the loyal son, provided an example of the successful assimilation of a Jew into an alien and hostile environment, while Moses, the fatherly leader of the Jewish people, represented a defiant rejection of oppressive authority in defense of the ideal of freedom. During adolescence, when Freud's interest in politics intensified, he found in historical and literary figures such as Brutus, Hannibal, and Karl Moor, the hero of Schiller's play *The Robbers,* ideal representations of the struggle for freedom and law against tyranny.

Shortly before he graduated from the Gymnasium, Freud decided against a possible career in law and politics in order to devote himself to science, but while he was a university student he continued to have strong political opinions. Over time, however, his political interests were gradually redirected and transformed into professional concerns that reflected his earlier radicalism; his fervent enthusiasm for Darwin, his professional iconoclasm, and in particular his interest in hysteria owed much to his former political views. That Freud's thoughts and feelings continued to be influenced by his political past long after he had consciously repudiated his youthful radicalism is particularly clear in the period from 1897 to 1900 when he was writing *The Interpretation of Dreams.* A close examination of his dreams from this period reveals that many of them—perhaps most—involved important allusions to the political events of the time. These events, particularly the 1897 crisis surrounding the language ordinances put forward by the government of Count Badeni, had profound emotional significance for both Jews and German nationalists, and Freud's dreams reveal that on an emotional level he identified with both groups. Because they came at a time when the death of his father had left him particularly vulnerable, and because politics had for him become weighted with personal, familial, and professional significance, these political events came to play a role in shaping the creative process at work in his central discoveries.

The question whether politics actually shaped his discoveries in a deep way or merely served as a symbolic medium of exchange for more personal forces that did the shaping cannot be answered through a study of Freud's dreams alone, however. In dreams the ordinary laws of causality are suspended, and since his personal, professional, and political concerns were so closely intertwined, the question of causal priority remains unclear. Nonetheless, when Freud's political dreams are carefully dated and chronologically aligned with these political events and the key intellectual steps which led to his discovery of psychoanalysis, a historically persuasive pattern emerges to suggest that politics did play a significant role in his creative process. Through their ability to carry him back emotionally to an earlier time in his life, political pressures served to facilitate Freud's solution to the major intellectual and personal problems posed by his adherence to the seduction theory. The political events he lived through stirred his own phantasies so powerfully and directly that Freud suddenly came to realize that phantasy could foster driving emotional forces as powerful as, or even more powerful than those generated by real events. When he came to this realization, late in the summer of 1897, it removed a barrier to his further psychological and intellectual development. On the personal psychological level, it helped him to resolve his conflicted feelings toward his dead father by leading to the understanding that his unconscious hostility was rooted as much in phantasy as in reality. Similarly, on the intellectual level, it allowed him to move toward a more unified conception of mental activity that removed the firm distinction between normal and abnormal by dissolving the boundary between phantasy and reality.

In writing *The Interpretation of Dreams,* Freud found an outlet for his political passions which served him well both emotionally and intellectually. Seizing on the myth of Oedipus to express his new theoretical insight, he sought to use his more advanced understanding of mental activity to exorcise the emotional ghosts within himself. His own Oedipal rivalry had assumed a political form in his Hannibal phantasy, and so he adopted an openly counterpolitical stance aimed at freeing himself from the power politics exercised on his inner feeling. Seeing a close parallel between the psychological dynamics of family relationships internalized by the individual and the dynamic forces at work in the sociopolitical realm, Freud used the parallel to work back and forth between the inner and outer worlds in developing and elaborating his theoretical structure. At the same time, in espousing a theory that gave psychological forces a position of primacy over those of history and politics, he hoped to offer himself and others a way out of a deterministically driven world in which sociopolitical and psychological forces interlocked to rob the individual and society of freedom. Psychoanalysis opened up a path to freedom through a deepened understanding of how these forces developed and worked. In his self-analysis Freud used himself as his own primary test case and moved to resolve his inner conflicts involving fathers, mothers, sisters, and brothers while simultaneously filling out the structure and details of his fundamental work. The book he regarded as his most enduring accomplishment thus became a vehicle for achieving, in the realm of personal psychology, the ideal of freedom that had inspired the political hopes of his youth.

Without denying that Freud abandoned the seduction theory, in favor of a psychological conception which placed phantasy in a central role, for clearly personal as well as objective, scientific reasons, I argue, in direct opposition to Masson and others, that this step represented an advance in both theoretical and personal insight. I also believe that a close examination of Freud's own life and work offers powerful support to this phantasy-oriented view of mental reality, and that understanding Freud's own phantasies provides the key to the uniquely personal dimension of his creativity. However powerfully the political and social forces of his time may have impelled him toward his psychological insights, it was his own particular mind and personality which finally produced those insights. Although such contemporaries as Schnitzler, Kafka, Mahler, and Hitler all paralleled Freud in displaying profound psychological sensitivity, each of them expressed their psychological insights differently. Although Freud acknowledged Schnitzler as his *Doppelgänger,*[8] nonetheless it was Freud rather than Schnitzler who discovered psychoanalysis and first understood the meaning of dreams. The recurrent patterns of Freud's phantasy life provide clues to

[8] Freud's May 14, 1922 letter to Schnitzler is reprinted in Jones, III:443.

this peculiarly individual element of creativity, to the enduring personality structures and conflicts which shaped the creative process from within.

Freud discussed the relevance of phantasy to creativity in his 1908 essay "Creative Writers and Day-Dreaming," where he compared artistic creativity to childhood play and to the adult predeliction for indulging in phantasies or daydreams. His concept of phantasy formation paralleled his explanation of dreams. He argued that "the motive forces of phantasies are unsatisfied wishes, and every single phantasy is the fulfilment of a wish, a correction of unsatisfying reality." He then went on to discuss the different temporal components of phantasy:

> We may say that it hovers, as it were, between three times—the three moments of time which our ideation involves. Mental work is linked to some current impression, some provoking occasion in the present which has been able to arouse one of the subject's major wishes. From there it harks back to a memory of an earlier experience (usually an infantile one) in which this wish was fulfilled; and it now creates a situation relating to the future which represents a fulfilment of the wish. What it thus creates is a day-dream or phantasy, which carries about it traces of its origin from the occasion which provoked it and from the memory. Thus past, present and future are strung together, as it were, on the thread of the wish that runs through them.[9]

The forward pointing component of phantasy which Freud isolated as one of its three temporal dimensions may represent the germ of truth in the popular myth that dreams foretell the future.

Particularly from the child's view, this future oriented element of phantasy is of great importance. Bruno Bettelheim shows this in *The Uses of Enchantment* where he observes, "Through most of man's history, a child's intellectual life, apart from immediate experiences within the family, depended on mythical and religious stories and on fairy tales. This traditional literature fed the child's imagination and stimulated his fantasizing." In addition to giving an inner spur to phantasy life, this material also fostered a relationship to the outer world: "Simultaneously, since these stories answered the child's most important questions, they were a major agent of his socialization. Myths and closely related religious legends offered material from which children formed their concepts of the

[9] Sigmund Freud, "Creative Writers and Day-Dreaming," *The Standard Edition of the Complete Psychological Works of Sigmund Freud* (hereafter *S.E.*), ed. and tr. James Strachey et al. (London: Hogarth, 1953–74), IX:146, 147–48.

world's origin and purpose, and of the social ideals a child could pattern himself after." Bettelheim makes the point that fairy tales go beyond this socializing agency in their ability to speak to the individual's innermost needs and thereby play a therapeutic role: "The fairy tale is therapeutic because the patient finds his *own* solution, through contemplating what the story seems to imply about him and his inner conflicts at this moment in his life. The content of the chosen tale usually has nothing to do with the patient's external life, but much to do with his inner problems, which seem incomprehensible and hence unsolvable."[10] Since the phantasy identifications of Freud's early years combined elements of both the socializing religious myth and the emotional-problem-solving fairy tale they were particularly potent. His boyish dreams of being Joseph in Egypt, or Karl Moor leading the robber band, powerfully engaged both his intellectual interests and his emotional needs. A consideration of their role in the history of Freud's intellectual development testifies strongly to the formative influence of childhood phantasy and its importance to adult creativity.

[10] Bruno Bettelheim, *The Uses of Enchantment, The Meaning and Importance of Fairy Tales* (New York: Vintage, 1977), pp. 24, 25.

1/

The Dream of Joseph

Sigmund Freud, the man whose discoveries opened up the world of the child within man, provided in his *Autobiographical Study* only the barest clues to the childhood origins of his own thought patterns. After indicating that he was born on May 6, 1856, in Freiberg, Moravia, then part of the Habsburg Empire, he went on to emphasize his Jewish background: "My parents were Jews, and I have remained a Jew myself." He sketched the movements of his ancestors as they fled persecution from Cologne in the Rhineland east to Lithuania and then back west and south through Galicia into German Austria, but alluded only briefly to the early wanderings of his own immediate family, noting that "when I was a child of four I came to Vienna, and I went through the whole of my education there." Although Freud did not expand on his early educational development, he did provide one additional observation of great importance: he indicated that his first stirrings of intellectual curiosity were "directed more towards human concerns than towards natural objects. . . . My deep engrossment in the Bible story (at a time almost before I had learnt the art of reading) had, as I recognized much later, an enduring effect upon the direction of my interest."[1]

Freud had written his *Autobiographical Study* in 1924, but since he added this last sentence in 1935, a year after completing a draft of *Moses and Monotheism,* it seems likely that one part of the Bible he had in mind was the story of Moses. Various scholars have pointed out the importance of the Moses image to Freud,[2] partic-

[1] Sigmund Freud, *An Autobiographical Study, S.E.,* XX:7–8.

[2] Martin S. Bergmann, "Moses and the Evolution of Freud's Jewish Identity," *The Israel Annals of Psychiatry and Related Disciplines* 14 (March 1976), 3–26; Marthe

ularly in his later life, and there is every reason to think that Freud's fascination with Moses began with the biblical studies of his childhood. In reading the Bible, however, Freud would have been introduced to the story of Moses through the story of Joseph, and in an important sense the stories form a symmetrical unit. They deal with the descent of the Jews into Egypt in search of prosperity and their ultimate flight from it in search of freedom, the process that transformed them from a family into a nation. Although the importance of Joseph to Freud has been less widely appreciated, Leonard Shengold has argued persuasively in his article "Freud and Joseph" that Freud's life can be seen as "living out a Joseph fantasy."[3] Moreover, the evidence of Freud's mature dream life suggests that Joseph ranked with Moses as an emotionally significant figure. In the various dreams analyzed in *The Interpretation of Dreams,* Joseph was the only biblical figure with whom Freud specifically admitted an identification. He explained the frequent occurrence of the name Joseph in his *Non vixit* dream by observing, "It will be noticed that the name Josef plays a great part in my dreams (cf. the dream about my uncle [with the yellow beard]). My own ego finds it very easy to hide itself behind people of that name, since Joseph was the name of a man famous in the Bible as an interpreter of dreams."[4] Moses was alluded to in Freud's dream of Rome in a mist and the dream of dissecting his own pelvis.[5] In Freud's "My son the Myops" dream the biblical allusions embraced the end of the Joseph story and the beginning of Moses' flight to freedom, recapitulating the biblical coherence of the two stories.[6] Other biblical figures appeared only fleetingly in Freud's dreams.

It will be useful to recapitulate here the chief elements of the Joseph story as Freud would have learned them in his childhood. The account of the descent into Egypt began with Joseph and his brothers tending their flocks in the land of Canaan. Joseph was seventeen, and since his father, Jacob, had given him a coat of many colors as a sign of his favored position, he was envied and disliked by his older half-brothers. One night Joseph had a dream,

---

Robert, *From Oedipus to Moses: Freud's Jewish Identity,* trans. Ralph Manheim (Garden City, N.Y.: Anchor Press, Doubleday, 1976); Leonard Shengold, "Freud and Joseph," in Kanzer and Glenn, *Freud,* pp. 81–83; Dennis B. Klein, *Jewish Origins of the Psychoanalytic Movement* (New York: Praeger, 1981), pp. 94, 140.

[3] Shengold, "Freud and Joseph," p. 67.

[4] Freud, *Interpretation, S.E.,* v:484.

[5] See below, Chap. 7.

[6] See below, Chap. 6.

which he told to his brothers. He dreamed they "were binding sheaves in the field and lo my sheaf arose and also stood upright; and behold your sheaves stood round about and made obeisance to my sheaf."[7] When they heard the dream, the brothers mocked him and "hated him yet the more," but then Joseph dreamed another dream in which the sun and the moon and the eleven stars made obeisance to him. When he told his father the dream, Jacob rebuked him for his arrogance in suggesting that even his father and mother would bow down to him. Later Jacob sent Joseph back to rejoin his brothers in order to help them with the flocks and to report on their activities. When the brothers saw Joseph coming from a distance, they decided to kill him by casting him into a deep pit without food or water. Then, thinking better of their sinful plans, they resolved to sell him to a passing caravan headed for Egypt. Jacob was overcome with grief at the loss of his favorite son and entered a period of deep mourning.

In Egypt, Joseph was sold to Potiphar, a high official of Pharaoh's court. In his work, Joseph's intelligence and excellence of character so distinguished him that he was soon entrusted with overseeing Potiphar's household. Being exceedingly well-favored, Joseph was asked by Potiphar's wife to lie with her; because he declined, she accused him of trying to seduce her and had him thrown into prison. But even here in the nethermost part of the Egyptian netherworld, Joseph's excellence of character distinguished him, and the jailer decided to entrust him with the overseeing of prison life. He then encountered two high officials of Pharaoh's court, both recently imprisoned. Each had a dream, and Joseph interpreted the dreams as meaning that the one man would be restored to power and the other executed. According to the Bible these events took place as predicted, but the high official who was restored forgot his promise to help free Joseph from his unjust bondage. Later, however, when Pharaoh had a striking pair of dreams that no one was able to interpret, the official remembered Joseph and had him brought out of prison to see if he could understand them. Pharaoh dreamed that seven fat kine came out of the river followed by seven lean kine, who devoured the fat kine. Then he dreamed that seven good ears of corn grew on a stalk and that seven withered ears sprang up after them and consumed the first. Joseph declared that both dreams had one meaning: Egypt would enjoy seven years of plenty followed by seven years of want. His interpretation was so persuasive that Pharaoh made him ruler over all Egypt second

[7] Genesis 37:7. All biblical quotations are from the King James version.

only to Pharaoh himself, with the understanding that Joseph would make provision for the years of hardship he had predicted.

The lean years came, and only in Egypt was there food, the food set aside through Joseph's foresight. The land of Canaan was also struck with famine, and Jacob, hearing that there was food in Egypt, sent his sons to buy provisions for their families. Except for Benjamin, the one remaining son of his beloved Rachel, they all went to Egypt, where they appeared before Joseph, whom they failed to recognize. Joseph did recognize them, but decided not to reveal himself until he could test their character and their attitude toward his younger brother, Benjamin. After inquiring of their family, he accused them of being spies, and decided to hold Simeon hostage while sending the rest back to bring Benjamin as proof of their story. Although Jacob at first refused to risk the loss of Rachel's only other son, he finally consented, and the brothers returned to Egypt with Benjamin. Then Joseph decided to test them further by first allowing them to leave with the necessary provisions, and then sending after them to arrest Benjamin on the grounds that he had stolen a silver cup. When Joseph threatened to punish Benjamin by keeping him as a servant, Judah came forward to argue that since the loss of this son would surely send their father, Jacob, to his grave, Joseph should take the older brother in place of Benjamin. This evidence of concern for his father and brother caused Joseph to reveal himself and forgive his brothers. He told them to go and return with Jacob, their families, and their flocks to live in the land of Goshen near Egypt, where he would provide for them through the years of hardship. The brothers returned with Jacob, whose joy at the recovery and triumph of his lost son was complete. Jacob lived out the rest of his days in Egypt, and before he died Joseph brought to him his two sons, Manasseh and Ephraim. Jacob adopted these two as his own sons and then proceeded to bless each of his sons according to his nature and deserts—Joseph most copiously of all. After a long and fruitful life, Joseph himself died, leaving his people prosperous and multiplying in Pharaoh's land.

It is easy to understand how the story of Joseph impressed itself deeply on the consciousness of the young Freud. Joseph's life was marked by an extraordinary capacity for achieving success in the face of obstacles. Time and again he was treated unjustly and punished harshly, only to surmount the difficulty and rise to some still higher position. Ultimately, his triumph was complete. His excellence of character and the intelligence he exhibited in understanding the mystery of dreams allowed him to rise to a position of unprecedented power. He came to hold sway over the very brothers who plotted his death, and after testing their characters, he forgave them. He assumed the role of protector of his younger brother and bestowed special favors on him. He returned to a father who thought him dead and brought the old man a degree of joy and satisfaction he had never before experienced. Finally, he saved his entire clan, Israel and all his children, from starvation by settling them in the land of Goshen where they could live in abundance.

The political conditions prevailing during Freud's childhood in Vienna served to enhance the attractiveness of the Joseph story as a guiding myth for the boy. The story of the Jew who rose to the pinnacle of power and wealth in a foreign land represented the assimilationist hope in its most extravagant form, and the various reforms of the 1860s seemed to suggest that such hopes were not completely unrealistic. After achieving virtually complete equality with other citizens during the liberal revolutions of 1848, Jews had seen many of the old restrictions reimposed during the reactionary 1850s.[8] When Austria was defeated in the Italian war of 1859, the country once again embarked on a liberal course, led by Anton von Schmerling, a man whose outlook had been shaped by the tradition associated with another Joseph much admired by Freud, the eighteenth-century emperor Josef II.[9] Jews had earlier experienced a period of liberalization during the reign of this enlightened despot, and his various reforms established the tradition of enlightened reform known as Josephinism. During the Schmerling period from the early to the mid-1860s, many of the restrictions on Jews were once again lifted, and finally, after the thoroughly liberal Bürgerministerium took power in 1867, Jews regained almost full equality with other citizens. The allusion in Freud's *Non vixit* dream to the biblical Joseph is associated with allusions to the emperor Josef II; since Freud first read the Bible in the mid-1860s, a self-consciously Josephinist period, it may be that the two names blended together then too. The values of the time, the apparent triumph of Josephinism, infused the Joseph story with particular magic.

With the installation of the Bürgerministerium militant liberalism came to power in Austria, and its first priority involved a full-scale assault on the entrenched position of the Roman Catholic church.

[8] Ernst Mischler and Josef Ulbrich, *Österreichisches Staatswörterbuch Handbuch des gesammten öffentlichen Rechtes* (Vienna: Alfred Hölder, 1895), 2:191–92.

[9] See Georg Franz, *Liberalismus, Die deutschliberale Bewegung in der habsburgischen Monarchie* (Munich: G. W. D. Callwey, 1955), p. 264.

The signing of a concordat between the pope and the emperor in 1855 had given the church an unprecedented degree of influence in public life, an influence liberals regarded as one of the most pernicious legacies of the neo-absolutist decade. The new government's successful efforts to force a revocation of the concordat culminated in the debate which occurred in the upper house over reform of the marriage laws in March 1868. Richard Charmatz has captured the drama of those heroic times: "There were some oratorical masterpieces. Cardinal Prince Schwarzenberg opposed the bill. . . . At the close of his speech Schwarzenberg demanded that his friends defy the attacks of the liberal journalists and form themselves into a loyal wall surrounding the throne, 'even if it should cost life or blood.' " He was opposed by Count Anton Auersperg, whose words were greeted with widespread applause: "He called the Concordat a 'published *Kanossa*' in which the Austria of the nineteenth century had to atone in sackcloth and ashes for the Josephinism of the eighteenth century." Then, reminding his listeners that in 1753 when Empress Maria Theresa had encountered the resistance of the clergy in an important matter, she had simply locked them up in Greifenstein Castle, he observed, "Freedom for the state; healthy freedom for all churches in the state; then it will be said of freedom for state and church: in this sign we shall conquer!"[10] Contrasting the liberal religion of freedom to the outworn dogmatism of the Catholic church, Auersperg captured the anticlerical sentiments of the day.

The Freud household greeted the advent of the Bürgerministerium with unrestrained enthusiasm. Freud later recalled how his father had brought home portraits of the new ministers, "and we had illuminated the house in their honour. There had even been some Jews among them. So henceforth every industrious Jewish schoolboy carried a Cabinet Minister's portfolio in his satchel."[11] The liberal government seemed to promise a new era of religious toleration and political progress, and the strong anticlerical campaign it launched against the concordat offered particular cause for enthusiasm since Freud, like the liberal reformers, regarded the Roman Catholic church as the chief enemy of toleration.[12] His earliest political ambitions developed in this context. As he later recalled, he was eleven or twelve (1867–68) when a restaurant fortune teller predicted that "I should probably grow up to be a

[10] Richard Charmatz, *Österreichs innere Geschichte von 1848 bis 1907* (Leipzig: B. G. Teubner, 1909), 1:83.
[11] Freud, *Interpretation, S.E.*, IV:193.
[12] Ibid., pp. 196–99.

Cabinet Minister. I still remember quite well what an impression this second prophecy had made on me. Those were the days of the 'Bürger' Ministry."[13] In dreaming of a ministerial career, young Sigmund built on an element of the Joseph story, for Joseph had also become a minister.

In addition to the external, broadly political factors that invested the Joseph story with meaning for Freud, more particular and internal factors made it emotionally significant. In his *Autobiographical Study*, as I noted, Freud introduced his reference to the influence of the Bible on his thought by mentioning the wanderings of his own family and their ancestors. The fate of Joseph, who moves from the backward countryside of Palestine to the splendor of the Egyptian court, was particularly relevant to the childhood situation of the young Freud, who had moved from rural Freiburg to imperial Vienna. As a young man, Freud looked back to his years in Freiberg with a certain sense of loss, and the move itself seems to have had a strong emotional impact. Later in life, he diagnosed a travel phobia in himself and traced it back to experiences involved in his family's early travels.[14] The sense of loss he associated with this move had to do in part with the division that occurred in his family at the time. In Freiberg, Freud's father, Jakob, had lived in close proximity to the sons of his first marriage, Emmanuel and Philipp, who were grown men when Freud was born. Emmanuel had even married and fathered a son, John, who was born a year before Freud, as well as a daughter, Pauline, who was Freud's age, and these two children were his earliest playmates. When the family left Freiberg, the two half-brothers moved to Manchester, England, while Jakob and his new family went first to Leipzig and then to Vienna. For the young Freud the move from Freiberg entailed the loss of these close childhood friends, as well as the disappearance of Emmanuel, whom he greatly liked, and Philipp, whom he didn't. Many of the dreams and slips Freud experienced in his adult years allude to various forms of sibling rivalry involved in his early experiences with John and Pauline or his half-brothers.[15] With the move from Freiberg they vanished from the outer reality of Freud's life and entered the phantasy world he was constructing within.

Freud's early years in Freiberg brought other experiences of loss as well, also involving sibling rivalry. Of the birth of his one-year-

[13] Ibid., p. 193.

[14] Schur, *Freud*, pp. 118–20, 100.

[15] On Freud's relationships with his various brothers, see Shengold, "Freud and Joseph."

younger brother Julius, who died in infancy, he later recalled that he had welcomed him "with ill wishes and real infantile jealousy and . . . his death left the germ of guilt in me."[16] The loss was desired, but its consequence was a strong feeling of guilt. The birth of another sibling, Anna, marked the occasion of yet another loss. In the course of his self-analysis, Freud came to realize that it was at the time his mother gave birth to Anna that the woman hired to care for him, Monika Zajic, was accused by his half-brother Philipp of being a thief.[17] Since Philipp had the woman prosecuted and imprisoned, Freud associated the loss of her love and attention with this half-brother and resented him for it.[18]

The theme of brother rivalry that marks many of the events of Freud's early life is yet another tie to the Joseph story. While Freud's feelings of sibling rivalry were in no way unusual, the peculiar overlapping of generations was, and as Ernest Jones has suggested, the family configuration may have influenced the direction of Freud's early thoughts and interests.[19] It was in this sphere that the Joseph story was perhaps most immediately relevant to the inner concerns of the young child, for Joseph had also grown up within an unusual family constellation, one with parallels to Freud's. Jakob Freud apparently married three times but his second marriage was childless and brief. Freud never referred to the existence of that wife; apparently he either did not know of her or repressed knowledge of her.[20] Freud's mother, Amalia, doted on her first-born son, and as he grew up he occupied a privileged position in the family; his parents granted him the luxury of a room to himself in their crowded Vienna apartment. Like Joseph, he was thus the favored elder son of a father named Jakob and his well-loved younger wife. As Leonard Shengold points out, "As a child, Freud's specific interest in the Biblical tale of Joseph must have been very great because it reflected his own family situa-

[16] Sigmund Freud, *The Origins of Psycho-Analysis, Letters to Wilhelm Fliess, Drafts and Notes: 1887–1902* (hereafter *Origins*), ed. Marie Bonaparte, Anna Freud, Ernst Kris, trans. Eric Mosbacher and James Strachey (New York: Basic Books, 1954), p. 219. As Shengold observes, "There can be no doubt of the tremendous effect of the death wish toward that first Julius which actually had coincided with his having been 'got rid of' " ("Freud and Joseph," p. 75).

[17] Ronald W. Clark, *Freud: The Man and the Cause* (New York: Random House, 1980), p. 11; This woman's name and many other details about Freud's early life were unearthed by Josef Sajner, "Sigmund Freuds Beziehungen zu seinem Geburtsort Freiberg (Pribor) und zu Mähren," *Clio Medica,* 3 (1968):167–180.

[18] Sigmund Freud, *The Psychopathology of Everyday Life, S.E.,* VI:49–52.

[19] Jones, I:3, 9.

[20] Clark, pp. 5, 7; Schur, *Freud,* p. 21.

tion. . . . Similarity and identity of names always impressed Freud."[21] These parallels predisposed him to seek in the Joseph story an ideal model for his developing self-identity.

That Freud did find such a model in Joseph can be demonstrated by a close look at a unique piece of evidence from his early years, his dream of the bird-beaked figures. Of the many dreams of his own that Freud analyzed in *The Interpretation of Dreams,* the dream of the bird-beaked figures was the only one he placed in his childhood. Discussing it as an example of anxiety dreams or nightmares, he wrote "It is dozens of years since I myself had a true anxiety-dream. But I remember one from my seventh or eighth year, which I submitted to interpretation some thirty years later."[22] His analysis indicated, however, that the dream alluded to an event which took place when he was almost nine-and-a-half, and for reasons to be considered below it seems more likely that it occurred then. Freud could understandably have been uncertain about the exact date after so many years, and it has also been suggested that the discrepancy can be explained by the possibility that the dream was actually a screen memory, or at least had the essential characteristics of one, in drawing together emotionally related issues over a period of time.[23] In either case the material is emotionally and intellectually relevant to understanding Freud's early years, and particularly important in that it came out of his reading of the Philippson Bible which he credits in his *Autobiographical Study* as the starting point for his later interests.

Freud's account of the dream reports: "I saw *my beloved mother, with a peculiarly peaceful, sleeping expression on her features, being carried into the room by two (or three) people with birds' beaks and laid upon the bed;* I awoke in tears and screaming, and interrupted my parents' sleep." Analysis of the dream reveals the mind of a child attempting to grapple with the eternal riddles faced by all children as they grow up—the problems of identity, love, death, and sexuality. The riddle on which Freud focused his own subsequent analysis was that of childhood sexuality and its relationship to anxiety. He argued

[21] Shengold, "Freud and Joseph," p. 68. See also K. R. Eissler, *Goethe, a Psychoanalytic Study,* (Detroit: Wayne State University Press, 1963), p. 1104.

[22] Freud, *Interpretation, S.E.,* v:583.

[23] Grinstein, p. 456. Screen memories present themselves to the consciousness as real memories of early experiences but decompose on analysis into dreamlike constructions held together by emotional rather than temporal coherence. So far as understanding Freud's childhood phantasy life is concerned, it matters little which of these alternatives is true. See also Eva M. Rosenfeld, "Dreams and Vision: Some Remarks on Freud's Egyptian Bird Dream," *International Journal of Psychoanalysis,* 37 (1956):97–105.

in discreetly veiled terms that the anxiety arose from a sexual longing for his mother, and that the dream attempted to hide this forbidden longing by presenting the anxiety as fear of his mother's death.[24] He indicated two sources for the bird-beaked figures. One was an experience with a young playmate, the caretaker's son, whose less proper upbringing had allowed him to become "well acquainted with the facts of life." From this young man, Freud first learned the German word *vögeln,* a vulgar term for sexual intercourse derived from the German word for bird—*Vogel.* As he wrote, "I must have guessed the sexual significance of the word from the face of my young instructor."[25] In the dream, the fact that his mother was carried to the bed by the bird-beaked figures directly expressed a sexual desire for her in visual language.

The second source for the bird-beaked figures was as lofty as the first was common. According to Freud, the figures derived "from the illustrations to Philippson's Bible," the Freud family Bible. This magnificent book was richly illustrated with etchings and drawings including many depicting Egyptian customs and religious beliefs. Among these were the sources for the bird-beaked figures: "I fancy," Freud wrote, "they must have been gods with falcons' heads from an ancient funerary relief." It was at this point in the dream interpretation that the thoughts of death entered—providing, according to Freud, the apparent cause of the dream's anxiety, the surface cause that masked the underlying sexual impulse actually motivating the dream.[26]

Since this dream clearly touched Freud at a delicate point, it is understandable that he carried its published analysis no further, but as was often the case with his self-censorship, he provided some clues to a more complete understanding of it. He said of the boy from whom he learned the word *vögeln,* "I am inclined to think [he] was called Philipp." As Alexander Grinstein points out, the fact that Freud should bother to mention the boy's name at all, as well as the allusion to the Philipp in Philippson, suggest that thoughts about Freud's half-brother Philipp were a motivating factor in the dream.[27] In the young Freud's mind, this half-brother played a major role with respect to questions of sex—that of nemesis. This role was dictated in part by the complexity of Freud's familial situation and the misconceptions which arose from his childish attempts to understand it. One of these involved the

[24] Freud, *Interpretation, S.E.,* v:583–84.
[25] Ibid., p. 583.
[26] Ibid.
[27] Cf. Jones, I:9n, and Grinstein, p. 455.

parentage of his younger siblings. Through his analysis of an early screen memory, Freud has revealed that in attempting to account for the birth of these unwanted rivals, he ignored the possible role of his beloved father and instead placed the blame on Philipp, who was the same age as his mother, Amalia, and unlike his other half-brother, Emmanuel, did not have a wife. As Freud indicated in *The Psychopathology of Everyday Life,* the analysis of the screen memory revealed that as a young child he had thought that "his big brother . . . had taken his father's place as the child's rival" and that "he had in some way introduced the recently born baby into his mother's inside."[28] Young Sigmund's erroneous conclusion thus fostered a strong sense of rivalry and dislike toward Philipp, while diverting natural hostility from his father.

Philipp was also disliked for his role in the disappearance of Monika Zajic; it was he who had gone to fetch the policeman and pressed charges of thievery against her.[29] She received a harsh ten-month jail term for her petty offenses, and when the child asked what had happened to her, Philipp replied humorously that she was *eingekastelt,* or boxed up. As a child, Freud had understood the term literally, and this misconception had helped to produce the subsequent screen memory in which "I was crying my heart out, because my mother was nowhere to be found. My brother, Philipp, . . . opened a cupboard *[Kasten]* for me, and when I found that mother was not there either, I cried still more, until she came through the door, looking slim and beautiful."[30] As the scene indicates, because he blamed Philipp for the disappearance of his nursemaid, Freud feared that he might have boxed up his mother as well.

Freud's analysis of the screen memory indicated further that the cupboard was a womb symbol and that his childhood anxiety had a sexual source. He was able to determine that the memory dated from a time shortly after the birth of his sister Anna; that it had been during his mother's confinement to bed that the nursemaid had committed her most extensive thefts; and that shortly thereafter, she had been dismissed.[31] The loss of the nursemaid and the arrival of unwanted siblings were thus tied together in the child's mind, and so it was that Philipp's joking use of the term "boxed up" pointed the way to the misconception about his role in the procreation of these rivals. As Freud indicated, "The child of not

[28] Freud, *Psychopathology, S.E.,* VI:51n.
[29] Freud, *Origins,* p. 222.
[30] Ibid.
[31] Freud, *Psychopathology, S.E.,* VI:51.

yet three had understood that the little sister who had recently arrived had grown inside his mother. . . . The wardrobe or cupboard was a symbol for him of his mother's inside."[32] Since in his mind it was Philipp who was responsible for putting people into boxes, the anxiety expressed in the scene involved not only the fear that he had lost his mother but also the suspicion that Philipp's boxing activities might have produced another rival. This connection explains his relief when his mother returned "looking beautiful and slim," a direct visual reassurance that she was not pregnant.[33]

Freud's nightmare of the bird-beaked figures bears a striking resemblance to this early screen memory in the nature and level of anxiety experienced. In both cases, his fear of maternal loss manifested itself with such frightening intensity that his crying stopped only when he actually saw his mother, and in both cases, the anxiety was tied to a sexual theme connected with the name Philipp. Furthermore, one of the details connected with the nightmare suggests that it was associated with the same problem which gave rise to the screen memory: the pregnancy of Freud's mother and the fear of loss that situation entailed. Freud associated the peaceful appearance of his mother's face in the dream with the view he had of his comatose grandfather a few days before his death. The grandfather died on October 3, 1865, and until recently analysts of this dream have failed to realize that at that time Freud's mother was pregnant with his younger brother Alexander.[34] The records of the city of Vienna indicate that Alexander was born on April 19, 1866.[35] By October 3 of the previous year, Amalia Freud would have been about two and one half months pregnant, enough for Sigmund to be aware of the fact. Even if the element of the grandfather's death was drawn in later, in the fashion of a screen memory, his mother's pregnancy remains just as relevant; since these two developments occurred simultaneously in October 1865, they would have been associated in Freud's mind, constituting one more instance of birth associated with loss.

By this time, Freud's experiences had given him ample cause to feel anxiety about his mother's pregnancies. The birth and death of Julius were associated with jealousy and guilt, the birth of Anna was joined to the memory of his nursemaid's disappearance, and the arrival of subsequent sisters had added still more claimants for

[32] Ibid., p. 51n.

[33] Ibid., p. 50.

[34] Marianne Krüll, *Freud und sein Vater, Die Enstehung der Psychoanalyse und Freuds ungelöste Vaterverbindung* (Munich: C. H. Beck, 1979), p. 196, does make this point.

[35] See the Heimat-Rolle, the citizenship records located in the Vienna Rathhaus.

parental attention. Until this time, however, his mother's only other son had been the ill-fated Julius, and the possibility that the new child might be a brother may have aroused guilty memories as well as fears of future brother rivalry. This latter possibility also pertains to the biblical background of the dream: Isaac and Ishmael, Jacob and Esau, Joseph and his brothers all came into conflict over their claims to inherit the paternal blessing; and the tradition clearly favored the younger son. Mark Kanzer has argued that Freud was in fact particularly sensitive about this issue of the more favored youngest son.[36] Seen in this light, the textual material associated with the nightmare suggests that it called up the central phantasy of the early screen memory as a way to focus both Freud's fear that the new child might be a son and his anger at Philipp for this threat to his status. *Philippson's* Bible is mentioned as one source for the bird-beaked figures, and *Philipp, son* of the caretaker was indicated as the other.[37] In this dream puzzle, the words Philipp and son represent the point of intersection between the two lines of associations leading from these sexual figures. In both instances Freud's clues to the meaning of the dream point to the psychological pattern of his early screen memory—the pattern that blamed Philipp for fathering the unwanted siblings. Moreover, there is important evidence that this pattern also influenced Freud's waking consciousness at the time. When Amalia Freud's second son was born in April 1866, Sigmund was allowed to choose his name, and he chose Alexander, after Alexander the Great, who was in fact a Philipp's son.[38] Shengold argues that Freud's attribution of the paternal role to Philipp was at least unconsciously implicit in this choice of a name,[39] and this third allusion to a Philipp's son further strengthens the evidence linking Freud's dream to his mother's pregnancy.

If the dream of the bird-beaked figures is approached from a point of view which takes into account both Freud's phantasies about his half-brother Philipp and the familial similarities that fostered his identification with Joseph, a deeper and more complete

[36] Mark Kanzer, "Sigmund and Alexander Freud on the Acropolis," Kanzer and Glenn, *Freud*, pp. 277, 275. On the biblical background of the dream, see Krüll, pp. 188–92.

[37] Freud's dreams often involved multilingual puns, and in this case the puns worked as well in German as in English.

[38] Jones, I:21. The name choice is also relevant to Freud's feelings of guilt about Julius (whom Freud associated with Julius Caesar in his later dreams) for in effect it invoked the memory of one military hero in place of another. See also Krüll, p. 196.

[39] Shengold, "Freud and Joseph," p. 73.

level of meaning emerges to confirm the connection. In the associative material of the dream, the name Philipp was linked to sex not only through the name of Freud's playmate, but also, as Grinstein suggests, because Freud learned something about sex from the Philippson Bible.[40] One passage connected with the Joseph story is particularly relevant to the sexual issues raised in the dream: the second half of Genesis 35. The chapter's early verses report that at Beth-el God appeared to Jacob and told him that from that time forward he would be called Israel. Verses 16 through 29 go on to reveal how Joseph lost his mother, Rachel: her death in giving birth to her second son, Benjamin, her burial, and Jacob's further travels. One then reads: "it came to pass when Israel dwelt in that land, that Reuben went and lay with Bilhah, his father's concubine: and Israel heard it. Now the sons of Jacob were twelve." There follows a listing of Jacob's sons by Leah, Rachel, Bilhah, and Zilpah, and a report of the death and burial of his aged father, Isaac.

The dream of the bird-beaked figures was associated with the prospective birth of Jakob Freud's last child, in effect the second son of his second family; Genesis 35 related the parallel event in the life of the biblical Jacob. If one examines the dream in the light of Freud's identification with Joseph, it can be seen that it alluded to all the crucial familial developments described in the biblical passage. Freud's phantasy that his half-brother Philipp had a sexual relationship with their father's wife was paralleled by the biblical statement that Joseph's half-brother Reuben had sexual intercourse with one of Jacob's concubines. The odd interpolation of the incident into the recounting of Jacob's progeny may even have suggested the further phantasy which Sigmund had associated with Philipp, the phantasy that he was the father of his siblings. The biblical passage also mentioned the death of Joseph's grandfather, Isaac, and Freud indicated that, in the dream, the peaceful look on his mother's face "was copied from the view I had had of my grandfather a few days before his death as he lay snoring in a coma." Finally, and most important, the passage from Genesis indicated that Joseph's mother died shortly after giving birth to his brother, and in Freud's dream of the bird-beaked figures, it was the fear that his mother had died that became the focus of anxiety in the dream. It seems evident that the dream's basic meaning centers on a Joseph identification and incorporates a full set of allusions to Genesis 35.

[40] Grinstein, p. 455.

As a mature scientist, Freud showed how the secret meaning of dreams could be found by translating the visual, pictographic language of the unconscious into the language of conscious communication. A careful consideration of the evidence suggested by the dream's visual elements, further reinforces the allusions to Freud's identification with Joseph, and Alexander Grinstein has provided a basis for understanding these visual materials. Starting from Freud's statement that the dream images derived from the illustrations in the Philippson Bible, Grinstein examined the more than five hundred woodcuts involved and discovered only four that closely enough approximated Freud's description of the dream figures to be possible sources for them. Grinstein suggests a number of possible thematic relationships which would tie three of the four illustrations and their associated texts to the dream. He presents a particularly strong argument for the illustration to 2 Samuel 3, a woodcut entitled "Bier from a Bas Relief in Thebes" (see Figure 1), which shows a figure with a peaceful expression lying on a bedlike bier with two "strangely draped and unnaturally tall figures" looking on.[41] Grinstein's argument for this illustration is persuasive since it is from a funerary relief, as Freud indicated, and its resemblance to the dream scene is striking. On the other hand, one essential element is missing: the figures do not have bird beaks.

By looking further at the passage from Genesis involving Benjamin's birth and the death of Rachel, one can supply the missing ingredient and show that the dream has a level of meaning overlooked in previous interpretations. Genesis 35 states that Rachel was buried near Bethlehem, and in a note Philippson referred to a later passage, 1 Samuel 10, that mentions the location of her grave: This involved Saul, the first king of Israel, who was anointed by Samuel and told "When thou art departed from me to-day, then thou shalt find two men by Rachel's sepulchre in the border of Benjamin['s province]." This was virtually the entire biblical text appearing on the page, most of which was devoted to a long footnote by Philippson, and with it appeared an illustration showing two bird-beaked figures in the act of anointing a young Egyptian (see Figure 2).[42] This illustration, though one of the four suggested by Grinstein as possible sources for Freud's dream, was the one for which he could offer no explanation on the basis of the associated

[41] Grinstein, pp. 451–53. Grinstein notes that in the text associated with this illustration, "The elements of death and castration . . . combine with the theme of murder and the possession of a forbidden woman" (pp. 452–53).

[42] *Die Israelitische Bibel* (hereafter Philippson), ed. Ludwig Philippson (Leipzig: Baumgärtners Buchhandlung, 1858), 2:287.

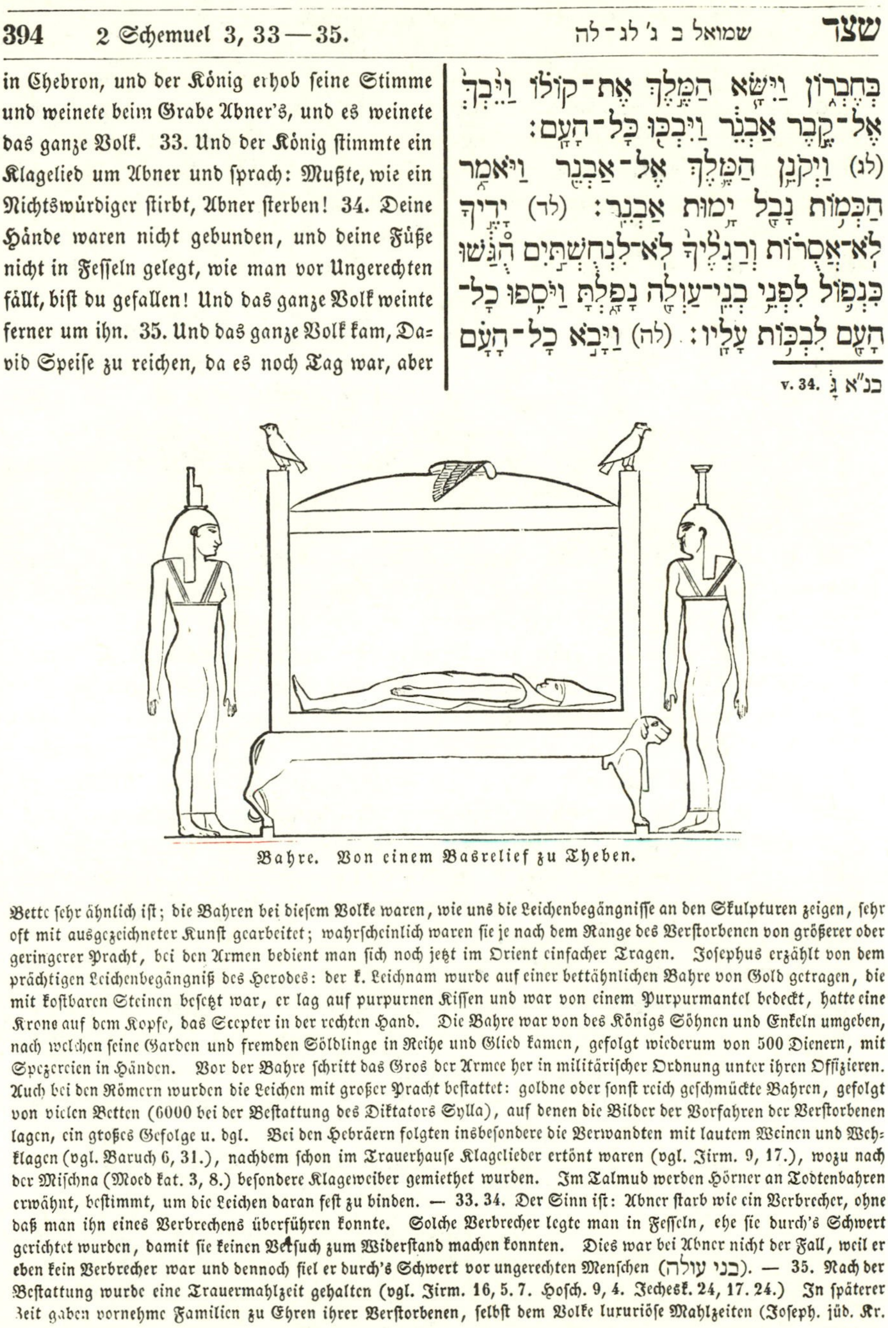

394 2 Schemuel 3, 33—35. שמואל ב ג׳ לג-לה שצד

in Chebron, und der König erhob seine Stimme und weinete beim Grabe Abner's, und es weinete das ganze Volk. 33. Und der König stimmte ein Klagelied um Abner und sprach: Mußte, wie ein Nichtswürdiger stirbt, Abner sterben! 34. Deine Hände waren nicht gebunden, und deine Füße nicht in Fesseln gelegt, wie man vor Ungerechten fällt, bist du gefallen! Und das ganze Volk weinte ferner um ihn. 35. Und das ganze Volk kam, David Speise zu reichen, da es noch Tag war, aber

בחברון וישא המלך את־קולו ויבך
אל־קבר אבנר ויבכו כל־העם׃
(לג) ויקנן המלך אל־אבנר ויאמר
הכמות נבל ימות אבנר׃ (לד) ידיך
לא־אסרות ורגליך לא־לנחשתים הגשו
כנפול לפני בני־עולה נפלת ויספו כל־
העם לבכות עליו׃ (לה) ויבא כל־העם

בנ"א ג v. 34.

Bahre. Von einem Basrelief zu Theben.

Bette sehr ähnlich ist; die Bahren bei diesem Volke waren, wie uns die Leichenbegängnisse an den Skulpturen zeigen, sehr oft mit ausgezeichneter Kunst gearbeitet; wahrscheinlich waren sie je nach dem Range des Verstorbenen von größerer oder geringerer Pracht, bei den Armen bedient man sich noch jetzt im Orient einfacher Tragen. Josephus erzählt von dem prächtigen Leichenbegängniß des Herodes: der k. Leichnam wurde auf einer bettähnlichen Bahre von Gold getragen, die mit kostbaren Steinen besetzt war, er lag auf purpurnen Kissen und war von einem Purpurmantel bedeckt, hatte eine Krone auf dem Kopfe, das Scepter in der rechten Hand. Die Bahre war von des Königs Söhnen und Enkeln umgeben, nach welchen seine Garden und fremden Söldlinge in Reihe und Glied kamen, gefolgt wiederum von 500 Dienern, mit Specereien in Händen. Vor der Bahre schritt das Gros der Armee her in militärischer Ordnung unter ihren Offizieren. Auch bei den Römern wurden die Leichen mit großer Pracht bestattet: goldne oder sonst reich geschmückte Bahren, gefolgt von vielen Betten (6000 bei der Bestattung des Diktators Sylla), auf denen die Bilder der Vorfahren der Verstorbenen lagen, ein großes Gefolge u. dgl. Bei den Hebräern folgten insbesondere die Verwandten mit lautem Weinen und Wehklagen (vgl. Baruch 6, 31.), nachdem schon im Trauerhause Klagelieder ertönt waren (vgl. Jirm. 9, 17.), wozu nach der Mischna (Moed kat. 3, 8.) besondere Klageweiber gemiethet wurden. Im Talmud werden Hörner an Todtenbahren erwähnt, bestimmt, um die Leichen daran fest zu binden. — 33. 34. Der Sinn ist: Abner starb wie ein Verbrecher, ohne daß man ihn eines Verbrechens überführen konnte. Solche Verbrecher legte man in Fesseln, ehe sie durch's Schwert gerichtet wurden, damit sie keinen Versuch zum Widerstand machen konnten. Dies war bei Abner nicht der Fall, weil er eben kein Verbrecher war und dennoch fiel er durch's Schwert vor ungerechten Menschen (בני עולה). — 35. Nach der Bestattung wurde eine Trauermahlzeit gehalten (vgl. Jirm. 16, 5. 7. Hosch. 9, 4. Jechesk. 24, 17. 24.) In späterer Zeit gaben vornehme Familien zu Ehren ihrer Verstorbenen, selbst dem Volke luxuriöse Mahlzeiten (Joseph. jüd. Kr.

Figure 1. Bier, from a bas-relief in Thebes. From the Philippson Bible, page 394.

text. Once the identification with Joseph is perceived, however, and the dream's allusions to the death of Rachel are understood, the relevance of the passage becomes clear: it referred to her place of burial and, through mention of Benjamin, alluded to the cause of her death. Moreover, the prediction that Saul would meet two men near Rachel's grave conjured up an image quite similar to the dream scene (and the illustration for 2 Samuel 3, on which Grinstein focuses primary attention). Furthermore, the passage from 1 Samuel 10 went on to say that Saul would next meet three men on the plain of Tabor, a statement reflected in Freud's uncertainty about the number of people involved in the dream: he saw his mother *"being carried . . . by two (or three) people with bird's beaks."* If one assumes that the dream condensed the two illustrations into one, it becomes possible to account for all its essential visual elements.

The plausibility of the combination can be seen by comparing the figures in the two pictures. In the funerary relief, the profiles are clearly human but highly stylized, with prominent noses and full, smoothly flowing hair reaching down over the shoulders. The hair of the bird-beaked figures is worn in exactly the same style. The resemblance in the profiles is striking, and it is easy to see how Freud's dream could compress the two and thereby include this allusion to Rachel's grave. In interpreting the dream, Freud found that, on one level, its meaning was "dass die Mutter stirbt, auch das Grab relief stimmt dazu [that my *mother* was dying—the *grave* relief also pointed to that]."[43] In the original German, the two emphasized words stood out, further suggesting an allusion to the grave of Joseph's mother.

Beginning with the basic elements suggested by Freud himself—the sexual longing for his mother and the strong sense of rivalry with his half-brother Philipp—one can see how the dream of the bird-beaked figures provided reassurance about the fears and desires evoked by his mother's pregnancy. Through the allusion to Genesis 35, it furnished an example of incest similar to the one he desired, while shifting the dangerous consequences to the disliked half-brother. With respect to the Joseph story as a whole, it provided the most reassuring possible answer to the young child's fears of rivalry with the older brothers or the younger one in his mother's womb. Joseph's triumph over his brothers was complete: he humbled the older ones and became the all-powerful protector of the

[43] Sigmund Freud, *Die Traumdeutung. Gesammelte Schriften* (hereafter *G.S.*)(Leipzig: Internationaler Psychoanalytischen Verlag, 1925), II:500.

287 1 Schemuel 10, 2. שמואל א י׳ ב רפז

zum Fürsten. 2. Wenn du heute von mir gehest, so wirst du zwei Männer treffen bei dem Grabe Rachel's im Gebiete Binjamin's, in Zelzach, und

(ב) בְּלֶכְתְּךָ הַיּוֹם מֵעִמָּדִי וּמָצָאתָ שְׁנֵי
אֲנָשִׁים עִם־קְבוּרַת רָחֵל בִּגְבוּל בִּנְיָמִן

frech von Neulingen nieder gerissen wird, was verhütet werden könnte, wenn die Erfahrung der Vorgänger zuvor die neuen Führer der Geschäfte selbst leitete. — Als eine weise Vorbereitung ist es anzusehen, daß dem zum Könige erkornen Manne diese Bestimmung eine Weile vorher bekannt gemacht, und er dabei durch eine Salbung zu der Würde eingeweiht wurde. Hätte er nicht eher, als in eben dem Augenblicke, da das Volk es vernahm, es auch erfahren, so würde wahrscheinlich seine Verlegenheit noch weit größer gewesen sein, als sie jetzt (V. 22.) ward, und er würde sich dem Volke in einem noch ungünstigern Lichte gezeigt haben. Indeß konnten in den Zeitumständen auch noch andere, von uns nicht zu errathende Gründe liegen, welche eine vorherige Privaternennung rathsam machten. — Die Salbung (s. Anm. 2 M. 30, 25. 3 M. 8, 12.) war unter den Hebräern und andern orientalischen Nationen ein Zeichen der Bekleidung mit königlicher Würde und ist noch jetzt ein Akt der Krönung in einigen europäischen Ländern. Bei den Hebr. war es aber der vornehmste, nicht der untergeordnete Akt der Investitur, doch müssen wir zwei Arten unterscheiden, die eine war privatim, die andere öffentlich. Jene, durch einen Propheten vorgenommen, gab noch kein besonderes Recht zum Throne, sie war nur das prophet. Symbol, daß der Gesalbte eventuell zum Königthum gelangen sollte, eine Symbolisirung höherer Bestimmung und geistiger Erhöhung durch göttliche Gnade. So wurde Schaul erst nach seiner Salbung König, so machte David, obgleich er schon zu Schaul's Zeit gesalbt wurde, während dessen Leben und selbst nachher keinen Anspruch auf die Königswürde, bis er vom St. Jehudah und sieben Jahre nachher von den anderen Stämmen zum Throne berufen wurde. In der That hat weder ein König in irgend einer Periode ein Recht aus seiner Salbung hergeleitet, noch das Volk sich an die Erwählung des Gesalbten gebunden erachtet, obgleich die Kenntniß der Faktums, daß Jemand gesalbt war, die Wirkung einer Prophezeiung hatte, indem sie die öffentliche Aufmerksamkeit auf ihn, als den zum Königthum bestimmten, lenkte. Die andere Salbung, nachdem der König feierlich vom Volke anerkannt worden, bildete die wirkliche Einweihungsceremonie, die Thatsache ihrer Wiederholung beweiset die so eben gegebene Ansicht von der prophetischen Salbung. Diese zweite, feierliche Salbung ward wahrscheinlich vom Hohenpriester vorgenommen, indessen scheint sie nie bei einem succedirenden König, dessen Vater schon König war, sondern nur bei dem Gründer einer neuen Dynastie und da geschehen zu sein, wo die Nachfolge bestritten wurde, und man dem Gesalbten somit eine Auszeichnung vor dem andern Prätendenten geben wollte. So wurde David, mit dem eine neue Dynastie begann, gesalbt, Schelomoh, dessen Rechte durch seinen ältern Bruder Adonijah bestritten wurden, Joasch, nachdem der Thron von Jehudah sechs Jahre durch Attaljah usurpirt war; Jehoachas, der Sohn des Joschijahu (2 Kön. 23, 30.), der einzige König in dem erblichen Königreich, von welchem gesagt wird, daß er gesalbt wurde, scheint beim ersten Anblick eine Ausnahme von dieser Regel zu machen, aber bei weiterer Forschung finden wir, daß wirklich eine Unregelmäßigkeit statt fand, denn es heißt, „daß das Volk (Pöbel) des Landes Jehoachas nahm und salbte," auch war sein Bruder Jehojakim älter als er (das. V. 31. 36.). — Dies ist die Ansicht, welche die jüd. Ausleger (Talm. Horijoth 11, 2. u. a. O.) von der Salbung proferiren, welche Ansicht wohl begründet scheint, wenn wir nicht annehmen wollen, daß von anderen Salbungen zufällig in den h. Büchern keine Rede ist. — Der Kuß Schemuel's (die Akkolade) war sicherlich ein Zeichen der Huldigung, wie der jisraelitische Gebrauch war (Ps. 2, 12.), er wurde von Schemuel wahrscheinlich auf die Stirn gegeben, da das Küssen der Hand, des Fußes oder des Kleides nur bei großem Unterschied des Standes üblich war. Die neueren Beduinen geben als Zeichen der Ehrfurcht noch einen Kuß auf die Stirn, die anderen orientalischen Herrscher lassen nur die niedrigste Art der Huldigung zu. Der Midrasch giebt den Kuß nur bei drei Akten zu, bei der Huldigung, beim Abschied (Ruth 1, 14.), beim Willkommen (2 M. 4, 27.). — Sept. fügen dem Verse hinzu (zum Fürsten): „über Jisrael und du wirst herrschen über das Volk des Herrn und wirst es retten aus der Hand seiner Feinde, und das soll dir das Zeichen sein, daß der Herr dich zum Herrscher über sein Erbtheil gesetzt hat." — 2. Als Wahrzeichen für Schaul werden allerdings die

Aegyptische Art der Salbung.

Figure 2. The Egyptian method of annointing. From the Philippson Bible, page 287.

younger one. Although the emotional price of this flattering identification with Joseph was quite high, since it implied the death of Freud's mother as a consequence of the prospective birth, the events of his childhood had already prepared him to expect such a loss. The unhappy experiences involving Philipp that congealed in the early screen memory, had established the link between the appearance of unwanted siblings and the loss of the nursemaid's maternal affection. Thus the dream could easily incorporate this allusion to his mother's death as the apparent cause of the anxiety already aroused by the sexual themes. The dream of the bird-beaked figures illustrates in a striking manner the way Freud's reading of the Philippson Bible channeled the direction of his thoughts and feelings as he attempted to define his identity in response to one of the ordinary crises of childhood. To the young child groping for answers to the complex and troubling questions of identity and sexuality, the story of Joseph provided reassurance and suggested an attractive pattern for his future.

Freud's conscious knowledge of the Bible was mediated through the mind of Ludwig Philippson. Philippson was a member of a Jewish family which rose to prominence toward the end of the era of the German Enlightenment. His father, Moses Philippson, taught himself to read German, studied the works of Kant, Lessing, and Moses Mendelssohn, and eventually devoted himself to publishing. He published various translations of parts of the Bible by himself and others; and his own translations were praised for the pure and "noble style" of his German.[44] Throughout his life he devoted himself to the task of facilitating, through education and publication, the exchange of ideas between Jews and Germans. As a descendant observed, he was a "true representative of the Enlightenment, he shared the optimism of his German contemporaries. He never lost courage in spite of all disappointments."[45]

Ludwig Philippson was only three when his father died in 1814, but under the influence of his mother and older brother, he came to share his father's ideals and outlook. He received his elementary education at the Franzschule in Dessau, where his father once taught, and then went on to attend the Gymnasium of the Francksche Stiftungen in Halle, where his brother lived. This famous Protestant school had been founded by the Pietist theologian August Hermann Francke, whose religious beliefs, following those of his teacher, Philipp Jakob Spener, emphasized the need for supple-

[44] Johanna Philippson, "The Philippsons, a German-Jewish Family," (hereafter Johanna Philippson), *Publications of the Leo Baeck Institute*, 7 (London, 1962), 98.
[45] Ibid.

menting Lutheran religious dogma with a strong emphasis on the inner spiritual life of the individual. The Pietists aimed at cultivating that inner spiritual freedom emphasized by Luther as an aspect of the deep faith which bound the individual Christian to God, and the Pietist tradition contributed in important ways to the thought of such prominent figures of the German Enlightenment as Lessing, Kant, and Goethe. Up to the time when Ludwig Philippson applied for admission to the Gymnasium of the Franckesche Stiftungen, no Jew had ever attended the school, and his first application was turned down by the headmaster. Thereupon, Ludwig's older brother, Phoebus, protested to the head of the foundation, Hermann August Niemeyer, and as Johanna Philippson notes in her history of the family, "Niemeyer, a true adherent of enlightenment, was shocked and decreed that 'the boy, Ludwig Philippson, be admitted to the school at once.' "[46] The assimilationist hopes and ideals of Moses Philippson thus found realization in the educational opportunities opened up to his son.

While at the Gymnasium, Ludwig Philippson began to write poetry, and the subjects of his creative efforts indicate interests and sympathies that remained with him for the rest of his life. In addition to a group of poems about Greek philosophers and a set of metrical translations of the Minor Prophets, he was led by a strong interest in German mythology to compose such works as *Proben der Blüten des Nordens, Wodanslieder,* and *Die Nornen.* He fully shared the pride in German culture and the growing sense of German national identity associated with *Sturm und Drang* literature, German idealism, and the early nineteenth-century Romantic movement. As Johanna Philippson noted, he was "an enthusiastic German patriot. He fights against too great an admiration and imitation of French civilization after the July Revolution of 1830 and praises the German *Genius* of Lessing."[47] After earning his doctorate in classics at the University of Berlin, Philippson was offered a position as preacher *[Prediger]* to the Jewish community of Magdeburg. When he accepted that position he decided to give up any further involvement in studies of the classics or of German philology. Even so, however, the imprint of these earlier studies can be seen in the scope and erudition that informed his commentary and translation of the Bible, a task in which he was engaged from 1838 to 1854. From 1837 to the end of his life in 1889, he also edited the *Allgemeine Zeitung des Judentums,* a newspaper that exposed cases

[46] Ibid., p. 100.
[47] Ibid., p. 103.

of Jewish persecution and fought vigorously for the political and social rights of Jews.[48]

Philippson's assimilationist outlook manifested itself directly in his Bible. Each page reproduced the biblical text in parallel columns of Hebrew and German with a German commentary underneath covering the full width of the page. For the early nineteenth-century German philologists whom Philippson admired so deeply, language was the essence of national identity, and in his Bible the two languages stood side by side in a relationship of mutual enrichment. The language of common discourse was German, the language of the enveloping outer culture, but the inner structure of the book was Jewish; the pages were turned from "back to front." Jewish identity was preserved intact to enrich a friendly and receptive foreign culture—a perfect reflection of the hopes which inspired this emancipated German Jew.

Philippson's fascination with the ideal of nationalism found specific intellectual expression in his commentary on the story of Joseph. Joseph was the instrument through which the children of Israel were brought into the land of Egypt where conditions were ideally suited to transforming them into a nation or *Volk,* and at the very beginning of the Joseph story Philippson emphasized the fact that this move represented the start of "an entirely new era: *the story of how the family chosen for the calling of Abraham became a nation.*" Conditions were favorable in Egypt because it stood in continuous, close relationship to the land of Canaan, and "its caste system and its hatred of foreigners created insuperable barriers to the intermingling of the tribe of Abraham with its native inhabitants, while at the same time its unity of nation and state *[Volk und Staatsverband]* gave an opportunity for the Israelites to educate themselves to nationhood."[49]

In emphasizing the importance of the Jews' development into a nation, Philippson necessarily cast Joseph in a heroic role, for it was by virtue of his skills and accomplishments that the way was prepared for the children of Israel "to receive a welcome acceptance in a country where a foreigner would usually not dare set foot." In terms of character and historical role, Philippson noted that Joseph was "always revered as one of the purest and noblest figures in the Holy Scriptures—particularly the favorite of the young, who observe with pleasure how their hero emerges from sorrowful darkness into the glory of the throne." This fairy-tale-like descrip-

[48] Ibid., p. 105.
[49] Philippson, p. 195.

tion might have kindled the phantasies of any child, a tendency reinforced in Freud's case by the strong personal factors which imparted significance to the story. Philippson's description of Joseph emphasized that "above all there stands out in him a delicate soul which is full of feeling *[gefühlvolles Gemüth]* . . . whose tenderness is described with equal feeling. Moreover, a properly measured, indeed statesmanlike reason *[Verstand]* (which at the same time has a colorful backdrop *[farbigen Hintergrund]* in the depth of his dream life) enables him to maintain a high position in a foreign country till the end of his life."[50] Philippson associated Joseph's success not only with his strength of feeling and sharpness of intellect, but also with the profundity of his dream life.

In depicting Joseph as an inward-looking man of feeling as well as a reasoning statesman, Philippson reflected once again the outlook of his time and the influences which shaped his education: the German Enlightenment and the Pietist heritage. The Pietists had long focused attention on the world of feeling and spirit, and during the late eighteenth century this tradition fed into, and found reinforcement in, the *Sturm und Drang* literary movement, as F. Ernest Stoeffler has shown. Stoeffler characterizes the *Sturm und Drang* movement as a "protest of the younger generation against the hegemony of the prevailing rationalism. The emphasis was upon man's inner experience, upon the legitimacy and significance of feeling. . . . It made room for the irrational aspects of man's experience and for his elemental needs."[51] In reaction to the French rationalist influences embodied in the practices of enlightened despotism, this reemphasis of the world of spirit and feeling was closely associated with the awakening sense of German national identity, and whether it was later synthesized with the rationalist tradition, as in the idealism of Kant and the classicism of Goethe, or emerged in a form antagonistic to it, as in the German romantic movement of the early nineteenth century, this *Innerlichkeit* remained a central element in the emerging national culture.[52] Philippson's characterization of Joseph reflected more the sense of balance and wholeness typical of the tradition's classical phase, but it was freighted with romantic allusions to the inner world of feeling and dreams.

Since Joseph's skill at dream interpretation was of central importance to his role in leading the Jews to nationhood, it is not

[50] Ibid.

[51] F. Ernest Stoeffler, *German Pietism during the Eighteenth Century* (Leiden: Brill, 1973), pp. 240–41. See also Friedrich Müller and Gerold Valentin, *Deutsche Dichtung* (Paderborn: Verlag Ferdinand Schöningh, 1958), p. 99.

[52] Müller and Valentin, pp. 89, 99, 134.

surprising that Philippson took the first mention of Joseph's dreams as the occasion for a lengthy discussion of the importance of dreams in the Bible as a whole.[53] It was through the dream world within man that God exercised his guiding influence. After noting that God warned Laban in a dream and that Jacob thus received a divine revelation, Philippson went on to observe that "with Joseph we have, then, three dreams which foretell the future in images *[in Bildern]* and which are described not only as having come from God in that he wanted to foretell the future through them, but also as being open to a true interpretation only as a result of divine influence—which is why Pharaoh attributes a divine spirit to Joseph." Philippson followed his analysis of biblical dreams with a discussion pointing out similar attitudes in the ancient world generally. The belief that in dreams, "a beneficent deity disclosed remedies and the future to men runs through antiquity, so that the Greeks erected temples to Aeskulapius in which those who were ill found remedies in dreams." As a mature scientist, Freud approached the world of dreams from a medical perspective; the Bible he read as a child suggested this same perspective.

Philippson concluded his discussion of dreams with various references to his own time, and here again the merging of Enlightenment and romantic influences can be seen. "Any impartial contemporary will confess, in any case," he wrote, "that however much the cool rationality which has completely altered the physiognomy of our spirit predominates within us, nevertheless no one can tear himself free from the mysterious weavings of the dream world . . ." Philippson pointed out that "from time to time at important moments in everyone's life one becomes aware of meaningful dreams, in which, however, the threads leading to the intentional *[Berechneten]* outer world are lacking, so that the dream image soon disappears among the noisy images of reality." He also referred to a mysterious phenomenon which had touched his own life: "somnambulism, which this writer—can he speak of it in so exalted a place—experienced in an irrefutable way in his own family, where quite definite opinions about distant and future matters were delivered with tested veracity."[54] Under such circumstances, he concluded, no sensible individual would shrug off the testimony of the Holy Scriptures on dreams.

By combining meticulous scholarship with a romantic faith in the phenomena of the inner spiritual world, Philippson's commen-

[53] Philippson, p. 197.
[54] Ibid.

tary cultivated an attitude of high seriousness toward the subject of Joseph and his dreams. In treating other facets of the Joseph story, Philippson likewise betrayed a fascination with the world of feeling. He noted that the narrative was for the most part simple and straightforward but that "where the soul of the actor is aroused in powerful surges, it resounds with the pulsating reality of life and rises to a genuinely unaffected but emotionally rich and effective eloquence."[55] When Joseph confronted his brothers on their second trip to Egypt and finally reached the point where he decided to reveal himself to them, Philippson drew attention to the way the Holy Scriptures emphasize Joseph's inner feelings: the news of his still mourning father "would assail his heart; and the Holy Scriptures—realistic as always—allow us to see into this agitation of Joseph's soul."[56] Philippson's commentary also stressed the psychological realism of the story at other points. When Jacob learned that his long-lost son was not only alive, but had risen to a position of almost supreme power in Egypt, his first reaction was a simple lack of comprehension. "Then the resilience *[Spannkraft]* of his soul revived as from a long oppression and once again reared itself in the sunshine of this magnificent and well-deserved joy. How psychologically accurate this is." Philippson then gave a rational psychological explanation of the traditional belief that the prophetic spirit disappeared from Jacob with the loss of Joseph and only returned when he learned that Joseph was still alive: "However much one may doubt this literally, still there lies within it the truth that a heavy loss stupifies even strong spirits to the lofty *[das Höhere]* and causes them to continue a gloomy life sunk in themselves whereas joy strengthens even an aged man and once again widens his view."[57] Here one sees in Philippson himself the same combination of emotional sensitivity and sharpness of intellect that he attributed to Joseph. By valuing the world of spirit and emotion and subjecting it to rational analysis he produced an interpretation rich in psychological insight.

In Philippson's commentary, even the dark, evil side of the world of passion was viewed in a positive light, as part of the instrumentality of God's directing influence. He pointed out that although the events of the Joseph story "find their beginning in evil, in brother hatred and human slavery, even so they are led by God's hand to a fortunate conclusion."[58] Perhaps still more suggestive to

[55] Ibid., p. 196.
[56] Ibid., p. 241.
[57] Ibid., p. 244.
[58] Ibid., p. 195.

the young Freud was Philippson's general characterization of the Jews as dynamic and passionate in contrast to the passive and intellectual Egyptians, whose life and culture he described in detail. Egypt was a land "where a scientific culture arose at an early point—and a significant body of philosophical ideas, clad in mysterious symbols, penetrated into the life of the people."[59] Philippson painted a vivid contrast between "the uniform, rectilinear calm of Egypt which always proceeds dispassionately along the same path" and "the inward [*innerlichen*] emotional character of the descendants of Abraham." This contrast echoed quite precisely the background out of which his own thought emerged, and provided him with a metaphor linking his subject to the culture of eighteenth-century Germany where enlightened despotism incorporated the scientific advances of the French Enlightenment as part of its rationalization of state and society, while the *Sturm und Drang* and Pietist movements turned inward to the realm of spirit and feeling to find a counterweight to this absolutist foreign influence. As a specific example of the differences between the Egyptians and the Jews, Philippson pointed out that "all Egypt calmly allowed itself to be subjugated to its king while in Jacob's small family his blessing inspired boundless confusion, rebellion against the father, and wild passion."[60] Depicting Egypt as absolutist establishment and Jews as passionate spiritual rebels, Philippson subtly associated the Jews with the patriotic and incipiently democratic movement that inspired his own political loyalties.

In the same passage, he went on to cite an example involving another part of the Bible of great importance to the young Freud, the story of Moses and the flight out of Egypt: "So it is indeed the sufferings of Israel and the exertions of Moses versus simply the stubbornness of Pharaoh (i.e., a holding fast to previously arranged relationships) that draws down heaven's wrath on Egypt—under which it nevertheless long endures in calm. It is into this land and among these people that Joseph is taken."[61] By pointing forward to the theme of Moses and freedom in his discussion of Joseph's journey to Egypt as a slave, Philippson emphasized the overall thematic coherence of the Joseph and Moses stories. During Freud's late childhood, the enlightened Josephin spirit of the day may have fostered an assimilationist mood in which identification with Joseph seemed natural, but the figure of Moses and the themes of his story were also important. As Ernest Jones observed, "There

[59] Ibid., p. 207.
[60] Ibid., p. 208.
[61] Ibid.

is every reason to suppose that the great figure of Moses himself, from Freud's early biblical studies to the last book he ever wrote, was of tremendous significance to him. Did he represent the formidable Father-Image or did Freud identify himself with him? Apparently both at different periods."[62] Or perhaps both during the same period; the two alternatives could have blended together in the mind of the developing child.

Since Jewish memories of persecution and oppression were quite recent, the story of Moses remained relevant as a vehicle for thoughts and feelings very different from those associated with Joseph. However powerful Joseph may have become in the land of Egypt, the Bible dwelt on him as a son and a brother almost to the very end of Genesis, as is evident in one of its concluding events. When Jacob adopted Joseph's two sons as his own and blessed them, he gave preference to the younger son, Ephraim, and in response to Joseph's protests in favor of Manasseh, Jacob asserted his fatherly prerogative to do as he intended. Until the family drama of inheritance was played out with the final bestowal of Jacob's blessing, power and wealth could not outweigh paternal authority, and Joseph remained a son. The acceptance of paternal authority expressed in this incident characterized Joseph's relationship to authority generally. Moses, in contrast, quickly assumed his essentially paternal role as defender and leader of the Children of Israel. The Holy Scriptures said little about his family and childhood before moving on to the event that revealed his most characteristic trait, his hot temper. One day, according to Exodus 2:12–13, "he spied an Egyptian smiting an Hebrew, one of his brethren. And he looked this way and that way, and when he saw that there was no man, he slew the Egyptian, and hid him in the sand." The incident showed Moses as a man of action, angry and fearless in response to the enemies of his people. Freud's later description of Michelangelo's Moses reflected this view of the awe-inspiring biblical figure: "How often have I mounted the steep steps from the unlovely Corso Cavour to the lonely piazza where the deserted church stands, and have essayed to support the angry scorn of the hero's glance! Sometimes I have crept cautiously out of the half-gloom of the interior as though I myself belonged to the mob upon whom his eye is turned."[63] Although Freud wrote this passage in middle age, the sense it conveyed was that of a small boy filled with a sense of sinful inadequacy as he confronted

[62] Jones, II:364–65.
[63] Sigmund Freud, "The Moses of Michelangelo," *S.E.*, XIII:213.

his angry father. The expression of the statue seemed to carry him back to that earlier time in his life when this mighty biblical figure symbolized so much of a deeply personal nature to him.

As with Joseph, Freud's early view of Moses was mediated through the lens of Ludwig Philippson's interpretive framework. Through his comments on the stirring events described in Exodus, Philippson conveyed a complex body of religious and philosophical ideas which built on the foundations laid down in his commentary on the Joseph story. The emotionally compelling story of Moses brought his metaphor to its point: the conflict between the forces of freedom and those of an oppressive authority. The conception of freedom developed in Philippson's commentary on the flight out of Egypt and the celebration of Passover reveals once again his profound debt to German Enlightenment thought. He emphasized that when they depart from Egypt, the Jews "become a nation and as such enter into their particular calling as the nation which recognizes and acknowledges one unitary God." In describing the way the Jews came to recognize and acknowledge their one god, he focused attention on the relationship between the inner world of spirituality and the multitude of precise rules governing the celebration of Passover. Because the mass of Jews had not yet reached the stage where they were capable of "a free spiritual recognition and inner vision of this single unitary God," it was necessary to embody the recognition in specific concrete forms which would be the "vehicle and instrument for spiritual realization."[64] On this basis he argued that the Passover rules represented not so much an arbitrary form as "an inner necessity which must be preserved in its entire conception as well as in its most specific regulations."[65]

This conception of an inner necessity based on law strongly echoed the moral philosophy of Kant, and Philippson's further comments on the significance of Passover reveal even more clearly the influence of the German Enlightenment's paramount philosopher. Philippson emphasized that "with their departure from Egypt the Israelites as individuals had to acknowledge themselves as Israelites in a *free* act . . . so that in opposition to the determinism of [external] relationships *[dem Drange der Verhältnisse]* room was given for *an expression of the freedom of the individual will.*"[66] This analysis reflected the basic Kantian philosophical framework of an outer phenomenal world ruled by causal necessity and an inner realm where freedom of will became possible through self-imposed

[64] Philippson, p. 354.
[65] Ibid., p. 355.
[66] Ibid.

law. Philippson's assimilationist outlook and the influence of his Pietist education were evident in this synthesis of Jewish tradition with the German idealist conception of individual freedom and autonomy. The story of the Jews' struggle for freedom from the oppression of their Egyptian taskmasters took on deeper significance as the reflection of a struggle within each individual to achieve autonomy and freedom of the will by imposing law on himself. The story of Moses and the Exodus represented the culmination of the Joseph story in two parallel senses. After Joseph had prepared the way for nationhood by leading Israel and his children into Egypt, Moses' celebration of the first Passover marked the coming of age of the Jewish nation, its moment of self-definition. Similarly, on an individual level, the stories presented a process of growth and development from Joseph the egocentric youth to Moses the mature and responsible leader.

The values and ideals conveyed through Philippson's Bible found fertile ground in the Jewish assimilationist culture of Freud's youth. He received instruction in Hebrew and in the Bible from Samuel Hammerschlag, a man whose outlook closely paralleled Philippson's. Freud remained on terms of close friendship with Hammerschlag up to the time of the latter's death in 1904, and wrote an obituary for the *Neue Freie Presse,* in which he described his teacher as "one of those personalities who possess the gift of leaving ineradicable impressions on the development of their pupils. A spark from the same fire which animated the spirit of the great Jewish seers and prophets burned in him." Like Philippson, Hammerschlag highly valued both the passionate and the rational dimensions of human experience. Freud noted that "the passionate side of his nature was happily tempered by the ideal of humanism of our German classical period which governed him,"[67] a description that echoed the theme of a balanced synthesis of thought and feeling sounded so frequently in Philippson's commentary.

In describing the impact of Hammerschlag's teaching, Freud noted that "religious instruction served him as a way of educating toward love of the humanities, and from the material of Jewish history he was able to find means of tapping the sources of enthusiasm hidden in the hearts of young people."[68] Hammerschlag's ability to grip the emotions of his students reflected the success of a well-articulated educational program, consciously aimed at shaping their emotional as well as their intellectual development. In 1869,

[67] Freud, "Obituary of Professor S. Hammerschlag," *S.E.,* IX:255.
[68] Ibid.

at a time when Freud was his student, Hammerschlag had occasion to describe his educational philosophy and methods in detail, when he published a long explanation of the principles underlying the new program of religious instruction at the Religion School of the Jewish community of Vienna. Time and again he emphasized the importance of employing educational techniques which would engage and direct the feelings as well as the thoughts of students. He argued that religious instruction "was a matter not just of accumulating a certain sum of facts and memorized details but at least as much a matter of stirring the heart *[Aufregung des Gemüthes]* and strengthening the will." He urged the use of methods "which would lead youth to the basic source of our whole religious life, to the Bible, in order to sharpen their perceptions as well as awaken and animate their feeling." For example, even though Hammerschlag called for more vigorous instruction in the Hebrew language, he believed that such instruction should not be intermingled with the dramatic presentation with which an instructor would begin treatment of a particular segment of the Bible. He argued that, after such a presentation, if the teacher tried immediately to use the passage for language instruction, "either the child's imagination *[Fantasie]* would have been so powerfully excited, his feelings so strongly set in motion by what he has just experienced, that his attention could absolutely never be captured for grammatical treatment of the material," or even worse, the moving effect of the initial presentation would be lost.[69]

The idea that religious instruction should try to mold feelings, ideals, and character was the accepted justification for requiring such instruction in almost all of Austria's public schools. The *Österreichisches Staatswörterbuch,* a nineteenth-century handbook of Austrian public law, notes in its article on religious instruction that its compulsory character "rests on the claim *[Forderung]* that heart and spirit *[Gemüth]* must just as necessarily be cultivated as understanding and reason and that religious instruction is the best means to this end."[70] This view exactly parallels what Hammerschlag saw as the chief advantages of focusing religious instruction for Jewish students on the Bible, "a source of instruction at the disposal of our youth from ancient times, the gripping, attractive power of which is unmistakable and uncontested; through which we are able to work an effect on the spirit *[Gemüth]* and the

[69] Samuel Hammerschlag, "Das Programm der Israel. Religionsschule in Wien," *Bericht der Religionsschule der Israelitischen Cultusgemeinde in Wien über die Schuljahre 1868 und 1869* (Vienna: Jacob Schlossberg, 1869), pp. 9 and 30.

[70] Mischler and Ulbrich, p. 991.

imagination *[Fantasie]*, on the understanding and the capacity for thought in such an excellent way."[71] As Freud's obituary of Hammerschlag indicated, these aims were certainly accomplished in his own case. Moreover, in calling for direct study of the Bible rather than a more abstract form of religious instruction, Hammerschlag cited the example of the Joseph story to prove his point. "Could . . . any sort of even carefully arranged systematic instruction give the child even roughly as firm and certain a perception of the power of divine providence; could it implant in him as firm a trust in its protection, as the recital of the Joseph story in the dramatic, vital, form in which the Bible offers it to us?"[72] The sense of security and trust that the Joseph story conveyed made it psychologically appropriate to the age at which Freud first became absorbed in the Bible, and as such it provided both historical and psychological preparation for the story of Moses, a figure whose aggressive leadership offered a model for emergence into manhood.

As a grown man, Freud always retained an interest in the history and artifacts of ancient Egypt, for they took him back to the phantasy world of his late childhood. The many Egyptian images and themes which appear in his writings and various references in his letters provide evidence that the stories of both Joseph and Moses continued to fascinate him into his final years. Max Schur recounts an illustrative incident. In 1936, at the time of Freud's eightieth birthday, Thomas Mann came to Vienna to celebrate the occasion by giving a talk entitled, "Freud and the Future." Schur arranged a meeting between the two world-famous men, and according to his account, "At tea and afterward, Freud and Mann engaged in a long and fascinating conversation, mainly about Joseph and Moses."[73] The theme was a natural one since Mann was then engaged in writing his Joseph tetralogy, and Freud was soon to publish the first parts of *Moses and Monotheism.* Mann's lecture and a letter Freud wrote Mann after their meeting illustrate a remarkable similarity of outlook in their approach to these biblical figures.

In his lecture Mann explored the ties between his own outlook and that of the psychoanalytic school by focusing on the concept of identification. He noted that in his own *Joseph,* "the fundamental motif . . . is precisely this idea of the 'lived life,' life as succession, as a moving in others' steps, as identification—such as Joseph's teacher, Eliezer, practices with droll solemnity. For in him . . . all

[71] Hammerschlag, p. 30.
[72] Ibid., p. 9.
[73] Schur, *Freud,* p. 481.

the Eliezers of the past gather to shape the Eliezer of the present."[74] Mann pointed out how this concept of identification, of the "lived vita" as he also called it, passed over into the mythical, "and that one may as well say 'lived myth' as 'lived life.' But the mythus as lived is the epic idea embodied in my novel." As Mann noted, this interest in myth "penetrates into the childhood of the individual soul" and leads to "a penetration into the childhood of mankind, into the primitive and mythical." He stressed the application of this concept to Freud's own life: "Freud has told us that for him all natural science, medicine and psychotherapy were a lifelong journey round and back to the early passion of his youth for the history of mankind, for the origins of religion and morality."[75] Focusing on this return to childhood, Mann observed:

> Infantilism—in other words, regression to childhood—what a role this genuinely psychoanalytic element plays in all our lives! What a large share it has in shaping the life of a human being; operating, indeed in just the way I have described: as mythical identification, as survival, as a treading in footprints already made! The bond with the father, the imitation of the father, the game of being the father, and the transference to father-substitute pictures of a higher and more developed type.[76]

This line of thought allowed Mann to establish a close tie between his work and Freud's psychoanalytic perspective.

Freud's letter to Mann, written some months later (November 29, 1936), recalled the writer's visit to Vienna as well as this central idea of his lecture: "The beneficient personal impressions of your last visit to Vienna keep coming back to my mind. Not long ago I laid aside your new volume of the Joseph legend with the melancholy thought that this beautiful experience is now over and that I shall probably not be able to read the sequel." Reading Mann's story and thinking about his ideas "of the 'lived vita' . . . and the mythological prototype" had prompted him, Freud wrote, to suggest the following theory: "I keep wondering if there isn't a figure in history for whom the life of Joseph was a mythical prototype, allowing us to detect the phantasy of Joseph as the secret demonic motor behind the scenes of his complex life. I am thinking of Napoleon I." He developed his case in detail, citing Napoleon's

[74] Thomas Mann, *Essays,* trans. H. T. Lowe-Porter (New York: Vintage, 1958), p. 316.

[75] Ibid., p. 317.

[76] Ibid., p. 322.

famous Egyptian campaign: "Where else could one go but Egypt if one were Joseph and wanted to loom large in the brothers' eyes?"[77] In discussing Freud's theory about Napoleon, Marthe Robert argues convincingly that here "Freud resumed the novelistic confession begun forty years before between the lines of the *Traumdeutung*, so that Freud was actually speaking of himself in his subtle analysis of an extraordinary destiny."[78] In support of this argument, it should be noted that in at least one instance Freud consciously acted out the Joseph role in the "lived vita" or "lived myth" sense. Samuel Rosenberg has called attention to an incident in which "Freud concealed two Egyptian statuettes in Karl Abraham's briefcase in a manner similar to that of the Biblical Joseph who had had his silver goblet concealed in the sack of his brother Benjamin, when he came to Egypt to get grain."[79] Here Freud consciously moved in Joseph's footprints in just the manner Mann later described. The dream of the bird-beaked figures reveals that he had begun moving in those footprints as a child.

As Mann emphasized, however, identification is a complex process, involving multiple objects, both phantasized and real, ranging from mythical identification to the "game of being the father," to the search for a more ideal father-substitute. What Robert observes of Freud's later life applies equally well to his childhood: "Freud lived on terms of natural intimacy with the great figures of the Bible; they were so much part of his inner life that he felt himself to be by turns Joseph, Jacob, and Moses."[80] The comparable example to Freud's conscious imitation of Joseph can be found in a letter he wrote to Jung in which he compared himself to Moses and suggested that Jung, like Joshua, would lead the Children of Israel into the promised land, and Freud also seemed to act out the role of Moses on other occasions in his later life.[81] After Vienna

[77] Sigmund Freud, *The Letters of Sigmund Freud* (hereafter Freud, *Letters*), ed. Ernst L. Freud, trans. Tania and James Stern (New York: McGraw-Hill, 1964), pp. 432–33.

[78] Robert, p. 154. Others have noted Freud's identification with Napoleon and Joseph in the context of his "Disturbance of Memory on the Acropolis." See Kanzer, "Sigmund and Alexander Freud," pp. 267–81, and Shengold, "Freud and Joseph," pp. 77–84.

[79] Sigmund Freud and Karl Abraham *A Psycho-Analytic Dialogue, The Letters of Sigmund Freud and Karl Abraham, 1907–1926*, ed. Hilda C. Abraham and Ernst L. Freud, trans. Bernard Marsh and Hilda C. Abraham (New York: Basic Books, 1965), p. 14; Samuel Rosenberg, *Why Freud Fainted* (Indianapolis/New York: Bobbs-Merrill, 1978), pp. 62–67. See also Grinstein, p. 485.

[80] Robert, p. 37.

[81] Sigmund Freud and Carl Jung, *The Freud/Jung Letters: The Correspondence between Sigmund Freud and C. G. Jung*, ed. William McGuire; trans. Ralph Manheim and R. F. C. Hull (Princeton: Princeton University Press, 1974), pp. 196–97; Robert, p. 38.

had been occupied by Hitler's troops, he wrote a letter to his son in England in which he seemed to blend the images of Moses and Jacob: "Two prospects keep me going in these grim times: to rejoin you all and—to die in freedom. I sometimes compare myself with the old Jacob who, when a very old man, was taken by his children to Egypt." As he went on to add: "let us hope that it won't also be followed by an exodus from Egypt."[82] Freud's mood and objective situation combined to call up whatever identification or combination of identifications suited the occasion best. As a child he would not have consciously understood his identifications in the way he later came to, but on the unconscious level their power may have been all the greater for it.

[82] Freud, *Letters,* pp. 442–43.

2 /

Adolescent *Sturm und Drang*

During his adolescence, Freud enjoyed considerable academic success at the Leopoldstädter Gymnasium, which he attended from 1865 to 1873. Except for one semester, he ranked first in his class, and for most but not all of the time, the school records indicate that he was a model student. Only in the second half of his sophomore year did his class rank slip to second, and there is evidence that in that term, and for several semesters thereafter, his usually exemplary behavior gave way to a more rebellious attitude.[1] During this season of discontent, Freud came under the influence of Heinrich Braun, a somewhat older classmate who usually ranked near the bottom of the class, and this friendship strongly shaped Freud's increasing interest in politics. Even earlier, however, Freud's strong political feelings had found an outlet in the world of phantasy influenced by his reading. His own later testimony and bits of evidence gleaned from his school records reveal his interest in a number of heroic political figures drawn from the pages of history and literature.

Freud's favorite heroes—the Carthaginian general, Hannibal; Marcus Brutus, the defender of the Roman Republic; and Karl Moor, the protagonist of Schiller's *The Robbers*—all shared a passionate dedication to freedom in the face of threatening tyranny. Freud's deep and lasting interest in them points up his own political

[1] This information is based on the still private school records of the Leopoldstädter Communal-Realgymnasium in Wien, the Haupt-Catalog der sechten Classe, Schuljahr 1870–71, the Haupt-Catalog der siebenten Classe, Schuljahr 1871–72, and the Haupt-Catalog der achten Classe, Schuljahr 1872–73. These records are now in the archive of the Bundesgymnasium located at Wohlmutstrasse 3. I am grateful to Anna Freud for giving me permission to consult these records.

sympathies and has an important bearing on his later intellectual and emotional development. Like the phantasies of his late childhood, the political passions of Freud's adolescence drew much of their power from psychological forces rooted in his family relationships. These inner forces influenced the direction of his interests over this whole period, from the early adolescent disillusionment with his father which fostered his Hannibal phantasy, to the longing for a maternal figure which subsequently played a part in his attraction to Gisela Fluss and the decision he made shortly before going to college to give up his plans for a political career to pursue one in science.

In *The Interpretation of Dreams,* Freud described in detail the experience of adolescent disillusionment which played so powerful a role in his emotional life from his teenage years until the time of his self-analysis, when he was over forty. According to Freud the experience occurred when he was about ten or twelve, but there is evidence that it may have been a year or so later.[2] Freud wrote that at this time his father "began to take me with him on his walks and reveal to me in his talk his views upon things in the world we live in." On one such occasion Jakob Freud told a story aimed at showing how much better conditions had become for Jews: " 'When I was a young man,' he said, 'I went for a walk one Saturday in the streets of your birthplace; I was well dressed, and had a new fur cap on my head. A Christian came up to me and with a single blow knocked off my cap into the mud and shouted: 'Jew! get off the pavement!' " When the young boy asked, "And what did you do?" Jakob Freud replied quietly, "I went into the roadway and picked up my cap." This example of "unheroic conduct on the part of the big, strong man"[3] conflicted sharply with the heroic image Freud had had of his father, undermining it at a crucial moment in the boy's emotional development.

Although disillusionment with parents occurs regularly in adolescence, Freud's own comments about this experience and the evidence of his later dream life suggest that he may have been particularly disturbed by it. His childhood had left him vulnerable to acute disappointment in several ways. In one of his self-analytic essays he pointed to a problem that had to do with his "criticism of his father, with the undervaluation which took the place of overvaluation of earlier childhood."[4] During his childhood, Freud's

[2] See below, pp. 81–82.
[3] Freud, *Interpretation, S.E.,* IV:197.
[4] Sigmund Freud "A Disturbance of Memory on the Acropolis," *S.E.* XXII:247. See also Schur, *Freud,* pp. 228–30.

Joseph identification, with its implicit respect for paternal authority, expressed this overvaluation, an attitude reinforced both by broad cultural influences and by factors specific to Freud's family situation. Leonard Shengold has noted that, not only in the Joseph story but in many other parts of Genesis, hostility toward the father is redirected toward brothers.[5] Erik Erikson has seen a similar desire to spare the father as characteristic of German middle-class families of the late nineteenth and early twentieth centuries: "When the father comes home from work, even the walls seem to pull themselves together. . . . The mother . . . hurries to fulfill the father's whims and to avoid angering him. The children hold their breath." Furthermore, Erikson notes a sharp contrast between the father's dominant position within the family and the weakness and subservience typically exhibited in the outer world in relationships with equals or superiors, a contrast that became apparent to the son only later and became the basis for adolescent disillusionment. The fact that Jakob Freud was already in his forties during his son's childhood would have reinforced the exaggerated deference that characterized the early stages of this culturally typical pattern of development.[6] Most important of all, the peculiar overlapping of generations in Freud's family created a psychological situation which added particular emphasis to this attitude. Both Freud's dream of the bird-beaked figures and his screen memory of his mother locked in a cupboard show the impact of a psychic confusion of brother and father. Shengold observes of the dream that it linked together incest, Philipp (not Jakob) as the boy's rival, "and Egypt—here connoting . . . the underworld, the sexual world, the land of the dead," and Freud's own analysis of the screen memory reflects the same connections.[7] The frequency of brother-father substitutions in the dreams, phantasies, and psychological slips that Freud recorded as an adult testifies to the continuing emotional power of the childhood phantasy that Philipp had fathered the siblings. As Shengold notes, "In his Oedipal fantasies, Freud spared the beloved, feared, and respected Jacob, focusing instead on Philipp as his rival."[8] The diversion of this hostility pointed Freud toward an unrealistic idealization of his father, and since few fathers could live up to such standards, the effect was to prepare the way for an unusually profound adolescent disillusionment.

[5] Shengold, "Freud and Joseph," p. 70.
[6] Erik H. Erikson, *Childhood and Society* (New York: Norton, 1963), p. 331–32.
[7] Shengold, "Freud and Joseph," p. 73, and Freud, *Psychopathology, S.E.*, VI:49–52.
[8] Shengold, "Freud and Joseph," p. 72.

In response to his father's disappointing conduct in the anti-Semitic incident, Freud conjured up a more satisfying alternative in phantasy. "I contrasted this situation with another which fitted my feelings better: the scene in which Hannibal's father, Hamilcar Barca, made his boy swear before the household altar to take vengeance on the Romans. Ever since that time Hannibal had had a place in my phantasies."[9] Since the Carthaginians, like the Jews, were a Semitic people, it was particularly easy for Freud to sympathize with them in their struggle against Rome, which he associated with Roman Catholicism. His knowledge of Hannibal's oath derived from Livy, who recounted the incident at the beginning of his history of the Second Punic War. In justifying his history, Livy noted the "high passions" at work throughout the struggle, and he told the story of the oath as an example of the Carthaginians' "bitter resentment of what was felt to be the grasping and tyrannical attitude of their conquerors."[10] Livy presented Hannibal and his family as the leaders of the popular political faction in Carthage, the faction opposed by Hanno and his aristocratic supporters, and in writing of his military prowess he emphasized Hannibal's closeness to the common soldiers. This democratic political dimension also extended directly into the campaign against Rome, for often Hannibal sought to win over Italian cities to his side by urging the commons to overthrow the senatorial order and abandon the alliance with Rome.[11] Freud's Hannibal phantasy fused a militant rejection of Catholic anti-Semitism with a strongly democratic opposition to clerical, aristocratic, and monarchical power, thereby recapitulating in more direct form the political message conveyed by metaphor in Philippson's commentary.

The phantasy also had direct and immediate significance as an expression of Freud's deep disillusionment with his father. Although it did not on the face of it denigrate Jakob Freud, it nonetheless set a standard he did not meet, and it masked a deeper level of hostility and rejection, feelings whose existence Freud revealed in the psychological slip he made in recounting the story of Hannibal's oath. In the first edition of *The Interpretation of Dreams,* Freud identified the father as Hasdrubal rather than Hamilcar Barca, even though he was thoroughly familiar with the names, relationships, and history of the ancient Carthaginian family. Since Hasdrubal

[9] Freud, *Interpretation, S.E.,* IV:197.

[10] Livy, *The War with Hannibal, Books XXI-XXX of the History of Rome from Its Foundation,* trans. Aubrey de Selincourt, ed. Betty Radice (London: Penguin, 1965), p. 23.

[11] Livy, Book XXIII (2), p. 168.

was the name of both Hannibal's much older brother-in-law and his brother (both of whom also fought against Rome), the slip in effect replaced the father with the brothers, and in his *Psychopathology of Everyday Life,* Freud indicated that the slip betrayed a hidden wish that he might have been born the son of his older half-brother Emmanuel, rather than of his own father. This was a wish he had consciously entertained at the age of nineteen when he visited Emmanuel Freud in England and was reunited with the playmates of his early childhood, his nephew John and his niece Pauline.[12] Since Emmanuel Freud's branch of the family, in contrast to the Viennese Freuds, enjoyed a substantial degree of material prosperity as well as the absence of any significant anti-Semitic pressure, Freud's wish implicitly criticized his father for his failure to provide these desirable conditions.

Although Freud's Hasdrubal–Hamilcar Barca slip falls into the psychologically characteristic pattern of brother-father substitutions, it exhibits a "reverse polarity" from the early screen memory and the nightmare of the bird-beaked figures: in the slip, the good brother, Emmanuel, replaced an inadequate father instead of the bad brother, Philipp, taking the place of an idealized father. This reversal points up a central unresolved problem of Freud's adolescence: his deep ambivalence toward father and brother figures. Freud's ambivalence took the form of an oscillation between two different mental states: one characterized by attitudes associated with Joseph, the successful, loyal, and favored son, and the other by the defiant, antipaternal, antiauthoritarian stance exemplified by Hannibal, the foremost of the brothers who banded together to overthrow the power of Rome. Freud himself saw this pattern in his personality and described it in a letter to his fiancée in February 1886, when he was twenty-nine. "One would hardly guess it from looking at me," he wrote, "and yet even at school, I was always the bold oppositionist, always on hand when an extreme had to be defended and usually ready to atone for it. As I moved up into the favored position of head boy, where I remained for years and was generally trusted, people no longer had any reason to complain about me." Further on in the letter Freud specifically tied his rebellious adolescence to his Jewish heritage: "I have often felt as though I had inherited all the defiance and all the passions with which our ancestors defended their Temple and could gladly sacrifice my life for one great moment in history."[13]

[12] Freud, *Psychopathology, S.E.,* VII:217–20.
[13] Freud, *Letters,* p. 202.

Here then are all the elements associated with the Hannibal phantasy, and a close examination of Freud's life reveals that the unresolved tension between his wish to play Hannibal, the bold oppositionist, and his desire to enjoy the security and comfort of Joseph, the paternal favorite, provides one of the central dynamics of his creative activity. At the same time, the fact that these opposing psychic impulses long went unreconciled may also account for much of Freud's continuing emotional discomfort, since it left him without an adequate model for the development of a mature masculine identity. In the eyes of the young boy, Jakob Freud had demonstrated his impotence in the face of the anti-Semitic insult, and that failure blocked the way to his providing a masculine model for his son.[14]

In his adolescence, as in his Hasdrubal–Hamilcar Barca slip, Freud substituted the brothers for the father. Swinging away from the father-oriented Joseph story, his imagination turned at that time toward brother figures for an understanding of his developing sexual identity. As was appropriate to this more aggressive phase of sexual development, Freud's Hannibal phantasy centered on a military hero in contrast to the decidedly pacific Joseph, a military hero representing a popular, revolutionary politics as opposed to Joseph's ministerial politics. Militant, revolutionary impulses had, of course, found expression in Freud's personality from early life on, and in *The Interpretation of Dreams* he indicated the childhood foundations of this powerful emotional complex, recalling, beneath the Hannibal phantasy, a similar fascination with Napoleon and his subordinate, Marshal Masséna, whom Freud mistakenly thought to be Jewish. Like Hannibal, Napoleon made military history by crossing the Alps; like Hannibal, he fought against the power of Rome; and like Hannibal, he was a revolutionary and popular leader. Beneath both these heroic historical phantasies, however, Freud discerned a still earlier, purely personal, basis for the powerful emotional forces expressed in them: "It may even be that the development of this martial idea is traceable still further back into my childhood: to the times when, at the age of three, I was in

[14] In *The Interpretation of Dreams* Freud discusses hats as symbols of male genital organs, and at one point he quotes one of his own observations to a patient: "It may seem strange, perhaps, that a hat should be a man, but you will remember the phrase 'Unter die Haube Kommen' ('to find a husband'—literally 'to come under the cap'). . . . At the time my patient told me this dream I had long been familiar with the hat symbol": *Interpretation, S.E.,* v:361. Whatever the general significance of hats as dream symbols, if one applies Freud's observation to this incident from his own life, it suggests that the knocking off of his father's hat could have directly symbolized to him the emasculation of Jakob Freud.

close relation, sometimes friendly but sometimes warlike, with a boy a year older than myself, and to the wishes which the relation must have stirred up in the weaker of us."[15] Freud referred here to his half-brother Emmanuel's son John, who despite his inferior position in the family hierarchy was both older and stronger than he. This "unjust" superiority provided the germ for what later became the antiauthoritarian political dimension of the Hannibal phantasy, for as Freud observed, "There must have been times when he treated me very badly and I must have shown courage in the face of my tyrant."[16]

Since Freud's half-brothers were much older than he, and his brother Alexander was not born until he was almost ten, his nephew John was, in a certain sense, the only real brother he knew during early childhood, and this relationship provided the model for all his subsequent brotherly ties. In *The Interpretation of Dreams* he wrote of John: "Until the end of my third year, we had been inseparable. We had loved each other and fought with each other; and this childhood relationship . . . had a determining influence on all my subsequent relations with contemporaries. Since that time my nephew John has had many re-incarnations which revived now one side and now another of his personality, unalterably fixed as it was in my unconscious memory."[17] In addition to playing the role of superior antagonist, John also provided the model for the beloved fellow conspirator, for it was in league with him that Freud first defied paternal authority to explore the forbidden realm of sex. In a letter to Fliess, Freud later recalled that he and his "companion in crime," nephew John, "seem occasionally to have treated my niece, who was a year younger, shockingly."[18] The strong libidinal ties forged in this common rebellion against authority were thus as much a part of Freud's relationships with John and the various brother figures who followed as were the feelings of competitive antagonism. As Freud himself observed in *The Interpretation of Dreams,* "My emotional life has always insisted that I should have an intimate friend and a hated enemy. I have always been able to provide myself afresh with both, and it has not infrequently happened that the ideal situation of childhood has been so completely reproduced that friend and enemy have come together in a single individual—though not, of course, both at once or with constant oscillations, as may have been the case in

[15] Freud, *Interpretation, S.E.,* IV:198.
[16] Ibid., V:424.
[17] Ibid.
[18] Freud, *Origins,* p. 219.

my early childhood."[19] In Freud's case, then, his brother band of rebels extended across time and included nephew John and all his many reincarnations. The close professional relationships with Josef Breuer and Wilhelm Fliess are but two of the subsequent examples in which Freud sought and found fellow rebels to share his defiance of authority in the exploration of sexuality, and in both cases the relationships eventually moved from the most intimate friendship to bitter antagonism.

That the feelings associated with Freud's brother relationships involved a strong homosexual component seems evident enough from what Freud himself revealed. Ernest Jones made this point in connection with Freud's anonymous analysis of his screen memory of the yellow flowers, a screen memory that involved childhood games with John and Pauline and took the form of "an unconscious phantasy of her being raped by John and himself together." Jones's conclusion that such "hunting in couples" gives evidence of Freud's bisexual disposition seems justified.[20] Homosexuality also figured in the story of Hannibal that so captured Freud's adolescent imagination. On the same pages where Livy recounted the story of Hannibal's oath, he alluded to the possibility of an earlier homosexual relationship between Hasdrubal and Hamilcar Barca as well as reporting accusations of a homosexual link between Hasdrubal and Hannibal. Some stirring of homosexual feeling occurs in most adolescents, and Erikson argues that it was a common aspect of the severe adolescent crisis typical of nineteenth-century German middle-class families.[21] Still, the peculiar configuration of Freud's family and his lasting disillusionment with his father seem to have left him open to the development of particularly intense homoerotic attachments to the various male friends who came to replace John.

The strong interest in politics that Freud developed during his adolescence drew much of its psychic energy from unresolved emotional problems involving brothers and fathers. He translated his family drama into a larger political drama, forming a set of emotional and intellectual connections which conditioned his thought from then on. This process of transformation can be seen in another of the adolescent phantasies that powerfully engaged his thoughts and feelings: that centered on Friedrich Schiller's play *The Robbers.* This heroic portrayal of the rebellious brother band, written when Schiller was himself an adolescent, occupied a unique place in Freud's psychic world, for it became associated with the return of

[19] Freud, *Interpretation, S.E.,* V:483.
[20] Jones, I:11. See below, Chapter 7.
[21] Erikson, *Childhood,* pp. 332–34.

his childhood "partner in crime." John came to Vienna for a visit when Freud was about fourteen, and at that time the two boys acted out a scene from *The Robbers* for an audience of children. This experience captured Freud's imagination and gave direction to his mood of antiauthoritarian disillusionment; decades later he had a dream (the *Non vixit* dream) which allowed him to understand the way the emotions rooted in it continued to influence his adult relations with friends and colleagues. His own full analysis of this dream in *The Interpretation of Dreams* testifies strongly to the lasting impact of his youthful encounter with Schiller's drama.[22]

Further evidence of the Schiller identification is offered by a slip that Freud discussed in the *Psychopathology of Everyday Life.* It involved the brother of one of his women patients, a young man (apparently Friedrich Eckstein) whom he saw frequently and customarily addressed by his first name. On one particular occasion Freud found that he could not recall that name though he had seen the young man earlier in the day. He wrote that he then "went out into the street to read the names over the shops, and recognized his name the first time I ran across it."[23] Attributing the slip to what he called his "family complex," Freud indicated that the analysis showed he had drawn a parallel between the young man and his own brother, a parallel facilitated "by the chance fact that in both cases the mothers had the same first name of Amalia. Later in retrospect," he wrote, "I also understood the substitute names, Daniel and Franz, which had forced themselves on me without making me any the wiser. These, like Amalia too, are names from Schiller's *Die Räuber* which were the subject of a jest made by Daniel Spitzer, the 'Vienna walker'."[24]

Daniel Spitzer was a popular Viennese journalist and *raconteur* whose stories appeared in a newspaper column entitled "Walks in Vienna." The particular anecdote to which Freud referred concerned a certain widow Spitzer had met in a park, a woman whose

[22] Freud, *Interpretation, S.E.,* V:421–25, 480–83. According to a letter Oliver Freud wrote to Bernfeld on April 13, 1944, when John was very young he lived for a year with his grandparents after they moved to Vienna, and then again later when he was fifteen or sixteen he visited for a winter in order to learn German. Peter Swales communicated this detail to me on the basis of his personal inspection of the Bernfeld papers at the Library of Congress (restricted access).

[23] Freud, *Psychopathology, S.E.,* VI:23. Although Freud provided few clues to the young man's identity it is evident that he was Friedrich Eckstein, one of Freud's frequent partners at cards and the brother of his patient Emma Eckstein. Their mother was named Amalia (see Masson, *Assault on Truth,* p. 233), which coincides with one of the clues Freud provided, and the forgotten name "Friedrich" connects with Friedrich Schiller in the memory lapse.

[24] Ibid., p. 24.

deep appreciation of Schiller was rooted in her conviction that his various dramas were written about the members of her own family. Pointing out examples to support her remarkable delusion, she concluded by noting that her brother's name was Karl—the name of the good brother in *The Robbers.* When she said that if she remarried she would look for someone with a Schillerian name, Spitzer teasingly asked if she would like a Franz—a reference to the evil brother in the play. Finally, she asked him his name, and when he replied, Daniel, she seized him by the arm and cried, "That is remarkable! . . . then you are indeed the faithful servant of the Moor family, the old Daniel with the shaking knees!" Spitzer quickly thanked her for reminding him that he had to get his legs to a spa as rapidly as possible and then "departed with youthful agility even if this did not conform with the intentions of the great poet."[25] Freud's mental lapse put him in the same position as the deluded woman in the joke, for the names that came to him, Franz and Daniel, were from *The Robbers,* and in taking action to solve the problem, he played the role of the narrator. Like the "Vienna walker," he "took a walk" which allowed him to break out of the web of Schillerian phantasy when he saw the right name on a sign. The slip demonstrated the momentary resurgence of an adolescent phantasy that had once enveloped him almost as fully as it did the woman in the joke.

A close examination of Schiller's drama reveals why it became a vehicle for the powerful feelings involved in Freud's "family complex." The story revolved around the intense rivalry between two brothers, Karl and Franz, sons of Count Maximilian von Moor. In failing health, Old Moor, as the father was called, was cared for by his young and beautiful niece, Amalia. In addition to their rivalry over the right to inherit their father's domain, the brothers were also rivals for Amalia's love, but she was interested only in Karl and despised the wicked Franz. When Franz succeeded in displacing Karl as his father's heir, Karl was driven to become the leader of a robber band in the hope that, like Robin Hood, he would be able to aid the poor and oppressed while fighting unjust wielders of power. Franz, however, took on just such a despotic role by imprisoning his own father and ruling in his place after spreading the story that the old man had died of shock over the report of Karl's death. Franz also attempted to use his power to subdue Amalia's stubborn resistance to his advances, but she re-

[25] Daniel Spitzer, *Gesammelte Schriften,* ed. Max Kalbeck and Otto E. Deutsch (Munich and Leipzig: George Müller, 1912), 2:136.

mained faithful to the memory of Karl. Eventually, Karl's growing disillusionment with his life of crime as well as his desire to overturn Franz's unjust rule drew him back to his childhood home. The robber band broke into the castle, and in the tragic conclusion both Franz and Amalia died, after which Karl decided to turn himself in to the authorities.

In many of its themes, particularly the central theme of brother rivalry for the father's inheritance, Schiller's drama was strikingly similar to the Joseph story, though it was strikingly different in emotional tone. Schiller himself played on this thematic similarity by referring directly to Joseph in the second act. Tricked by the machinations of Franz into believing that Karl was dead, Old Moor was overwhelmed by grief, and when Franz complained that he had cried enough for Karl considering that he still had him as a son, Old Moor replied, "Jacob's sons were twelve, but for the one he wept tears of blood." In an attempt to deal with his feelings of loss, the bereaved father then said to Amalia, "Go and fetch the Bible, my daughter, and read me the story of Jacob and Joseph! It moved me always so to hear it, and then I was not yet a Jacob."[26] As Amalia read the part of the story involving Jacob's deep mourning over the report of Joseph's death, the old man was so overcome that he fell into a deathlike coma.

This thematic link to his favorite Bible story must have struck the adolescent Freud as particularly appropriate when he first read Schiller's play, for in the drama the "family complex" that had earlier drawn him to Joseph now took on a form more emotionally appropriate to adolescence. Significantly, in contrast to the father-centered Joseph identification which had been facilitated by the coincidence that Freud's father had the same name as Joseph's, the Schiller phantasy exploited the coincidence of names between Freud's mother and the Amalia who was the heroine of *The Robbers.* Just as this name drew together the different elements of Freud's memory slip, so the figure of Amalia provided the focus for the romantic emotions of the Schiller phantasy. The drama's portrayal of the beautiful young Amalia caring for the old father provided a framework into which Freud could easily fit his own family story of an old father with a young wife much desired by the brothers. Moreover, since Amalia was desired by both Karl and Franz, the romantic line of the drama accommodated the sexual phantasy of "hunting in couples" that Freud associated with his nephew John.

[26] Friedrich Schiller, *The Robbers,* trans. R.J. Lamport (New York: Penguin, 1979), p. 69.

Finally, yet another name in the play provided a link to Freud's early childhood. In connection with one of his dream analyses in *The Interpretation of Dreams,* he noted, "It appears that I came into the world with such a tangle of black hair that my young mother declared I was a little Moor."[27] No wonder Freud appreciated Daniel Spitzer's story about the woman who believed that Schiller's plays were written about the members of her own family!

The Robbers at once reflected and helped shape the thoughts and feelings of Freud's adolescent years, and the evidence of his later dream life suggests that the scene he acted out with his nephew John was particularly important in this respect. The scene offers a clear example of how the drama served to translate emotionally charged familial relationships into passionately held political views, a process that provides the key to understanding how and why the world of politics exerted so strong an effect on the thoughts and emotions of the adult Freud. Occurring near the end of Act IV, shortly before the story reached its tragic climax, this scene involved a moment of profound reflection on the part of Karl Moor, whose robber band had returned to the vicinity of his ancestral home and awaited his orders to strike. With his men asleep around him, Karl restlessly took up his lute to play "the Roman's song," which told of a dialogue between Brutus and Caesar, encountering each other as shades in the underworld. In this dialogue Freud played the part of Brutus and John the part of Caesar.[28] Brutus came to Hades fresh from the defeat at Philippi where he, Cassius, and the other defenders of republican freedom went down to defeat at the hands of Mark Antony's forces. To the great German classicists Schiller and Goethe, the battle of Philippi symbolized the demise of freedom in the ancient world. As Brutus said when Caesar asked about the state of Rome,

> Triumph not, proud mourner, in thy spite!
> Upon Philippi's brazen altar smokes
> The final sacrifice of freedom's blood;
> While Rome upon the bier of Brutus chokes.

Caesar's answer overlooked the political reasons for Brutus' part in his assassination and pointed only to the personal dimension of the crime, describing it as parricide. As bearer of the title "father of his country," Caesar could legally call any Roman citizen his

[27] Freud, *The Interpretation, S.E.,* IV:337.
[28] Schiller, pp. 128–30.

child, and according to some legends he was the natural father of Brutus. Caesar declared:

> Thou also, Brutus, thou?
> My son—thy father—son, didst thou not feel,
> The earth entire to thee should homage vow?
> Go—thou as the noblest Roman art renowned,
> Since in thy father's breast thou plunged thy sword.

Brutus' final response accepted the description of himself as son, but went on to reaffirm his deed.

> Father stay!—Upon the earth so wide
> I have never known but one
> Fit to stand at mighty Caesar's side:
> It was he whom you called son. . . .
> Where Brutus lives, for Caesar is no room.

In the figure of Caesar political tyranny was fused with paternal authority, and in that of Brutus political freedom emerged as the justifying ideal of the rebellious son. Psychologically, the scene allowed for the expression of a powerful (even murderous) anti-paternal affect by transforming it into the passionately held political feelings of an ardent republican.

Within the drama as a whole, the Brutus-Caesar scene reflected Karl Moor's tangled relationships with both his father and his brother. Shortly thereafter, Karl discovered his father (whom he thought dead) imprisoned in a tower where Franz had sent him to die. Finding the old man near death, he concealed his identity so that his father would not learn that his favorite son had become an outlaw. Later, in a scene reminiscent of the biblical story in which Jacob stole the blessing of his father, Isaac, Karl went to Old Moor and still without revealing himself, implored his blessing as the old man's deliverer. Old Moor agreed and kissing him said, "Imagine that it was a father's kiss; and I will imagine that I am kissing my son."[29] Here phantasy expressed the deeper reality, as father and son were reunited in the world of their imaginations. Their reunion echoed the encounter between Brutus and Caesar in the underworld, and like it, ended by reaffirming the son's tragic destiny to be the destroyer of his father. When the robber band returned with Amalia, who recognized Karl, he could no longer conceal his true identity and in anguish cried out to Old Moor,

[29] Ibid., p. 153.

"Die Father! Die through me a third time! These your rescuers are robbers and murderers! Your Karl is their captain!"[30] With this Old Moor did indeed finally die, fulfilling Karl's prophetic words.

Although Karl Moor felt deeply guilty for his unwitting part in his father's destruction, the drama actually depicted his competitive and hostile impulses as directed not at his father but at his brother, and through him at the political system he represented. When Karl finally learned how Franz had tricked him into a life of crime as well as plotting their father's destruction, the full force of his anger burst out: "Thus I curse every drop of brother's blood before the face of heaven! . . . I swear, and may nature spew me forth from her creation like a venomous beast if I break this oath, swear never to greet the light of day again, until the blood of my father's murderer, spilt before these stones, shall smoke beneath the sun."[31] From the beginning of the play, Karl set himself against the political order of princely despotism and aristocratic privilege represented by Franz, who was depicted as a ruthless tyrant. After gaining control of his father's domain, Franz himself gleefully described the harsh regime he would impose on his subjects and contrasted it with his father's mild rule: "My father sugared his commands, made his territories one happy family, sat smiling at the gate and called everyone brother and sister. . . . I am not one for stroking and fondling. I will set my pointed spurs into your flesh and see what a keen whip will do."[32] The clash between Karl Moor's revolutionary dedication to freedom and his brother's thirst for tyrannical power drove home the radical political message of Schiller's play, a message that found its most pointed expression in the Brutus-Caesar scene.

Viewed as a study in family dynamics, Schiller's play, in effect, removed the father from the all-important struggle for power and love which preoccupied the brothers, and the adolescent disillusionment Freud had experienced inclined him to identify his own family complex with that depicted in *The Robbers.* In the play, Old Moor emerged from the outset as a weak and ineffectual, though well-meaning, man whose fate was determined by the powerful forces and characters around him. Even toward the end, where the imagery tended to associate him with God the Father, he remained a vague and overidealized figure. Freud's childhood and adolescent experiences disposed him to a similar ambivalence toward his father. The unrealistic measure of heroism expected in child-

[30] Ibid.
[31] Ibid., pp. 136–37.
[32] Ibid., pp. 70–71.

hood phantasy prepared the way for bitter disappointment when his father failed to respond adequately to "the enemies of our people." From that time until much later in his life, Freud's attitude remained split between feelings that his father had proved a failure and feelings of vague affection for the old man's good qualities. In Marthe Robert's discussion of one of Freud's dreams, she observes that it seemed to imply feelings of resentment at his father's failure "to provide his children with a more cheerful and less precarious future. In this respect, Jacob Freud had been a 'vague' father; he had chosen the shaky solution of pseudo-assimilation, which put his son in a false position just where he had the greatest need of stability and truth. Resigned, irresponsible, pusillanimous toward 'the other side,' he had doomed his children by leaving them no other possibility than submission to outward oppression or a shameful inner exile."[33] In its treatment of the father-figure, as in so many other ways, Schiller's play provided a parallel for the unresolved conflicts involved in Freud's "family complex," and in so doing, it strengthened and directed his developing political radicalism. In the wake of his disillusionment with his father, the play helped to crystallize a shift from the optimistic, paternalistic, political inclinations of his Josephin youth toward the rebellious, antiauthoritarian politics represented by the brother band.

Despite the fact that Schiller's play contrasted strongly with the Joseph story in emotional tone, the drama's intellectual content was strikingly similar to what Freud had encountered in Philippson's commentary. One particularly important element of continuity involved the attention focused on inner emotions. Schiller developed a strong contrast between the passionate strivings of Karl Moor's robber band and Franz Moor's "enlightened" despotism—enlightened in the negative sense that he used the tools of Enlightenment thought and science to manipulate emotions to his own advantage. The play also echoed the Bible story and Philippson's commentary in its emphasis on the importance of dreams. At its climax, Franz had a terrifying nightmare which he was unable to forget or dismiss. In his attempts to convince himself that it had no significance, he turned to the old family servant Daniel for reassurance, but in response to his master's skeptical comments Daniel simply repeated his belief that "dreams come from God."[34] Then in the final scenes, some of the most frightening elements of the dream came true as the robber band broke into the castle and it was consumed in

[33] Robert, *From Oedipus to Moses*, p. 119.
[34] Schiller, p. 143.

flames. The drama conveyed much the same attitude toward dreams as that imparted by Philippson's commentary: dreams were mysterious, but highly significant phenomena, which no one should dismiss lightly.

The political themes of Schiller's play must also have struck a familiar chord in Freud's mind, for the work directly portrayed the world of the 18th-century German Enlightenment that so strongly influenced Philippson. The play was written at the time of the *Sturm und Drang* literary revolt against French classicism, and when it was first produced in 1782, the wildly enthusiastic audience clearly saw it as a revolutionary work. One eye-witness reported of that first performance: "The theatre resembled a mad-house—with rolling eyes, clenched fists, and passionate outcries in the theatre hall. Total strangers fell sobbing into each other's arms while women fainted near the door."[35] It was against the backdrop of a prerevolutionary Germany dominated by petty despots who modeled themselves on the example of Louis XIV that Karl Moor delivered his stirring cry, "Give me an army of fellows like me to command and I'll turn Germany into a republic that will make Rome and Sparta look like nunneries."[36] The play's radical political thrust also found direct expression in the portrayal of Franz Moor, who gained success in his ruthless quest for power by making use of the various scientific and rational advances which the French Enlightenment had put at his disposal. In his scornful rejection of religious faith as well as his carefully thought-out use of medical knowledge to hasten his father's death, Franz stood for all those aspects of enlightened despotism that so many eighteenth-century German intellectuals rejected as dangerous and foreign to Germany's spiritual tradition.

Yet *The Robbers* also included other themes, drawn from the German spiritual tradition, that substantially modified its radical thrust and have provided a basis for nonrevolutionary interpretations of the play from the time of its first performance to the present. Modern representatives of this point of view have seen in the drama's religious themes an attempt on the young Schiller's part to deal with the question of justifying God's works in the face of the evil existing in the world, and certainly the poet's early religious training and the drama itself provide evidence for this position.[37] There is, however, no need to choose between these

[35] Müller and Valentin, *Deutsche Dichtung*, p. 113.
[36] Schiller, p. 37.
[37] Friedrich Burschell, *Schiller* (Reinbek bei Hamburg: Rowohlt, 1968), p. 97.

two lines of interpretation, for as Friedrich Burschell points out in his study of Schiller, "It is rather the case that in *The Robbers* two currents of the time are still contending strongly with each other: the undeniable will to freedom and to the transformation of social conditions with the no less powerful belief in the plan of a supernatural order against which one cannot rebel without punishment." Burschell goes on to note, "The young Schiller had certainly turned aside from his childhood [religious] beliefs, but the heritage of Swabian Pietism lived on in him and Klopstock's ecstasies only further strengthened his enthusiasms."[38] For Schiller, as for Philippson and so many other thinkers of the German Enlightenment, the Pietist tradition served to sanctify an inner spiritual realm into which the all-pervasive power of enlightened despotism could not penetrate. From this inner realm the creative artists and thinkers of the time drew reinforcement for a wide range of political, moral, and religious beliefs at odds with the expanding claims of the secular order. In Schiller's play this realm of spiritual feeling provided the source for the demonic, revolutionary elements of Karl Moor's personality as well as for his belief in the moral imperatives of a supernatural order. The balance between revolutionary ardor and moral duty in this early play differed from that struck in Schiller's later works, but the issues posed in *The Robbers,* as well as the overall intellectual framework within which they were raised, remained important to Schiller over the course of his career.

Freud's adult dream life reveals that for him, as for so many Austrians, Schiller was the German freedom poet par excellence,[39] and as Erik Erikson notes, adolescence is the time in the life cycle when ideological issues generally, and the issue of freedom in particular, first tend to assume great importance.[40] Schiller's explanation of the meaning of freedom was central to the political and moral issues developed in *The Robbers,* and no concept was of greater importance to Freud's emerging political consciousness. At the lowest level, the concept of freedom functioned in the play as a rallying cry for the robbers in their opposition to the existing legal and political order. When Karl Moor made his first appearance, he denounced the constraints laws had imposed on him and declared: "The law has cramped the flight of eagles to a snail's pace.

[38] Ibid., p. 98.
[39] See below Chap. 6, p. 267.
[40] Erik Erikson, *Insight and Responsibility* (New York: Norton, 1964), pp. 91, 127–31, 171.

The law has never yet made a great man, but freedom will breed a giant, a colossus."[41] Yet even in the early stages of the dramatic development, voices were raised by the more responsible members of the robber band to warn that untrammeled freedom could also be a destructive force. When the robbers discussed their need for a leader, one of them, a man named Roller, observed: "The beast must have its head . . . Even liberty must have its master. Without a head, Rome and Sparta were destroyed." Another quickly agreed: "Yes . . . Roller is right. And the head must be a brilliant one. Do you understand? A shrewd political head it must be."[42] Although Karl Moor and his robber band justified their freedom from the constraints of law on the basis of their determination to help the poor and oppressed, the drama's unfolding action revealed that this kind of freedom degenerated all too often into wantonly destructive violence. Karl Moor came to be haunted by the band's crimes.

Karl's brother, Franz, also came to be punished for his far more villanous crimes, but in his career it was the limits of power that were tested rather than those of freedom. In the play's opening scene Franz declared his belief that might makes right, and then went on to speak derisively of certain social contracts *[gemeinschaftliche Pakte]* which have been formed. He was particularly contemptuous of the idea that conscience should play a role in questions of political power: "Conscience—yes indeed! an excellent scarecrow, to keep the sparrows from cherry-trees!"[43] These comments expressed the scorn Franz felt for the Rousseauian ideas that inspired the young Schiller, and in the final scenes of the drama the poet exacted a heavy vengeance for this contemptuous attitude toward the inner voice of morality. When, in the last act, Franz appealed to a pastor whose religious views he had formerly scorned, the latter told him, "A tribunal within, that your sceptical speculations will not be able to silence, will then awake, and sit in judgement upon you."[44] Such was indeed his fate, for as he approached his final hours he was virtually driven mad by the nightmares aroused by what he had done.

In contrast, Karl went to his death with a clear conscience based on a new understanding of the relationship between law and man's inner freedom of will. In Act IV, immediately after the Brutus-

[41] Schiller, p. 36.
[42] Ibid., p. 47.
[43] Ibid., p. 33. In this translation *gemeinschaftliche Pakte* is inadequately translated as "conventions."
[44] Ibid., p. 146.

Caesar song epitomizing the drama's basic conflict between freedom and authority, Karl's deep confusion led him to contemplate, and then reject, the possibility of suicide. Confronted with the insoluble riddles of death and eternity, he found support within himself: "Be what you wilt, nameless Beyond—if but my own self to me is true. . . . Externals are but the varnish upon a man—I am my heaven and my hell."[45] Then, in the final scene of Act V, Karl's experiences brought him to realize the futility of the lawless freedom espoused by the robbers. As he renounced any further involvement with the band, Karl declared, "Oh, fool that I was, to suppose that I could make the world a fairer place through terror and uphold the cause of justice through lawlessness."[46] To atone for what he had done he thereupon decided to deliver himself into "the hands of the law" of his own free will. As he explained, he had no doubt that "the powers above" would eventually bring him to justice in any case, but he feared it might happen in such a way that he would be deprived of "dying for justice of my own free will *[mit Willen].*"[47] Karl Moor's action reflected what might later have been called a Kantian moral decision, though when these lines were written Kant had not yet elaborated his epoch-making conception of morality as the exercise of freedom based on inner law. As a mature thinker, Schiller was to become an outspoken Kantian, but at the time he wrote *The Robbers* he drew from the same Rousseauian sources upon which Kant himself relied in the development of his moral philosophy.

For both Rousseau and Kant the concept of autonomy provided the key to any true understanding of morality. Both argued that man's capacity to impose on himself laws of universal scope made possible the only genuinely moral actions, those based on freedom from external or personally interested motives. Karl Moor behaved in this way at the end of the drama when he decided to turn himself in. Having realized the necessity of obedience to law, he decided to submit himself to its punishment of his own free will. He thereby imposed the law on himself, even though it was against his most vital personal interest, the preservation of his own life. Even at the very end, however, Karl Moor remained true to his earlier ideal of helping the poor. He decided to go to the home of a poor worker nearby in order to allow this man to turn him in and thereby collect the reward for his capture.

[45] Ibid., p. 131.
[46] Ibid., p. 159.
[47] Ibid., p. 160.

The various themes linking Schiller's play to Freud's earlier readings in Philippson's Bible and his later scientific work suggest the development of a basic mind set. In addition to the concern with an inner world of dreams and emotions, another element of intellectual continuity involved the emphasis on freedom within the ordering force of law. The conception of psychoanalysis Freud developed in *The Interpretation of Dreams* involved just this idea of achieving freedom from the driving forces of the unconscious by using the rules of psychoanalysis to achieve a greater degree of inner psychic order, and Freud's early readings laid a philosophic and literary foundation for this concept. Freedom and law were, of course, the fundamental issues around which the story of Moses revolved, and their treatment in Philippson's commentary pointed in the same direction as did the final scene in Schiller's drama. As a hot-spirited young man, Moses, like Karl Moor, took up the cause of freedom for his oppressed people and, in murdering the anti-Semitic Egyptian committed a crime as serious as any on Karl Moor's conscience. Yet finally, Moses too came to understand and exemplify the need for basing freedom in law. Philippson's discussion of the first Passover emphasized its significance as an outward manifestation of the struggle going on within each Jew to achieve freedom through self-imposed law. Looked at from a political perspective, the story of Moses, like that of *The Robbers,* justified revolt against the arbitrary power of an established authority in the name of a new and universal law that man could affirm within himself of his own free will.

The political radicalism that figured so prominently in Freud's adolescent phantasy life also found direct expression in his youthful friendships, most particularly in his relationship with his fellow student Heinrich Braun. Braun went on to become a prominent sociologist and politician in Germany, and many years later when his fourth wife, Julie Braun-Vogelstein, decided to write his biography, she contacted Freud to ask for any relevant letters or information he might have. Freud's answering letter, written in October 1927, provides valuable insight into the nature of the friendship. He wrote, "I know that I made Heinrich Braun's acquaintance during the first school year on the day of the first annual report, and that we soon became inseparable friends. I spent every hour not taken up by school with him, mostly at his place." Braun, he recalled, "encouraged me in my aversion to school and what was taught there, aroused a great many revolutionary feelings within me, and we encouraged each other in overestimating our critical powers and superior judgment. He directed my interest toward books like Buckle's *History of Civilization* and a similar work by Lecky."[48] These works by Henry Thomas Buckle and W. E. H. Lecky exemplified the progressive, reformist spirit of English liberalism, and Lecky's *History of the Rise and Influence of the Spirit of Rationalism* may have stimulated Freud's first interest in hysteria. Its first chapter, entitled "On the Declining Sense of the Miraculous," began with a long discussion of magic and witchcraft. One of the bearers of the spirit of rationalism who appeared in its early pages was an obscure sixteenth-century physician named Johann Weier, a man whose scientific accomplishments Freud later (1907) compared with those of Copernicus and Darwin.[49] Freud admired him as one of the early forerunners of the modern understanding of hysteria; in opposition to the practice of witch-hunts Weier argued that many supposed witches were actually mentally ill.[50] Lecky presented him as a "learned and able physician. . . . He was convinced as a doctor that many of the victims were simply lunatics; and, being a very humane man, was greatly shocked at the sufferings they endured. He was a Protestant; and therefore, perhaps, not quite as much trammelled by tradition as some of his contemporaries."[51] After discussing Weier's ideas in some detail Lecky went on to describe his conflict with the illustrious Jean Bodin, regarded by many as the most learned man of his day. Lecky characterized Bodin's attitude toward Weier's writings as follows: "He could scarcely find words to express the astonishment and the indignation with which he had perused it. That a puny doctor should have dared to oppose himself to the authority of all ages . . . was, in truth, the very climax of human arrogance."[52] The rebellious, antiauthoritarian attitude Freud shared with Heinrich Braun found an ideal representative in this enlightened physician who attacked the deepest prejudices and superstitions of medieval Catholic culture and was opposed by the leading defender of Catholic orthodoxy.

Despite the tone of amused irony which Freud's letter to Julie Braun-Vogelstein conveyed as he looked back on his youthful rebelliousness from a distance of more than half a century, he did not attempt to disguise the intense admiration he had felt for his

[48] Freud, *Letters*, p. 379.

[49] Sigmund Freud, "Contribution to a Questionnaire on Reading," *S.E.*, IX:245.

[50] See Peter J. Swales, "Freud, Johann Weier, and the Status of Seduction: The Role of the Witch in the Conception of Fantasy" (privately published by the author, 1982), pp. 20–22.

[51] William Edward Hartpole Lecky, *History of the Rise and Influence of the Spirit of Rationalism in Europe* (London: Longmans, Green, 1900), p. 85.

[52] Ibid., p. 89.

bold and handsome friend: "I admired him, his energetic behavior, his independent judgment, compared him secretly with a young lion and was deeply convinced that he would one day fill a leading position in the world. A learner he was not, but . . . I guessed that he possessed something which was more valuable than any success at school and which I have learned since to call 'personality'." In this adolescent relationship, Braun's charismatic personality clearly gave him the dominant role. As Freud observed, "Neither the aims nor the means of our strivings were very clear . . . but it was understood that I would work with him and never let down his side. Under his influence I also decided at that time to study law at the university."[53] This friendship filled the psychic gap left by Freud's disillusionment with his father over his "cowardly" response to anti-Semitism. In it, he found a place for his adolescent phantasy of a brother band of rebels striving heroically against the forces of oppression, and he readied himself for the coming political struggles by preparing to pursue a career in law.

In his investigation of Freud's early life, Siegfried Bernfeld, the first great pioneer of Freud research, uncovered a considerable body of material that he was unable to publish before his death, and one of the working notes left among his papers (now in the Library of Congress) provides strong support for this picture of Braun's relationship with Freud. Bernfeld's note indicates that when Braun was away attending high school in Leipzig for a number of terms Freud corresponded with him, and in one letter applied to himself a line from Schiller's *The Robbers:* "Why did nature burden me with this ugliness?" According to Bernfeld, Braun's description of Freud reveals that during his high school years he was a timid and anxious boy who was quite fearful of his father. Braun recalled that once when he visited Freud's house and engaged in a lively conversation with his father, Freud had afterward expressed his great admiration for his ease in this man-to-man exchange.[54] The line from Schiller was spoken in the opening scene by Franz Moor, comparing himself to his good brother as a possible object of Amalia's affection. In quoting it to Braun, Freud directly acknowledged his friend as the embodiment of his Karl Moor phantasy and expressed his own inadequacy in the brothers' competition. Not only would Braun, Freud thought, win the favors of an Amalia, but he was able to hold his own with Jakob Freud and speak to

[53] Freud, *Letters,* p. 379.

[54] Schiller, p. 33; Peter Swales communicated the contents of this note to me on the basis of his personal inspection of the Bernfeld papers, Library of Congress (restricted access).

him man to man. Bernfeld's note supports the idea that a fundamentally important element of the adolescent Freud's psychological configuration involved the conflation of father and older brother images in his relationship with Braun.

Since the Gymnasium which Freud and Braun attended published detailed yearly reports that still exist, it is possible by comparing them with Freud's own later recollections to fill out with greater chronological precision some of the details of this important and largely unexplored phase of his development. In his letter to Julie Braun-Vogelstein, Freud wrote that after he met Braun during their first year at the school they soon became close friends and that "the first interruption of our relationship occurred when he—I think it was in the 'Septima,' the highest class but one—left school, unfortunately not of his own free will."[55] The school reports, however, indicate that Braun was a student there during his first and second years (1865–66 and 1866–67) as well as during his sixth, seventh, and eighth years (1870–71, 1871–72 and 1872–73), but during the intervening time period his family lived in Leipzig and he attended school there.[56] Braun was forced to leave the Leopoldstädter Gymnasium during the middle of the final year, but the fact that Freud forgot about the first three-year interruption in their relationship strongly suggests that the friendship became close only during the later two-and-one-half-year period of Braun's attendance at the school. Moreover, that Freud said of Braun "a learner he was not" further supports this conclusion, for the school reports indicate that during their first two years Braun and Freud were both near the top of their class, but during the 1870–73 period, though Freud remained there, Braun did not.[57] Furthermore, the school reports show that it was during the fifth year, 1869–70 in Freud's case, that the Latin class began the study of Livy with readings that included the passage containing the account of Hannibal's oath to take vengeance on the Romans.[58] Although Freud could have read the Livy earlier, this fact raises the possibility that his disillusionment with his father may have occurred several

[55] Freud, *Letters,* pp. 379–80.

[56] *Zweiter Jahresbericht des Leopoldstädter Communal-Realgymnasiums in Wien* (hereafter *J.B.d.L.C.-R.,* preceded by the number of the volume and followed by the year published in parentheses), ed. Alois Pokorny, (Vienna: Gerold, 1866), p. 26. 3d *J.B.d.L.C.-R.* (1867), p. 49; 7th *J.B.d.L.C.-R.* (1871), p. 78; 8th *J.B.d.L.C.-R.* (1872), p. 58. The published school records do not indicate that Braun was a student during his final (eighth) year, but the private records of the school do: Haupt-Catalog der achten Classe, Schuljahr 1872–73.

[57] 2d *J.B.d.L.C.-R.* (1866), pp. 27–28; 3d *J.B.d.L.C.-R.* (1867), p. 49; 7th *J.B.d.L.C.-R.* (1871), p. 78; 8th *J.B.d.L.C.-R.* (1872), p. 58.

[58] 5th *J.B.d.L.C.-R.* (1869), p. 91; 6th *J.B.d.L.C.-R.* (1870), p. 53.

years later than his own estimate of ten or twelve, close to the time of Braun's return to Vienna and the beginning of the intense phase of their friendship—a psychologically plausible juxtaposition. In this new friend Freud found someone ideally suited to take the place of his father as a masculine model. Even though he and Freud were in the same class, Braun was two years older, and as one of his several wives later noted, his good looks made him highly attractive to women at an early age.[59] Braun exemplified in real life the combination of political and sexual potency, which Freud seems to have missed in his father, and which he sought for himself in his phantasized identification with Karl Moor. Such an intermingling of the political and the sexual retained its fascination for Freud throughout much of his lifetime.

As Freud indicated in his letter to Julie Braun-Vogelstein, the revolutionary feelings he shared with Braun found an outlet in his attitude toward what was taught at his Gymnasium. In *The Interpretation of Dreams,* he told of an incident which illustrated this point.[60] Freud wrote, "We had hatched a conspiracy against an unpopular and ignorant master, the moving spirit of which had been one of my school-fellows who since those days seemed to have taken *Henry VIII* of *England* as his model." (Henry VIII was, of course, a model combination of political power and sexual vigor.) In this rebellion against "the school tyrant, the German language teacher," Freud also played an important role: "The leadership in the chief assault was allotted to me, and the signal for open revolt was a discussion of the significance of the Danube to Austria." By comparing Freud's account of the rebellion with the published and unpublished school records, we can identify the other individuals involved and determine its approximate date. Freud mentioned that "one of our fellow-conspirators had been the only aristocratic boy in the class, who, on account of his remarkable length of limb, was called 'the Giraffe'," and it seems highly likely that this was Robert Edler von Siebenrock. There were actually no members of the aristocracy in Freud's class proper nor in that ahead of his, but Robert von Siebenrock was in the class behind, along with Freud's close friend Eduard Silberstein.[61] Furthermore, it seems clear that von Siebenrock was close to Freud and Silberstein because he was one of the handful of Gymnasium students Freud referred to later in his correspondence with Silberstein. Von Siebenrock

[59] Julie Braun-Vogelstein, *Heinrich Braun* (Stuttgart: Deutsche Verlag, 1967), p. 22.

[60] Freud, *Interpretation, S.E.,* IV:211–12.

[61] See 7th *J.B.d.L.C.-R.* (1871) and 8th *J.B.d.L.C.-R.* (1872).

could also have shared a German class with Freud even though he was a year behind, because the published yearly report for 1871 indicates that German was taught to both the fifth and the sixth class by the same man, A. J. Seidl.[62] This man was probably the "school tyrant" of Freud's account, and he could easily have combined the two years into a single class since both groups were quite small. The date of the event is suggested by the unpublished school records, which indicate that in the second semester of the 1870–71 academic year (Freud's sixth year) his grades in deportment, along with those of most of the other members of his class, suffered a precipitous decline: Freud fell from "musterhaft" (outstanding) to "entsprechend" (satisfactory), a drop of two full levels.[63] During the next year and a half, he rose one notch to "lobenswert" (praiseworthy), but not until his final semester, the semester Heinrich Braun was expelled from the school, did his deportment grade once again reach the highest level.[64] This dating of the "revolt" in the spring semester of 1871 coincides exactly with Freud's statement that he was fifteen at the time.

Freud's account of this classroom conspiracy against the "school tyrant" echoes the political desire expressed in his Schiller phantasy to play Brutus against the tyranny of Julius Caesar, and the school records indicate that he actually played this role more than once. As well as acting out the Brutus-Caesar dialogue from *The Robbers* with his nephew when he was fourteen, he took the part of Brutus in a reading at his school when he was fifteen. The published yearly report for 1870–71 indicated that on July 29, 1871, as part of the school's annual concluding festivities, Freud and another student read the dialogue between Brutus and Cassius from Act IV, Scene 3 of Shakespeare's *Julius Caesar.* In this scene the conspirators fell out over Cassius' lenient attitude toward corruption, and even though they achieved a reconciliation, it provided an opportunity for showing the purity of Brutus' motives. Near the beginning of the dialogue Brutus declared:

> Remember March, the ides of March remember!
> Did not great Julius bleed for justice' sake?
> What villain touch'd his body that did stab,
> And not for justice? What! shall one of us,
> That struck the foremost man of all this world

[62] 7th *J.B.d.L.C.-R.* (1871), p. 73.
[63] Haupt-Catalog der sechsten Classe, Schuljahr 1870–71.
[64] Haupt-Catalog der siebenten Classe, Schuljahr 1871–72, Haupt-Catalog der achten Classe, Schuljahr 1872–73.

> But for supporting robbers,—shall we now
> Contaminate our fingers with base bribes. . . .

The passage Freud read defended Brutus' assault on tyranny in the name of justice, a theme sounded again in one of his earliest letters. Writing to his friend Emil Fluss on March 17, 1873, Freud reported that he and his sisters performed a theatrical piece for Purim, the Jewish holiday celebrating the deliverance of the Jews from massacre by Haman. Freud did not say what they performed, but in referring to Purim he noted that "it fell on the—to all of us holy—13th of March, on which of course Caesar was also murdered."[65] This remark reveals quite clearly the way the subject of Jewish persecution directly activated Freud's profound feelings of opposition to tyranny. Since relatively little evidence from his adolescent years remains, these repeated instances of his acting out the role of Brutus, the tyrannicide, testify persuasively to the emotional depth of his antiauthoritarian political phantasies. He clearly missed no opportunity for giving expression to his radical political feelings, and these feelings strongly influenced his closest friendships, his performance at school, and his plans for a career.

During Freud's final year at the Leopoldstädter Gymnasium, his professional plans underwent an important change. He decided to enter the field of medicine rather than law, a crucial decision that seems to have been linked to the experience he later described as his first "calf-love." In the summer of 1872, when he was sixteen, Freud returned to Freiberg, Moravia, to spend the vacation at the home of the Fluss family, whom Freud and his family had known from the time of their earlier residence there. He recounted his experience in his 1899 paper on screen memories where, under the cloak of anonymity he wrote, "in the family where I was staying there was a daughter of fifteen, with whom I immediately fell in love. It was my first calf-love and sufficiently intense, but I kept it completely secret."[66] Gisela Fluss, the object of Freud's secret admiration, soon departed none the wiser, and as Freud indicated,

[65] Ernst L. Freud, "Jugendbriefe Sigmund Freuds," *Neue Rundschau* 80 (1969) (hereafter *Jugendbriefe*):684.

[66] Freud, "Screen Memories," *S.E.*, III:313. See K. R. Eissler, "Creativity and Adolescence: The Effect of Trauma on Freud's Adolescence," *The Psychoanalytic Study of the Child*, ed. Ruth S. Eissler et al., vol. 33 (New Haven: Yale University Press, 1978), pp. 467–77. Eissler also connects the Gisela episode with Freud's decision to enter medicine, but his treatment of the experience as "tragic" seems overdrawn and romantic. It also seems questionable to ignore the impact of the adolescent trauma on which Freud himself focused attention when dealing with this period of his life: his disillusionment with his father.

"it was this separation after such a short acquaintance that brought my longings to a really high pitch. I passed many hours in solitary walks through the lonely woods that I had found once more and spent my time building castles in the air." In his imagination, Freud conjured up a picture of what life would have been like if he had grown up in Freiberg with the young woman for whom he now longed: "And then if only I had followed my father's profession and if I had finally married her. . . ." The phantasy created a comfortable if unambitious alternative to the highly competitive Viennese milieu he had momentarily escaped. It offered easy answers to the most important decisions facing him at that point in his life, the choice of a profession and the choice of a wife.

Freud's first encounter with the charms of the opposite sex made so deep an impression on him that it contributed to the formation of a screen memory which subsequently became the subject of his own self-analytic investigation. Disguising the screen memory and the experiences associated with it as those of a former patient, Freud's published analysis provides a framework for understanding the nature of the experience and his reaction to it. The memory, or pseudomemory as he sometimes more accurately called it, involved a childhood scene: "I see a rectangular, rather steeply sloping piece of meadow-land, green and thickly grown; in the green there are a great number of yellow flowers—evidently common dandelions. At the top of the meadow there is a cottage and in front of the cottage door two women are standing chatting busily, a peasant woman . . . and a children's nurse. Three children are playing in the grass."[67] The three children were Freud himself between the age of two and three, his nephew John, and his niece Pauline. Freud's account continued: "We are picking the yellow flowers and each of us is holding a bunch of flowers we have already picked. The little girl has the best bunch; and as though by mutual agreement, we—the two boys—fall on her and snatch away her flowers. She runs up the meadow in tears and as a consolation the peasant woman gives her a big piece of black bread." When the two boys saw this, they threw away their flowers and ran off to get some bread too. "And we are in fact given some; the peasant woman cuts the loaf with a long knife. In my memory the bread tastes quite delicious." Although this seemed to be a memory of early childhood, Freud's analysis revealed that it emerged only well after the visit to Freiberg in 1872.[68] He came to the conclusion that

[67] Freud, "Screen Memories," *S.E.*, III:311.
[68] Ibid., pp. 313–15.

even though it may have been based on an early memory trace, its emotional significance and many of its details had to do with the experiences associated with the visit.

Since a screen memory serves the psychological function of masking an experience of great emotional intensity, it seems likely that the visit to Freiberg marked an important point in Freud's emotional development. Ernest Jones has provided a central clue to its significance. In an unpublished letter of October 28, 1883, Freud mentioned this visit and his momentary infatuation with Gisela Fluss to his fiancée, Martha Bernays, and Jones summarizes its contents: "On looking back he attributed his infatuation to Gisela's black hair and eyes and to the deeply moved state of mind that the visit to his birthplace had induced. It was evidently not the girl's charms themselves, since he commented on his lack of taste—so it was love of some internal image of his own plainly derived from far deeper sources but associated with his early home."[69] Jones's final comment and various details of the screen memory associated with the visit point to the regressive nature of the feelings it involved. The screen memory masked a sexual phantasy to which the yellow flowers provided the key. As Freud pointed out in his analysis, "Taking flowers away from a girl means to deflower her. What a contrast between the boldness of this phantasy and my bashfulness on the first occasion. . . ." The phantasy took the place of the action he did not have the courage to undertake or even to consider consciously. As he observed, "It is precisely the coarsely sensual element in the phantasy which explains why it does not develop into a *conscious* phantasy but must be content to find its way allusively and under a flowery disguise into a childhood scene."[70] In the phantasy, his longing for Gisela Fluss found expression in the yellow dandelions. As he later recalled, "I can remember quite well for what a long time afterwards I was affected by the yellow colour of the dress she was wearing when we first met."[71] The necessity for the flowery disguise suggests that during adolescence Freud found the thought of heterosexual intercourse frightening, and the same thing is suggested by the screen memory itself. In it Freud was assisted in deflowering the girl by his older nephew, and then both boys turned away from the aggressive genital activity symbolized by the flower snatching to the passive oral satisfaction represented by the woman giving them bread. The phantasy was both bisexual and regressive.

[69] Jones, I:33.
[70] Freud, "Screen Memories," *S.E.*, III:316, 317.
[71] Ibid., p. 313.

Why did female sexuality present so frightening a face to the adolescent Freud? In part, he was a victim of the highly restrictive moral code of his day. The all-male school he attended actively discouraged social contacts with girls even when they were of an altogether innocent character. When they were not, and this was discovered, it severely punished those involved. The school records tell of one particularly revealing episode involving three members of Freud's class who were bold enough to explore their awakening sexual impulses. They must have bragged about their adventures to their fellow students, and when the school authorities heard about them they held a full-scale inquiry into the matter. Freud, who was thirteen years old at the time, was among the students called to testify against the three, and as a result of the investigation, the boys were expelled from school.[72] From Freud's point of view, this episode provided impressive evidence that sexual involvement with women could be a dangerous thing. Still, his exaggerated and highly ambivalent reaction to Gisela Fluss makes it seem probable that the repressive sexual climate only reinforced a more basic personal factor involving the longing for a maternal figure expressed in his Freiberg experiences and in the desire for Amalia associated with his Schiller phantasy. In the screen memory, the presence of the two women by the hut recalled the two mother figures Freud associated with his early years in Freiberg. The nursemaid was directly represented, and the peasant woman took on a maternal role by providing the children with nourishment and comfort. Freud's screen memory of his mother locked in the cupboard and his nightmare of the bird-beaked figures both testify to the powerful feelings of loss which he associated with these early memories of maternal affection, and a sense of loss also characterized his experience with Gisela Fluss. As he said of her departure, "it was this separation after such a short acquaintance that first brought my longings to a really high pitch." The next sentence is also revealing. Freud reported that after Gisela left, "I passed many hours in solitary walks through the lonely woods *that I had found once more. . . .*" His correspondence with Eduard Silberstein reveals that he himself was aware at the time of a maternal dimension to his feelings for Gisela Fluss. In a letter of September 4, 1872, he discussed his attraction openly and observed that he had "transferred the esteem of the mother as friendship to the daughter. I am, or consider myself to be, a sharp observer. My life in a numerous

[72] Renée Gicklhorn, "Eine Episode aus. S. Freuds Mittelschulzeit," *Unsere Heimat*, 36 (1965):18–23.

family circle where so many characters developed, has sharpened my eyes and I am full of admiration for this woman, none of whose children can completely come up to her." After devoting several pages to a paean of praise for Frau Fluss, Freud concluded by observing that she "cared for me as for her own child."[74] Freud's Freiberg visit revolved around feelings of the loss of something that had been regained only to be lost once more, and because there is evidence that these feelings, which he focused on Gisela Fluss, contained a strong component of Oedipal longing for his mother, it is possible to understand both their intensity and their frightening character.

In its allusion to aggressive sexual conquest, Freud's screen memory of the yellow flowers fitted in with the adolescent phantasies in which he saw himself as Hannibal, Karl Moor, or Brutus. These heroic men had joined with bold companions to lead a fight against unjust privilege or oppression, and the same pattern characterized the screen memory, since the desired conquest it represented challenged the most sacred of paternal privileges. Moreover, because such a challenge seemed to involve formidable dangers, Freud's phantasy depicted his older nephew as his companion in the deflowering symbolized by the *Löwenzähne* (dandelions—literally, lion's teeth) just as he looked in real life to the *junge Löwe* (young lion), Heinrich Braun, to lead the way in the planned assault on political authority.

In certain important ways, however, the screen memory reveals a vulnerable underside to these heroic phantasies. It shows that Freud also felt a powerful desire to withdraw from aggressive conflict and return to an unconflicted parent-child relationship—which is not unlike what he actually decided to do. Jones noted that after his encounter with Gisela Fluss, "it was ten years before he ventured to fall in love again,"[75] and during that time he avoided the dangerous allure of female sexuality in favor of his studies. Moreover, it was not long after his return from Freiberg that he decided to abandon his plans for a political career in favor of becoming a medical scientist. Just as the events of the screen memory pointed in a regressive direction, from active to passive gratification, so his career choice turned from an active determination to transform the world toward a passive desire to observe and understand the workings of nature. In place of Hannibal the warrior, the model of Joseph the scientist returned to guide his aspirations.

[74] Cited in Clark, *Freud,* p. 25.
[75] Jones, I:33.

Although Freud did not even speak to Gisela Fluss about his feelings during his stay in Freiberg, he did write her brother, Emil, after returning home to begin his last year at the Leopoldstädter Gymnasium. These letters illuminate the process of change and development going on within him during that final year of preparation for entry into the more adult world of university life. In them Freud alluded briefly to his romantic interest in Gisela, but his distanced treatment of the subject betrays the strength of his defenses against the feelings he had experienced. He assured his friend that "there was more irony—indeed disdain—involved in the whole flirtation than seriousness,"[76] and he referred to her under the code name Ichthyosaura, which was the name of a prehistoric reptile. This name involved a pun on her last name, Fluss, meaning "river." Being a female member of the Fluss family made her a *weibliches Flusswesen* (female river creature), like the Ichthyosaura.

The bearing of this episode on Freud's decision to become a scientist can be seen in the letter containing his first mysterious hint that he had decided to change his professional plans. On March 17, 1873, he first mentioned his friend's apparently successful pursuit of a girl named Ottalie and declared that if—as Emil apparently assumed—he (Freud) had been jealous, "still the reason for continuing to feel that way has now disappeared." Then, after a few further comments about Emil and Ottalie, he added, "As for myself, I could report to you a piece of news which is probably the most important of my miserable life. If the latter is ever to have any value it will be because of this event."[77] Having offered this tantalizing statement, he then declared that the matter was not yet ripe for discussion and that he would tell Emil more later. Still, he assured his friend that while he should not expect too much, it was also "no empty flirtation *[leere Tandelei]*."[78] As Freud had doubtless intended, Emil drew from these ambiguous remarks the erroneous conclusion that his friend referred to a new romance or even a "relationship," but as the next letter made clear, Freud's romance involved mother nature: "Will you not be disappointed when I lift the veil? Well, give it a try: I have decided to become a scientist *[Naturforscher]* and I therefore give back to you your promise to let me try all your cases."[79] The harmless joke that Freud perpetrated on his friend provides an important clue to the

[76] *Jugendbriefe*, p. 681.
[77] Ibid., p. 684.
[78] Ibid., p. 686.
[79] Ibid.

unconscious motivation underlying his change of career plans: it suggests that his turn toward science had a sexual motive, and this takes on particular significance in the light of his later work as a scientist of sexuality.

Freud's own subsequent account of his change of career plans provides further evidence that unresolved sexual issues were deeply involved in this decision. In *An Autobiographical Study,* he wrote that "it was hearing Goethe's beautiful essay on Nature read aloud at a popular lecture by Professor Carl Brühl just before I left school that decided me to become a medical student."[80] Alexander Grinstein has found a newspaper announcement of Brühl's lecture series which indicates that it was scheduled to begin on February 9, 1873, but it may have been postponed; there is no subsequent evidence that the opening lecture was actually delivered on that date.[81] That it must have been then or shortly thereafter, however, is indicated by the story Freud later told his friend Friedrich Eckstein about how he came to attend the lecture.[82] According to Eckstein, Freud told him that a friend had been assigned by his newspaper to cover Brühl's opening lecture and had persuaded Freud to go in his place and write the report for him. It is clear from Eckstein's description that the friend was Heinrich Braun. Julie Braun-Vogelstein, in her biography of Braun, noted that Braun received his job as a journalist by presenting himself to the editor of the *Neue Wiener Tagblatt,* who demanded that he prove himself by submitting a report on a lecture being given that evening. According to her account, the lecture concerned Goethe, and when Braun submitted the report, the editor was so impressed he hired him on the spot at a salary of 100 gulden a month.[83] She also indicated that this occurred very near the time when Braun was forced to leave school. The unpublished records of the Gymnasium show that he was expelled on March 15, 1873—which fits closely with the March 17 letter to Emil Fluss where Freud first alluded to his decision to become a scientist.[84] The evidence suggests that Braun probably owed his job to the writing skills of his young friend and that the lecture Freud attended in his place occurred between mid-February and mid-March 1873.

As various Freud scholars have observed, the essay on nature to which Freud referred presented an erotic description of nature as

[80] Freud, *Autobiographical Study, S.E.,* xx:8.

[81] Grinstein, p. 263.

[82] Friedrich Eckstein, *"Alte unnennbare Tage!" Erinnerungen aus siebzig Lehr und Wanderjahren* (Vienna: H. Reichner, 1936), p. 21.

[83] Braun-Vogelstein, p. 23.

[84] Haupt-Catalog der achten Classe, Schuljahr 1872–73.

an enveloping, all-sustaining mother.[85] It began "Nature! We are surrounded by her, embraced by her. . . . We live in her midst, and yet we are strangers to her. She speaks constantly with us, but betrays not her secret to us. . . . She dwells in none but children; and the mother, where is she." The importance of approaching nature as a trusting child was further emphasized: "Him who follows trustingly she folds like a child to her heart. Her children are innumerable. To no one is she niggardly but she has favorites upon whom she lavishes much and to whom she shows great devotion."[86] These words echoed a primary assumption of Freud's Joseph identification, the assumption that he was his mother's favorite. Moreover, like his screen memory of the yellow flowers, the essay, in its undertone of erotic Oedipal longing, pointed in a psychologically regressive direction. "Nature's crown is love," it emphasized. "Only through it does one draw near her. . . . With a draft or two from love's beaker she compensates for a life of toil and trouble."[87] As Fritz Wittels has observed, the outlook the essay conveyed coincided with that expressed near the beginning of Goethe's *Faust,* where Faust's desire to plumb nature's depths took the form of an erotic quest and he was moved to ask, "Where shall I grasp thee, boundless nature? Where are your breasts from which all life doth flow?"[88] The hero of Goethe's drama personified the scientist who approached nature in the manner suggested by the essay, and as he was later, during the period of his most fundamental scientific discoveries, Freud was here apparently being guided by a Faustian model. An examination of the essay on nature makes clear how appropriate it was that in his letter to Emil Fluss he should mask his decision under the guise of a new romance. The decision offered an outlet for the immature but powerful sexual feelings that continued to be directed toward his mother, and it did so in a way that presented none of the dangers involved in the open challenge to paternal privilege implicit in his earlier plans for a political career.

Nonetheless, Freud's letters to Fluss give evidence that he by no means intended to abandon radicalism altogether. The March 17 letter that first hinted at the new romance with science also contained the first openly political remark to be found in this correspondence, and the next letter, which formally announced his

[85] Fritz Wittels, *Freud and His Time* (New York: Grosset & Dunlap, 1931), pp. 34–35; Schorske, *Vienna,* p. 193.
[86] Wittels, pp. 31, 32.
[87] Ibid., p. 33.
[88] Ibid., p. 34.

decision, began on a radical note with an extended satirical comment on the celebration of the emperor's twenty-five-year jubilee. During these ceremonies, Freud observed, "an almost Siberian coldness prevailed, a democratic rain soaked roads and meadows . . . while the worthy populace covered themselves with umbrellas and scarcely tipped their hats." Proudly noting that he certainly did not tip *his* hat to the emperor, he took satisfaction in his own position "as a thinking man and an upright citizen." He also referred derisively to the aristocracy as "that bunch of crowned heads whose very existence is the best evidence against the doctrine of a purposeful universe, for they are not even good at serving the purpose of drones in a beehive; moreover we do not need them for that."[89] With this final adolescent sexual dig, Freud depicted the nobility as socially and sexually useless. Only three paragraphs later did Freud turn to his decision to become a scientist, and when he did so, he used punning language: "I will seek insight into the centuries-old laws *[Akten]* of nature and perhaps even become aware of her eternal process *[Prozess]*."[90] By using legal terminology—"Akten" meaning laws and "Prozess" meaning trial or case as well as process—to describe his scientific aims, Freud employed the language appropriate to his former political plans to serve his new scientific concerns. As his later political dreams show, this intermingling of scientific and political themes proved to be an enduring characteristic of his thought. Freud's puns and his political comments in these two letters seem aimed at compensating for his abandonment of his political plans; they signaled the transference of his radicalism into his scientific work, where it was to become a driving force in the development of his revolutionary theories.

The various heroes around whom Freud spun his adolescent phantasies of greatness reveal much of importance to an understanding of his emerging personality and thought processes. Hannibal, Karl Moor, Brutus, and Faust caught the attention of his lively, youthful, imagination; and previous scholars have demonstrated the importance of others.[91] Whether historically real or the

[89] *Jugendbriefe*, p. 685.

[90] Ibid., p. 686.

[91] Walter Schönau, *Sigmund Freuds Prosa: Literarische Elemente seines Stils* (Stuttgart: Metzler, 1968), pp. 115–21; Harry Trosman, "The Cryptomnesic Fragment in the Discovery of Free Association," in *Freud: The Fusion of Science and Humanism*, ed. John E. Gedo and George H. Pollock, *Psychological Issues*, IX, nos. 2/3, Monograph 34/36 (New York: International Universities Press, 1976; hereafter Gedo and Pollock, *Fusion*), pp. 229–53. See also John E. Gedo and Ernest S. Wolff, "The Ich. Letters," pp. 71–86 in this collection. Gedo and Wolff emphasize the importance of Freud's capacity for developing selective identifications as evidenced by his letters

products of literary imagination, the stories of these heroic figures struck in Freud a deep emotional chord that allowed them to serve as vehicles for the expression of his unconscious desires. Examining these stories against the background of his early life makes it possible to detect certain recurrent patterns of familial relationships which suggest how and why they held deep emotional significance for him, from his youth into his creative adult years. Furthermore, the ideas and intellectual traditions associated with these figures also fall into a coherent pattern in that they form a series of links between the intellectual framework of the Philippson Bible, which influenced Freud's thoughts and feelings in late childhood, and a number of the most fundamental elements of his outlook as an adult. During his adolescence, Freud found in such works as *The Robbers* abundant resources for the development and elaboration of a world view rooted in the culture of the late German Enlightenment with its interest in the exploration of dreams, emotions, and the other mysterious phenomena of man's inner world. The readings of Freud's youth provided his phantasy life with a pantheon of heroes who were to affect his thoughts and feelings for many years to come.

---

to Emil Fluss. They argue that "he was an adolescent in search of greatness. He needed ideal imago figures for the consolidation of his self-esteem" (p. 86). These authors also stress the connection between Freud's frequently noted ability to draw the maximum benefit from such deeply revered teachers as Charcot and Breuer and the "use of a similar mechanism of selective identifications" with such writers as Horace and Goethe in the development of his literary style (pp. 82–85).

3 / Professionalization: The Double Approach to Mental Activity

The political drives that fired Freud's imagination during his days as a Gymnasium student underwent a fundamental metamorphosis during his university and early professional years, when his ambitions were directed toward becoming a scientist. As a university student Freud continued to be concerned with political questions, but gradually these interests were rechanneled in a way that transformed the political radical into a revolutionary scientist. According to Friedrich Eckstein, Freud later told him that "only after a decade-long detour by way of the medical-biological sciences . . . had he been able at an advanced age to return once again to the problems of his early years, to the problems of philosophy and religious psychology."[1] Although previous treatments of Freud's intellectual development have largely ignored it, the scientific concerns that became central to his professional career bore a direct relationship to these early interests and the political issues underlying them.[2]

[1] Eckstein, *"Alte unnennbare Tage!,"* p. 21.

[2] Jones, following Bernfeld, consistently underestimates the importance of philosophy to Freud's intellectual development, particularly in the case of Franz Brentano (Jones, *Life and Work,* 1:37). The Silberstein correspondence reveals that Bernfeld was dead wrong in arguing that "it is impossible that Freud at that time [his university years] or at any time for that matter was a follower of Brentano. One even wonders whether he would have cared to understand the finer points of his arguments": Sigfried Bernfeld, "Freud's Scientific Beginnings" (hereafter Bernfeld 1949), *American Imago,* 6 (1949):190. Paul Ricoeur provides a valuable corrective to this view of Freud in his *Freud and Philosophy,* trans. Denis Savage (New Haven: Yale University Press, 1970).

The aspect of philosophy that most intrigued Freud during his first years at the university involved problems of psychology, particularly the psychology of religion, and much of his interest in the latter subject had to do with politics. One of the first important philosophers to arouse his enthusiasm was Ludwig Feuerbach, whose psychological analysis of religious faith constituted the foundation of his political radicalism. Freud's philosophical approach to psychology received further reinforcement from Franz Brentano, with whom he studied, as well as from Schopenhauer, whose ideas were important to his teachers. Even the work of Charles Darwin, which inspired Freud's earliest biological research efforts, had important philosophical and theological implications with a direct bearing on current political issues. Both the political and the philosophical elements of Freud's earlier outlook remained important during his university education. The intellectual legacy of the late German Enlightenment, with its dual approach to the material and spiritual worlds and its emphasis on the psychological phenomena which united them, provided a solid foundation for Freud's work as a scientist. Approaching his professional development from this perspective reveals the close relationship between his early interests and the scientific accomplishments of his mature years.

Although a number of Freud's Gymnasium friends went on to attend the University of Vienna as he did, his particularly close friend Eduard Silberstein did not, and it is to this fact that we owe the possibility of a detailed understanding of Freud's intellectual development during his university years. Silberstein (1856–1925), whose family lived in Braila, Rumania, nonetheless attended Gymnasium in Vienna, presumably because it offered much better educational opportunities than Rumania, which was then quite backward. While attending the Leopoldstadt Gymnasium where he and Freud became friends, he lived with a relative, and when he graduated (a year behind Freud) he went on to study law at the University of Leipzig. After this friendship became close, Freud corresponded with Silberstein whenever they were separated by summer vacations, and later, when Silberstein went to Leipzig, he kept in touch with him on a weekly basis, writing long and detailed letters about every aspect of his personal and intellectual life. As the years passed, the pace of the correspondence gradually slackened, and it came to an end in the early 1880s. These still unpublished letters spanning Freud's university years provide an unusually rich source of information about this period of his life.[3]

[3] Heinz Stanescu, "Young Freud's Letters to His Rumanian Friend Silberstein," *The Israel Annals of Psychiatry and Related Disciplines,* 9 (December 1971):197–98.

During the summer before the start of his university career, Freud's letters to Silberstein reveal his continuing fascination with the political themes of his high school years. In his letter of August 2, 1873, for example, he said that he had attended two different performances of Schiller's *The Robbers* in two weeks, one at the Burgtheater and the other at the Wiener Stadt Theater. He also mentioned activities involving his political friend Heinrich Braun; in a letter of August 16, he reported that the next day he and Braun would study French together in the morning and philosophy in the afternoon. Braun seems to have been less interested than he in these scholarly pursuits, however, for Freud observed that he had united himself "with a very lazy comrade who always feigns fatigue" and proceeded with "irrational slowness."[4] The comment suggests the diverging paths of the two adolescent rebels; Braun, the man of action, longed to leave scholarship for politics while Freud prepared to follow a philosophical course to intellectual radicalism.

Freud's intention manifested itself in the goal he set for this first year of study. On July 11, 1873, he wrote Silberstein, "About the first year at University I can tell you that I shall spend it entirely in studying humanistic subjects which have nothing at all to do with my future profession but which will not be useless to me."[5] Further on in the same letter he declared that he would pursue this intention by enrolling in the philosophical rather than the medical faculty. As he looked forward to his first year of university life, Freud exhibited a philosophical orientation toward science similar to that of the Goethe essay which had inspired his choice of a medical career, and this approach was to be of central importance to the shape of his professional education.

Despite the radical political views he held as a university student, Silberstein eventually followed in his father's footsteps and went into banking in Braila, but he and Freud continued to meet and exchange greetings occasionally later in their lives. When Silberstein died in 1925, Freud sent a warm letter of tribute to those honoring his memory. Although an edition of these letters is being prepared, the manuscripts, which are in the possession of the Library of Congress, have not yet been made available to the scholarly public. I am grateful to Sigmund Freud Copyrights Ltd. of Colchester, England, for giving me permission to quote passages from the letters in German and in my own English translation. In citing these letters I will refer simply to Silberstein and the date or dates of the letter unless these are immediately clear in the text; I will also provide the original German text and in the case of passages in Spanish or English indicate that those are the original languages.

[4] Stanescu, "Young Freud's Letters," p. 208 (I have translated this passage from the Spanish).

[5] Quoted in ibid., p. 198.

In the fall of 1873, however, when Freud enrolled at the University of Vienna, he did not carry out his summer plan for a broad humanistic course of study. Instead, he became a student in the medical faculty, and his first semester involved twelve hours a week of anatomy classes, six of chemistry, and related laboratory work. During the second semester his philosophical impulse did find an outlet in at least one of his courses: in addition to anatomy, botany, chemistry, microscopy, minerology, and physiology, he signed up for "General Biology and Darwinism."[6] In Catholic Austria of the 1870s, the ideas of Charles Darwin and the philosophical framework implicit in his work represented a controversial and intellectually radical point of view, a point of view highly congenial to the iconoclastic temperament of the young Freud. As his subsequent letters to Silberstein reveal, he was to become deeply involved in Darwin's theories and the theological issues they raised.

Freud also found an outlet for his broader intellectual and political interests in the Leseverein der deutschen Studenten Wiens, a radical student society which he joined during his first year. This organization, which counted among its members young men who were to become some of the most important political and intellectual figures of late-nineteenth-century Vienna, had as its central purpose the stimulation of a strong sense of German nationalism. The fact that Freud joined the Leseverein as a first-year student and remained a member until 1878, the year the society was dissolved, testifies to the strength of his commitment to the German nationalist cause during these years. Leseverein membership also provided an opportunity to explore other radical and reformist political issues as well as various philosophical, literary, and cultural topics, and Freud's letters to Silberstein reveal his active involvement in the whole range of the society's activities.

A mention of one of the Leseverein discussions in *The Interpretation of Dreams* provides evidence about the course of Freud's intellectual development during this period. In connection with the analysis of his 1898 revolutionary dream, he indicated that at the time of the discussion he was "so full of materialistic theories" that he put forward "an extremely one-sided point of view,"[7] and got into a verbal duel with an older student. Since the Silberstein

[6] Siegfried Bernfeld, "Sigmund Freud, M.D., 1882–1885" (hereafter Bernfeld 1951), *International Journal of Psychoanalysis,* 32 (1951):216.

[7] Freud, *Interpretation, S.E.,* IV:212. I have written a detailed account of the history of the Leseverein and briefly described Freud's involvement in it in my *Dionysian Art and Populist Politics in Austria* (New Haven: Yale University Press, 1974).

correspondence shows that Freud had begun to refer to himself as a "former materialist" by April 1875,[8] his one-sided materialist phase must have belonged to his first year and a half at the university. Such a chronology is further suggested by his changing view of Carl Brühl, the man whose lecture on nature philosophy had inspired him to go into medicine. Freud mentioned Brühl in a March 6, 1874 letter to Emil Fluss in which he contrasted the inspiring ideas of the previous year with his "insipid *[wässerig]*" performance in the 1874 lecture series which Freud had persuaded Fluss to attend with him. Freud was particularly incensed that Brühl could say of Darwinism "that it did not help the natural scientist to understand nature (!) which even an embittered opponent of it would scarcely say."[9] Freud's enthusiasm for Darwinism allowed him to complement the political radicalism of his German nationalist views with a modern scientific position radically opposed to traditional religious beliefs, and pushed him away from Brühl's sort of mystical nature philosophy.

Freud's letters to Silberstein during the summer vacation of 1874 provide further evidence of his political and philosophical radicalism. In his letter of August 22 he expressed his deep contempt for members of the aristocracy and their privileged station in society. He referred sarcastically to the coming of age of the Austrian crown prince, mocking the newspapers for the attention they devoted to the event by observing that "still such days are always noteworthy since they point to the little known phenomenon that even crown princes become a year older every 365 days." Later in the same letter, Freud wrote with equal sarcasm of an encounter between the Archduke von Oldenburg and an innkeeper, an encounter in which the two came to blows. He had nothing but scorn for the deference the police exhibited toward the great aristocrat.[10] Although Freud was less open about his scientific radicalism, one of the books he mentioned in a letter written nine days earlier indicates his growing interest in a "materialistic" point of view on scientific and philosophical questions.[11] He reported that he was reading a book by the German scientist Hermann Helmholtz, who, as Ernest Jones has emphasized, was the leading member of a scientific circle devoted to showing that "no other

[8] See below, pp. 117–19.
[9] *Jungendbriefe,* p. 691.
[10] Cited in Heinz Stanescu, "Unbekannte Briefe des jungen Sigmund Freud an einen rumänishchen Freud," *Neue Literatur, Zeitschrift des Schriftstellerverbandes des R.V.R.* 16 (June 1965):127.
[11] Silberstein, Aug. 13, 1874.

forces than the common physical-chemical ones are active within the organism."[12] This exclusively physicalist approach aimed at destroying the influence of the vitalist nature philosophy which dominated the thought of an earlier generation of scientists. That Freud was reading Helmholtz is further evidence that his first year at the university, which included a course with Helmholtz's close associate Ernst Brücke, had won him over to the new outlook.

Freud's enthusiasm for scientific materialism, however, involved less of a break with the ideals and values of his youth than he may have realized at the time. Scientific modernism and anticlerical liberalism encouraged in him an antagonistic attitude toward religious belief, but the "enlightened" religious outlook expounded in Philippson's commentary retained an influence in the form of a secularized philosophical framework. This can be seen in Freud's comments on one of the books he mentioned in his August 13 letter to Silberstein. The book was *Sartor Resartus,* one of the first major works of Thomas Carlyle, published in 1833–34. Carlyle had previously published a book on Schiller and his intense admiration for the great poet of German idealism may have been one of the factors that drew Freud to his work. A. B. Tennyson notes that in *Sartor Resartus* (The Philosophy of Clothes), "Carlyle was able to embody his own double awareness that everything has two aspects, the spiritual and the material." Playing on the Kantian distinction between a phenomenal world of appearances and a noumeral world of essences, Carlyle employed the theme of clothes to convey "the double vision of material and spiritual, the stripping away of old clothes, the irreducible mystery and divinity of man."[13] Freud's letter to Silberstein shows that he saw essentially the same meaning in the work. After summarizing the story, he noted that it "is in part done as parody and in part as an intelligent viewpoint which proceeds from the assumption that the clothes are a representation of the apparent and the material behind which the spiritual hides itself in shame."[14] Anthony Cockshut has noted that the work's "main theme is that the intellectual forms in which men's deepest convictions have been cast are dead and that new ones must be found to fit the times,[15] a statement that seems

[12] Jones, 1:40.

[13] A. B. Tennyson, *Sartor Called Resartus* (Princeton: Princeton University Press, 1965), pp. 285, 287.

[14] Silberstein, Aug. 13, 1874: ". . . ist zum Theil parodistisch gehalten, zum Theil aber eine geistreiche Anschauung, die von der Voraussetzung ausgeht, dass die Kleider eine Darstellung des Scheinbaren u. Körperlichen überhaupt seien, hinter denen sich das Geistige aus Scham verbirgt."

[15] Anthony O. Cockshut, "Thomas Carlyle," *Encyclopedia Britannica* (1965), 4:923.

particularly relevant to Freud's comment and to this early materialistic stage of his intellectual development. Even as a convinced disciple of the scientific outlook, he retained his interest in the great spiritual and religious issues and attempted to reappropriate them within the framework of the new scientific system.

Indeed, even after a year in the medical curriculum, which certainly insured a close view of the material world, Freud still wanted to pursue his interest in the spiritual by taking other courses. In his September 4, 1874 letter to Silberstein, he argued that "one can find interesting matters enough within one's self and in what changes and remains around us, if one just becomes accustomed to paying attention to it. Apropos of that, I gladly confess to you my need to be instructed even in what is developing in the other faculties and other branches of knowledge in order to avoid the danger of insensibility (for example, typical Bohemian, typical M.D.) to which every individual working in his own field is exposed."[16] During his first year at the University of Vienna, Freud found little opportunity to realize his desire for educational breadth. In his second year he was much more successful in expanding the range and direction of his interest in human behavior. The detailed letters Freud wrote to Silberstein during the 1874–75 academic year indicate that he was beginning to lay down the intellectual foundations for his scientific approach to psychology.

Freud's first letter of the winter term, (October 22/23, 1874) conveyed a strong sense of excitement about both the intellectual and the political climate of university life. He began by describing the situation surrounding the inauguration of the new rector of the university, Dr. Emil Wahlberg. Toward the end of the previous rector's term, the minister of education, Dr. Carl von Stremayr, had sharply criticized the students for cutting classes and had threatened disciplinary measures. Simultaneously, he had alienated the professoriat by criticizing their conduct of examinations. In response, the students had planned a massive demonstration which, as Freud put it, "would remind his Excellency Privy Councillor Minister von Stremayr somewhat forcefully about academic freedom."[17] The students were caught off guard, however, by the

[16] "Zudem gestehe ich Dir gerne mein Bedürfnis, auch von dem, was an anderen Facultäten u. in anderen Wissenschaften vorgeht, unterrichtet zu sein, um der Gefahr der Verstockung (Z.B. Stockböme, Stockmediciner), der ein jeder in seinem Gebiet arbeitende Mensche ausgesetzt, ist, zu entgehen."

[17] ". . . den Herrn Minister Dr. v. Stremayr Excellenz u. Geheimrat etwas nachdrücklich an die akademische Freiheit erinnern sollte."

decision to install the new rector quickly before the protesters had time to organize. Nonetheless, the students found their basic desires realized by none other than the new rector himself, whose acceptance speech was in Freud's words an act of "truly shameless audacity . . . for a Hofrat and Rector Magnificus." Wahlberg declared that it was impossible to expect the university to return to its medieval role of serving the church or the state, and he demanded "unrestricted freedom of scholarship in experiments, research and criticism."[18] This powerful defense of academic freedom elicited stormy approval from the students, and their response stood out in sharp contrast to the hisses they directed at Minister von Stremayr as he left the ceremony.

Freud's letter then went on to tell Silberstein what major fields of study the various members of their Gymnasium circle had chosen. Despite their diverse choices and course schedules, Freud wrote, "we all meet together at Brentano's lectures. He is teaching two courses which we attend regularly: Wednesday and Saturday evenings, selected metaphysical questions, and Friday evenings a work by Mill on the utility principle. Brentano reminds me that you had the idea of going to Fechner's classes, and I urge you to write and tell me what and how he teaches."[19] This passage reveals that Ernest Jones misjudged Freud's interest and involvement in philosophy during his second year in writing "Once a week, however, he took a glance at Philosophy in Brentano's reading seminar."[20] Jones seriously underestimated Brentano's influence, for as this and many subsequent letters reveal, it was the courses with Franz Brentano that most excited Freud during that semester. In another letter written two weeks later (November 8, 1874) he again returned to the subject of philosophy and noted that Silberstein, the law student, had decided to neglect philosophy while, as he put it, "I godless medical man and empiricist attend two philosophy courses and in common with Paneth read Feuerbach. One of the courses is about—listen and be amazed—the existence of God. Professor Brentano who teaches it is a magnificent man, scholar, and phi-

[18] "Für einen Hofrat u. Rector Magnificus war eine solche Rede eine wahre Unverschämtheit. . . . unumschränkte Freiheit der Wissenschaft in Experiment, Forschung u. Kritik."

[19] ". . . in Brentano's Vorlesungen treffen wir alle Zusammen. Brentano liest zwei Collegien, Mittwoch u. Samstag Abends ausgewählte metaphys. Fragen, u. Freitag Abends eine Schrift von Mill über das Nützlichkeltsprincip, die wir regelmässig besuchen. Bei Brentano erinnere ich mich, dass Du die Absicht hattest den Fechner zu hören u. ersuche Dich mir zu schreiben, was u. wie er vorträgt."

[20] Jones, I:37.

losopher although he finds it necessary to support this airy existence of God with his arguments."[21]

With respect to Brentano's religious convictions, Freud's attitude combined deep interest with open skepticism. In his November 8 letter, for example, he promised Silberstein that as soon as Brentano got beyond the preliminaries and actually presented his arguments for the existence of God he would pass them on in order, as he ironically observed, "to avoid cutting you off from the path to salvation through faith."[22] Freud's presentation of himself as a "godless medical man and empiricist" was an accurate description of his consciously held philosophical position. The plans he mentioned to Silberstein in a letter of January 24, 1875, testify to the depths of his commitment to this materialist, empiricist outlook during the early months of his second year. He wrote, "I have decided, and my father agrees . . . to spend the winter semester of 1875–76 in Berlin in order to take courses from [Emil] Du Bois-Reymond, Helmholtz and [Rudolf] Virchow. I am as happy as a child about it.[23] These men were, of course, the patron saints of the modern "materialist," physicalist, scientific school to which Freud's teacher Brücke and Freud himself belonged. The idea of becoming their disciple found an appropriate personal analogue in the suggestion broached to Silberstein in his next letter (January 30, 1875): Freud proposed that if he went to Berlin, Silberstein might come too and both might room with their politically revolutionary friend Heinrich Braun, who also planned to be there. Freud's plan to study in Berlin represents the high-water mark of his "one-sided" enthusiasm for this scientific school. Before long the countervailing influence of Franz Brentano modified both his enthusiasm and his plan.

In addition to describing the political scene and his course work, Freud's letters to Silberstein reveal much about his extracurricular activities during his second year. His letter of December 6 mentioned that he and a group of friends had just put out the second issue of a journal, "containing: the critique of Lipiner's essay on

[21] ". . . Ich gottloser Mediciner, u. Empiriker 2 philosoph. Collegien höre u. in Gemeinschaft mit Paneth den Feuerbach lese. Eines davon handelt—höre u. staune!—über das Dasein Gottes u. Prof. Brentano, der es liest, ist ein prächtiger Mensch, Gelehrter u. Philosoph, obwol er es für nötig hält, dieses luftige Dasein Gottes mit seinen Gründen zu stützen."

[22] ". . . um Dir den Weg zur Rettung in den Glauben nicht abzuschneiden."

[23] "Ich bin entschlossen u. mein Vater stimmt dem bei, . . . das Wintersemester 1875/6 in Berlin zuzubringen, um Du Bois-Reymond, Helmholtz u. Virchow zu hören. Ich freue mich daruf wie ein Kind. . . ."

the telelogical argument authored by me, the foundations of materialistic ethics by Paneth, and On Spinoza's Proof for the Existence of God, . . . by Emanuel Loewy."[24] The intellectual fare of this short-lived journal clearly owed much to the philosophical issues raised in Brentano's class, and it seems likely that all the various contributors attended it. Freud's letters reveal that Josef Paneth (1857–90) definitely attended, and the philosophical friendship Freud formed with him at this time was to endure throughout their university years. Another of the contributors, Siegfried Lipiner, had been at Freud's Gymnasium, and even though he was not in Freud's class, they may have known each other there. The annual report of the Gymnasium for the year after Freud graduated indicates that one of the ceremonies included the reading of a literary piece composed by Lipiner and delivered by Richard Wahle, one of three Wahle brothers who were close to Freud and Silberstein.[25] Lipiner was soon to become one of the leading lights of the Leseverein der deutschen Studenten and the Pernerstorfer circle, the group that dominated the intellectual life of the Leseverein.[26]

Freud's letters show that he took an active part in the activities of the Leseverein during the 1874–75 academic year, a particularly important one for the society. During this time student membership increased by more than 50 percent, from 297 to 466, while the number of professors who belonged grew to include almost the entire professoriat of the three Viennese universities.[27] Dr. Emil Wahlberg, the new rector who so inspired the students with his inaugural speech, also belonged to the society and seems to have been well-disposed toward it; its yearly report noted that "he repeatedly took the opportunity to assure the society of his good will and to support it energetically for which we here extend our sincere thanks."[28] One reason for the gain in student membership was that closer ties were established between the Leseverein and the Burschenschaften, the fraternities which had long provided centers for student political and social activity. The Burschenschaften had boycotted the Leseverein in its early years, but during the

[24] ". . . enthaltend: die Kritik über Lipiner's Aufsatz über das teleolog. Argument autore me, Die Grundlagen der material. Ethik von Paneth und über Spinoza's Beweis für das Dasein Gottes . . . von Emanuel Loewy."

[25] 10th *J.B.d.L.C.-R,* p. 57; Jones, I:163.

[26] McGrath, *Dionysian Art,* chaps. 2–5.

[27] *Jahresbericht des Lesevereines der deutschen Studenten Wiens über das IV. Vereinsjahr 1874–75* (hereafter *J.B. Leseverein*) (Vienna: Leseverein d.d.S., 1875), pp. 4–5.

[28] Ibid., p. 5.

1874–75 academic year, when some of them began to lend their support, their members began to join the society *en masse.*[29] Freud viewed these fraternities with disapproval. In his letter to Silberstein of December 6, 1874, immediately after mentioning the journal he had put out with Paneth and Lipiner, he noted the formation of a new Burschenschaft called Austria, named five students (presumably mutual acquaintances) who had joined, and went on: "I expect from you that you will never run off and join any kind of fraternity, which is also my firm resolution.[30] All five students mentioned were members of the Leseverein, although two of them left the society in the course of the year.[31] One of these two, Samuel Fleicher, was mentioned again in a letter of January 1, 1875, where Freud indicated that he had been expelled from the Leseverein for creating a scandal. Freud felt that particularly in Vienna the members of the Burschenschaften tended to be lacking in seriousness. As he observed to Silberstein in his December 11, 1874 letter, the Burschenschaft members were "high-spirited fellows who instead of studying, drink, gossip, and brew up political nonsense."[32] Freud seems to have had little use for this boistrous side of student life; he preferred more serious activities.

Mentioned or alluded to in his letters are various lectures sponsored by the Leseverein, including one delivered on December 14, 1874 by Dr. Karl Grün entitled "The Three Ages of the Human Spirit."[33] The speaker was the editor of Ludwig Feuerbach's correspondence, and Freud's description of the lecture to Silberstein (March 7, 1875) indicates his enthusiasm for both Grün and Feuerbach. The talk, he wrote, "culminated in a glorification of modern science and our most modern saints such as Darwin, Haeckel, etc.," and he added, "Since the man has, moreover, published a biography of Feuerbach which does justice to the significance of this man whom I honor and admire more than any other philosopher, for that reason I esteem him and rejoice at having such a staunch fighter for 'our' truths."[34]

[29] Ibid., p. 4.

[30] "Ich erwarte von Dir, dass Du niemals in irgendwelchen Farben anlaufen wirst, wie es auch mein fester Vorsatz . . . ist."

[31] They were Victor Schmeidel, Emil Baiersdorf, Hermann Müller, Konrad Löw, and Samuel Fleicher. *J.B. Leseverein,* pp. 24–25.

[32] ". . . zu den hochmütigen Kerlen gehören, die anstatt zu studieren, saufen u. schwätzen und politische Faseleien bebrühten. . . ."

[33] *J.B. Leseverein,* p. 10; see also Silberstein, March 7, 1875, April 11, 1875 and Nov. 21, 1875.

[34] ". . . in einer Glorifizirung der moderne Naturwissenschaft u. unserer modernsten Heiligen wie Darwin, Haeckel u.s.w. gipfelte. . . . Da der Mann überdies eine Biographie Feuerbach's hat erscheinen lassen, die der Bedeutung dieses Mannes,

Ludwig Feuerbach (1804–72), a thinker who also exercised an important influence on Marx and Engels, had achieved his most profound effect through his studies of religion. His most famous work, *The Essence of Christianity* (1841), a book included in Freud's library,[35] approached religion in a way highly congenial to the young Freud's outlook. The Philippson commentary had offered countless anthropological, psychological insights into the nature of religious belief; in Feuerbach this anthropological approach found a much more thoroughgoing and systematic realization. Feuerbach described himself as a materialist, and as Marx Wartofsky observes, it was a kind of materialism "whose attack is on the mystification and alienation of everyday life. . . . This materialism, therefore, transfers, in Marx's own phrase, the critique of the Holy Family to the critique of the earthly family, turns attention from heaven to earth, from theology to this-worldly salvation."[36] Freud expressed precisely this point of view in his February 21, 1875 letter to Silberstein, in which he cautioned his friend "not to act too much like a Tannhäuser in Leipzig: today no one any longer believes in the healing power of the Pope; think not of the impermanence of the earthly but of its importance."[37] This comment, written during the period when Freud was studying Feuerbach, surely reflects the influence of the latter's religious views, and it further supports suggestions of a link between Feuerbach and Freud's later works on religion such as *The Future of an Illusion.* Wartofsky notes that

---

den ich unter allen Philosophen am höchsten verehre u. bewundere, gerecht wird, achte ich den Mann u. freue mich eines so gesinnungstüchtigen Kämfers für 'unsere' Wahrheiten." It seems likely that it was during the discussion following Grün's lecture that Freud became involved in the verbal duel with Viktor Adler to which he refers in analyzing his 1898 "revolutionary dream" in *The Interpretation of Dreams* (*S.E.*, IV:212): "There was a discussion in a *German* students' club on the relation of philosophy to the natural sciences. I was a green youngster *[Ich, grüner Jugend]* full of materialistic theories, and thrust myself forward to give expression to an extremely one-sided point of view." Although Freud does not further identify the lecture, this association to the revolutionary dream seems to allude to Karl Grün through the words "grüner Jugend." The same dream involves a similar word play on the color brown *(braun)* and Freud's friend Heinrich Braun. Furthermore, the reference to materialistic theories and the relation of philosophy to the natural sciences fits, since these were the main themes of Grün's work. Finally, Freud's letter to Silberstein describing the lecture and discussion has an unusually agitated and bitter quality, which suggests that the subject may have been a source of conflict.

[35] Harry Trosman and Roger Dennis Simmons, "The Freud Library," *Journal of the American Psychoanalytic Association,* 21 (1973):661.

[36] Marx W. Wartofsky, *Feuerbach* (Cambridge: Cambridge University Press, 1977), p. 18.

[37] ". . . vertannhäusere nicht zu sehr in Leipzig, es glaubt heut ja niemand mehr an lösende Kraft der Päpste; denk nicht etwa an die Vergänglichkeit, sondern an die Wichtigkeit des Irdischen."

Adolf Weser, in an unpublished doctoral dissertation, has argued that Freud's definition of "illusion" is directly borrowed from Feuerbach.[38] Philip Rieff writes that Freud "privately . . . admitted to remote intellectual connections—with Kant, Voltaire, Feuerbach,"[39] but the Silberstein correspondence reveals that his connections with Feuerbach were far more direct.

In *The Essence of Christianity,* Feuerbach argued that "the fundamental dogmas of Christianity are fulfilled wishes of the heart—the essence of Christianity is the essence of feeling *[des Gemüths]*"[40] and as Simon Rawidowicz points out, this argument contains the fundamental elements of Freud's later treatment of religion as "projection."[41] Both Feuerbach and Freud saw religious beliefs and institutions as outward projections or realizations of emotional needs. Beyond what this similarity reveals about the debt of Freud's later religious works to Feuerbach, it also indicates that Freud came to his study of psychology in part through his interest in religion and that Feuerbach's psychology of religion influenced his movement in this direction. In the foreword to *The Essence of Christianity,* Feuerbach explained that in his book, "theology is not treated as a mystical pragmatology as in Christian mythology, nor as ontology, as in speculative philosophy of religion, but rather as psychic pathology."[42] Another dimension of Feuerbach's psychological view of religion that may have attracted Freud involved the subject of dreams and their relationship to feelings. In Freud's favorite readings as a child and adolescent, the subject of dreaming had loomed large, so it seems plausible that he would have read what the philosopher he most admired said about dreams. Feuerbach wrote: "Feeling is of a dreamlike nature; therefore there is nothing more blessed, more profound than the dream. But what is the dream? It is the reversal of waking consciousness. In dreaming the active is the passive; the passive the active. In dreaming I take . . . my changes of feeling *[Gemüthsbewegungen]* as events, my ideas and sensations as things true outside of myself." He went on to declare that "feeling is dreaming with open eyes; religion is the dream of the wakened consciousness; the dream is the key to the secrets of

[38] Wartofsky, p. 446.

[39] Philip Rieff, *Freud: The Mind of the Moralist* (New York: Viking Press, 1959), p. 24.

[40] Ludwig Feuerbach, *Sämtliche Werke,* ed. W. Bolin and F. Jodl (Stuttgart: Frommann Verlag, 1960), 6:168.

[41] Simon Rawidowicz, *Ludwig Feuerbachs Philosophie: Ursprung und Schicksal* (Berlin: Walter De Gruyter, 1964), p. 349.

[42] Ludwig Feuerbach, *Das Wesen des Christenthums* (Leipzig: n.p., 1841), p. vi., cited in Wartofsky, p. 253.

religion. The highest law of feeling is the immediate unity of will and deed, of wish and reality."[43] Wartofsky argues that in this passage "Feuerbach explicitly suggests the psychological explanation of dreaming as wish fulfillment. Though his analysis deals specifically with religion, and he does not generalize the suggestion in so many words, it is clear that Feuerbach anticipates the Freudian dream theory in its essential particulars."[44] Since more than twenty years elapsed between Freud's reading of Feuerbach and the elaboration of his dream theory, the possibility of direct influence here remains an open question, but there can be little doubt that Feuerbach's psychological orientation did help point Freud toward the professional study of psychology, which he began in the 1874–75 academic year. Freud's enthusiasm for Feuerbach, his repeated references in the letters to Silberstein to the psychologist Theodor Fechner,[45] and his developing relationship with Franz Brentano all fit into a pattern that testifies to the increasingly central position of psychology in his academic interests at this time.

Freud's letters to Silberstein also show that as he began to focus his studies on psychology, he began to lose some of his longstanding interest in politics. The first indication of this important development appeared in the same letter of March 7, 1875 where Freud referred with such enthusiasm to Feuerbach. After discussing Grün's Leseverein lecture he went on to say, "I am so down on politics that I can scarcely say any longer that I have a political opinion."[46] The date of this uncharacteristic statement indicates the probable cause of Freud's disillusionment. He wrote at a time when many of Vienna's university students shared the sentiment, for only a week earlier the widely publicized Ofenheim scandal had reached its climax with the acquittal of Ofenheim on charges involving bribery. Ritter von Ofenheim had made his fortune in railroad construction, and in the wake of the financial crash of 1873 an official investigation had revealed evidence of corruption linking him with some of Austrian liberalism's most prominent representatives. Although he was acquitted of the charges brought against him, few believed him actually innocent. Along with Karl Giskra, a former interior minister, and Anton Banhans, the minister of trade, Ofenheim was severely compromised. The open immo-

[43] Feuerbach, *Wesen*, p. 169.

[44] Wartofsky, pp. 283–84. Feuerbach may also have indirectly influenced Freud through Josef Popper-Lynceaus; see Rawidowicz, p. 350.

[45] Silberstein, Oct. 22–23, 1874, Nov. 8, 1874.

[46] "In der Politik bin ich so herabgekommen, dass ich kaum mehr sagen, ich habe eine pol. Meinung."

rality and cynicism that the trial revealed severely undermined the fragile political prestige of Austrian liberalism.[47]

Freud indicated his own specific feelings about Ofenheim in a subsequent letter (April 11, 1875) where he referred with pride to the Leseverein's reaction to the scandal. Since Ofenheim belonged to the society as one of its supporting members, the scandal touched it directly, and it moved quickly to distance itself from him. Freud wrote, "Our Leseverein is playing a powerful role in nationalist politics and reformist strivings; when the famous Ofenheim was acquitted it undertook through the arbitration committee to have him removed from the membership lists (a proposal which I supported, by the way)."[48] He then discussed the differences in newspaper reaction to the event. In contrast to the liberal *Neue Freie Presse,* which greeted Ofenheim's acquittal with relief and which ignored the action of the Leseverein, the more nationalistic *Deutsche Zeitung,* as well as several provincial papers, had raised the society "on their shield" when they learned of Ofenheim's expulsion. With evident satisfaction Freud wrote, "As I know from a reliable source, Ofenheim was very angry about it. Further, a philosopher, Dr. [Johannes] Volkelt, has presented to the discussion section of our society a lecture directed against the whole Ofenheim clique which was lucid, well delivered, appropriate, important, and well justified."[49] Volkelt's address, delivered on March 10, 1875, contained a stinging indictment of Ofenheim and the whole moral, economic, and political system that had produced him. He contrasted the high idealism of Kant with the moral decay of Ofenheim and such liberal politicians as Karl Giskra. Referring sarcastically to the "heroes of the stock exchange," he declared, "In the eyes of these men of paper and gold who have lost their souls in the rising and falling tides of the money market, reliability has long since been discarded from the order of the day; morality is regarded as something purely conventional, something manufactured from social considerations."[50] So enthusiastic was the Leseverein's response to this lecture that it took the unprecedented step of having

[47] McGrath, *Dionysian Art,* pp. 47–52.

[48] "Unser Leseverein macht stark in vaterländischer Politik u. reformatorischen Bestrebungen; als der famose Ofenheim freigesprochen wurde, hat er es unternommen, ihn durch das Schiedsgericht aus der Mitgliederliste streichen zu lassen (welchen Antrag ich übrigens unterschrieben habe)."

[49] "Ofenheim soll sie, wie ich aus guter Quelle weiss sehr gekränkt haben. Gegen die ganze Ofenheim-Clique hat nun ein Philosoph Dr. Volkelt in der Redehalle unseres Vereins einen Vortag gehalten, der klar u. schön gehalten, angemessen, gross u. sehr berechtigt ist."

[50] Johannes Volkelt, *Kants kategorischer Imperativ und die Gegenwart* (Vienna: Leseverein d.d.S., 1875), p. 17.

it printed along with a statement fully endorsing the views it contained.[51] Freud clearly shared this enthusiasm, and in his April 11 letter he told Silberstein that he was sending him a copy of the lecture.

The discrediting of liberalism brought about by the Ofenheim scandal had the effect of impelling the Leseverein toward a more radical political position, one emphasizing a more socialist—though no less nationalist—outlook, but in Freud's case the process of disillusionment seems to have pushed him toward transforming political into intellectual radicalism. This process was evident in the March 7 letter where he expressed his disappointment with politics and his enthusiasm for Feuerbach. In the following paragraph he referred somewhat skeptically to Silberstein's Social Democratic friends, observing "It would be very interesting to me to know if your Social Democrats are also revolutionary in philosophical and religious matters; I am of the opinion that one can more easily learn from this relationship than from any other whether or not the basic trait of their character is really radical."[52] Freud was saying, in essence, that the philosophical and religious radicalism of someone like Feuerbach (or himself) was more central to a revolutionary position than the political radicalism of Social Democracy. He returned to this issue in subsequent letters, as on April 11, when he wrote to Silberstein: "You are seeking the truth in life just as fervently as I intend to seek it in science. The great question on which you like to speculate daily is for you third or fourth estate, Republican or Social Democrat; for me it is theist or materialist, causal law or skepticism."[53] The subject appeared once again in a brief comment on June 13, 1875, when he regretted that Silberstein's interest in politics had completely driven science from the field. Freud, the most political of adolescents, turned in the wake of his political disillusionment to the philosophical, scientific realm to express his radical impulses. Whereas Silberstein still hovered between moderate and radical left in the seemingly dubious world of politics, Freud had moved on to stake out the exactly analogous position between moderate and radical on the

[51] McGrath, *Dionysian Art,* pp. 50–51.

[52] "Sehr interessieren würde es mich zu erfahren, ob Deine Socialdemokraten auch auf philosophischen u. religiösem Gebiet revolutionär sind; ich meine, man kann leichter aus diesem Verhältniss erfahren, ob der Grundzug ihres Characters wirklich der Radicalismus ist, als aus irgend einem andern."

[53] "Du suchst die Wahrheit eben so dringend im Leben als ich in der Wissenschaft zu suchen meine, die grosse Frage, an die Du täglich denken magst, heisst für Dich dritter oder vierter Stand u. Republikaner oder Socialdemokrat, für mich heisst sie Theist oder Materialist, Causalgesetz oder Skepsis."

great questions of the day in the philosophy of science. From this time forward his interest in politics manifested itself primarily as an undercurrent in his intellectual life—though a strong one—appearing usually in jokes, allusions, asides, and unconscious connectives.

In fact, although Freud's enthusiastic reaction to Johannes Volkelt's Leseverein lecture specifically emphasized the talk's political subtheme involving the attack on Ofenheim and the failures of the liberal order, both the principal theme and the speaker himself also bore a relationship to philosophical issues that increasingly concerned him. The lecture, entitled "Kant's Categorical Imperative and the Present," began with an explication of the fundamental elements of Kant's system, with its central dichotomy between the physical, phenomenal world of nature, which was open to scientific exploration and prediction, and the inner world of spirituality and morality, the essence of which could never be known by scientific, cognitive reason. Here again Freud encountered the theme of the two aspects of reality, the material versus the spiritual, the theme which had interested him most recently in *Sartor Resartus* but which went back to the very beginning of his intellectual development within the German idealist framework of Philippson's commentary. Both Carlyle and Philippson relied on Kant for their understanding of this dualistic outlook, and Freud's letter to Silberstein of April 11, 1875 revealed in its discussion of Kant's concept of synthetic a priori judgments and his *Critique of Practical Reason* Freud's highly sophisticated grasp of the Kantian framework. Although Freud's remarks also show that he by no means fully accepted that framework, it was nonetheless relevant to his developing approach to psychology. Volkelt's own scholarly work may also have interested Freud. Although still quite young at the time of his lecture, Volkelt had already published on Hegel, Schopenhauer, and Eduard von Hartmann, all philosophers with a profound interest in human psychology. Volkelt carried on this interest with the publication in 1875, the year Freud heard his lecture, of his *Traum Phantasie,* a study of dreams that Freud cited extensively in his *Interpretation of Dreams.* Since it is impossible to know when Freud read Volkelt's book, the question of its influence remains open, but it is noteworthy that whenever he referred to Volkelt's work he always did so with warmth and respect, even when he disagreed with it. Freud obviously liked and continued to respect Volkelt's idealist orientation whatever else he knew and retained of his psychological theories.

The philosopher who most decisively shaped Freud's emerging interest in psychology was Franz Brentano (1838–1917), and the Silberstein correspondence reveals for the first time just how direct and profound an influence he exercised. One can well understand Freud's admiration, for Brentano was a remarkable man with a most unusual background. A member of a prominent German family (his brother was the well-known economist Lujo Brentano), Franz decided to become a Catholic priest, and after pursuing theological studies he was ordained in the Dominican Order. As a theologian, however, he opposed the doctrine of papal infallibility then under dicussion, and when it was promulgated he resigned his university position and left the priesthood. Brentano was appointed professor at the University of Vienna in 1874, the year Freud first enrolled in his courses. He came as a controversial figure since his appointment was opposed by both the emperor and the cardinal.[54] Freud's Hannibal phantasy would certainly have predisposed him to admire a man who had first defied the pope in resigning from the priesthood and had then defied both emperor and cardinal in accepting the Vienna position. Furthermore, the phenomenon of Brentano's continuing religious faith combined with his dedication to the English empiricist philosophical tradition (which Freud also followed) deeply fascinated Freud.

Even in the early weeks of the winter term, Freud's letters show that Brentano's philosophy course had already sparked a lively interest in various theological questions, questions Freud pursued with the fellow students who joined together to publish the journal mentioned in his letter of December 6. Most of the Gymnasium friends he had known in common with Silberstein had decided to pursue interests different from his, and this divergence created an impetus for establishing closer ties with new friends such as Josef Paneth.[55] As Freud wrote to Silberstein, "Only in the case of Wahle has my involvement become more active, because his idealistic naivete predisposes me toward him, and with Paneth I stand in a relationship of lively intellectual exchange fostered by the similarity of our studies and aspirations. But Paneth, although otherwise a charming man, is so drunk with his own perfection that it scarcely occurs to him to seek any completion through a friend."[56] None-

[54] James R. Barclay, "Franz Brentano and Sigmund Freud," *Journal of Existentialism*, 5 (1964):8.

[55] Silberstein, Jan. 30, 1875.

[56] Dec. 11, 1874: "Blos mit Wahle hat sich mein Verkehr herzlicher gestaltet, da seine idealistische Naivität mich für ihn eingenommen u. mit Paneth stehe ich in

theless, the friendship with Paneth did prove to be an important long-term relationship for Freud, and when he told Silberstein on January 30, 1875 that the journal founded earlier in the term had expired, he added, "From now on I will have to keep my philosophical thoughts purely to myself or pass them on to Paneth in unimproved condition."[57] Before long, however, Freud and Paneth sought to pursue their philosophical discussions directly with Brentano. In his letter of March 7, 1875, Freud reported to Silberstein: "We two (Paneth and I) have entered into a closer relationship with him. We sent him a letter with objections [to his ideas]; he invited us to his house, proved us wrong, appeared to take an interest in us . . . and now, after we sent him a second letter with objections, he has once again invited us to come see him."[58] These two meetings brought Freud directly under the spell of Brentano's magnetic personality and changed the direction of his university education.

James Barclay, who established a compelling case for the influence of Brentano on Freud even before the evidence of their close personal relationship came to light, emphasizes Brentano's commanding presence as a teacher and quotes a description of him by Alfred Kastil, one of his students who later wrote on his philosophy: "The many years since our last meeting cannot blot out in me the picture of his overwhelming personality. But in those who did not know him I cannot make it real. This unity of strength and gracefulness, of immanent priestliness and aristocratic world-knowledge, of deep seriousness, responsible spirit of inquiry mixed with playful levity."[59] If anything, Freud's letters to Silberstein paint an even more glowing portrait of Brentano, whom he referred to as "this remarkable man and in many respects ideal human being (he is a believer in God, a teleologist (!) and Darwinian and a damned clever fellow, indeed one of genius)." He went on to announce the important news that "especially under Brentano's influence the

---

lebendigem Gedankenaustausch, der durch die Gleichheit der Studien u. Ähnlichkeit der Bestrebungen gefördert wird. Aber Paneth, obwohl sonst ein liebenswürdiger Mensch, ist von der eigenen Vollkommenheit so trunken, dass ihm kaum einfällt, eine Ergänzung in einem Freund zu suchen."

[57] "Von nun an muss ich meine philosoph. Gedanken rein für mich behalten oder sie in unverreiztem Zustand an Paneth vergeben."

[58] "Zu ihm sind wir beide (ich u. Paneth) in nähre Beziehung getreten, wir überschickten ihm einen Brief mit Einwänden, er lud uns in seine Wohnung, widerlegte uns, schien ein Interesse an uns zu finden, . . . u. hat uns jetzt, nach dem wir ihm einen zweiten Brief mit Einwänden überreicht, von Neuem zu sich beschieden."

[59] Barclay, p. 10.

determination has ripened within me to pursue a Ph.D. in philosophy and zoology. Further negotiations are in progress to bring about my enrollment in the philosophy faculty either next semester or next year."[60] At the end of his first semester with Brentano, Freud found himself so caught up in the intellectual problems raised by this man that he seriously considered altering the whole framework of his professional education.

The change Freud envisioned—and partly realized—meant reconsidering one of his most cherished dreams, the idea of spending a semester or a year in Berlin taking courses with Helmholtz, Du Bois-Reymond, and Virchow. After telling Silberstein of his intention to pursue the double Ph.D., Freud added, "My plan to go to Berlin has therefore undergone an important modification. I will remain here during the next winter term."[61] Initially, he intended only to postpone the Berlin plan but eventually he dropped it completely. The Silberstein correspondence reveals that the reason for the postponement was not financial, as Ronald Clark has suggested, but intellectual.[62] Brentano's philosophical influence had begun to alter Freud's "one-sided" materialism, and though he continued to admire and believe in the great Berlin scientific school, he now determined to supplement its approach with one shaped by Brentano.

During the next few weeks, from early March to mid-April 1875, Freud's letters to Silberstein returned again and again to the subject of Brentano and the impact of his thought and personality. This impact was felt on a range of issues of great importance to Freud: from the possibility of a double course of study, to the subject of philosophical methodology, to the most profound metaphysical questions. Moreover, these various issues were closely bound up with each other. Freud's plans for a double Ph.D. bore a clear and important relationship to his philosophical dualism, the idea of a dual approach to understanding the material and the spiritual aspects of reality. His first semester of work with Brentano made him realize that he had found a thinker whose approach to phi-

[60] Silberstein, March 7, 1875: ". . . diesem merkwürdigen (er ist Gottesgläubiger, Teleolog (!) u. Darwinianer, u. ein verdammt gescheidter, ja genialer Kerl) u. in vielen Hinsichten idealen Menschen. . . . dass zumal unter dem zeitigem Einfluss Brentano's in mir der Entschluss gereift ist, das Doctorat der Philosophie auf Grund von Philosophie u. Zoologie zu erwerben—weitere Verhandlungen sind im Zuge, um entweder vom nächsten Semester oder vom nächsten Jahr an, meinen Eintritt in die phil. Facultät zu bewerkstelligen."

[61] Ibid., "Mein Plan, nach Berlin zu gehen, hat demnach, eine wichtige Modification erfahren. Nächtes Wintersemester bleibe ich hier, . . ."

[62] Clark, *Freud*, p. 36.

losophy and psychology offered a similar, highly congenial framework, a framework within which Freud was later to make his own revolutionary discoveries.

The dualistic structure of Brentano's approach manifested itself throughout his most famous and important book, *Psychology from an Empirical Standpoint,* which was published in 1874, the year Freud first enrolled in his courses. In this work Brentano observed: "All the data of our consciousness are divided into two great classes—the class of physical and the class of mental phenomena. We spoke of this distinction earlier when we established the concept of psychology and we returned to it again in our discussion of psychological method."[63] In attempting to place the relatively new science of psychology in relationship to the natural sciences, Brentano argued that "just as the natural sciences study the properties and laws of physical bodies, which are the objects of our external perception, psychology is the science which studies the properties and laws of the soul, which we discover within ourselves directly by means of inner perception, and which we infer by analogy, to exist in others."[64] Through his concept of inner perception, which he distinguished from the more vague and unscientific notions of introspection or inner observation,[65] Brentano sought to establish psychology and philosophy on a foundation as firm as that of the natural sciences. He pointed to the "noteworthy trend which is now bringing philosophy and the natural sciences closer together" and argued that just as the physical world of nature conformed to certain laws so too did the inner world explored by psychology: "The same thing is true of psychology. The phenomena revealed by inner perception are also subject to laws. Anyone who has engaged in scientific psychological research recognizes this."[66] Within a necessarily dualistic approach to the study of consciousness, Brentano recognized one scientific standard as valid in both realms.

Brentano also recognized that the boundary between physical and mental phenomena was by no means clear and absolute. "As always happens when two sciences touch upon one another, here too borderline cases between the natural and mental sciences are inevitable." He went on to point out that "the facts which the physiologist investigates and those which the psychologist investi-

[63] Franz Brentano, *Psychology from an Empirical Standpoint,* trans. A. C. Rancurello, D. B. Terrell and L. L. McAllister (New York: Humanities Press, 1973), p. 77.

[64] Ibid., p. 5.

[65] Ibid., p. 29. Freud used the same term, "inner perception" *(innere Wahrnehmung)* in *The Interpretation of Dreams, S.E.,* v:608.

[66] Brentano, pp. 11, 12.

gates are most intimately correlated, despite their great differences in character. We find physical and mental properties united in one and the same group. Not only may physical states be aroused by physical states and mental states by mental, but it is also the case that physical states have mental consequences and mental states have physical consequences."[67] Brentano regarded these borderline questions as particularly interesting, and it was precisely in this region that Freud, once having achieved a thorough grounding in both physiology and psychology, went on to his first scientific breakthrough in the investigation of hysteria. One example of mental states having physical consequences involved phenomena such as blushing or trembling, and Brentano took occasion, in his discussion of this topic, to caution against any exclusive reliance on a purely physical approach to such questions: "It is not possible, therefore, as many people have quite foolishly wanted to make us believe, that this external and, as it was pretentiously called, 'objective' observation of mental states could become a source of psychological knowledge quite independently of inner 'subjective' observations." In Brentano's view this external approach alone led nowhere, but "together with subjective observation . . . it will do a great deal to enrich and supplement our own inner experiences by the addition of what others have experienced in themselves, and thus to correct the self delusions into which we may have fallen."[68] His words seem particularly appropriate as a corrective to what Freud himself called his one-sided materialism. Moreover, the method Brentano recommended, a scientific working back and forth between the evidence of the inner "subjective" world and the outer "objective" world, was in fact exactly what Freud so often did as a mature scientist. It was the guiding principle behind his experiments with cocaine, his understanding of dream interpretation, and his discovery of psychoanalysis. In all these cases Freud used himself as his principal laboratory to provide a basis of comparison for what he learned from his patients or from some other external source. Brentano's methodology provided the foundation for Freud's whole approach to psychological investigation.

Freud's plan to enroll simultaneously in the philosophical and medical faculties proved impossible, as he reported to Silberstein in his letter of March 13, but at that point he still hoped to pursue the double course of study by another route and take doctoral exams in both zoology and philosophy. He indicated that he and

[67] Ibid., p. 6.
[68] Ibid., p. 40.

Paneth, who had the same intention, would seek Brentano's advice on the subject when they paid their second visit to his house early the next week, and he also listed his prospective courses for the coming semester, including a course on logic and another called "Philosophical Readings," both taught by Brentano. On March 15, Freud continued his letter with a detailed description of the visit to Brentano, who had reacted warmly to the plan for a double course of study: "it was completely possible and quite fine if we worked for a doctorate in philosophy as well as one in medicine."[69] Impressed with their promise, Brentano went on to suggest that they might well end up in philosophy and told them that the minister of education had particularly urged him to train new teachers *(Dozenten)* of philosophy. Freud obviously felt flattered, but he remained cautious. As he observed later in the letter, "He is a man who came here to found schools and win followers and who thus directs his warmth and friendliness to anyone who asks something of him. I have not, however, been able to escape his influence. I am not capable of disproving a simple theistic argument which forms the crown of his expositions. . . . He proves to me the existence of God with as little partiality and as much exactitude as someone else might present the advantages of the wave over the particle theory."[70] Brentano's combination of religious conviction with a logical and scientific method of argument deeply fascinated Freud, for it drew together the spiritual and material worlds in a way which seemed to promise answers to some of their most profound secrets. Freud's letter also expressed admiration for Brentano's philosophic method in connection with the latter's comments on J. F. Herbart. Paneth had pressed Brentano during their visit to express his opinion of this philosophical psychologist, and Freud reported that "he thoroughly damned his a priori psychological constructions, regarded it as unforgivable that he never thought to turn to experience or experiment to see if they agreed with his arbitrary assumptions." Freud wrote that Brentano declared himself "without reservation a member of the empiricist school which

[69] ". . . es sei ganz gut möglich u. recht schön, wenn wir das Doctorat der Philosophie neben dem der Medicin anstrebten, . . ."

[70] "Er ist eben ein Mann, der hierher gekommen ist, Schule zu machen, Anhänger zu gewinnen u. deshalb seine Lust u. Freundlichkeit an jeden wendet, der etwas von ihm bedarf. Seinem Einfluss bin ich indessen nicht entgangen—ich bin nicht im Stande, ein einfaches theistisches Argument zu widerlegen, das die Krone seiner Ausführungen bildet. . . . Er beweist mir Gott, mit sowenig Parteilichkeit u. soviel Exactheit, als ein anderer den Vorzug der Undulations—vor der Emissionstheorie darthut."

carries over the methods of the natural sciences into philosophy and particularly psychology (in fact this is the chief advantage of his philosophy, which alone makes it acceptable to me)," According to Freud, Brentano then went on to offer various examples which demonstrated "the emptiness of Herbartian speculation."[71] Since Freud said nothing in defense of Herbart and clearly sympathized with Brentano's position, this passage argues against Ernest Jones's attempts to suggest a significant Herbartian influence on Freud.[72]

The subject of discussion which twice brought Freud and Paneth to write Brentano and visit him at home was nothing less than the existence of God. Within Brentano's philosophic system, this issue fell into that important borderline area between the spheres of psychology and the natural sciences, an area involving questions he called "numerous and important enough for there to be a special field of study devoted to them,"[73] a field he termed metaphysics. One of Freud's winter-term courses with Brentano was on "selected metaphysical questions," and the intellectual issues that inspired the visits to Brentano sprang directly from work in this course. When Freud and Paneth followed up their second letter disputing Brentano's arguments for the existence of God by reappearing at his home for another round of direct discussion, he once again easily disproved their objections. Nonetheless he warmly supported their spirit of inquiry and praised the fact "that even though of a contrary opinion we kept ourselves free of any pre-judgment (he knows very well that we are materialists)."[74] By the time he wrote these lines, however, Freud's commitment to the materialist position had already been severely shaken by Brentano's arguments, for he says toward the end of the letter, "At the moment I am no longer a materialist but not yet a theist." He also declared that "I do not intend to surrender myself so quickly or completely. In the course of several semesters I mean to become thoroughly acquainted with

[71] "Er verdammte gründlich dessen aprioristische Constructionen der Psychologie, hielt es für unverzeihlich, dass es ihm nie eingefallen sei, die Erfahrung oder das Experiment zu Rate zu ziehen u. nachzusehn, ob diese auch mit seinen willkürlichen Annahmen stimmten, bekannte sich unumwunden zur empiristischen Schule, die die Methode der Naturwissenschaften auf die Philosophie u. besonders die Psychologie überträgt (in der That ist das der Hauptvorzug seiner Phil., die sie allein mir erträglich macht) u. erzählte uns einige merkwürdige psychologische Beobachtungen, die die Haltlosigkeit der Herbart'schen Speculation zeigen."

[72] Jones, I:372–76.

[73] Brentano, p. 6.

[74] Silberstein, March 13–15, 1875: ". . . dass wir, obwohl entgegengesetzter Meinung, uns durch kein Vorurtheil abhalten liessen (er weiss sehr wohl, dass wir Materialisten sind)."

his philosophy and until then to reserve judgment on it as well as to hold off a decision between theism and materialism."[75]

In his following letters (March 27 and April 11, 1875) Freud returned to the subject of this fundamental shift in his philosophic assumptions. Having admitted the possibility of the existence of God, he now felt open to various other beliefs which he would once have rejected out of hand. On March 27 he wrote, "Since Brentano [proved] to me the existence of his God in such a ridiculously easy way, I am afraid of being captured by . . . spiritualism, homeopathy, Louise Lateau, and so forth."[76] Louise Lateau, a young woman who was alive at the time Freud wrote, was a world-famous example of stigmatization; Peter Swales writes that she "displayed stigmata—blood issuing forth from her hands, feet, forehead and abdomen—while witnessing the spectacle of Christ's passion during ecstatic trance states; and she was the subject of a 'scientific' investigation published by D. M. Bourneville in 1875."[77] Brentano had opened up to Freud the possibility of directing serious scientific attention at a whole range of strange phenomena, and Freud found the prospect both intriguing and disturbing, as he wryly admitted: "It is unfortunately a slippery slope which one treads in admitting the concept of God. We will have to wait and see how far we will fall."[78] He was long to maintain this interest in the exotic phenomena of mental and spiritual life, and since it pointed him toward some of his most important discoveries the cultivation of it should be seen as one of the routes through which Brentano helped to stimulate Freud's scientific creativity.

Brentano also provided a model of argumentative skill. In his letter of March 27, Freud wrote, "In short Brentano cannot possibly be disproved before one has heard, studied, and plundered him. So sharp a dialectician demands that one sharpen one's strength on his before measuring oneself against it."[79] Having suffered such

[75] Ibid.: "Vorläufig bin ich nicht mehr Materialist, auch noch nicht Theist. . . . ich habe nicht die Absicht, mich so schnell oder so vollständig gefangenzugeben. Im Laufe mehrerer Semester gedenke ich seine Philosophie gründlich kennen zu lernen u. mir von ein Urtheil darüber sowie eine Entscheidung über Theism und Materialism vorzubehalten."

[76] "Seit Brentano auf so lächerlich leichte Weise . . . mir seinen Gott [bewiesen] hat, fürchte ich . . . für den Spiritismus u. die Homeopathie u. die Luise Lateau u. s. w. gefangen zu werden."

[77] Swales, "Weier," p. 17.

[78] Silberstein, March 27, 1875: "Es ist leider eine abschüssige Bahn die man mit dem Zugeständnis des Gottesbgriffs betritt. Wir wollen abwarten, wie weit wir fallen können."

[79] "Kurz, Brentano kann unmöglich widerlegt werden, bevor man ihn gehört, studiert u. geplundert hat. Ein so scharfer Dialektiker verlangt, dass man seine eigne Kraft an der seinigen schärft, bevor man sie misst."

quick defeat in philosophical contests with Brentano, Freud now confessed his ignorance and prepared himself for the future. On April 11 he wrote Silberstein, "For the moment I must acknowledge that I crudely misunderstood the nature of the question . . . and that I possessed a complete lack of philosophical insight. The rueful confession of a formerly fashionable and defiant materialist!" But, he went on to add, "I also do not feel at all comfortable in my new coat and have therefore felt it best to set aside a decision [between materialism and theism] for a long time until I am more skillful in philosophy and more mature in natural science."[80] By following Brentano's dualistic approach combining a philosophic with a natural scientific viewpoint, Freud hoped eventually to establish himself in a stronger intellectual position to argue these questions and determine his own beliefs.

The views Freud expressed on the existence of God in the Silberstein letters of March and April 1875 also shed additional light on the centrally important relationship between politics and psychology in his intellectual development. The transferral of his radicalism from the world of politics to the inner world of psychological investigation is suggested by the repeated comparison he established between Silberstein's choice between the republican or the Social Democratic positions and his own choice between theism or materialism. Freud's line of argument with Silberstein seemed to suggest that an inner-oriented philosophic radicalism was more basic than political radicalism, a view that reflected Freud's own increasing concentration on this inner psychological realm. One illuminating sentence occurred in the same paragraph where he mentioned his concern that Brentano's proof of God's existence might eventually lead him to other exotic beliefs: "I scarcely know how to explain to you how much my trust in the generally accepted position has disappeared and my inclination to the viewpoints which have remained in the minority has increased."[81] These lines reveal his path from religious defiance to political rebellion to psychological radicalism. Freud's sympathy for the minority position was really a constant, but its forms changed.

[80] "Vorläufig muss ich bekennen, dass ich die Natur der Fragen, . . . gröblich misskant u. völligen Mangel an philosoph. Einsicht besessen habe. Das reumütige Geständnis eines ehemaligen feschen u. trotzigen Materialisten! . . . auch im neuen Rock fühl' ich mich gar nicht behaglich u. habe darum für das Beste gehalten, die Entscheidung für lange Zeit auszusezten, bis ich in Philosophie gewandter u. in Naturwissenschaft gereifter bin."

[81] Silberstein, March 27, 1875: "Wie sehr mein Vertrauen in das allgemein für richtig Gehaltene geschwunden u. eine geheime Neigung zu den in der Minorität gebliebenen Anschauungen zugenommen hat, kann ich Dir kaum deutlich machen."

His early sense of belonging to a religious minority and the associated defiance, translated during adolescence into sympathy for political radicals who opposed themselves to the existing order, became retranslated during his university years into an interest in the sometimes bizarre psychological and spiritual questions on which Brentano wished to focus scientific investigation.

Brentano's own writings, which posed the possibility of a close relationship between politics and psychology, may have helped to encourage this retranslation. In the opening paragraph of his *Psychology from an Empirical Standpoint,* Brentano argued that not only was psychology "the pinnacle of the towering structure of science, on the one hand; it is destined to become the basis of society and of its noblest possessions . . . as well."[82] Later in the chapter he argued more specifically that "no truly great statesman" had yet appeared in history "because there has been no systematic application of psychological principles in the political field until now." In his view the advances in knowledge that had led to the emergence of a scientific psychology promised a bright hope for society in the future. "How many evils could be remedied, both on the individual and social level, by the correct psychological diagnosis, or by knowledge of the laws according to which mental states can be modified."[83] Freud wrote in this spirit in his letter of April 11 when he observed, "For you must make no mistake about it, the existence of God is not to be resolved through society debates or parliamentary speeches nor through speculative thought, but only through logical and psychological investigations."[84] Since the questioning of God's existence posed a basic threat to the established religious order, this issue held great political significance both for Silberstein's Social Democrats and for the authorities of Catholic Austria, and Freud believed it should be left to philosophical and psychological experts rather than politicians. It is noteworthy that he developed this view in the same letter in which he discussed the Ofenheim scandal; his psychological outlook advanced its claim to dissolve the problems of politics as early as 1875 in the wake of his first political disillusionment.

The translation of Freud's radicalism from politics into psychology can also be seen in his comments on Friedrich Hebbel in the March

[82] Brentano, p. 3.
[83] Ibid., pp. 21, 22.
[84] Silberstein, April 11, 1875: "Denn sie mögen sich darüber nicht täuschen, die Existenz Gottes ist nicht durch Vereinsdebatten oder Parlamentsreden auszumachen, auch noch nicht durch speculat. Denken, blos durch logische u. psycholog. Untersuchungen, . . ."

27 letter to Silberstein. After concluding his discussion of Brentano, Freud told his friend that he was using the library of the Leseverein der deutschen Studenten to fill in the gaps in his knowledge of contemporary literature and that he had "wolfed down" a half dozen plays by Hebbel. This important north German dramatist grew up in conditions of dire poverty which strongly influenced his viewpoint and choice of themes. Freud's opening comments indicated that he appreciated the social-critical thrust of Hebbel's work, but he then went on to concentrate far more attention on its psychological significance. He wrote of Hebbel, "His essence is sharply revolutionary, full of bitter criticism."[85] Then, comparing him to Shakespeare, he noted that "what he likes best is if someone goes to ruin as a consequence of passion; all his heroes are defiant types who beat their brains out on each other. He portrays the passions with such grandeur that it is worth his poetic effort to illuminate them and—perhaps if one understands Hebbel correctly to forgive them." Commenting on specific plays, he wrote in an almost clinical style: "His Judith is very beautiful—a sexual problem—an unusually strong woman defies an overpowering man and revenges herself on him for the inferiority she suffers because of her sex."[86] He complained that he did not enjoy *Marianne* because "such intricate and dangerous psychological experiments have something improbable about them."[87] He reported of Hebbel's masterpiece, *The Ring of Gyges,* that it "is again a sexual problem, moreover often really lovely."[88] Concluding with a discussion of Hebbel's preference for female heroes, he argued that "the poet favors women as the poetically more warm-blooded animal for besides the obstinacy which they share with men, they can also have glowing feelings."[89] To Freud's eyes, Hebbel's revolutionary essence seemed to manifest itself far more in his skill at psychological portrayal than in his critical view of society.

[85] "Sein Wesen ist herb revolutionär, voll von bitterer Kritik."

[86] ". . . am wolsten ist ihm, wenn sich jemand durch Consequenz der Leidenschaft zu Grunde richtet, alle seine Helden sind Trotzköpfe, die sich gegenseitig die Schädel einrennen, die Leidenschaften schildert er immer so gross, dass es dem Dichter die Mühe lohnt, sie zu beleuchten u.—vielleicht, wenn man Hebbel recht versteht, zu entschuldigen. Sehr schön ist die Judith, ein sexuelles Problem, eine überstarke Frau trotzt einem übergewaltigen Mann u. rächt sich an ihm für die durch das Geschlecht ihr zu Theil gewordene Inferiorität."

[87] ". . . so verwickelte gefährliche psycholog. Experimente haben etwas Unwahrscheinliches."

[88] ". . . widerum ein sexualles Problem, übrigens oft recht lieblich."

[89] ". . . der Dichter bevorzugt die Frauen als die poetisch warmblütigern Thiere, weil sie neben dem Starrsinn, den sie mit den Männern theilen, auch glühende Gefühle haben können."

In the spring of 1875 Freud looked forward to the start of the second semester (which ran from late April to the end of July) with great enthusiasm. Although plans for the double doctorate had by then undergone modification, he felt that he had realized the spirit of his intention in his course schedule. On April 11 he wrote, "We stand on the threshold of the second semester—for me a new life, in which I can for the first time pass as philosopher and zoologist, since I will be attending psychology, logic and two zoology courses."[90] This passage reveals that one of the courses Freud took with Brentano that semester—the course with the general title "Philosophical Readings"—was actually a course on psychology. The second course was on logic, not on Aristotle as Bernfeld says, or Aristotelian logic as Jones says.[91] It is particularly important to know that Freud took this psychology course because Brentano's manuscript lecture notes for the course in psychology he taught during his last year at Würzburg (1872–73) have survived, and even though the course Freud took two years later may not have been identical, it is very likely that many of the same topics were covered. Freud's attitude as he looked forward to the beginning of classes could not have been more receptive. After listing his courses, he added, "I have never before enjoyed the lovely feeling which one calls academic bliss and which, for the most part, consists in the awareness of sitting at the source from which knowledge pours forth in its greatest purity and taking a good deep drink of it."[92]

In his "Franz Brentano and Sigmund Freud," James Barclay provides a summary of Brentano's course notes and points out many points of contact between Brentano's psychology and that of Freud. One of the most important involves the topic of the association of ideas. For Freud the technique of free association and the tracing out of the links which cause ideas to be associated in mental processes were to be the indispensable tools of psychoanalysis and dream interpretation. In his *Psychology*, Brentano pointed to the goal of working out the "Laws of Association of Ideas," and

[90] "Wir stehen ja an der Schwelle des zweiten Semesters, für mich ein neues Leben, wo ich zuerst als Philosoph u. Zoolog gelten kann, da ich Psychologie, Logik u. 2 zoolog. Collegien hören werde."

[91] Bernfeld 1951, p. 204. Bernfeld's error resulted in not correctly reporting the information contained in the full list of courses provided at the end of his article (pp. 216–17). Jones compounded the error in his account, I:37.

[92] Silberstein, April 11, 1875: "Ich habe niemals noch vorher die schöne Empfindung genossen, die mann akademisches Glück nennen kann u. die zumeist in dem Bewusstsein besteht, an der Quelle aus der Wissenschaft am reinsten strömt, zu sitzen u. einen guten, ächten Trank aus ihr zu thun."

although he cited the work of John Stuart Mill as providing a valuable beginning he did not develop the subject in detail.[93] His lecture notes, however, devoted much more attention to it. "The discussion in his notes," Barclay says, "is grouped around primary association, conditions which determine the recall of ideas, and observations concerning dream phenomena." The category of primary association was passed over quickly on the grounds that its laws were not yet understood. But on the subject of acquired associations, Barclay says, he argued that they were "more strong and durable because of the force of habit connected with them. Brentano stated almost as a law that once a sense impression had taken place—if there be no hindrance—a similar sense impression will appear in consciousness as soon as a phenomenon formerly connected with it recurs." In discussing the conditions that led to the recall of an idea, Brentano "felt that the more common circumstantial denominatives present, the more likely it is that there would be an association. Also, strong excitement, such as a vivid phantasm or mental image, tends to create a strong association."[94] These observations on the nature of mental associations closely parallel the assumptions underlying Freud's psychology, and although Freud cited Brentano only in his *Psychopathology of Everyday Life,* he did use the phrase "the laws of association governing the sequence of ideas" when he discussed this subject in *The Interpretation of Dreams.*[95]

It is also significant that Brentano carried his discussion of association into the area of dreams, insanity, and other bizarre mental phenomena. Barclay writes that in his lecture notes "he spoke of the influence of foreign or alien experiences on dreams, the peculiar association of sensations in dreams, and the exploration of prophetic dreams as instances of recurring memory phenomena. His final remarks related to the almost inseparable nature of acquired associations."[96] It seems likely that his course reinforced and refined the interest in dreams which had been nourished in Freud since childhood.

Another important subject treated much more extensively in Brentano's lecture notes than in his book was that of psychological development, and here too there are numerous parallels to Freud's thought. Barclay writes that in Brentano's discussion of how we build up a picture of outer reality, "he stated in his outline that

[93] Brentano, pp. 12–13.
[94] Barclay, p. 14.
[95] Freud, *Interpretation, S.E.,* IV:58.
[96] Barclay, p. 14.

instinctive inclinations are stronger than judgment. Instinctive inclinations are not based on inferences or deductions, but on the original inclination of the organism to assent to each mental image."[97] Brentano's outline went on to suggest the stages through which this would occur: "In the development process of knowing reality, instinctual propensities first identified with psychic imagery. The early organism naturally assumes the validity of its own acts. Subsequently through experience and development, the primitive reliance on instinctual images is altered through the process of distinguishing other psychic beings and identifying them in accord with sensory memories.[98] Brentano also attributed a prominent role in psychic development to what he called the phenomena of love-hate. According to Barclay, Brentano's lecture notes show that he "inclined toward the belief that the original motivation of love-hate phenomena was a need for incorporation. He admitted that the original motivating force might also be *Lust* and *Unlust.*" Finally, Brentano turned to the role of these phenomena in acts of will, and according to Barclay, "the end result of this discussion of the phenomena of love-hate and their relationship to the act of will seems to be that phenomena of love-hate are the motivating agents behind will activities."[99] Particularly in the prominence accorded to the role of instinct, Brentano's conception of psychic development anticipated many elements of Freudian theory.

A unifying strand within such elements of Brentano's psychology as his discussion of association and his analysis of changing emotional states was his important and original conception of intentionality. Of all the intellectual links between his ideas and those of Freud, it may be the most central. In his *Psychology,* Brentano described intentionality, "the inexistence of an object," as characteristic of all mental phenomena: "Every mental phenomenon includes something as object within itself, although they do not all do so in the same way. In presentation something is presented, in judgment something is affirmed or denied, in love loved, in hate hated, in desire desired and so on." Intentionality provided so basic and general a concept for Brentano that he employed it as the defining characteristic to distinguish mental from physical phenomena. He wrote, "We can, therefore, define mental phenomena by saying that they are those phenomena which contain an object intentionally within themselves."[100] The importance of this concept of inten-

[97] Ibid., p. 20.
[98] Ibid.
[99] Ibid., p. 21.
[100] Brentano, pp. 88, 89; see also p. 91.

tionality for Freud has been pointed out by Paul Ricoeur in his *Freud and Philosophy* and before him by James Barclay. The phenomenology of Brentano's student Edmund Husserl provided Ricoeur with the philosophic lens through which he viewed Freud. In this context he vividly conveyed the relevance of intentionality to the Freudian unconscious: "Intentionality concerns our meditation in the unconscious inasmuch as consciousness is first of all an intending of the other, and not self-presence or self-possession. Engrossed in the other, it does not at first know itself intending. The unconsciousness that attaches to this bursting forth from self is that of the unreflected."[101] Ricoeur argued that this made it possible "to give a direct definition of the psychism—as the mere intending of something, as meaning—without appealing to self-consciousness. But this as one writer has said, contains the whole of Freud's discovery: 'the psychical is defined as meaning, and this meaning is dynamic and historical.' Husserl and Freud are seen to be the heirs of Brentano."[102] Although this claim may go too far, its basic substance seems justified.

By considering Brentano's concept of intentionality within his framework of an outer physical world and an inner mental realm, Barclay discovered additional points of contact with Freud's thought. He notes that according to Brentano even if something were a real—or as he called it, an "effective"—object in the outer world, it could "exist in the mind only as an intentional object," but that even so, "this very intentional existence is for the mind an effective [real] existence. Because the intentional existence is for the mind an effective existence, all psychic activity is directed toward these intentional creations with the dual aspect of relationship to the outward object and the inner needs of the self."[103] As Freud put it in an 1899 letter to Fliess, "Reality—wish-fulfillment: it is from this contrasting pair that our mental life springs."[104] Barclay points out that although Brentano many years later abandoned his concept of intentionality, he was thoroughly committed to it during the period when Freud came into contact with him."[105] As the Silberstein letters reveal, Brentano could have had no more attentive and appreciative a student than the young Freud, so there is every reason to believe that Brentano exerted a profound influence on the development of Freud's psychology.

[101] Ricoeur, pp. 376, 378.
[102] Ibid., p. 379.
[103] Barclay, p. 18.
[104] Freud, *Origins,* p. 277.
[105] Barclay, p. 18.

The double approach to mental processes which Freud cultivated in his work with Brentano pointed him toward the problem that was to concern him throughout his professional life, the mind-body problem, as it had traditionally been called—or the mind-brain problem in its more modern formulation. Brentano taught Freud that the only truly scientific approach to it involved both inner psychological investigation and external physiological and biological research. Only with this dualistic approach could one hope eventually to gain a better understanding of the interactions between the psychological and the physiological. An appreciation of Brentano's powerful influence thus helps to resolve the long-standing dispute among Freud scholars about the relative importance of Freud's biological and psychological background to his fundamental discoveries. Nor was Brentano exceptional among Freud's teachers in taking this approach. Peter Amacher notes that in Brücke's lectures on mental phenomena he assumed that they were simultaneously paralleled by physical phenomena: "Because it was so orthodox to conceive of the relationship of mind and body in this way, he did not discuss his assumption. It allowed him to work from both sides of the parallelism, to describe a process partly in physical and partly in psychological terms." Amacher concludes that "this unrestrained shifting from descriptions in terms of mind to descriptions in physical terms was characteristic of the work of Freud's teachers and of Freud."[106] This dualistic approach is apparent in the pattern of Freud's scientific work leading up to and including *The Interpretation of Dreams,* and the close relationship with Brentano revealed in the letters to Silberstein further illuminates its origin and nature. Certainly Freud's intellectual background, his thorough grounding in the dualisms of such German idealists as Schiller and Kant, had well prepared him for Brentano's approach, but Brentano carried the understanding of the dualism substantially further and brought to his discussion of it a degree of scientific precision that rendered it immediately useful to Freud. Although Brentano recommended to Freud and Paneth that they read and study Kant (in contrast to Schelling, Fichte, and Hegel

[106] Peter Amacher, "Freud's Neurological Education and Its Influence on Psychoanalytic Theory," *Psychological Issues,* 4, no. 4, monograph 16 (New York: International Universities Press, 1965), pp. 16–17. See also Amacher's discussion of Meynert on pp. 40–41. Even Frank Sulloway agrees that Freud's approach was firmly dualistic: Sulloway, *Freud,* pp. 48, 50–51. See also Hannah S. Decker, *Freud in Germany: Revolution and Reaction in Science, 1893–1907* (New York: International Universities Press, 1977), pp. 201–5; and Barry Silverstein, "Freud's Psychology and Its Organic Foundation: Sexuality and Mind-Body Interactions," *Psychoanalytic Review,* 72 (Summer 1985):203–28.

whom he condemned as charlatans), he was highly critical of many aspects of Kant's thought, and attributed most of what was useful in it to the influence of Hume.[107] Brentano's strong preference for the English empiricist tradition found a reflection in one of Freud's letters discussing Kant and his critics. Noting that Kant's position stood or fell on the correctness of his concept of synthetic a priori judgments, Freud wrote, "All of a great and exact scientific school, that of the English empirical philosophers, strongly contests the possibility of such judgments. They say, 'All of our knowledge not only begins with experience but also stems from it,' which certainly sounds materialistic enough, and in any case is more scientific than the assumption of inborn categories of reason."[108] The statement indicates that Freud followed Brentano and the English empiricists in abandoning any belief in the Kantian realm of the thing-in-itself. The two worlds were in fact one world which could be experienced two ways, through outer observation and inner perception. Freud's dualistic approach rested firmly on his sophisticated view of reality. The inner-oriented disciplines of philosophy and psychology offered one view of the reality of mental processes while physiology and neurology studied that same reality from the other side of the mind-brain duality.

During the second semester of his second year—having achieved philosophic clarity on his educational aims—Freud plunged into the ambitious course schedule designed to further his double doctorate. In addition to his two courses with Brentano, he also took three with Carl Claus and two with Ernst Brücke, the two professors who most strongly shaped the natural sciences half of his studies. Claus, the professor from whom Freud had taken the course in general biology and Darwinism during his first year, had, like Brentano, just arrived at the University of Vienna. Bernfeld reported that "in the fall of 1873 Claus had come from Goettingen to Vienna with the intent and assignment to modernize the zoological department."[109] Freud's letters reveal that Brentano had come with a similar commission in philosophy, so his twofold course of study had aligned him with two of the most modern and forward-looking personalities at the university. The course on Darwinism

[107] Silberstein, March 15, 1875.

[108] Silberstein, April 11, 1875: "Eine ganze grosse u. exacte wissenschaftliche Schule, die der empirischen Philosophen in England bestreitet entschieden die Möglichkeit solcher Urtheile. 'All unser Wissen beginnt nicht nur mit, sondern stammt auch aus der Erfahrung' sagen sie, was doch materialistisch genug klingt u. jedenfalls wissenschaftlicher ist als die Annahme von uns angeborenen Verstandesformen; . . ."

[109] Bernfeld 1949, p. 166.

offers further evidence of this. Claus was at the forefront of the scientific investigations emerging from Darwin's revolutionary work, and he, along with Brücke, helped to direct Freud's first biological research projects toward this area.

By the summer of 1875, with Darwin providing the dominant influence in his zoological studies, and the English empiricists regnant in his philosophical-psychological education, Freud had firmly allied his scientific ambitions with the most modern intellectual traditions of liberal England, and in this context the visit he made to England at that time to see his half-brothers in Manchester brought out in him a psychological reaction of great importance for his future development. In the course of his later self-analysis Freud became very interested in the thoughts and feelings evoked by the visit, and he covertly described it in his essay on screen memories and alluded to it in both the *Psychopathology of Everyday Life* and *The Interpretation of Dreams.* In his *Psychopathology* Freud brought it up in the course of explaining a slip he made in the first edition of *The Interpretation of Dreams,* where he substituted the name Hasdrubal for that of Hamilcar Barca. He explained that his relationship with his father was changed by the visit "which resulted in my getting to know my half-brother, the child of my father's first marriage, who lived there. My brother's eldest son is the same age as I am. Thus the relations between our ages were no hindrance to my phantasies of how different things would have been if I had been born the son not of my father but of my brother." According to Freud, "these suppressed phantasies falsified the text of my book . . . by forcing me to put the brother's name for the father's."[110] He somewhat clarified the nature of these suppressed phantasies in the account of the visit included in his essay on screen memories. In the guise of the fictional patient he revealed that his father and half-brother "concocted a plan by which I was to exchange the abstruse subject of my studies for one of more practical value, settle down, after my studies were completed, in the place where my uncle [half-brother] lived, and marry my cousin [niece]. No doubt when they saw how absorbed I was in my own intentions the plan was dropped; but I fancy I must certainly have been aware of its existence."[111] Freud also discussed the visit in his analysis of the Hollthurn dream (July 1898), in which the theme of flight from the problems and pressures

[110] Freud, *Psychopathology, S.E.,* VI:219–20.
[111] Freud, *Screen Memories, S.E.,* III:314.

of Vienna to the security and prosperity of England played a prominent role.[112]

The psychological pattern that emerges from Freud's various references to his trip to England closely resembles that of his earlier Freiberg visit, when he became infatuated with Gisela Fluss. His accounts of both visits revolve around the "if only . . ." phantasies connected with his feelings of his father's inadequacies, and in both accounts the highly competitive and demanding life in Vienna provided the real-world alternative to the phantasies. Whether they involved the peace and security of a country life with Gisela Fluss or the prosperity and social acceptance that would come with marrying Pauline Freud, these phantasies tempted Freud to flee the intense pressures of Vienna. That he felt the temptation at the time, and not just in his retrospective construction of the screen memory, can be seen in his contemporary report of the visit to Silberstein. In the long description written on September 9, 1875, shortly after his return to Vienna, he declared, "I would much rather live there than here despite fog and rain, drunkenness and conservatism."[113] Observing that there were many peculiarities of the English temperament that particularly suited him, he speculated that after completing his studies "a favorable wind" might bring him back to England "to achieve practical results."[114] Then he added a "confession" which reveals the polarity of ambition and practicality discussed in the screen memory paper. "I now have more than one ideal; in addition to the theoretical one of earlier years, a practical one has been added. Last year, in answer to the question what my highest wish would be I would have answered: a laboratory and free time or a ship on the ocean with all the instruments which a researcher needs. Now I am uncertain whether I should not rather say: a large hospital and plenty of money."[115] Further on in the letter he indicated that he had also grown more distrustful of philosophy. His theoretical interests, whether in evolutionary biology or philosophical psychology, demanded keen

[112] See below, Chap. 6.

[113] ". . . ich dort lieber wohnen würde als hier trotz Nebel u. Regen, Trunkenheit u. Conservativismus."

[114] "Vielleicht, lieber Freund, dass mich nach Beendigung meiner Studien ein günstiger Wind nach England zum practischen Wirken hinüberweht."

[115] "Ich habe jetzt mehr als ein Ideal, zu dem theoretischen der früheren Jahre noch ein practisches hinzugekommen. Voriges Jahr hätte ich auf die Frage, was mein höchster Wunsch sei, geantwortet: Ein Laboratorium u. freie Zeit oder ein Schiff auf dem Ocean mit allen instrumenten, die der Forscher braucht; jetzt schwanke ich, ob ich nicht lieber sagen sollte: ein grosses Spital u. reichlich Geld, . . ."

ambition and drive in the highly competitive scholarly world; in the psychological atmosphere created by his Manchester visit, Freud felt tempted by the relatively safe career of a medical doctor.

Although Freud eventually achieved a satisfactory compromise on this issue, in the short run his theoretical ambitions and his respect for English science and philosophy won out over safety. In the letter, his desire for scientific greatness appeared not only in the reference to his wish to sail the ocean on his own research ship, but also in a list of leading English scientists whose works he had come to admire. He argued that his acquaintance with English scientific literature would make it possible in his studies "always to hold to the side of the English who now enjoy a highly favorable prejudice with me: Tyndall, Huxley, Lyell, Darwin, Thomson, Lockyer, as well as others."[116] Freud's reference to his earlier wish for a ship alluded not only to Darwin, whose voyages had produced revolutionary discoveries, but also to Sir Charles Wyville Thomson, whose book *The Depths of the Sea* had appeared just two years before. In it Thomson described the research efforts through which he had demonstrated the existence of abundant sea life at great depths. In recognition of his important achievement he was then put in charge of the scientific staff of the H.M.S. *Challenger* on a three-and-a-half-year, around-the-world expedition to investigate ocean life and conditions. The *Challenger* expedition was underway at the time Freud wrote his letter, and his thoughts followed it in phantasy. At least two of the other scientists listed, Thomas Huxley and Sir Charles Lyell, had also done important work involving ocean animal life, and Freud's own interest in sea creatures found direct expression in the preceding paragraph of the letter, where he told how he "followed the waves of the sea as they rumbled back from the land, and caught crabs and starfish on the shore!"[117] Freud elaborated on this detail of his visit in his analysis of the Hollthurn dream, where he wrote, "When I was nineteen years old I visited England for the first time and spent a whole day on the shore of the Irish Sea. I naturally revelled in the opportunity of collecting the marine animals left behind by the tide and I was occupied with a starfish . . . when a charming little girl came up to me and said: 'Is it a starfish? Is it alive?' 'Yes,' I replied, 'he is alive,' and at once, embarrassed at my mistake, repeated the sentence cor-

[116] ". . . immer auf Seite der Engländer zu halten, die nun einmal ein höchst günstiges Vorurtheil bei mir haben: Tyndall, Huxley, Lyell, Darwin, Thomson, Lockyer u. a."

[117] ". . . bin den Wellen der Flut, wie sie das Land grollende verliessen, nachgegangen u. habe Krabben u. Seesterne am Ufer gefangen! !"

rectly."[118] As Freud noted in his analysis, the mistake (he for it) provided an innocent example of bringing in sex when it did not belong, a theme which pertained to the 1898 context of the dream. This sexual theme also had a direct bearing on the 1875 scene that surfaced in the dream, for it pointed in the direction of his first scientific research efforts.

The little girl who encountered Freud on the beach that day could hardly have known that she directed her innocent question at a budding expert on the subject of sea creatures and their sexuality. It almost seems odd that he would have considered the answer he gave her a mistake, but since he had by that time taken five courses in biology, Darwinism, and zoology with Carl Claus, whose particular research specialty involved the sexualty of sea creatures, Freud did not take the issue of their sexuality for granted. Here his analysis of the Hollthurn dream illuminates the 1875 letter. He introduced the recollection of his encounter by the seashore as an association to an element of the dream in which an English brother and sister commented on a row of books and Freud committed a verbal error in his attempt to say in English that one of the books was by Schiller. The various psychically significant elements that came together in the dream were also closely associated in the much earlier letter, where his discussion of the English books he had come to admire immediately followed the paragraph in which he mentioned finding the starfish. Four paragraphs earlier he had also referred to the English brother and sister (John and Pauline Freud) in the course of explaining to Silberstein the exotic family constellation which had produced a nephew and niece his own age. He then proceeded to mention the plan for moving to England once his studies were complete, and since we know from the screen memory paper that marriage to Pauline constituted part of the plan, the theme of "bringing in sex where it does not belong" pertains to the letter as well as the dream, because such a marriage would have come close to incest.[119] Within the theoretical versus practical polarity that Freud set up in the letter, the theoretical (scientific) alternative to the emigration and marriage plan thus constituted a defense against incest, and the actual subject of his future research, the sexuality of sea creatures, has the character of a psychic compromise between desire and defense. What Freud called his "family complex," the exotic family constellation which aroused his curiosity about sex at an early age,

[118] Freud, *Interpretation, S.E.,* v:519.
[119] Mischler and Ulbrich, *Österreichisches Staatswörterbuch,* I:302–3.

can be seen here as a factor pointing him toward his first scientific study of sexuality.

Further evidence of his psychic compromise on this issue can be found in the remarkable fact that Gisela Fluss reemerged as a subject in Freud's correspondence at just this time—remarkable in that she, by virtue of her comic nickname Ichthyosaura, had earlier brought together the subject of sexuality and sea creatures in Freud's mind. On October 2, 1875, Freud sent Silberstein an epic poem commemorating the approaching marriage of Gisela Fluss, and the first line, "Sing to me, Muse, the fame of the Ichthyosauri communes," set a tone of comic satire which he maintained through various references to the nature and history of this prehistoric water creature (actually a reptile rather than a fish). In the accompanying postscript he described his letter as "a mixture of the sad and the humorous," thus indicating that his feelings were in fact affected. He also referred to himself in a geologic vein as he took leave of his romantic illusions: "Herewith ends this stratum [*Formation*—Freud used the term to refer to geologic strata in the opening of the poem]; here I let fall the magic wand which led to its creation; a new time without secretly working forces has dawned, one which needs no poetry or phantasy."[120] Gisela Fluss, who was psychologically tied to Freud's interest in "secretly working forces" *(Naturphilosophie)*, had been overlayered in his mind by the new Du Bois-Reymond/Helmholtz reality. Then, in the next sentence Freud returned to the theoretical versus practical alternative posed in his previous letter. With the object of his adolescent infatuation gone, Freud was ruefully forced to conclude that "no one seeks a one and only [*Princip*—his code word for girlfriend][121] anywhere else than in the present, in the *Alluvium* or *Diluvium*, nowhere else than among the children of mankind, not in the terrifying primeval past, when wild creatures unpunished by man consumed the oxygen of the atmosphere."[122] Yet he was to study just such primeval times and creatures during the academic year which began later that month.

[120] Silberstein, Oct. 1, 1875: "Singe mir, Muse, den Ruhm der Ichthyosauri communes . . . . Oct. 1/2: "ein Gemisch von Traurigem u. Scherzhaftem . . . Hiermit endet diese Formation, hier versenke ich den Zauberstab, der zu ihrer Bildung beigetragen; eine neue Zeit ohne geheim wirkende Kräfte breche herein, die keiner Poesie u. Phantasie bedarf."

[121] See Stanescu, "Young Freud's Letters," pp. 202, 206n15.

[122] Cited by Heinz Stanescu, "Ein Gelegenheitsgedicht des jungen Sigmund Freud—Hochzeitscarmen," *Deutsch für Ausländer*, ed. Hermann Kessler (Königswinter, Verlag für Sprachmethodik, 1967), p. 16.

Freud's travels seem to have had the effect of exposing him to regressive moods, in which the thoughts and feelings of earlier times reemerged to influence the direction of his development. The Manchester visit recalled the trip to Freiberg and the sexual feelings he had focused on Gisela Fluss, and just as the various maternal elements of that attraction called up connotations of incest which pushed him away from acting on those feelings, so too did the incestuous dimension of the Manchester visit. Freud returned from Manchester, as he had from Freiberg, with the underlying conviction that it was safer to explore the world of sexuality in scientific theory than in practice.

During his third year at the university (1875–76) Freud continued his two-track educational program with a philosophy course from Brentano each semester, a broad range of science courses, and specialized work in zoology and physiology with Claus and Brücke. His first research project (which eventuated in his second publication) came out of his work with Claus, and it involved the sexuality of the eel. This subject had been a matter of mystery from ancient times. The animal was thought by some to be hermaphroditic, and in myth it was linked to Tireseis, the prophet Oedipus scorned at such great personal cost. As Bernfeld noted, this research topic reflected the speciality of Freud's teacher: "Though Claus' main interest was in coelenterata and crustaceae, the problem of the eels was closely linked to his own earlier studies on hermaphroditism in animals."[123] Claus set Freud the problem of confirming a recent scientific claim that testes had been discovered in a mature eel, and he sent his student to carry out the research at the new zoological experiment station in Trieste, the establishment of which he had obtained in 1875. Its funding included money to support a few students each year for several weeks of study and research, and Freud departed for the first of two research trips to Trieste in March 1876.

Freud's letters from Trieste provide a detailed account of his life and work there. He explained to Silberstein the nature of his scientific problem, traced its history from Aristotle through the middle ages up to his own time, and also reported that as of April 5 his efforts had been in vain since "all the eels which I cut open are of the tender sex."[124] The letters also cast some light on the unconscious ties between his research and his underlying personal

[123] Bernfeld 1949, p. 166.

[124] Silberstein, April 5, 1875: ". . . alle Aale, die ich aufschneide, sind vom zarteren Geschlecht."

attitudes toward sexuality and politics, the two driving interests Freud transferred into his scientific work. Although he expressed a sexual interest in the women of Trieste, he did so only from a distance. In an undated letter he wrote that on his arrival there "it truly seemed to me as if only Italian Goddesses inhabited Trieste,"[125] but that after that they all disappeared. His April 5 letter confirmed the testimony of his postscript to the Ichthysaurus poem: that he preferred to view sexuality through the lens of scientific observation. He reported that after spending his days at the dissection table he went for walks in the evening, but that he saw "only very little of the physiology of Trieste's women." Further on, he described their typical features and added, "So much for anatomical characteristics: physiologically the only thing I know of them is that they like to go for walks."[126] After reporting that very young girls used makeup, he wrote "I actually have nothing at all to do with them since one is not allowed to dissect humans."[127] As Kurt Eissler observes, "But what he was dissecting in reality were eels, descendents of ichthyosauri."[128] Freud's comments were part of the generally playful tone of his letter, but as he was later to observe, "where he makes a jest, a problem lies concealed," and in this case the problem involved the highly personal origins of his scientific interest in sexuality.[129]

Freud's only political comment in the letters from Trieste also has the status of a humorous aside. Noting that after a week of glorious weather the previous Sunday had been cold and rainy, he remarked, "I believe it is a kind of anticlerical demonstration on the part of the Adriatic which perhaps, as a true Italian, hates the Pope, priests and Sunday."[130] Freud's former interest in politics had largely given way to his scientific work, but his comment reveals the persistence of a radical anticlerical orientation on this half-buried level of consciousness. The remark was altogether appropriate to the intellectual context of his scientific research, as Bernfeld indicated in describing the background to Freud's second

[125] Silberstein, n.d. (circa April 1876): ". . . schien es mir zwar, als ob lauter Italienische Göttinnen Triest bevölkern würden. . . ."

[126] ". . . nur recht wenig von der Physiologie der Triestiner . . . Soviel antom. Merkmale, physiologisches weiss ich von ihnen nur, dass sie gern spazleren gehen."

[127] Silberstein, April 5, 1876: "Da es nicht gestattet ist, die Menschen zu seciren, habe ich eigentlich gar nichts mit ihnen zu thun."

[128] Eissler, "Creativity and Adolescence," p. 471.

[129] Freud quoted this observation by Goethe in *Introductory Lectures on Psychoanalysis*, *S.E.*, xv:38.

[130] Silberstein, April 5, 1876: "Ich glaube, es ist das eine Art anticlerikale Demonstration von Seiten der Adria, die vielleicht als echte Italienerin den Papst, die Pfaffen u. den Sonntag hast."

project, which concerned the spinal cord of the Amocoetes or Petromyzon. This investigation, which grew out of his work in the laboratory of his teacher, Ernst Brücke, involved interesting and controversial issues, including the question whether the nervous systems of the higher vertebrates differed from those of the lower animals merely in the complexity of the basic units or in some more fundamental way. "The philosophical and religious implications seemed to be very disturbing," Bernfeld wrote. "Are the differences in the mind of higher and lower animals only a matter of degree of complication? Does the human mind differ from that of some mollusk—not basically but correlative to the number of nerve cells in both and the combination of their respective fibers? Scientists were searching for the answers to such questions in the hope of gaining definite decisions—one way or another—on the nature of man, the existence of God and the aim of life."[131] The Silberstein correspondence shows that Freud saw his work in just such a broad context, and his comments on Brentano specifically involved these large metaphysical questions. In the letter of March 13–15, 1875, where he discussed his movement from a materialist toward a theist position, he did so specifically within the framework of the debates over Darwinism. He went on to say of Brentano, "he himself argues for the descent of man from animals; he contests Darwinism, and has . . . shaken my conviction in it; but even if Darwinism remains tenable, as I hope, it does not contradict his theology and his God."[132] Needless to say, Freud did retain his faith in Darwinism, and the radical implications of this outlook undoubtedly constituted one of its attractions for him.

Frank Sulloway has clarified the significance of Freud's work on the Petromyzon by explaining its place within the Darwinist theoretical framework of the day. The discovery by Alexander Kovalevski that the larval form of the sea squirt or ascidian possessed a rudimentary notochord and was therefore related to the most primitive of all true vertebrates held important implications for Darwin's theory of evolution. As Sulloway explains, "The ascidians were consequently recognized as animals, not plants, and were considered by many to be a 'missing link' between invertebrates and the lowest true vertebrates."[133] Darwin quickly incorporated this discovery into his theory to argue that two evolutionary branches

[131] Bernfeld 1949, p. 176.

[132] "Die Descendenz des Menschen vom Thier vertritt er selbst; den Darwinismus bestreitet er, u. hat ihn . . . bei mir erschüttert; aber selbst wenn der Darwinism, wie ich hoffe, haltbar ist, widerspricht er nicht seiner Teleologie u. seinem Gott."

[133] Sulloway, p. 153.

of an original primitive form of ascidian had developed, one leading to the vertebrates, the other to the modern ascidian. Darwin also regarded the ascidian as a possible missing link in the sexual evolution of the higher animals. Working from the observation that the embryonic forms of the vertebrates displayed both male and female sexual organs before one set atrophied in the middle stages of development, he argued in *The Descent of Man* that "some extremely remote progenitor of the whole vertebrate kingdom appears to have been hermaphrodite or androgynous."[134] He believed that the hermaphrodic ascidians were likely candidates for this missing bisexual link. Freud's research project for Brücke had a direct relationship to these issues, for as Sulloway points out the Petromyzon was not only bisexual but was also, at least in theory, a close zoological relative of the ascidian."[135] In investigating the Petromyzon, Freud discovered that certain anomalous cells (Riessner cells) observed on the surface of the spinal cord represented an evolutionary link between cells of the central and of the peripheral ganglia. This finding allowed him to argue that "it is not surprising if, in an animal that in many respects represents a permanent embryo, there are cells that have remained behind and that indicate the path the spinal ganglia cells once travelled."[136] The evolutionist framework of this early research project resulted in published findings which put Freud at the forefront of some of the most exciting scientific developments of his day.

Freud's paper on the Petromyzon appeared in the January 1877 issue of the Reports of the Imperial Academy of Science, and he followed this first, perhaps too hasty, publication with a much more thorough and polished one in July 1878.[137] (After additional work on the problem of sex in eels, carried out during a second stay in Trieste in the fall of 1876, he published a paper on that subject in the same bulletin in 1877.) The success represented by the publication of the two papers which emerged from Freud's first research project for Brücke encouraged him to pursue his further work under Brücke's guidance. As he observed in his *Autobiographical Study,* "At length, in Ernst Brücke's physiological laboratory, I found rest and satisfaction—and men, too, whom I could respect and take as my models: the great Brücke himself, and his assistants Sigmund Exner and Ernst Fleichl von Marxow. With the last of these, a brilliant man, I was privileged to be upon terms of friend-

[134] Quoted in ibid., p. 159.
[135] Ibid., p. 160.
[136] Quoted in ibid., p. 267.
[137] Bernfeld 1949, p. 177.

ship."[138] During the academic years 1875–76 and 1876–77, Freud enrolled in no fewer than six courses with Fleichl and three with Exner.[139] Brücke's laboratory also provided the setting for Freud's continuing research efforts. "I worked at this Institute, with short interruptions, from 1876 to 1882," he wrote, "and it was generally thought that I was marked out to fill the next post of Assistant that might fall vacant there."[140] Two other projects that Freud carried out in Brücke's laboratory also resulted in publications. The first, which appeared in 1879, concerned a new chemical method for preparing nerve tissues for microscopic examination, and the second, involving the nerve cells of the crayfish, was published in 1882.[141] By the time he was twenty-six years old, Freud had no less than five publications to his credit, all in the field of biological research.

There is no reason to regard this concentration on biological research as evidence of a departure from Freud's intellectual ideal of a two-sided approach to knowledge. Brentano firmly believed in this kind of rigorous investigation of physical reality, and in search of a deepened understanding of mental processes he sought to combine it with the study of internal perception, logic, and the other subjects included in philosophy and psychology. During the 1875–76 academic year, when Freud was carrying out his research projects for Claus and Brücke, he continued his course work with Brentano, bringing the total number of courses taken with him to five plus at least one other which Freud audited. Even after this formal course work ended, Brentano continued to further Freud's involvement in philosophy. The translation of four essays by John Stuart Mill which Freud began in the fall of 1879 resulted from Brentano's recommendation that Theodor Gomperz consider Freud for the job which fell vacant when the translator originally commissioned to do it suddenly died. Freud reported much later in a letter to Gomperz's son Heinrich, who was writing a biography of his father, that the elder Gomperz had mentioned his problem to Brentano at a party and that the philosopher, "whose student I then was or had been at a still earlier time, named my name."[142] The Silberstein correspondence reveals that Mill was the first name Freud mentioned in connection with Brentano's courses, and in both his published work and his lectures Brentano displayed the

[138] Freud, *Autobiographical Study, S.E.*, xx:9.
[139] Bernfeld 1951, p. 216.
[140] Freud, *Autobiographical Study, S.E.*, xx:10.
[141] Bernfeld 1949, pp. 178, 181.
[142] Ibid., pp. 189–90.

greatest admiration for Mill and the philosophical tradition he represented. Since he spoke as an expert on Mill, Brentano's recommendation carried considerable weight, so his suggestion of Freud's name should be seen as a mark of great respect for his former student. Heinrich Gomperz, himself a philosopher, commented on Freud's intellectual relationship to Brentano, which he regarded as a significant one: "May we speak, perhaps, of a certain after effect of the influence of a psychologist, who, more than any other, distinguished between 'physical' and 'psychic' phenomena and erected his whole doctrine on the basis of this distinction?"[143] Although Bernfeld argued the contrary, Freud's letters to Silberstein leave no doubt about a positive answer to this question.

Freud's friendships during this period also bespeak a continuing interest in the philosophical approach to psychology. In his letter to Silberstein of September 7, 1877, he mentioned various mutual friends including Josef Paneth and Siegfried Lipiner, both of whom had been members of the short-lived philosophical discussion group Freud wrote about in the fall of 1874. His comment on Lipiner is particularly interesting: "I had a lengthy conversation with him and will perhaps cultivate an acquaintance with him—that is, if he gives me the opportunity. I have no idea what to make of him; I have neither taken the measure of his accomplishments nor determined the weight of his personality."[144] He went on to indicate that he did not share the negative view of Lipiner held by one of their mutual friends: "In general, I incline . . . rather to a very favorable view of him."[145] Freud's deferential attitude toward a student who had been two years behind him at the Leopoldstadt Gymnasium may seem odd, but since Lipiner at that time enjoyed the esteem of such men of genius as Friedrich Nietzsche, Richard Wagner, and Gustav Mahler, respect was not out of place. Lipiner had in common with Freud a consuming interest in psychology, and at the time of their conversation he was in the process of establishing a personal link between Nietzsche and the Pernerstofer circle, the intellectual leaders of the Leseverein der deutschen Studenten.[146] Josef Paneth, the constant companion of Freud's earlier philosophical explorations, was also interested in Nietzsche.

[143] Quoted in ibid., p. 190.

[144] ". . . ich habe ein längeres Gespräch mit ihm gehabt u. werde sein Bekanntschaft vielleicht—d. h. wenn er mir Gelegenheit gibt, cultiviren. Ich bin gar nicht einig, was ich aus ihm machen soll, ich habe weder das Mass seines Geistes genommen, noch das Gewicht seiner Persönlichkeit bestimmt."

[145] "Im Allgemeinen neige ich aber nicht zu Wahle's Verurtheilung, eher zu einer sehr günstigen Ansicht über ihn."

[146] McGrath, *Dionysian Art*, pp. 69–70.

He lectured on his ideas to the Leseverein and like Lipiner eventually established a friendship with him. Although Freud specifically denied reading Nietzsche until late in life, it seems quite probable that his philosophic friendships with Lipiner and Paneth brought him at least a general knowledge of Nietzsche's outlook much earlier. As Freud observed in a 1934 letter, "In my youth he signified a nobility to which I could not attain. A friend of mine, Dr. Paneth, had got to know him in the Engadine and he used to write me a lot about him."[147] Like so many other important Austrian intellectuals of the *fin de siècle,* Freud shared the admiration for Nietzsche which the members of the Pernerstofer circle cultivated within the Leseverein in the late 1870s, as part of their crusade to develop a more psychologically sensitive culture.

Freud's early interest in hypnotism also testifies to his continuing interest in the purely psychological aspect of mental activity even during his years at Brücke's institute. In his *Autobiographical Study* he wrote of his first encounter with hypnotism: "While I was still a student I had attended a public exhibition given by Hansen the 'magnetist,' and had noticed that one of the subjects experimented upon had become deathly pale at the onset of cataleptic rigidity and had remained so as long as that condition lasted. This firmly convinced me of the genuineness of the phenomena of hypnosis."[148] One of Freud's letters to Silberstein offers some clues to the date of this encounter: in a note dated February 3, 1880 and written in English, he said that he would not attend Hansen's demonstration since it might disrupt his work schedule, but his reference to him as "my Mr. Hansen" suggests a previous familiarity with him. Freud also admonished his friend to "keep your mind skeptical and remember 'wonderful' is an admission of ignorance and not the acknowledgment of a miracle."[149] In the letter, as in the later comment in his autobiography, Freud combined an openmindedness toward this previously scorned psychological phenomenon with a keen scientific eye as to its authenticity.

Freud's broad range of interests figured in the unusually long time he took to complete his medical degree, for it was only in 1880 and 1881 that he took and passed the necessary series of final exams in the required subjects. He was awarded his M.D. in early 1881 after seven and a half years instead of the usual five, and both his letters and his course schedule make it evident that his love of theory (be it philosophy, psychology, or Darwinism)

[147] Quoted in Jones, III:460.
[148] Freud, *Autobiographical Study, S.E.,* XX:16.
[149] Silberstein, Feb. 3, 1880, written in English.

accounted for much of the delay. Freud betrayed a sensitivity about this subject in various dreams involving examinations. In the analysis of one he wrote, "The *five years* which are prescribed for medical studies were once again too few for me. I quietly went on with my work for several more years; and in my circle of acquaintances I was regarded as an idler and it was doubted whether I should ever get through."[150] Another dream involved allusions to the botany exam which he took on June 9, 1880: "In my preliminary examination in botany I was also given a Crucifer to identify—and failed to do so. My prospects would not have been too bright, if I had not been helped out by my theoretical knowledge." Further on in his analysis of related themes in this dream, Freud noted that they involved his *"favorite hobbies."*[151] This seems to be associated with a comment he made in an 1895 letter to Fliess where he observed that he could not live "without a hobby-horse, a consuming passion—in Schiller's words a tyrant. . . . My tyrant is psychology; it has always been my distant, beckoning goal."[152] Although Freud always defended himself against these dream accusations of being dilatory, it seems odd that even his most worshipful biographers, Bernfeld and Jones, have lent substance to them by suggesting that the course work of his second, third, and fourth years involved an aimless departure from the straight path of medical education.[153] Perhaps Freud did engage in a certain amount of sophomoric exploration, but even if so, it should be more fully appreciated that the love of theory which drove him to it bore a most important relationship to his later discoveries.

Important as Freud's love of theory may have been, however, the practical problem of earning a living could not be ignored. In view of the unlikelihood that either Exner or Fleichl would soon leave their positions at the physiological institute, Brücke finally, in 1882, urged Freud to resolve his dilemma by becoming a practicing physician—"advising me," Freud wrote later, "in view of my bad financial position, to abandon my theoretical career. I followed his advice, left the physiological laboratory and entered the General Hospital as an *Aspirant* [clinical assistant]. I was soon afterwards promoted to being a *Sekundararzt* [junior or house physician] and worked in various departments of the hospital, among others for more than six months under Meynert, by whose work and personality I had been greatly struck while I was still a stu-

[150] Freud, *Interpretation, S.E.,* v:450.
[151] Ibid., iv:171–72, 173.
[152] Freud, *Origins,* p. 119.
[153] Bernfeld 1951, pp. 204–5; Jones, i:36–39.

dent."[154] In 1877–78, as an undergraduate, Freud had taken a course in clinical psychiatry from Theodor Meynert, and since Meynert also gave frequent lectures on this topic to the Leseverein it is very likely that Freud was familiar with the work of this internationally known scientist even before he enrolled in his course.[155] The position in Meynert's division of the General Hospital that Freud secured in 1883 represented an important step in his attempt to achieve a compromise between his theoretical interests and the practical demands of life. He earned only a nominal salary, but since Meynert specialized in the anatomy of the brain, it meant that even during his clinical training as a physician Freud could continue his theoretical interests, both biological and psychological. As he observed in his autobiography, "In a certain sense I nevertheless remained faithful to the line of work upon which I had originally started. The subject which Brücke had proposed for my investigations had been the spinal cord of one of the lowest of fishes *(Ammocoetes Petromyzon);* and I now passed on to the human central nervous system."[156] Even before beginning his work with Meynert in the General Hospital, Freud had been allowed to enter his Institute of Cerebral Anatomy (autumn of 1882), and there he wrote several papers on the anatomy of the medulla oblongata. During the period before his trip to Paris, Freud's relationship with Meynert became quite close. Freud reported that "one day Meynert, who had given me access to the laboratory even during the times when I was not actually working under him, proposed that I should definitely devote myself to the anatomy of the brain, and promised to hand over his lecturing work to me.[157] Although Freud declined this offer, it demonstrates that Meynert shared the high regard for the young scientist that Brentano, Claus, and Brücke had felt and, like them, sought to foster Freud's career.

Freud also admired Meynert, referring to him in *The Interpretation of Dreams* as "the great Meynert, in whose footsteps I had trodden with such deep veneration."[158] This was high praise, considering the antagonism which subsequently developed between them, and it acknowledged a substantial intellectual debt extending well beyond the specifics of brain anatomy. Meynert's work offered Freud a dynamic model of mental activity, a model he closely followed in evolving his own psychoanalytic theories a decade later. A man

[154] Freud, *Autobiographical Study, S.E.,* xx:10.
[155] McGrath, *Dionysian Art,* pp. 42–44.
[156] Freud, *Autobiographical Study, S.E.,* xx:10.
[157] Ibid., p. 11.
[158] Freud, *Interpretation, S.E.,* v:437.

of broad artistic, political, and philosophical interests, Meynert developed his research on cerebral anatomy within a sophisticated psychological-philosophical framework. This aspect of his work served to reinforce in Freud Brentano's ideal of a dual physical-psychological framework for understanding mental processes, and Meynert and Brentano were in fact close friends. They socialized and vacationed together, and as Meynert's daughter indicated in her biography of her father, he and the entire family felt the deepest admiration and respect for this priestly philosopher.[159]

The importance of Meynert's influence on Freud has long been appreciated, but its nature has been misunderstood. Maria Dorer, one of the earliest scholars to trace the genealogy of Freud's thought, pointed out as early as 1932 the close similarity between the dynamic elements of Meynert's psychology and Freud's dynamic conception of conscious-unconscious interaction. She also suggested, without substantial evidence, that Meynert drew his conception of a dynamic unconscious from J. F. Herbart.[160] This erroneous conclusion that Freud, via Meynert, was influenced by Herbart has been uncritically accepted by virtually all the scholars who have written on this subject from Bernfeld and Jones to Sulloway.[161] In fact no substantial evidence has yet been brought forward to show any Herbartian influence on Freud. In Freud's entire *Collected Works* the only index entries for Herbart involve editorial references to the Bernfeld-Jones theory of a Herbartian influence. Freud himself did not mention Herbart's name in any of his published works. As a well-educated man, Theodor Meynert undoubtedly knew Herbart's work, but he rarely referred to him and in fact disagreed with his psychological theories. Erna Lesky, in her outstanding history of the Vienna medical school, points out that in 1865, when Maximilian Leidesdorf prepared a new edition of his textbook on mental disorders, he allowed Meynert, who was his student, to do certain sections of it, including the part on psychological theory. In this section Meynert discarded the Herbartian framework of

[159] Dora Stockert Meynert, *Theodor Meynert und seine Zeit* (Vienna: Österreichischer Bundesverlag, 1930), pp. 149–53, 155–56.

[160] Maria Dorer, *Historische Grundlagen der Psychoanalyse* (Leipzig: Felix Meiner, 1932), pp. 149–50, 158–70.

[161] Bernfeld and Jones also supported their theory of a Herbartian influence on Freud with one other, equally questionable, piece of evidence. The Bernfelds discovered that a textbook on psychology in use in Freud's Gymnasium during his last year there was written by a Herbartian, G. A. Lindner, and on this basis Jones argued that Herbart's ideas strongly influenced Freud (Jones, I:371–76). No evidence has ever been offered that Freud read the book, even though Sulloway elaborates on this particular myth by saying that Freud was "known to have read" it (Sulloway, p. 67).

Wilhelm Griesinger, whom Leidesdorf had followed in the earlier edition and continued to use in his own segments of the new edition of the book.[162] Moreover, the Silberstein correspondence indicates that Freud had no argument with Brentano's utter condemnation of Herbart. It appears highly unlikely that the dynamic elements of Freud's psychology derived in any way from Herbart.

The crucial philosophical-psychological influence on Meynert came not from Herbart but from Schopenhauer, as Meynert readily acknowledged and various contemporary writers who discussed his work recognized. Meynert shared this philosophical orientation with his patron, colleague, and close friend, Karl von Rokitansky, the moving spirit in the development of the great medical school of nineteenth-century Vienna. From the outset of his long, energetic, and successful career Rokitansky set himself a goal which, as Erna Lesky observes, "he considered an urgent requirement of his time. To arouse German medicine from its natural-philosophical dream and to base it on solid, unchangeable, material facts, was the task he set himself." Although it may seem paradoxical, it is important to emphasize that in pursuing this goal, which closely resembled that of the Du Bois-Reymond/Helmholtz school, Rokitansky was at one with that school and with many other prominent scientists in adhering to the German idealist tradition represented by Kant and Schopenhauer. Within the Kantian framework there was no contradiction in the belief that the unchangeable, scientifically predictable, material world of nature was also a world of appearances or phenomena; and scholars familiar with the idealist tradition have understood its importance to the science of Freud's time. Erna Lesky discusses Rokitansky's interest in this Kantian tradition which culminated in his acceptance of "the philosophy of Schopenhauer as the interpretation of the world most appropriate to his nature."[163] Freud's friend Siegfried Lipiner, himself a Schopenhauerian, also had occasion to write about this element of Rokitansky's thought. In an 1881 newspaper review of two of his essays Lipiner observed, "Rokitansky is a student of Kant and Schopenhauer, and more of the latter than the former. He is a Schopenauerian with body and soul and in every respect."[164] Wilhelm Jerusalem, a prominent contemporary scholar of this intellectual tradition, pointed out its widespread influence in an 1892

[162] Erna Lesky, *The Vienna Medical School,* trans. L. Williams and I. S. Levij (Baltimore: The Johns Hopkins University Press, 1976), p. 158.

[163] Ibid., p. 107.

[164] Siegfried Lipiner, "Zwei Schriften von Rokitansky," *Deutsche Zeitung,* no. 3435, July 27, 1881, p. 1.

Neue Freie Presse review of a book of essays by Meynert. He argued that "Rokitansky and Meynert as well as Helmholtz and Du Bois-Reymond are firm idealists and true adherents of Kant and Schopenhauer. They are all firmly convinced of the fact that the world which we have before us is only an appearance and that we can never fathom the somewhat hidden essence behind the appearance."[165] Meynert's central debt to Schopenhauer involved the dynamic psychological model which emerged from this philosopher's transformation of Kant.

Meynert introduced a discussion of his psychological system into almost all his lectures whether on brain anatomy or on more general topics, and he also expounded it in somewhat greater detail in his *Psychiatry,* a book devoted primarily to the anatomy of the brain. He would usually begin his discussion with a reference to the Kantian tradition and would often allude to a particular remark of Schopenauer's about Kant's theory of knowledge. As he put it in an 1872 lecture, "According to Schopenhauer, our head was in space before Kant; but since Kant space is in our head."[166] This reference to Kant's "Copernican Revolution" was a paraphrase of the concluding line of section 30 of Schopenhauer's *Parerga and Parilipomena,* a line that prepared the way for a detailed summary of the main elements of Schopenauer's own philosophical system. In his 1872 lecture and in various others, Meynert went on from this reference to explain the relationship of brain anatomy to the psychology of consciousness, which in his view revolved about the interaction between a primary and a secondary ego impelled by motives of aggression and defense. A comparison of his discussion with the extended context of the passage from Schopenhauer reveals that Meynert's ideas emerged directly from this section of *Parerga and Parilipomena.*

Working within the framework of Kant's dualism between the world of phenomenal appearances and the noumenal essence of things, Schopenhauer transformed Kant by asserting that the thing-in-itself for all things was the will, which he conceived of as blind and irrational. In section 32 of *Parerga* he pointed out the implications of this with respect to the knowing subject: "To us the will is of course the thing-in-itself, existing for itself, a purely desiring

[165] Wilhelm Jerusalem, *Gedanken und Denker, Gesammelte Aufsätze* (Vienna: Wilhelm Braumüller, 1905), p. 151. The difficulty in grasping this point of view which underlies Freud's two-sided approach to mental activity may account for the failure of Jones and other scholars to appreciate the importance of the idealist tradition to Freud's work.

[166] Theodor Meynert, *Sammlung von Populär–Wissenschaftlichen Vorträgen über den Bau und die Leistangen des Gehirns* (Vienna: Braumüller, 1892), p. 23.

[Wollendes], rather than a knowing thing." To the knowing subject, then, the will appeared as body, and he knew his own will only in the objectified form of his own body with the physical feelings which arose from it. Schopenhauer thus argued that "knowing is a secondary and mediated function that does not immediately belong to the will, to that which is primary in its own essence."[167] This view provided the basis for Meynert's psychology of the primary and secondary ego. As he observed in an 1890 lecture, "We must, however, also consider, as does Schopenauer, that our head is in space but that at the same time space is in our head; that our body—taken in the truest sense as 'ego'—is an object [or ingredient—*Bestandtheil*] of our outer perception."[168] Meynert saw the differentiation between this primary, body ego and a self-conscious secondary ego in a developmental context. "The ego begins . . . as the *primary* ego of the child; its only contents are bodily feelings. As an association attaches to it from the outer world, what pleases or displeases the bodily feelings causes this new association to be met with movements either of possession *[Ergreifen]* or defense *[Abwehr]*. Without defense the child cannot delimit the components of its ego." Meynert believed that over time contact with the outer world led to the development of a secondary ego in the child: "So far as its position in the world is concerned it is at first a parasite of maternal love and then later depends on the help of others. But with just such strong associations, the *primary* ego developing and expanding adds to itself even more elements from the external world and without firm boundaries develops from a primary ego into a *secondary* ego."[169] This statement closely followed Schopenhauer's assertion that "the intellect . . . is nothing more than a receptivity to external impressions."[170] Schopenhauer's conception of a primary will versus a secondary intellect, which led to Meynert's primary ego–secondary ego system, pointed forward to Freud's distinction between id and ego, between the primary process and secondary process levels of mental activity.

How closely Freud approximated Schopenhauer in this distinction can be seen in a passage from section 40 of *Parerga:* "One might almost believe that half of all our thought occurs unconsciously. . . . I can search my memory for days to recall a name that has escaped me, and then when I am not thinking about it at all it

[167] Arthur Schopenhauer, *Sämtliche Werke*, ed. Paul Deussen, vol. 5 (Munich: R. Pier, 1913), p. 54; henceforth cited as Deussen ed.

[168] Meynert, *Sammlung*, pp. 227–28.

[169] Ibid., p. 228.

[170] Deussen ed., p. 59.

suddenly occurs to me, as though it had been whispered in my ear."[171] Schopenhauer described a similar conscious-unconscious interaction in the occurrence of profound thoughts which emerged suddenly into consciousness: "They are, however, clearly the result of long unconscious meditation and of countless *aperçus* that often lie in the distant past and are individually forgotten. . . . One might almost venture to suggest the physiological hypothesis that conscious thought takes place on the surface of the brain and unconscious in the innermost recesses of its medullary substance."[172] Meynert also followed this latter conceptualization in his anatomical brain research where, as Erna Lesky notes, he developed "his fundamental view that the phylogenetically older basal ganglia—the site of involuntary movements—are functionally inhibited by the cortex of the brain, which reaches maturity later. This functional antagonism between cortex and nuclei of the brain . . . would later become the determining factor of Meynert's complete psychiatric system."[173] Meynert undoubtedly carried Schopenhauer's ideas much further and refined them considerably, but in the basic conception of two dynamically interacting levels of mental activity as well as in the anatomical localization of these areas of activity he closely adhered to them.

Meynert's conception of defense also constitutes a link between Schopenhauer and Freud. In the treatment of memory that starts in section 36 of *Parerga,* Schopenhauer began by observing that in the mind "one could say that genius lives only one floor above madness." He went on to point out that even those who were rational were not always rational, and then, on the basis of these and other observations, put forward an explanation for this intermittent operation of rational consciousness. "All of this appears to point to a certain ebb and flow of the vital fluids of the brain or to a tension and relaxation of its filaments."[174] Schopenhauer thus translated his psychological system into a physiological theory, and Meynert's concept of defense built on that relationship. Erna Lesky notes that "Meynert recognized only two types of affect, that of attack and that of defense, and these . . . were merely an expression of a special nutritive phase of the brain."[175] In the discussion of defense contained in his *Psychiatry,* Meynert considered the impact

[171] Ibid., pp. 63–64.

[172] I have followed the Payne translation here: Arthur Schopenhauer, *Parerga and Parlipomena,* trans. E. F. J. Payne (Oxford: Clarendon Press, 1974), 2:56; see also Deussen ed., p. 64.

[173] Lesky, p. 336.

[174] Deussen ed., p. 58.

[175] Lesky, p. 338.

of a traumatic event such as news of the death of a loved one, a person whose image "when presented to the brain would arouse all sorts of secondary presentations and pleasurable emotions." According to Meynert "such news, I repeat, would cause inhibition of all these associations. . . . A physiological process occupying much time and consisting in the dissolution of now purposeless associations and the formation of new ones, precedes the introduction of this death news into the web of associations." He then sought to connect the psychological with the physiological process: "Inhibition is attended by emotion and psychical pain. With inhibition and psychical pain there is connected increase of arterial pressure. . . . Inhibition or resistance on the lines of nerve-conduction through the gray substance, as well as increased arterial pressure in consequence of strong sensory impressions, are physiological facts." After discussing certain of the chemical elements of these processes he continued, "Sensation itself is the subjective form of perception of all these physiological processes; it is, as it were, the expression of a special sense concerned with the nutritive phases of the cortex."[176]

Wilhelm Jerusalem has provided a particularly clear discussion of the psychological dimension of Meynert's conception of defense and its place in his two ego system. In an account of Meynert's lecture "Brain and Morality," he observed that "brain physiology now teaches us, however, that the function of the surface of the brain [the seat of the secondary ego] primarily consists in restraining *[hemmen]* the impulses emanating from the subcortical brain centers, the drives of the primary egotistical ego."[177] In another article on Meynert he indicated that defense operated on the levels of both primary and secondary ego, and that in the latter case the influence of such abstractions as nation, state, and society could become deeply integral components of the self. "We defend this integrity vigorously and tenaciously, often with more vigor and tenacity than we defend our primary ego, our own body."[178]

Although Meynert's ambitious attempt to bring together psychology, physiology, and anatomy in the explanation of mental processes necessarily contained many untested theoretical links, it offered Freud a useful framework for his own advancing understanding of this subject. There can be no doubt that Freud possessed

[176] Theodor Meynert, *Psychiatry: A Clinical Treatise on Diseases of the Fore-Brain Based upon a Study of Its Structure, Functions and Nutrition,* trans. B. Sachs (New York: Putnam, 1885), pp. 192–93.

[177] Jerusalem, p. 128.

[178] Ibid., p. 148.

a thorough understanding of Meynert's ideas.[179] Otherwise Meynert would not have invited him to take over his classes. Moreover, Freud employed Meynert's conceptual terminology in his essay *On Cocaine,* written and published in the summer of 1884, at a time when he was very much under Meynert's influence. He drew a parallel between the euphoria produced by cocaine and that resulting from general good health: "One may perhaps assume that the euphoria resulting from good health is also nothing more than the normal condition of a well-nourished cerebral cortex."[180]

Tracing in detail the intellectual path from Schopenhauer's *Parerga* through Meynert to Freud helps resolve a mystery pointed out by Freud in his *History of the Psychoanalytic Movement.* In recounting the history of his concept of repression he noted that at the time of his close association with Breuer, "I looked upon psychical splitting itself as an effect of a process of repelling which at that time I called 'defense,' and later, 'repression.' "[181] Although Freud regarded this fundamentally important concept as his own discovery, he later became aware of the close parallel between this idea and an element of Schopenhauer's philosophy. He noted that Otto Rank eventually pointed out to him "the passage in Schopenhauer's *World as Will and Idea* in which the philosopher seeks to give an explanation of insanity. What he says there about the struggle against accepting a distressing piece of reality coincides with my concept of repression so completely that once again I owe the chance of making this discovery to my not being well-read."[182] The passage to which he referred closely paralleled the context and content of the passage from *Parerga* on which Meynert rested his concept of defense. In a discussion of the relationship between genius and madness, Schopenhauer pointed to the impact of "unexpected and terrible events" on the memory: "Now if such a sorrow . . . is so harrowing that it becomes positively unbearable, and the individual would succumb to it, then nature, alarmed in this way, seizes on *madness* as the last means of saving life. The mind, tormented so greatly, destroys as it were, the thread of memory, fills up the gaps with fictions, and thus seeks refuge in madness from the mental suffering that exceeds its strength."[183]

[179] See Dorer, pp. 149–50; also Jones, I:375–77.

[180] Sigmund Freud, *Cocaine Papers* (hereafter Freud, *Cocaine*), ed. Robert Byck (New York: Stonehill, 1974), p. 60.

[181] Sigmund Freud, "On the History of the Psycho-Analytic Movement," *S.E.*, XIV:11.

[182] Ibid., p. 15.

[183] Arthur Schopenhauer, *The World as Will and Representation,* trans. E. F. J. Payne (New York: Dover, 1969), p. 193.

One need not doubt Freud's honesty in disclaiming any early knowledge of this passage; the Schopenhauerian basis of Meynert's ideas largely explains the mystery of the close parallel between Freud's concept of repression and Schopenhauer's thought.

Although Freud had seen his decision to leave Brücke's physiology institute as a choice for practical rather than theoretical work, his association with Meynert allowed him to find a middle way between these apparent alternatives. Meynert's influence contributed in important ways to the development of a sophisticated theoretical framework for psychiatric work, and the hospital training Freud received represented at least a step toward the practical goal of becoming a physician. On two previous occasions in his life when he had confronted the choice between theory and practice, the trips to Freiberg and to Manchester, romantic interests had figured prominently in his thoughts and feelings, and that was the case on this occasion as well. Bernfeld has pointed out that even though Freud stressed the importance of Brücke's advice in making this decision, it must also have been influenced by the beginning of his relationship with Martha Bernays. He met Martha in the spring of 1882, became formally engaged to her on June 17, and entered the General Hospital in July. Less than a year later, when he became a *Secundarartzt* and worked in Meynert's psychiatry section, he secured a free room in the hospital and was able for the first time to move out of his parents' house.[184] Even so, he was far from being able to afford marriage, and his work on brain anatomy offered little prospect of earning a living. As he observed in his autobiography: "From the material point of view, brain anatomy was certainly no better than physiology, and with an eye to pecuniary considerations, I began to study nervous diseases. There were, at that time, few specialists in that branch of medicine in Vienna, the material for its study was distributed over a number of different departments of the hospital, . . . and one was forced to be one's own teacher."[185] Bernfeld has suggested that Freud formulated this plan to become a neurologist in 1883,[186] and Freud's letters to his fiancée, who lived far away in Hamburg, indicate that by July of that year the close relationship that he had formed with Josef Breuer had expanded to include discussion of one of Breuer's most important neurological cases, Bertha Pappenheim (Anna O), who happened to be a friend of Martha Bernays.[187] In deciding

[184] Bernfeld 1951, pp. 208–9, 211.
[185] Freud, *Autobiographical Study, S.E.*, xx:11.
[186] Bernfeld 1951, p. 211.
[187] Freud, *Letters*, p. 41.

to become a neurologist Freud made further progress in achieving a compromise that allowed him to combine many of his theoretical and practical aims. "In the distance shone the great name of Charcot; so I formed a plan of first obtaining an appointment as Lecturer *[Dozent]* on Nervous Diseases in Vienna and of then going to Paris to continue my studies."[188] With the additional luster he would gain from a university position and the practical experience in working with nervous disorders that he had largely missed in Vienna, Freud could hope for enough income from a private practice to support himself and his future wife while also being able to continue his research career.

During the period from 1883 to 1885 when Freud was working to achieve these immediate goals, he supplemented his research in brain anatomy with experimental work on cocaine, work that allowed him for the first time to realize Brentano's ideal of a scientific, experimental approach to inner perception. Freud's research on cocaine proved to be deeply frustrating. First he narrowly missed gaining credit for discovering its value as an anesthetic in eye operations—the discovery that made his friend Karl Koller famous. Then later Freud was widely criticized in the scientific community for having incautiously advocated its general use as an anesthetic, a use proved to be dangerous when the drug's addictive properties came to be more fully understood. With respect to understanding the intellectual path to Freud's later discoveries, however, the primary importance of the cocaine episode lies in the example it provides of the way Freud used himself as his principal psychological laboratory, the practice he brought to perfection in *The Interpretation of Dreams.* In his *On Coca,* which appeared in July 1884, he began part v, "The Effects of Coca on the Healthy Human Body" by declaring, "I have carried out experiments and studied in myself and others the effect of coca on the healthy human body; my findings agree fundamentally with Mantegazza's description of the effect of coca leaves."[189] He then provided a detailed account of his initial mood, the smell and taste of the drug, its exhilarating effect, the changes in sense perception it produced, and various other physical effects. From there he moved on to an equally careful account of the drug's psychic effects. He thus followed the basic approach advocated by Brentano, making a close scientific examination of both the physical and the psychic sides of mental phenomena, and then proposed a theoretical link between the two,

[188] Freud, *Autobiographical Study, S.E.,* xx:11.
[189] Freud, *Cocaine,* p. 58.

suggesting *à la* Meynert that the euphoria produced by cocaine had to do with "a well-nourished cerebral cortex." The essay also provides yet another example of the importance of religion in Freud's approach to psychological investigation: after beginning with a brief description of the plant and its production, it turns to a more extensive account of the drug's place in the religious customs of the Incas as well as the religious opposition of the conquering Spaniards, who regarded its effects "as the work of the devil."[190] Freud's scientific investigation of the drug and his strong enthusiasm for it put him in the position of justifying the pagan Incas against the prejudices of their Catholic conquerors. His standpoint here echoed his adolescent Hannibal phantasy and showed the tendency nourished by Philippson, Schiller, and Brentano, to see a close tie between religious and psychological phenomena.[191]

Although Freud's work on cocaine eventually brought him more professional grief than profit, his initial publication and his role in the discovery of the drug's anesthetic properties added to the impressive list of scholarly accomplishments which soon gained him the university association he had set as his goal. As he wrote in his *Autobiographical Study*, "In the spring of 1885 I was appointed Lecturer *[Dozent]* in Neuropathology. . . . Soon afterwards, as a result of a warm testimonial from Brücke, I was awarded a Travelling Bursary of considerable value. In the autumn of the same year I made the journey to Paris."[192] Freud's stay in Paris and his contact with Charcot had the effect of focusing his professional interest on hysteria, and this subject provided an ideal vehicle for exploring further that border area Brentano had pointed to between the physical and psychological sides of mental life. Freud's work on hysteria, which also drew on his earlier political and religious interests, ultimately led him to his greatest discoveries.

[190] Ibid., p. 50.

[191] Freud's *On Coca* also points forward to his developing interests in hysteria and sexuality. In section VI, "The Therapeutic Uses of Cocaine," he noted that it had been prescribed "for the most diverse kinds of psychic debility—hysteria, hypochondria, melancholic inhibition, stupor and similar maladies; . . . and according to Caldwell it is the best tonic for hysteria" (Freud, *Cocaine*, p. 65). Although Freud did not in this essay explicitly link the subjects of hysteria and sexuality, he did go on to discuss the latter topic separately in a section near the end entitled "Coca as an Aphrodisiac." He began by observing, "The natives of South America, who represented their goddess of love with coca leaves in her hand, did not doubt the stimulative effect of coca on the genitalia." After this historical religious note he went on in the next paragraph to give the results of his own research efforts: "Among the persons to whom I have given coca, three report violent sexual excitement which they unhesitatingly attributed to the coca" (ibid., p. 73).

[192] Freud, *Autobiographical Study, S.E.*, XX:12.

4/

The Architecture of Hysteria

Freud found Paris exotic and fascinating. He later recalled, "The platform of Notre Dame was my favorite resort in Paris; every free afternoon, I used to clamber about there on the towers of the church between the monsters and the devils."[1] This supreme monument of medieval architecture provides an appropriate symbol for the new phase in Freud's development initiated by his studies with Jean Martin Charcot. On December 3, 1885, he wrote to Minna Bernays that Parisians "are people given to psychical epidemics, historical mass convulsions, and they haven't changed since Victor Hugo wrote *Notre Dame.* To understand Paris this is the novel you must read. Although everything in it is fiction, one is convinced of its truth."[2] Both the novel and the church itself served to link in Freud's mind a highly political view of the Catholic middle ages and a growing interest in various phenomena of mass psychology. This mix provided a congenial context for Charcot's approach to hysteria.

Freud's studies with Charcot shaped his research on hysteria over the decade following his return to Vienna, and the political dimension of Charcot's work proved especially important to him. What Jan Goldstein says of the hysteria diagnosis developed by Charcot and his followers: that it "contained within itself all the rudiments of an anticlerical campaign,"[3] also has a bearing on Freud's approach to the subject. The close correlation which Charcot and Désiré Magloire Bourneville saw between hysteria and

[1] Freud, *Interpretation, S.E.,* v:469.
[2] Freud, *Letters,* p. 188.
[3] Jan Goldstein, "The Hysterical Diagnosis and the Politics of Anticlericalism in Late Nineteenth-Century France," *Journal of Modern History,* 54 (June 1982):238.

certain repressive aspects of medieval Catholic culture harmonized well with Freud's own anticlerical political position. He brought their psychological analysis of medieval culture to bear on his developing conceptions of hysterical repression and defense as well as on the relationship between hysteria and sexuality. Moreover, during the period following his father's death in late 1896, when Freud himself began to exhibit hysterical symptoms, the deterioration of sociopolitical conditions in Vienna made the anticlerical dimension of the hysteria diagnosis immediately relevant to his situation. The triumph that the anti-Semitic, Catholic clerical forces achieved in the spring of 1897, with the confirmation of Karl Lueger as mayor of Vienna, represented a threat to everything Freud believed in and hoped for. Their victory so intensified his own inner turmoil that it helped reveal to him from within the relationship between hysteria and intense psychic conflict. When he summarized his new insights into the nature of neurotic disorder in a series of notes he sent to Fliess in May 1897, he gave them a title which provides a valuable clue to the origins of his ideas: "The Architecture of Hysteria" recalled not only his recent visit to Nürnberg and the medieval architecture he had seen there, but also his earlier trip to Paris, where he had been so impressed with Charcot that he could declare, "I sometimes come out of his lectures as from out of Nôtre Dame, with an entirely new idea about perfection."[4] Freud's studies in Paris drew together scientific, historical, and political issues of the greatest importance to his further intellectual development.

In describing Freud's reaction to Paris, Carl Schorske has noted how vividly it contrasted with his earlier impressions of England: "England was good order, morality and liberal rationality. . . . Paris was the very opposite: a city of danger, of the questionable, of the irrational. Freud accepted, but richly elaborated, Paris as the wanton, the female temptress; he approached it in a spirit of adventure at once thrilling and terrifying."[5] Schorske notes that in his letters from Paris "Freud seems to have opened himself to the whole world of forbidden *fleurs du mal* that Freud the Anglophile and liberal Jew had until then rejected or avoided: The Roman Catholic Church, the bewildering power of the female, and the power of the masses."[6] Freud's travels often evoked regressive feelings of longing for a mother figure, and the themes associated

[4] Freud, *Letters,* p. 185.

[5] Carl E. Schorske, "Freud: The Psycho-archeology of Civilizations," *Proceedings of the Massachusetts Historical Society,* 92 (1980):57.

[6] Ibid., p. 58.

with his trip to Paris recall his "second mother," the lower-class Roman Catholic woman whose disappearance had jarred his early childhood.[7]

Freud's regressive moods also tended to recall memories of his political radicalism, and this reaction manifested itself strongly in his Paris letters. In his political debates with Silberstein during their college years, Freud had always held to a republican position—radical enough in imperial Austria—and his arrival in Paris, the capital of the one important republic in Europe, revived that enthusiasm. "The Republic is pleased that I am in Paris," he wrote in one of his first letters.[8] In a letter of October 19, 1885, he commented on the frequently interrupted history of the Republic as well as on the current electoral contests between monarchists and republicans, and reported with relief that after earlier gains by the monarchists "these bye-elections are now Republican."[9] This political theme also found a more personal expression in his description of a Paris park. He wrote, "On the benches sit wet nurses feeding their babies, and nursemaids to whom the children dash screaming after they have had a quarrel. I couldn't help thinking of poor Mitzi, and grew very, very furious and full of revolutionary thoughts." The very next sentence, which concerned an Egyptian obelisk from Luxor, reveals the undercurrents of his thoughts and feelings. "Imagine a genuine obelisk, scribbled all over with the most beautiful birds' heads, little seated men and other hieroglyphs, at least 3000 years older than the vulgar crowd around it, built in honor of a king whose name today only a few people can read and who, but for this monument, might be forgotten!" The thought that his sister Mitzi had a servile position led his mind back to Egypt, the biblical land of oppression, and to the folly of monarchical pretensions. Further on in the same paragraph he described the collection of the Louvre, with its "Egyptian bas-reliefs, decorated in fiery colors, veritable colossi of kings, real sphinxes, a dreamlike world."[10] The images and associations of Freud's earlier historical and political interests frequently recurred in the letters he wrote from Paris.[11]

These interests, as well as the religious concerns that underlay them, had a direct bearing on the scientific subject which came to fascinate him in Paris: hysteria. By the time Freud encountered

[7] Freud, *Origins*, pp. 220–22.
[8] Freud, *Letters*, p. 184.
[9] Ibid., p. 174.
[10] Freud, *Letters*, pp. 173–74.
[11] See Freud, *Letters*, nos. 86, 87, 90–91, 94.

him, Charcot had become an honored luminary of the Third Republic. Jan Goldstein, who has explored the highly political context and significance of Charcot's work on hysteria, notes that "at just the time when Charcot and his school were rising to prominence, they formed part of a tight network of republican politicians and scientist-politicians. The cast of characters . . . included Gambetta, Paul Bert, Charcot and Désiré-Magloire Bourneville." She points out that, "Charcot, though not a political actor, was clearly politically affiliated, entertaining Gambetta at his soirées on the boulevard St. Germain, called to Gambetta's bedside as a consulting physician during the politician's fatal illness, the father-in-law of Gambetta's political ally Waldeck-Rousseau."[12] Freud fully appreciated Charcot's associations with the republican left. In a letter of October 21, 1885, he described the atmosphere of Charcot's clinic as "very informal and democratic,"[13] and in his 1893 obituary of Charcot he noted that "the government, at the head of which was Charcot's old friend, Gambetta, created a chair of Neuropathology for him at the Faculty of Medicine."[14] Goldstein argues that the establishment of this chair and Charcot's appointment to it were closely tied to the anticlerical policies of Gambetta and the republican left. "The program of the newly republicanized Republic of the late 1870s and 1880s was dominated by an anticlerical crusade, and the psychiatrists of the Salpêtrière school participated in it enthusiastically."[15]

By the time Freud arrived in Paris, however, Charcot's political position had begun to change as he deemphasized the anticlerical implications of his work and cultivated the image of the dispassionate scientist standing above the political fray. During this time his personal relationships involved him with a wide variety of political figures ranging from aristocratic revivalists such as the Goncourt brothers[16] to leaders of the liberal Catholic movements such as Cardinal Lavigerie.[17] Later, by the early 1890s, Charcot was close to those promoting the *ralliement*, the attempt to reconcile bourgeois republicanism with liberal Catholicism.[18] His family back-

[12] Goldstein, p. 222.
[13] Freud, *Letters*, p. 176.
[14] Sigmund Freud, "Charcot," *S.E.*, III:16.
[15] Goldstein, pp. 230, 233.
[16] Debora Leah Silverman, "Nature, Nobility and Neurology: The Ideological Origins of 'Art Nouveau' in France, 1889–1900," Ph.D. diss., Princeton University, 1983, p. 53.
[17] Georges Guillain, *J.-M. Charcot, 1825–1893: His Life—His Work*, ed. and trans. Pearce Bailey (New York: Paul B. Hoeber, 1959), p. 25.
[18] Silverman, pp. 71, 179–92.

ground had involved him as a young man in the decorative arts, and in his mature years he and his family founded a studio devoted to interior decoration and furniture making, achieving great prominence in the world of high taste. This artistic side of Charcot's personality also influenced his medical work, as can be seen not only in his strong emphasis on the visual, but also in a book he published in 1887, *Les démoniaques dans l'art.* In this study embracing works of art from the early medieval through the early modern period, Charcot sought to show how various images of supernatural possession and satanic convulsions were accurate renderings of what were later identified as symptoms of nervous degeneration and the phases of attacks of hysteria.[19] Although his science clarified the meaning of the art it also affirmed its truth and to some extent the truth of the religious experiences depicted, redefining the meaning of these experiences while affirming their reality. In this way the artistic side of Charcot's personality tended increasingly in his final years to undercut his earlier positivistic radicalism. Freud's own comments, however, suggest that he was more comfortable with the image of the earlier, more radical Charcot, the friend of Gambetta.[20]

One of the central figures in the alliance between psychiatry and anticlerical politics was Désiré Magloire Bourneville, a man whose political views may have made him particularly appealing to Freud. A close associate of Charcot at the Salpêtrière and an active politician, Bourneville had—either directly or indirectly—stirred Freud's interest in hysterical phenomena a decade earlier in 1875 with his work on Louise Lateau. This study of the Belgian stigmatist was of a piece with a larger project undertaken in close cooperation with Charcot; Bourneville edited a series of books on witchcraft and demonology called the *Bibliothèque diabolique,* which, as Peter Swales notes, was part of Charcot's larger endeavor "to demonstrate comprehensively how all of the somatic symptoms of hysteria corresponded minutely to the various symptoms attributed in the Middle Ages to witchcraft and possession."[21] A. R. G. Owen points out that often "suspected witches had anesthetic points, so beloved of such old witch-finders and witch-prickers as the English Matthew Hopkins, and Charcot equated these with the anesthetic areas found in so many hysterics."[22] This modern psychological explanation of

[19] Ibid., pp. 180, 189–92, 186; on Charcot as a *visuel,* see pp. 179–81.
[20] Freud, "Charcot," *S.E.,* III:18–19.
[21] Swales, "Weier," p. 7.
[22] Alan R. G. Owen, *Hysteria, Hypnosis and Healing: The Work of J.-M. Charcot* (London: Dobson; New York: Garrett, 1971), p. 70.

medieval Catholic witch-hunting bore a direct relationship to Bourneville's political activity, for as a member of the Paris municipal council he led the anticlerical campaign to laicize the public hospitals. The campaign succeeded in 1883, and Bourneville then went on to secure election to the national Chamber of Deputies, where he served from 1883 to 1887.[23] Just as his scholarship sought to show that medieval Catholic religious beliefs were based on misunderstood hysterical phenomena, so his politics invoked the name of modern science to wrest control of the hospitals from the church.

Freud's knowledge of Feuerbach and his work with Brentano on religious psychology had well prepared him to appreciate the importance of the view of witchcraft developed by Charcot and Bourneville. His acquaintance with the specific subject of witchcraft as a psychological phenomenon probably went back even earlier to his Gymnasium days and his friendship with Heinrich Braun, which had led him indirectly to a knowledge of the views of Johann Weier. Bourneville also admired the enlightened spirit of Weier's work and had it republished as part of the *Bibliothèque diabolique* in 1885, the year Freud arrived in Paris. Freud found in Charcot a modern-day defender of the tradition established by men like Weier, for as Goldstein shows, Charcot's conception of hysteria allowed "a smooth transformation of religious meaning into scientific meaning, a transformation which took on the air of a victory."[24] Freud could share in the victory since his own political outlook perfectly coincided with that underlying the historical use of the hysteria diagnosis. Freud had long seen the Roman Catholic church as his own particular nemesis, so the political implications of studying hysteria with Charcot could only have reinforced his interest in the subject.

Above all, Freud saw Charcot as a liberator, a view perhaps enhanced because it was set against the background of Charcot's great interest in the medieval. Owen writes of his house: "The mansion was furnished luxuriously to Charcot's visual taste, which inclined to the medieval: tapestries, stained-glass windows, wrought iron chandeliers, wood paneling and dark wooden columns. . . . The stained-glass windows gave a somewhat 'dim religious light'."[25] Freud described Charcot's study as "a room worthy of the magic

[23] Goldstein, pp. 231, 223.

[24] Goldstein writes, "This hysteria concept was a kind of capsule of the eighteenth-century Voltairean mentality, of the assault upon the clerical world view by the scientific world view. . . . " pp. 237–38.

[25] Owen, p. 229.

castle in which he lives," and characterized Charcot himself as being "like a worldly priest."[26] Nonetheless, to Freud Charcot was principally a man standing out against this medieval background as an enlightened secularizer, determined to free his patients from the oppressive weight of dogmatic misconceptions. In his obituary of Charcot, Freud wrote, "In the hall in which he gave his lectures there hung a picture which showed 'citizen' Pinel having the chains taken off the poor madmen in the Salpêtrière. The Salpêtrière, which had witnessed so many horrors during the Revolution, had also been the scene of this most humane of all revolutions."[27] Philippe Pinel was one of Charcot's predecessors as physician-in-chief at the Salpêtrière, and Freud drew an analogy between his historic act of liberation and Charcot's work with hysterics, who at that time suffered under the opprobrium directed at them by the medical profession generally. As Freud observed, "This, the most enigmatic of all nervous diseases . . . had just then fallen into thorough discredit; and this discredit extended not only to the patients but to the physicians who concerned themselves with the neurosis. . . . The first thing Charcot's work did was to restore its dignity to the topic. Little by little, people gave up the scornful smile with which the patient could at that time feel certain of being met. She was no longer necessarily a malingerer." Freud saw this accomplishment as worthy of the great Pinel: "Charcot had repeated on a small scale [i.e., on the individual level] the act of liberation in memory of which Pinel's portrait hung in the lecture hall of the Salpêtrière."[28] Freud's view of the new treatment of hysterics as a process of liberation was to be carried on in his own work on hysteria in the 1890s.

The dualistic scientific approach Freud drew from the German idealist tradition and refined through his philosophical studies with Brentano also found reinforcement in his work with Charcot. In this regard Freud came into contact with Charcot at an opportune moment in his career. As Freud noted in the obituary, in the early 1880s "a change occurred in the direction of Charcot's scientific pursuits, and to this we owe the finest of his work. He now pronounced that the theory of organic nervous illnesses was for the time being fairly complete, and he began to turn his attention almost exclusively to hysteria." Charcot's approach to hysteria emphasized what he called nosography, the most meticulous observation and description of its symptoms and phases, but he also

[26] Freud, *Letters*, pp. 194, 173.
[27] Freud, "Charcot," *S.E.*, III:18.
[28] Freud, "Charcot," *S.E.*, III:19.

offered insight into its inner psychological nature, an insight which, according to Freud, "assured him for all time . . . the fame of having been the first to explain hysteria." This came about as a result of Charcot's use of hypnosis: "He had the idea of artificially reproducing those paralyses, which he had earlier differentiated with care from organic ones. For this purpose he made use of hysterical patients whom he put into a state of somnambulism by hypnotizing them. He succeeded in proving, by an unbroken chain of argument, that these paralyses were the result of ideas which had dominated the patient's brain." Freud saw this demonstration as evidence that hysteria involved "dissociation of consciousness" and pointed out the medieval parallel: "By pronouncing possession by a demon to be the cause of hysterical phenomena, the Middle Ages in fact chose this solution; it would only have been a matter of exchanging the religious terminology of that dark and superstitious age for the scientific language of to-day."[29] Although Charcot himself did not emphasize the importance of dissociation, this use of hypnotism to reveal the nature of hysteria, Freud wrote, "was afterwards taken up by [Charcot's] own pupil, Pierre Janet, as well as by Breuer and others, who developed from it a theory of neurosis which coincided with the mediaeval view—when only they had replaced the 'demon' of clerical phantasy by a psychological formula."[30] Freud sought to apply his dualistic approach to mental phenomena directly in the area where Charcot had made his most significant advance, as is evident in a research project he proposed: "Before leaving Paris I discussed with the great man a plan for a comparative study of hysterical and organic paralysis. I wished to establish the thesis that in hysteria paralysis and anaesthesias of the various parts of the body are demarcated according to the popular idea of their limits and not according to anatomical facts."[31] Charcot approved of the project but evinced no enthusiasm for it, so Freud did not pursue it immediately. Nonetheless the proposal pointed toward a connection between societal values and the genesis of hysterical symptoms that later became central to Freud's concepts of psychological defense and censorship.

On his return to Vienna, after writing a travel report which enthusiastically described Charcot's work on hysteria and his use of hypnosis, Freud took the important step of renting an office and formally opening his private practice. In a clear act of defiance toward the religious establishment, he chose to open his office on

[29] Ibid., pp. 19, 22, 20.
[30] Ibid., p. 22.
[31] Freud, *Autobiographical Study, S.E.,* XX:13–14; Jones, *Life and Work,* I:233.

Easter Sunday, April 25, 1886, a day when every other office and business in Catholic Vienna would have been closed—thereby signaling his intent to carry the anticlerical campaign of Bourneville and Charcot to Vienna. Freud's pugnacious attitude may have helped produce what he, at least, regarded as an unenthusiastic reaction to his new interests on the part of the Viennese medical authorities. In his *Autobiographical Study* he described his fall from favor in the years following his return from Paris when he realized "that the high authorities had rejected my innovations . . . and with my hysteria in men and my production of hysterical paralyses by suggestion I found myself forced into the Opposition."[32] The stance Freud assumed on his return from Paris reveals the way his oppositionist impulses moved from anticlerical politics to scientific theory.

A decade earlier, in March and April 1875, political disillusionment had seemed to foster a shift of Freud's radicalism from politics into philosophic theory, and a similar process may have been at work in the mid-1880s. By that time the German nationalism which had formerly engaged his political passions had turned increasingly anti-Semitic. In the 1870s many of the most important student leaders of the nationalist movement were Jews who believed in the superiority of German culture and saw themselves as thoroughly assimilated into it.[33] However, within a few years of the launching of the Pan-German movement in 1882, Georg von Schönerer, the movement's leader, adopted a strident racial anti-Semitism and forced his party to accept it as well. This development roughly coincided with Richard Wagner's espousal of racial anti-Semitism as part of his German nationalism and with an increasing emphasis on race and racial theories across Europe. Since many of the students and professors at the University of Vienna idolized both Wagner and von Schönerer, anti-Semitic pressure greatly intensified in Freud's immediate work environment and in Vienna generally. Mounting racism may account for the political ambivalence Freud described in his Paris letter of February 2, 1886. In it he mentioned a party he had attended at Charcot's house and a political conversation he had there with Giles de la Tourette, "who predicted the most ferocious war with Germany. I promptly explained that I am a Jew, adhering neither to Germany nor Austria. But such conversations are always very embarrassing to me, for I feel stirring within me something German which I long ago decided to sup-

[32] Freud, *Autobiographical Study, S.E.,* xx:15–16.
[33] McGrath, *Dionysian Art,* p. 6.

press."[34] Freud's suppressed political feelings were to be stirred with increasing force as the 1880s gave way to the 1890s and the Austro-Hungarian nationality conflict intensified. His dreams of the late 1890s reveal that, despite his conscious renunciation of a German nationalist position, he found himself increasingly conflicted as an ever more strident German nationalism continued to engage his unconscious loyalties.

The changing political scene, with its increasing emphasis on race, may also have influenced Freud's changing assessment of Charcot's important theoretical assumption that hysteria was linked to hereditary predisposition. Charcot emphasized both hereditary predisposition and trauma as the essential aetiological factors in hysteria, and initially Freud accepted this view, as is evident in the last letter he wrote his fiancée from Paris. He there discussed his own family from this hereditary point of view and noted that two paternal uncles had families with extensive mental problems. One uncle, who lived in Breslau, had only one normal child out of four. Freud wrote, "I had so completely forgotten this uncle that I have always thought of my own family as free of any hereditary taint. But since I have been thinking about Breslau it all came back to me." He then referred to another uncle living in Vienna whose son died an epileptic and concluded that he had "to acknowledge to a considerable 'neuropathological taint' as it is called." Most interesting of all, he added at the end of the paragraph: "These stories are very common in Jewish families. But now that's enough about medicine."[35] Larry Stewart has traced Freud's gradual abandonment of this hereditary view for a sexual aetiology of hysteria through the late 1880s and early 1890s and has argued that it was motivated by a concern for the racist and anti-Semitic implications of an emphasis on heredity. He notes that Eduard Drummont, in his anti-Semitic best seller *La France juive,* which appeared in 1886, made use of Charcot's statements on the illnesses of Russian Jews "to assert that neuroses were particular maladies of the Jews." Stewart follows Hannah Decker in pointing out that in Germany the resistance to Freud's emphasis on sexuality in hysteria "did not lie solely in any supposed puritanism on the part of the medical establishment. Far more important was the belief of German psychiatrists in the organic origins of nervous disease. This concept of predisposition to mental illness received 'enormous support from the theories of *racial* or *family "degeneracy"* in vogue at the turn

[34] Freud, *Letters,* p. 203.
[35] Ibid., p. 210.

of the century.' "[36] Hannah Decker notes that many German physicians "regarded hysteria as an 'un-Germanic' disease, existing primarily in 'degenerate races.' "[37] Given Freud's sensitivity to any hint of anti-Semitism, the argument that this upsurge of racist sentiment pushed him away from an emphasis on heredity seems plausible.

As Freud indicated in his *Autobiographical Study,* the period immediately following his return from Paris saw an important change in his life, with a strong shift from the theoretical to the practical: "During the period from 1886 to 1891 I did little scientific work, and published scarcely anything. I was occupied with establishing myself in my new profession and with assuring my own material existence as well as that of a rapidly increasing family."[38] He had married Martha Bernays in the fall of 1886, and by 1891 they had three children, so the increased demands of family life and his practice combined to reinforce his sense of alienation from the scholarly community in Vienna. During such periods of being "in the Opposition," Freud invariably sought the support of a brother figure and in this instance found it in Josef Breuer. Freud had made Breuer's acquaintance in the late 1870s while working in Brücke's laboratory, and by the early 1880s they had become close friends. They had conversations about hysteria well before Freud's trip to Paris, and even then he was convinced that the case study of Bertha Pappenheim, which Breuer discussed with him, "accomplished more toward an understanding of neuroses than any previous observation. I determined to inform Charcot of these discoveries when I reached Paris, and I actually did so. But the great man showed no interest."[39] Freud continued his discussions of this case with Breuer on his return to Vienna and thereby became familiar with Breuer's "cathartic" method of treatment. Breuer had learned that the patient "could be relieved of . . . clouded states of consciousness if she was induced to express in words the affective phantasy by which she was at the moment dominated." From this he evolved a means of treatment: "He put her into deep hypnosis and made her tell him each time what it was that was oppressing her mind. After the attacks of depressive confusion had been overcome in this way, he employed the same procedure for removing her inhibitions and physical disorders."[40] Freud's use of

[36] Larry Stewart, "Freud before Oedipus," *Journal of the History of Biology,* 9 (Fall 1976):220.

[37] Decker, *Freud in Germany,* p. 182.

[38] Freud, *Autobiographical Study, S.E.,* xx:18.

[39] Ibid., pp. 19–20.

[40] Ibid., p. 20.

the cathartic method under hypnosis in his own expanding practice revealed various problems with it, such as the difficulty of hypnotizing certain patients. As a result, Freud gradually moved away from the use of hypnotism as an aid in recalling early memories and substituted a technique of applying pressure with his hand on the patient's forehead while urging the patient to concentrate. In this way he gradually moved toward the technique of free association, which seems to have been employed as early as 1889 in the treatment of Emmy von N., the first of his cases to be presented in the *Studies on Hysteria.*[41]

Although Freud wrote relatively little in the years from 1886 to 1891 when he was perfecting his techniques for the treatment of hysterical patients, the few works he did publish indicate the continuing importance to him of the dualistic conceptual framework he had developed. For example, in the 1888 preface to his translation of Hippolyte Bernheim's book on hypnotic suggestion, he wrote, "We must agree with Bernheim, however, that the partitioning of hypnotic phenomena under the two headings of physiological and psychical leaves us with a most unsatisfied feeling: a connecting link between the two classes is urgently needed."[42] Freud's pursuit of this connecting link not only in hypnotic but in all mental phenomena pointed him toward the great discoveries of the 1890s. He emphasized this conceptual framework with particular clarity in his first book, *On Aphasia,* which appeared in 1891. In support of Hughlings Jackson's warnings against the prevalent confusion of the physical with the psychic in the study of speech, he wrote: "The relationship between the chain of physiological events in the nervous system and the mental processes is probably not one of cause and effect. The former do not cease when the latter set in; they tend to continue, but from a certain moment, a mental phenomenon corresponds to each part of the chain or to several parts. The psychic is, therefore, a process parallel to the physiological, 'a dependent concomitant.' "[43] Here again, the two worlds were actually one world experienced two ways, the view advanced by Schopenhauer, Brentano, Meynert, Wilhelm Jerusalem and many other leading scientific thinkers.

[41] Josef Breuer and Sigmund Freud, *Studies on Hysteria,* (hereafter *Studies*), *S.E.,* II:107–11, 56.

[42] Sigmund Freud, "Preface to the Translation of Bernheim's Suggestion," *S.E.,* I:81.

[43] Sigmund Freud, *On Aphasia: A Critical Study* (New York: International Universities Press, 1953), p. 55. On this dualistic scientific tradition, see also Decker, pp. 201–5.

As Sulloway observes, *On Aphasia* has been described as the first Freudian book. In it Freud attacked the then current Wernicke-Lichtheim theory that speech disorders could be traced to localizable brain lesions, and advanced in its place a position much closer to the modern view. Sulloway notes that "Freud was particularly emphatic about the difficulty of knowing whether a lesion is *in* a certain speech center or is merely disturbing the paths of association *between* centers; and because of this difficulty, a rigid appeal to localized lesions seemed both premature and grossly oversimplified."[44] Again following Hughlings Jackson, Freud advanced a more functional and developmental view, which attempted to explain how a lesion might affect the whole system dynamically. He wrote, "we are adopting as a guiding principle Hughlings Jackson's doctrine that all these modes of reaction represent instances of functional retrogression (dis-involution) of a highly organized apparatus and therefore correspond to earlier states of its functional development." As he went on to point out, "This means that under all circumstances an arrangement of associations which, having been acquired later, belongs to a higher level of functioning, will be lost, while an earlier and simpler one will be preserved. From this point of view, a great number of aphasiac phenomena can be explained."[45] As Sulloway shows, this theory of aphasia points directly toward Freud's later conception of libidinal regression, and here too Freud saw the closest tie between the physiological and the psychological. In a 1907 letter in which he discussed certain regressive aspects of mental illness, he expressed his support for "the general pathological view that illness always implies a regression in development. (The *evolution* and involution of British authors)."[46] Freud's increasing emphasis on the developmental aspects of psychology doubtless also drew reinforcement from his work with children at the Kassowitz Institute for Children's Diseases, where he accepted a position as director of the neurological section in 1886. *On Aphasia* reveals the path Freud traveled from cerebral localization to disinvolution to regression, and the increasing concern with mental dynamics, childhood, and development fed directly into his work on hysteria.

Of all the intellectual ingredients that contributed to Freud's discovery of psychoanalysis as a method of treating hysteria, the two he most emphasized were his belief "that the source of the driving forces of neurosis lies in the sexual life" and the "theory

[44] Sulloway, *Freud,* p. 271.
[45] Freud, *On Aphasia,* p. 87.
[46] Quoted in Sulloway, p. 272.

of repression," which he described as "the corner-stone on which the whole structure of psycho-analysis rests."[47] In the development of Freud's ideas through the late 1880s and early 1890s, these two basic concepts and the close relationship between them are central to his continuing quest for the "connecting link" between the psychological and the physiological, the mind and the body. As Jones observes, "The suggestion may be ventured that Freud's interest in sexual activities, like that in the aphasia disturbances of speech, came from the fact that sexuality has so obviously both physical and mental components. Is Libido a mental or physical concept in its origin? So here again might be found a clue to the riddle of the relation of body to mind."[48]

Freud's exploration of sexuality was directly in line with the central interests of his whole scientific career, and in his writings it emerged in a context with strong political and religious overtones. The close relationship which he saw between hysteria and medieval culture is illustrative here. After his exposure to Charcot and his school, the medieval framework became a standard feature of Freud's attempts to define and describe hysteria. For example, in the report on his work abroad which he submitted on his return to Vienna in 1886, he wrote that in recent times "a hysterical woman would have been almost as certain to be treated as a malingerer, as in earlier centuries she would have been certain to be judged and condemned as a witch or as possessed of the devil." He even argued, "In another respect there has, if anything, been a step backward in the knowledge of hysteria. The Middle Ages had a precise acquaintance with the 'stigmata' of hysteria, its somatic signs, and interpreted and made use of them in their own fashion."[49] Freud's use of the term "stigmata" to describe hysterical symptoms, a use he derived from Charcot and shared with Breuer, represented but one of many medieval elements in his conceptualization of hysteria. In the 1888 article on hysteria written for Villaret's medical encyclopedia, he introduced the medieval framework in the first paragraph: "In the Middle Ages neuroses played a significant part in the history of civilization, they appeared in epidemics as a result of psychical contagion, and were at the root of what was factual in the history of possession and witchcraft. Documents from that period prove that the symptomatology has undergone no change up to the present day." Further on, in the section on symptomatology, he observed; "Disturbances of sensibility are the

[47] Freud, "On the History of the Psycho-Analytic Movement," *S.E.*, XIV:12, 16.
[48] Jones, I:272.
[49] Sigmund Freud, "Report on My Studies in Paris and Berlin," *S.E.*, I:11.

symptoms on which it is possible to base a diagnosis of hysteria, even in its most rudimentary forms. In the Middle Ages the discovery of anaesthetic and non-bleeding areas *(stigmata Diaboli)* was regarded as evidence of witchcraft."[50]

In his encyclopedia article, Freud established no link between sexuality and the medieval view of hysteria and indeed his intent was to diminish the significance of sexuality in hysteria altogether, an intent motivated by his belief in Charcot's hereditary emphasis. He argued that the aetiology of hysteria should be sought entirely in heredity, that hysterics were always hereditarily disposed to disturbances of nervous activity, and later in the paragraph he added, "As regards what is often asserted to be the preponderant influence of abnormalities in the sexual sphere upon the development of hysteria, it must be said that its importance is as a rule over-estimated." What Freud had in mind primarily, however, was the physical aspects of sexual abnormality (such as immaturity or lack of genitalia) for as he went on to observe, "It must, however, be admitted that conditions related *functionally* to sexual life play a great part in the aetiology of hysteria (as of all neuroses), and they do so on account of the high psychical significance of this function especially in the female sex."[51] Here, in what seems to be Freud's earliest (1888) formulation of a link between sexuality and the aetiology of hysteria, he specifically emphasized the psychical significance of sexuality, but since the statement was confined within the framework of Charcot's hereditary theory, it has not been sufficiently appreciated as a precursor of Freud's later view.

By the early 1890s, as Freud's belief in the hereditary factor waned, his emphasis on the role of sexuality increased, and in the writings of that period the all-important link between sexuality and repression emerged from the medieval context which shaped his view of hysteria. For example, in "A Case of Successful Treatment by Hypnotism," which was published in two installments, in December 1892 and January 1893, he discussed the role of "distressing antithetic ideas (inhibited or rejected by normal consciousness) which press forward at the moment of disposition to hysteria and find their way to the somatic innervation." Freud drew his supporting evidence from medieval religious history: "It is owing to no chance coincidences that the hysterical deleria of nuns during the epidemics of the Middle Ages took the form of violent blasphemies and unbridled erotic language or that (as Charcot remarked

[50] Sigmund Freud, "Hysteria," *S.E.*, I:41, 45.
[51] Ibid., pp. 50, 51.

. . .) it is precisely well-brought-up and well-behaved boys who suffer from hysterical attacks in which they give free play to every kind of rowdiness, every kind of wild escapade and bad conduct." The common characteristic linking the medieval nuns and the modern well-brought-up boys was repression, and from Freud's examples it seems plain that the "distressing antithetic ideas" he was considering were primarily sexual in nature. He postulated a relationship between them and what he described at the time as a "counter-will": "It is the suppressed *[unterdrückten]*—the laboriously suppressed—groups of ideas that are brought into action in these cases, by the operation of a sort of counter-will, when the subject has fallen a victim to hysterical exhaustion. Perhaps, indeed, the connection may be a more intimate one, for the hysterical condition may perhaps be *produced* by the laborious suppression." This latter alternative contained the basic elements of Freud's theory of repression even though he did not use the term. He did not pursue the idea in this context, however, but continued to develop his theory of the counter-will in a medieval religious vein. He wrote, "This emergence of a counter-will is chiefly responsible for the daemonic characteristic which hysteria so often exhibits—the characteristic . . . of doing the exact opposite of what they have been asked to do, and of being obliged to cover everything they most value with abuse and suspicion." Then, in considering what actually became of the "inhibited intentions" he argued, "they are stored up and enjoy an unsuspected existence in a sort of shadow kingdom, till they emerge like bad spirits and take control of the body, which is as a rule under the orders of the predominant ego-consciousness."[52] Here Freud's unconscious was the realm of a devil who lay in wait to seize control of his exhausted victims. Freud left open the question of what set the demonic counter-will in motion. Was it simply the victims' exhaustion or was it indeed the result of their laborious resistance?

Freud's first published use of the term "repression" came at virtually the same time as the appearance of "A Case of Successful Treatment by Hypnotism." He used it in the paper he published jointly with Josef Breuer in January 1893, entitled "On the Psychical Mechanisms of Hysterical Phenomena: Preliminary Communication," the paper that later formed the first chapter of *Studies on Hysteria.* Its context involved the relationship of memory and trauma. In explaining why certain traumas were not sufficiently "abreacted," he mentioned several possibilities: "because the nature of the trauma

[52] Sigmund Freud, "A Case of Successful Treatment by Hypnotism," *S.E.*, I:126–27.

excluded a reaction, as in the case of the apparently irreparable loss of a loved person or because social circumstances make a reaction impossible or because it was a question of things which the patient wished to forget, and therefore intentionally repressed from his conscious thought and inhibited and suppressed." Then, almost as if it were a signature indicating the origin of the concept, he added, "It is precisely distressing things of this kind that, under hypnosis, we find are the basis of hysterical phenomena (e.g., hysterical deliria in saints and nuns, continent women and well-brought-up children)."[53] The editors of the Standard Edition have noted that the joint example of the nuns and the well-behaved boys appeared frequently in Freud's writings of this period, but they have not appreciated its centrality to his evolving theoretical structure. Sexual denial ran through the instances of the example and there was implicit in it a view of medieval Catholic culture as sexually, religiously, and politically repressive.

Two other references to the nuns and well-behaved boys appeared in Freud's writings at this time in connection with important theoretical insights. One use of the example came in an early draft of the "Preliminary Communication," dated November 1892, in the context of a particularly clear statement of the mechanism of repression, although Freud did not use the term: "If a hysterical subject seeks intentionally to forget an experience or forcibly repudiates, inhibits and suppresses an intention or an idea, these psychical acts, as a consequence enter the second state of consciousness; from there they produce their permanent effects and the memory of them returns as a hysterical attack. (cf., hysteria in nuns, continent women, well-brought-up boys. . . ."[54] The second instance, which occurred in the footnotes to the translation of Charcot's *Tuesday Lectures,* reveals Freud's growing interest in dreams and the application of his theoretical insights to their interpretation. The passage in Charcot's lecture involved cases of the well-brought-up boys, and Freud added his nuns in the footnote. He referred to "the familiar fact that the hysterical deleria of nuns revel in blasphemies and erotic pictures. In this we may suspect a connection which allows us a deep insight into the mechanism of hysterical states. There emerges in hysterical deleria material in the shape of ideas and impulsions to action which the subject in his healthy state has rejected and inhibited—has often inhibited by a great psychical effort." Then, in an anticipation of his later concept of

[53] Breuer and Freud, *Studies, S.E.,* II:10–11.

[54] Sigmund Freud, "Sketches for the 'Preliminary Communication' of 1893," *S.E.,* I:153.

the "day residue" in dreams he added, "Something similar holds good of a number of dreams, which spin out further associations which have been rejected or broken off during the day."[55] The example of the nuns and boys provided an insight that formed the nucleus of the theoretical structure Freud would soon use to interpret a whole range of mental phenomena, from dreams and neuroses to jokes and slips of the tongue.

By 1895, when he published *Studies on Hysteria* with Breuer, Freud's theoretical structure had filled out considerably, as is indicated in the discussion of "defense" contained in part IV of that work. This passage suggests a coming together of the concept of defense derived from Schopenhauer and Meynert with the complex of ideas associated with medieval culture and Charcot. Referring to the kind of ideas that became pathogenic in the patients he had treated, he noted that "they were all of a distressing nature, calculated to arouse the affects of shame, of self-reproach and of psychical pain, and the feeling of being harmed; they were all of a kind that one would prefer not to have experienced, that one would rather forget. From all this there arose, as it were automatically, the thought of *defence.*" He then went on to define defense in a way highly reminiscent of Meynert: "It has indeed been generally admitted by psychologists that the acceptance of a new idea (acceptance in the sense of believing or recognizing as real) is dependent on the nature and trend of the ideas already united in the ego, and they have invented special technical names for this process of censorship to which the new arrival must submit."[56] This was Freud's first published use of the term "censorship," and it anticipates elements of the concept that he later recognized as one of the two interacting forces in the formation of dreams. It should be noted, however, that the allusion in this 1895 passage was to the ancient Roman censor, rather than to the contemporary political censorship which underlay his use of the term in *The Interpretation of Dreams.* It was the Roman censor who drew up the lists of those to be admitted to the Senate, and admission depended on the "new arrival" being appropriate to the existing membership. Freud went on in the same paragraph to relate this process of censorship to the concepts of repression, resistance, and conversion. By this time, then, the theoretical arsenal of psychoanalysis was almost complete, and one of the most important concepts still lacking was added in the summer of 1895. It came with Freud's

[55] Sigmund Freud, "Extracts from Freud's Footnotes to His Translation of Charcot's Tuesday Lectures," *S.E.*, I:138.
[56] Breuer and Freud, *Studies, S.E.*, II:269.

explicit statement of the theory that dreams were wish fulfillments, an insight he gained in July 1895 through understanding the dream of Irma's injection and proclaimed in his draft "Project for a Scientific Psychology" later that year.[57]

Even with the development of this theoretical vocabulary, however, Freud still lacked an overall comprehension of the nature and origins of hysteria. Moreover, in these last years before his self-analytic breakthrough, he developed an aetiological hypothesis that led him far astray. In his "History of the Psycho-Analytic Movement," he said of his progress toward the discovery of psychoanalysis during this period: "On the way, a mistaken idea had to be overcome which might have been almost fatal to the young science. Influenced by Charcot's view of the traumatic origin of hysteria, one was readily inclined to accept as true and aetiologically significant the statements made by patients in which they ascribed their symptoms to passive sexual experiences in the first years of childhood—to put in bluntly, to seduction."[58] The stories Freud heard from his patients were undoubtedly an important factor in influencing him to subscribe to this view, and Masson argues quite specifically, that Emma Eckstein was the patient who provided Freud with the seduction theory.[59] But although Emma Eckstein certainly played a prominent role in Freud's movement toward the theory, it seems more likely that he derived it from multiple sources. In addition to the testimony of various patients and the influence of Charcot which he mentions, he may also have been influenced by the conception of trauma developed by Meynert out of Schopenhauer.

In Charcot's view heredity was the primary factor in the origin of hysteria and trauma was accorded only a secondary, triggering, role. In his 1888 encyclopedia article, which largely followed Charcot, Freud wrote, "The aetiology of the *status hystericus* is to be looked for entirely in heredity; hysterics are always hereditarily disposed to disturbances of nervous activity, and epileptics, psychical patients, tabetics, etc. are found among their relatives." Then, after discussing the misunderstood role of sexuality in hysteria, he passed on to the subject of trauma without connecting it in any way to sexuality. Arguing that "trauma is a frequent incidental cause of hysterical illness," he assumed that it initiated hysteria only in those with a hereditary predisposition to it.[60] In Meynert's two-ego psy-

[57] Freud, *Origins,* p. 402.
[58] Freud, "On the History of the Psycho-Analytic Movement," *S.E.,* XIV:17.
[59] Masson, *Assault on Truth,* p. 87.
[60] Freud, "Hysteria," *S.E.,* I:50, 51.

chology, however, trauma played a much more basic role. The example central to both Schopenhauer and Meynert involved the trauma of loss, the death of a loved one, and its impact on rational functioning. Moreover, for both men the discussion of trauma was closely tied to a conception of psychological defense, with trauma initiating the defense process. In the early 1890s, when Freud's patients testified to bizarre sexual events in their past and he drew on Charcot's medieval framework to find a parallel with the erotic nuns, it was only logical to consider the possibility of a link between sexuality and Meynert's more dynamic conception of trauma.

One of the earliest pieces of evidence that Freud was considering the role of "seduction" in hysteria came in a letter to Fliess written on May 30, 1893, only a few months after the spate of references to erotic nuns and well-behaved boys. He wrote that he believed he had come to understand the origin of anxiety neuroses in young people who were "virgins with no history of sexual abuse." He indicated that the analyses of two such cases showed that "the cause was an apprehensive terror of sexuality; . . . thus the aetiology was purely emotional, but still of a sexual nature."[61] The reference to sexual abuse shows that Freud was at least weighing the possible role of "seduction" at that time, although the passage also shows the simultaneous consideration of a view much closer to his final position. By 1895 his belief in the seduction theory had begun to solidify, and on November 2 of that year, he wrote to Fliess that one of his cases "has given me what I was waiting for (sexual shock, i.e. infantile abuse in a case of male hysteria!). . . ."[62] Freud adhered to this theory for almost two more years, until it fell victim to his self-analysis.

As with so much involving hysteria, Freud dressed his seduction theory in medieval garb, drawing a close and elaborate parallel between it and medieval practices in a series of letters to Fliess written in January 1897. On January 17 he asked Fliess if he realized that "all of my brand-new prehistory of hysteria is already known and was published a hundred times over, though several centuries ago? Do you remember that I always said that the medieval theory of possession held by the ecclesiastical courts was identical with our theory of a foreign body and the splitting of consciousness?"[63] Freud's next questions alluded directly to his patients'

[61] Freud, *Origins*, p. 73; see also p. 71.

[62] Freud, *Origins*, p. 132.

[63] Freud, *Complete Letters*, p. 224. Although strictly speaking Freud's seduction theory was not brand new, his strong adherence to it was, and his belief that fathers and older brothers were the primary seducers added an important new dimension.

stories of seduction: "But why did the devil who took possession of the poor things invariably abuse them sexually . . . ? Why are their confessions under torture so like the communications made by my patients in psychical treatment?"[64] In a letter of January 24 he wrote, "The parallel with witchcraft is taking shape; and I believe it is conclusive." After he had elaborately developed the parallels between hysteria and medieval deviltry, he added that he was "beginning to dream of an extremely primitive devil religion the rites of which continue to be performed secretly. . . . The links are abundant." Further on he pointed specifically to the role of the father in the seduction theory, arguing that the excessively high standards demanded by hysterics in love reflected, "the influence of the father-figure. The cause is . . . the immense elevation from which the father condescends to the child's level. . . . That is the reverse side of the medal."[65] The over-idealization of the father figure and his reincarnation as devil could both be understood as aspects of mental dissociation arising from the trauma of paternal seduction.

Freud's association of hysteria with repressive medieval culture was complemented by his alignment of psychoanalysis with the ideal of freedom. In a January 3, 1897 letter to Fliess, Freud mentioned a quotation intended as the heading for the "therapy" chapter in his book on neuroses: *Flavit et dissipati sunt* [He blew and they were dispersed]."[66] Later, in *The Interpretation of Dreams,* he explained the words as an allusion to the defeat of the Spanish Armada, for a medal with this inscription was struck to commemorate the English victory. The inscription could also be read "Jehovah blew and they were dispersed," since, as Freud noted, "The English medallion bears the deity's name in Hebrew lettering on a cloud in the background. It is so placed that it can be taken as being part either of the design or of the inscription."[67] He wrote that he "had thought, half seriously" of using the inscription "as the heading to the chapter on 'Therapy,' if ever I got so far as producing a detailed account of my theory and treatment of hysteria."[68] As an ironic joke, the words "he blew and they were dispersed" alluded

[64] Ibid. Freud referred here to the reports of his patient Emma Eckstein, and his further comments in the letter concerned her and Fliess. Max Schur first provided the censored pieces of this letter and explained in detail the complex situation involving Fliess, Freud, and Emma, a situation which figures in Freud's dream of Irma's injection (Schur, "Day Residues").

[65] Freud, *Origins,* pp. 188, 189, 190.

[66] Ibid., p. 184.

[67] Freud, *Interpretation, S.E.,* IV:214n.

[68] Ibid., p. 214.

to the "talking cure" Freud employed, for the discussion of a hysterical disorder carried on between analyst and patient had the effect of dissipating its symptoms. In terms of historical reference, they represented another of the many congruent allusions to the struggle between tyranny and freedom—between the Catholic tyranny of the Spanish Habsburg, Philip II, whose fleet was destroyed, and the freedom which Freud always associated with Protestant England and which God presumably helped preserve by sending a storm to disperse the fleet. Jehovah's name written in Hebrew on a cloud also recalled the world of Exodus, where Jehovah acted in a similarly decisive fashion to make possible the freedom of the Jews from an oppressive Pharaoh. In considering this quotation an emblem for the therapy of hysterical disorders, Freud symbolically aligned his conception of analytic treatment not only with the freedom of the Protestant Reformation, but also with that of Passover and the Exodus—the two religious traditions drawn on in Philippson's biblical commentary.

Freud's evolving conception of hysteria and his emphasis on the role of the father in the seduction theory were strongly influenced by the momentous personal event that occurred at the end of 1896, the death of his own father. Freud's life was transformed by this loss, and out of it psychoanalysis was born. It gave Freud to himself as patient by plunging him into a mental crisis he recognized and acknowledged as hysterical. His own mental disturbance opened up to him the possibility of understanding hysteria directly through internal perception as well as external observation, the two approaches Brentano had stressed as essential to scientific psychological investigation. This internal insight into the nature of hysteria crystallized Freud's understanding of the subject and led to the closely related triumphs involved in carrying out his self-analysis and writing *The Interpretation of Dreams.*

In the preface to the second edition of *The Interpretation of Dreams,* Freud observed that after completing his book he realized that it was "a portion of my own self-analysis, my reaction to my father's death—that is to say, to the most important event, the most poignant loss, of a man's life."[69] Freud's father died on October 23, 1896, and these words suggest both the intensity of feeling called up by this event and the deeply personal nature of his most important work. Carl Schorske's insightful analysis shows that if attention is focused on the order in which Freud presents his own dreams in the book, "one becomes aware of three layers in a

[69] Ibid., p. xxvi.

psychoarcheological dig: professional, political and personal." Moreover, Schorske goes on to observe, these elements "that appear in the dream arrangement as three clear layers were also constituents of a wracking crisis Freud experienced in the 1890's."[70] During the year following his father's death, this multidimensional crisis passed into an acute stage as conflicting pressures mounted in each of these three important spheres. If Freud's dreams are examined in conjunction with the unfolding of the important theoretical advances which also marked this year, it becomes clear that the advances were pushed forward by the interplay of conflicting pressures.

The most deeply personal problem confronting Freud during this period involved his conflicted attitude toward his father. Shortly after Jakob Freud's death, his son described the emotional turmoil produced by this event in a letter to Fliess. "At a death the whole past stirs within one," he wrote. "I feel . . . torn up by the roots," and he went on to relate a dream he had had the night after the funeral. In it he found himself in a shop where he saw a notice saying, "You are requested to close the eyes," and his interpretation indicated that the notice had a double meaning reflecting the ambiguity of his feelings about his father.[71] On one level the notice referred to the need to close the dead man's eyes, that is, "to do one's duty toward the dead." In this literal sense it signified Freud's filial obligations to carry out the funeral arrangements. On a second level, however, the notice seemed to raise doubt that these obligations were being adequately fulfilled. In the somewhat different version included in *The Interpretation of Dreams,* Freud wrote that the notice read either "You are requested to close the eyes" or "You are requested to close an eye," and the latter alternative suggested the idea of "winking at" or overlooking unfulfilled obligations.[72] As he indicated to Fliess, it constituted "an apology, as though I had not done my duty and my conduct needed overlooking." It expressed the feelings "of self-reproach which a death generally leaves among the survivors."[73] One element of Freud's inner conflict over his father thus concerned the question of whether or not he had lived up to paternal expectations. It seems evident, however, that there were deeper levels of conflict that his analysis did not touch. As Marthe Robert observes in drawing attention to the superficial character of Freud's analysis of this dream, "Freud

[70] Schorske, *Vienna,* p. 184.
[71] Freud, *Origins,* pp. 170, 171.
[72] Freud, *Interpretation, S.E.,* IV:317.
[73] Freud, *Origins,* p. 171.

was able to distract his attention for the time being from the cluster of violent and conflicting desires that he would be obliged to confront later on. In other words, he obeyed the command to 'close the eyes' employed by the dream in the intention of absolving and at the same time accusing him."[74] During the year following this dream, the key to Freud's progress, both personal and intellectual, would lie in his ability to explore the sources of these inner conflicts regarding his father, thereby preparing the way for a resolution of his deeply felt ambivalence. In the months immediately following his father's death, however, Freud's tightly controlled emotions allowed for no such exploration.

Besides experiencing a sense of deep inner turmoil during these months, Freud also found himself in an ambiguous situation with respect to his professional ambition to secure a permanent appointment at the University of Vienna. On January 24, 1897, he told Fliess that he had once again been passed over for an appointment in his field.[75] A few weeks later, however, on February 8, he reported to his friend that his earlier news was incorrect and that three of his senior colleagues were going to propose him for a professorship. This pleasing news, however, was balanced by the realization that his promotion might well encounter anti-Semitic opposition within the Ministry of Education. Hermann Nothnagel, the colleague who informed Freud of his proposed appointment, cautiously added "You know the further difficulties. It may do no more than put you on the *tapis*," and Freud told Fliess that he realized there was only a slight chance "that the Minister will accept the proposal."[76]

[74] Robert, *From Oedipus to Moses*, p. 92. Edith Buxbaum, "Freud's Dream Interpretation in the Light of His Letters to Fliess," *Bulletin of the Menninger Clinic*, 15, no. 6 (1951):197–212, points out allusions to Freud's fear of dying and to his fear of travel in the dream, thereby suggesting the way his own neurotic symptoms were aroused by his father's death. See also Anzieu, *L'auto-analyse de Freud* (1:233–40), who emphasizes the self-analytic content of the dream.

[75] Freud, *Origins*, p. 190.

[76] Ibid., p. 191. The importance of anti-Semitism in delaying Freud's appointment as Ausserordentliche Professor has been questioned by Josef and Renée Gicklhorn, *Sigmund Freuds akademische Laufbahn* (Vienna: Urban & Schwarzenberg, 1960), and by Henri F. Ellenberger, *The Discovery of the Unconscious: The History and Evolution of Dynamic Psychiatry* (New York: Basic Books, 1970), pp. 452–54. K. R. Eissler, *Sigmund Freud und die Wiener Universität* (Bern: Verlag Hans Huber, 1966), has attempted to refute the Gicklhorns' argument point by point. The key factor in dealing with Freud's dreams and emotional reactions involves his subjective impression that anti-Semitism would block his promotion, and there is no reason to doubt its significance on that level, as the Gicklhorns readily concede (p. 44). Furthermore, as they also show (p. 19), Freud's close friend Leopold Königstein, one of the Jewish colleagues he refers to in his analysis of the uncle dream, had already waited almost three years for his appointment to be confirmed by the Ministry of Education. So

In telling Fliess about the proposal for his appointment as professor, Freud played down his hopes, but his dream of his uncle with the yellow beard (February 1897) shows how deeply the prospect of this appointment moved him.[77] One of the inciting causes of the dream was a visit from his friend R. (presumably Dr. Leopold Königstein), whose situation vis-à-vis a university appointment was the same as Freud's; he too had been proposed for appointment, and he too had apparently been blocked by anti-Semitic pressure within the Ministry of Education. Tired of waiting, this friend told Freud that he had sought out the minister himself and asked him point-blank if denominational considerations were the cause of the delay. In circumlocutory language, the minister finally conceded that this was the case. Freud reacted to this discouraging news with restraint: "It was not news to me, though it was bound to strengthen my feeling of resignation; for the same denominational considerations applied to my own case." During the night following the visit, Freud dreamed that *"my friend R. was my uncle. I had a great feeling of affection for him."*[78] He then saw before him a distorted vision of his friend's face with a yellow beard. In analyzing the dream, Freud discovered that it centered around his conversation with R. and a similar conversation several days earlier with his friend N., yet another Jewish academic who

---

there was certainly ample objective cause for Freud's apprehensions. Ellenberger (p. 453) accepts the Gicklhorns' explanation that a May 28, 1898 change in the rules governing these academic appointments accounts for the delay in Freud's case and that it was simply his bad luck that the changes occurred at that time. This reasoning ignores the year delay which occurred before the change in the rules, and it is also naive in that it fails to consider the possibility that the changes were instituted to cut down the number of Jews receiving these appointments. The Gicklhorns note that of the ten cases held up (including Freud's) seven involved Jews (p. 19). It also seems naive to ignore the prevailing political situation of early 1897 when the anti-Semites achieved their greatest success with the confirmation of Lueger. Since Count Badeni's government had to rely on the anti-Semitic Christian Socials for parliamentary support, his ministers may well have felt it necessary to delay the promotion of Jews at the university even if they themselves were not anti-Semitic. On the whole, the evidence in this question supports the view that anti-Semitism was not only subjectively important as a fear in Freud's mind, but also objectively important as a factor in delaying his promotion.

[77] This is an approximate date, based on a comparison of Freud's Feb. 8, 1897 letter to Fliess and his preamble to the dream, both of which mention the same events. The time mentioned in the English edition of *Interpretation* (*S.E.*, IV:136), the spring of 1897, is a mistranslation of the German "Im Frühjahr, 1897," *G.S.*, II:139.

[78] Freud, *Interpretation, S.E.*, IV:136–37. My assumption that R. is Leopold Königstein is based on Freud's statement that R. had been waiting a long time for action on his case and on information provided by the Gicklhorns in *Freuds akademische Laufbahn*, p. 19, that Königstein's case had been put forward to the ministry almost three years earlier, on March 10, 1894.

had been proposed for appointment and blocked by anti-Semitic pressure. The dream wish, Freud found, accused R. of being a simpleton and N. of being a criminal so that the delay on their appointments would be seen as resulting from these causes, rather than anti-Semitism.[79] In this way the wish underlying the dream—that Freud's appointment not be blocked by anti-Semitism—found fulfillment.

In his further analysis of the dream, Freud found that in the second part of it he had revenged himself on the minister by taking his place in office. "I was behaving as though I were the Minister . . . He had refused to appoint me *professor extraordinarius* and I had retaliated in the dream by stepping into his shoes." In recognizing this wish, Freud realized that his dream had carried him "back from the dreary present to the cheerful hopes of the days of the Bürger Ministry and that the wish that it had done its best to fulfill was one dating back to those times."[80] When the Bürgerministerium took office in late 1867, the young Freud had shared his proud parents' hopes that the dawning liberal era would allow him to pursue a political career and fulfill the Prater fortuneteller's prophecy that he would one day become a cabinet minister. In the dream this early hope found expression.

An even deeper level of meaning in the dream took Freud back still further into his childhood to his phantasized identification with the biblical Joseph. This identification surfaced most clearly and obviously in the name Joseph, which immediately occurred to Freud as the name of the uncle appearing in the dream. The power of the name was indicated by the fact that it blotted out the memory of all his other uncles at the moment he began analyzing the dream. As he free associated to the phrase "*R. was my uncle,*" he thought "What could that mean? I never had more than one uncle—Uncle Josef," but as he pointed out in a footnote, this was a conscious memory lapse, for he actually had five uncles.[81] Freud himself must have realized that this phantasy operated within the dream, for when he later mentioned his identification with Joseph in connection with the *Non vixit* dream, he cited the uncle dream as one of the examples of the name's figuring prominently in his dream life.[82]

Understanding the role of this phantasy identification greatly clarifies the basic meaning of the dream. Perhaps its most puzzling element involves the apparent ambiguity of Freud's attitude toward

[79] Freud, *Interpretation, S.E.,* IV:193.
[80] Ibid.
[81] Ibid., p. 138. See also Shengold, "Freud and Joseph," p. 77.
[82] Freud, *Interpretation, S.E.,* V:484.

anti-Semitism. The dream expressed a wish that anti-Semitism not affect his chances of academic promotion, but his final observation in the analysis of the dream was, "In mishandling my two learned and eminent colleagues because they were Jews, and in treating the one as a simpleton and the other as a criminal, I was behaving as though I were the Minister, I had put myself in the Minister's place."[83] Although this might seem an expression of anti-Semitism on Freud's own part, the dream allusions to his Joseph phantasy explain the apparent contradiction without resort to theories of Jewish self-hate. Joseph had become prime minister of Egypt, a land which traditionally evidenced deep suspicion and dislike of foreigners, and at one important point in his career he behaved in a way very similar to that of the minister in Freud's dream. When Joseph's brothers came to Egypt to buy food, he hid his identity and treated them with the suspicion and hostility appropriate to his being an Egyptian, to test their loyalty to their father and their repentance for their crime against him. Part of his strategy was to persuade the brothers to return with Benjamin, to see if they would stand up for him in the way they had failed to do for Joseph. When Jacob refused to allow Benjamin to go, Reuben, whose foolishness had earlier been demonstrated in his affair with his father's concubine, suggested that, as a guarantee of Benjamin's safety, he would allow Jacob to execute his own sons if Benjamin did not return. Jacob scornfully rejected this idea, and in his commentary Philippson made mention of Reuben's foolishness.[84] Then later, when Benjamin was brought to Egypt, Joseph arranged to make it look as though he had attempted to steal a goblet. So in the Bible story one of the brothers appeared to be a simpleton and the other a criminal, just as in Freud's dream.

Another link connecting the dream to the Joseph story was the theme of "grey hair." A central element of the dream's manifest content was the yellow beard of Freud's friend R. In Freud's own analysis, he observed that "the fair beard emerged prominently from a face which belonged to two people and which was consequently blurred; incidentally, the beard further involved an allusion to my father and myself through the intermediate idea of growing grey."[85] As Freud noted, when his uncle Josef became "involved in a transaction of a kind that is severely punished by the law . . . he was in fact punished for it. My father, whose hair turned grey from grief in a few days, used always to say that Uncle Josef was

[83] Ibid., IV:193.
[84] Philippson, p. 230.
[85] Freud, *Interpretation, S.E.*, IV:293.

not a bad man but only a simpleton."[86] Jakob Freud's grief and the consequent greying of his hair were strongly reminiscent of the situation confronting the biblical Jacob as a result of Joseph's decision to test his brothers' loyalty. When the brothers returned from their first trip to Egypt and told their father that Simeon had been left as hostage until they returned with Benjamin, Jacob was reminded of his earlier loss of Joseph. Since it seemed to him that he was losing his sons one by one, his grief was intense. He initially refused their request for Benjamin declaring that "if mischief befall him by the way . . . , then shall ye bring down my gray hairs with sorrow to the grave" (Gen. 42:38). As Philippson observed in his commentary, the expression "bring down my gray hairs with sorrow to the grave" recurred frequently in this incident and it "is the most extreme and bitter utterance possible for a deeply depressed old man. The father of numerous sons and now robbed of one after another of his heart's supports, he would take leave of a painful life with a dissatisfied and broken soul."[87] It was from this extreme depth of grief that Joseph ultimately rescued his father when he revealed, first to his brothers and then to Jacob, that he was not only alive, but had risen to the position of prime minister of Egypt.

Seen in the light of Freud's Joseph phantasy, the graying hair element of the uncle dream takes on deeper significance, reflecting Freud's reaction to the recent death of his father. His daytime hope for the prestige and security of an academic promotion and the dream's exaggeration of this hope to include a ministerial appointment were both the kind of thing that a son would be proud to be able to reveal to his father as proof of his success. At this point, Freud was still early in the traditional eleven-month period of mourning for his father, and the dream expresses contradictory wishes—to have (or be) a father with the dignity and majesty of the biblical Jacob as well as to be a son who is all-powerful, but still a son.

Freud's uncle dream opens up a number of important insights into the workings of his thoughts and feelings at the beginning of 1897. Appropriately, given his hope for promotion, his emotions pointed toward accommodation to, and acceptance by authority. The dream also reveals the way the political pressures of the late 1890s had the effect of reviving memories and feelings of the 1860s and 1870s. Freud feared that his ambition to become a professor

[86] Ibid., p. 138. On Josef Freud's crime, see Krüll, *Freud und sein Vater,* pp. 193–95.
[87] Philippson, p. 230.

was threatened by the political issue of anti-Semitism. To resolve this anxiety his dream wishes transported him back to the time in his life when his political consciousness was first taking shape, to a time when even a Jew could hope to become a cabinet minister.

The uncle dream shows that Freud entered the opening months of 1897 in a politically sensitized state, and for him, as well as for Jewish-German liberals generally, it was a particularly cruel spring. In the final months of 1896, the Austrian minister-president, Count Kasimir Badeni, the leader of a parliamentary coalition of Slavic and conservative parties, had secured passage of a new electoral law creating a limited number of new seats to be chosen by members of the working classes. In March 1897 the voters went to the polls after an intense and spirited campaign which saw the two rival parties of the masses, the Social Democrats and the anti-Semitic Christian Socials, competing for the new seats. Although the hopes of the liberals and the socialists had been high, the outcome was a further decline for the German liberals, a relatively modest advance for the Social Democrats, and a substantial gain for the Christian Socials.[88]

Before and after the elections, Count Badeni carried out extensive negotiations on the formation of a new coalition. He anticipated that the election results would require some participation by the German liberals in the government coalition, and he hoped that Josef Baernreither's group, the moderately liberal Deutschen Grossgrundbesitzer, would provide a crystallization point for the adherence of other moderate German liberal elements.[89] At the same time, Badeni's negotiations with the rival Young Czech faction had already committed him to the promulgation of new language ordinances aimed at substantially increasing the use of Czech and decreasing that of German in the administrative bureaucracy of Bohemia and Moravia. Behind this maneuvering lay Badeni's naive hope that he could bring both the German liberals and the Czechs into his coalition, thereby avoiding an alliance with the clerical conservatives. The effect, however, was to escalate the problem of the language ordinances into a major political crisis.[90]

In pursuit of the virtually impossible task of satisfying both the Czechs and the Germans, Badeni continued his flirtation with the German liberals through late March, when he allowed himself to

[88] Charmatz, *Österreichs innere Geschichte,* II:106.

[89] Berthold Sutter, *Die Badenischen Sprachverordnungen von 1897* (Graz-Cologne: Verlag Hermann Böhlaus, 1960), I:142.

[90] Ibid., p. 140.

be interviewed anonymously by a Bohemian newspaper. It was immediately apparent to the public that the "leading statesman" in question was Badeni, and in the interview he attempted to reconcile the German public and their parliamentary representatives to his forthcoming ordinances by suggesting that he would make only relatively modest concessions to the Czechs.[91] Meanwhile the clerical conservatives and the Bohemian aristocrats had been carrying on their own negotiations aimed at thwarting Badeni's movement away from them and toward the German liberals. When, at the end of March, Baernreither's Grossgrundbesitzer faction realized the extent of the concessions being made to the Czechs and expressed its opposition to the proposed ordinances, the conservative factions seized the opportunity to resolve the situation in their own favor.[92] Making contact with the Young Czechs, they succeeded in outbidding Badeni for their support and, with them and other Slavic groups, established a tenuous Slavic/clerical conservative majority against Badeni's wishes. Confronted with a *fait accompli,* Badeni offered his resignation. When the emperor refused it, Badeni finally accepted this group as his new coalition, and on April 5 issued the language ordinances favoring the Czechs.[93]

For Jewish-German liberals such as Freud, these events represented a major political setback, and it is clear from Freud's dreams that on an emotional level the emerging political crisis powerfully engaged him. His dream of a street corner in Rome occurred immediately after the promulgation of the language ordinances, and it reveals that Freud's emotions were strongly on the German side. In the dream he found himself in Rome, "but I was astonished at the quantity of German posters at a street-corner. The latter point was a wish-fulfillment, which at once made me think of Prague."[94] In effect, his dream repealed the language ordinances by giving German new prominence on the streets of Prague. According to Freud, the dream expressed a desire "probably dating back to my student days, that the German language might be better tolerated in Prague."[95] He indicated that "the wish itself may perhaps have dated from a German-nationalist phase which I passed through during my youth, but have since got over."[96] In his analysis

[91] Ibid., pp. 181–82.
[92] Ibid., pp. 205–6.
[93] Charmatz, II:107.
[94] Freud, *Interpretation, S.E.,* IV:323.
[95] Ibid., p. 196.
[96] Ibid., p. 323.

of the dream, Freud tied it to his apprehension about a projected meeting with Fliess in Prague. He noted that the day before the dream he had written his friend to say that he "thought Prague might not be an agreeable place for a German to walk about in."[97] Freud's correspondence reveals that on April 6, 1897 he wrote Fliess to say "I prefer Nürnberg to Prague," and he added that he would prefer Venice even more "if Venice were a city where one could take walks."[98] This and a subsequent letter indicate that the dream occurred on the night of April 6–7 and that it reflected the tensions associated with the political situation which had so greatly stimulated national feeling among Czechs and Germans.[99] In such a situation, Freud's reluctance to go to Prague would be understandable.

Freud's dream of a street corner in Rome, like that of his uncle with the yellow beard, shows that the political events of early 1897 were able, because of his sensitized state, to call up the unresolved hopes and conflicts of his childhood and early adolescence. As he indicated in his own analysis, the whole series of Rome dreams that he had at this time reflected his phantasized identification with Hannibal, itself closely tied to the antiauthoritarian German nationalism of his adolescence. Freud's further comments on the street corner dream indicated, however, that the political events which triggered these adolescent memories also helped revive still deeper and earlier ones. Since the language ordinances, the subject of Badeni's intense negotiations, concerned the use of German and Czech in Bohemia and Moravia, they affected the area where Freud had lived as a small child, and the street corner dream reflected the stirring of thoughts and feelings from that period of his life. As he observed, "Incidentally, I must have understood Czech in my earliest childhood, for I was born in a small town in Moravia which has a Slav population. A Czech nursery rhyme, which I heard in my seventeenth year, printed itself on my memory so easily that I can repeat it to this day, though I have no notion what it means. Thus there was no lack of connection with my early childhood."[100] Since the young Freud's knowledge of Czech must have come primarily through his Roman Catholic Czech nurse, these comments point to her as an underlying presence in the

[97] Ibid., p. 195.

[98] Freud, *Complete Letters,* p. 234.

[99] Freud's December 3, 1897 letter (ibid., pp. 284–85) confirms the connection between the dream and the April 6 letter.

[100] Freud, *Interpretation, S.E.,* IV:194.

dream. In this light the wish to go to Rome suggests a desire for the maternal affection the woman represented.

Taken together, Freud's dream of his uncle with the yellow beard and the dream of a street corner in Rome reveal the depth of the psychic conflict into which he was plunged in early 1897, during the months following his father's death. His intense desire for academic promotion and for the financial security such promotion would bring called up the assimilationist mentality of his childhood Joseph phantasy with its respect for a powerful father and its acceptance of a hierarchical authority structure. The wish of the uncle dream to become a minister meant working within the system, as Joseph had done with such success. On the other hand, as the street corner dream reveals, political pressures and events pushed his thoughts and feelings in the opposite direction. The continuing pressure of demagogic anti-Semitism posed a direct threat to the realization of his hopes for promotion, and the developing language conflict between Czechs and Germans worked to revive his rebellious adolescent impulses. These impulses, expressed in his adolescent enthusiasm for *The Robbers,* with its image of a weak father and its antiauthoritarian political radicalism, were directly at odds with the emotional thrust of the Joseph phantasy. These two opposing complexes represented the fundamental alternatives of assimilation or defiance open to a Jew in a foreign culture, and the professional and political pressures which powerfully activated and reinforced them in early 1897 deepened Freud's difficulties in resolving his conflicted attitude toward his father.

Within this personal context, the culminating development of the March-April political crisis took on profound significance. With the resolution of the cabinet crisis in the direction of a clerical conservative/Slavic government, Badeni had to give up his hopes for an accommodation with the moderate German liberal factions, and to ensure a majority of sufficient size to move the new language ordinances through parliament, he made a covert arrangement with Karl Lueger's anti-Semitic Christian Socials. They assured him of their support or abstention in parliament in return for the emperor's long-denied confirmation of Lueger as mayor of Vienna. Although the deal was concluded behind the scenes, it was soon obvious to all what had happened. In its lead article of April 9, the *Neue Freie Presse* outlined these suspicions and called for a public explanation, noting that because "the authority of the crown is involved in the mayorality question in a previously unprecedented way, *we regard this unclarified point as one of the darkest in the history of the Badeni ministry*."[101] This development offered cause for profound anxiety to all Jews living in Vienna.

Although Freud did not comment on these events in his published correspondence, there is evidence of his hostile attitude toward Lueger earlier, at the time of his 1895 bid for office, and also later, in 1899, after he had served as mayor for two years. In a letter to Fliess of September 23, 1895, Freud described the results of the recent city elections in terse language that expressed the depth of his discouragement. He reported that "in the third electoral district the Liberals were beaten by 46 seats to nil, and in the second district by 32 seats to 14. I voted after all. Our district remained Liberal."[102] On this earlier occasion, however, Freud's despair eventually gave way to elation when Franz Josef stood fast against the anti-Semitic tide and refused Lueger the necessary confirmation. On November 8, 1895, Freud wrote Fliess that, as prescribed, he had maintained almost complete abstinence from cigars, and had indulged himself only on one day out of "joy at Lueger's non-confirmation in office."[103] Nor did Freud soften his opposition to Lueger after he became mayor. On May 25, 1899, Freud reported that his wrath had been aroused by one of Fliess's friends, a man named Dernburg, because of "his tolerant evaluation of our Lueger." He wrote, "I treated him badly on account of this. D. wanted to persuade us that here all is very well . . . and that we are unfair in complaining so bitterly. I still think we know better."[104] Considering Freud's strong and consistent antagonism to Lueger over this period, the anti-Semitic demagogue's moment of political triumph in April 1897 must have been deeply disappointing, particularly since it occurred in a context that seemed to threaten Freud's career hopes and to betray his basic interests as both a German and a Jew.

The political and religious oppression that Lueger's confirmation seemed to portend fitted into the long tradition of Jewish oppression going back to Moses, so it was ironically apt that in the wake of this event Freud took flight from Vienna for his Nürnberg meeting with Fliess on the evening of Friday, April 16, at the beginning of Passover.[105] Although Freud would not have marked the holiday as a religious event, he could certainly empathize with its central

[101] Sutter, I:216.
[102] Freud, *Origins*, p. 124.
[103] Ibid., p. 133.
[104] Freud, *Complete Letters*, p. 351.
[105] Ibid., p. 234.

theme: the longing for freedom from religious persecution. It had been important in his emotional and intellectual development from childhood to maturity, from the Bible story of the flight out of Egypt, through his adolescent fascination with Hannibal and Schiller, to his recently developed conviction that analysis could dissolve medieval religious superstition and offer freedom from the emotional tyranny of hysteria. Freud may also have found some satisfaction in demonstrating his own freedom from the shackles of religious custom by ignoring the ban on travel imposed by the holiday. Even if the conjunction of his departure from Vienna with the beginning of Passover was pure coincidence, its symbolic significance could not have been lost on his feelings. The longing for freedom appropriate to Passover was further reinforced by its resonance with the idealistic freedom of the German nationalist tradition, the tradition threatened by the new language ordinances, and Freud's destination expressed his reaction to this threat. The decision to meet Fliess in Nürnberg, a city within the German Empire, and one that symbolized the greatness of medieval German culture, instead of Prague, the city where German culture was threatened by increasing Czech nationalism, again shows how the political events of spring 1897 reawakened in Freud the political feelings of his adolescence.

This resurgence of feelings and memories played an important role in the burst of intellectual creativity Freud experienced that May. The central problem confronting him in his work on hysteria revolved around his adherence to the seduction theory. Although Freud saw that the traumatic sexual incidents reported by his patients had the character of phantasies, he believed that analysis would eventually be able to recover memories of actual events responsible both for the phantasies and for the hysterical symptoms. The implications of this theory, however, tended to reinforce his conflicted attitude toward his father. Freud had voiced suspicions of neurotic behavior in himself to Fliess as early as 1894, and in a letter of April 16, 1896, he listed a range of symptoms associated with an attack of death anxiety. As Schur observed, "On this specific occasion, he had recognized that it was neurotic, based on a neurotic identification with the dead sculptor Tilgner."[106] In the summer of 1897, suffering under increasing pressure from internal and external conflicts, Freud began to refer frequently to what he sometimes called his neurosis and sometimes his hysteria. He men-

[106] Schur, *Freud*, pp. 100, 539.

tioned it in his letters of June 22, July 7, August 14, and August 18.[107] Since his seduction theory had come to focus increasing attention on fathers as the prime seducers, his observation of various hysterical symptoms both in his siblings and in himself cast suspicion on Jakob Freud, a suspicion intolerable to the respect demanded during the period of mourning.[108]

The best illustration of the way this emotional conflict interlocked with Freud's scientific work on hysteria can be seen in his Villa Secerno dream, which occurred on the night of April 27, 1897, soon after he had returned from his Nürnberg meeting with Fliess. The dream concerned Fliess, directly.[109] Instead of returning to Berlin, he had traveled on to Italy, and Freud felt irritated at not having his friend's precise address so that he could communicate with him. In the dream he received "a telegram containing this address. I saw it printed in blue on the telegraph form. The first word was vague: *'Via'*, perhaps or *'Villa'* or possibly even *('Casa');* the second was clear: *'Secerno.'* The second word sounded like some Italian name and reminded me of discussions I had had with my friend. . . . It also expressed my anger with him for having kept his address *secret* from me for so long." Freud went on to say that each of the words *Via, Villa,* and *Casa* "turned out on analysis to be an independent and equally valid starting point for a chain of thoughts."[110]

Freud reported and analyzed the dream in a letter he sent to Fliess as soon as he received his address. In it he referred to his regret at not hearing from him and to his need to have Fliess serve as "audience" for his latest ideas. At the end of the paragraph he concluded that since he still had doubts himself "in the matter of fathers *[im Sachen der Väter],* my touchiness is intelligible. The dream thus collected all the irritation with you that was present in my unconscious."[111] Freud thus acknowledged to Fliess directly

[107] Freud, *Origins,* pp. 210–11 (misdated June 12 in *Origins;* see Schur, *Freud,* p. 112), 212, 213, 214.

[108] Freud, *Complete Letters,* pp. 231–32. In this letter to Fliess of Feb. 11, 1897, Freud expressed such suspicion about his father as a seducer: "Unfortunately, my own father was one of these perverts and is responsible for the hysteria of my brother (all of whose symptoms are identifications) and those of several younger sisters." Freud had doubts about his theory even then, since he added, "The frequency of this circumstance often makes me wonder."

[109] Freud, *Origins,* p. 193.

[110] Freud, *Interpretation, S.E.,* IV:317.

[111] Freud, *Origins,* p. 194. I have retranslated the second passage from the original German to give a more literal reading. See Sigmund Freud, *Aus den Anfängen der Psychoanalyse, Briefe an Wilhelm Fliess, Abhandlungen und Notizen aus den Jahren 1887–1902* (hereafter Freud, *Anfängen*), introduction by Ernst Kris, ed. Marie Bonaparte, Anna Freud, and Ernst Kris (London: Imago, 1950), p. 207.

that he had cast him in a fatherly role, and he also seemed to suggest that his touchiness arose from his uncertain views concerning his own father. Freud's awareness of his own neurotic condition, which manifested itself in his acute travel anxiety, drew together his thoughts about the role of the father in the seduction theory and his doubts about his own father. This conflicted attitude toward the father also appeared in the word choices of the dream. In the letter to Fliess, Freud associated visual images with two of the three choices, and each of these images seems to have a clear and opposite significance with respect to his attitude toward his father and to his scientific work on hysteria.

Freud associated the word "via" with "Pompeii streets which I am studying,"[112] suggesting an archaeological image highly appropriate to the nature of psychoanalytic work. Throughout his life, Freud associated analysis with archaeology in his imagery, for both sought to dig through the layers separating the present from the past and thereby recover the remnants of an earlier age. But the map of Pompeii, at that time even more than today, was incomplete since large sections of the town remained obscured by the layer of lava and ash deposited by the disastrous eruption of Vesuvius. The image as a whole suggested that the work of analysis involved undoing the consequences of an exceptional traumatic incident, symbolism strongly suggestive of Freud's seduction theory with its inherent assumption of paternal responsibility for hysterical disorders.

The other visual image pointed in the opposite direction. Freud's associations with the word "villa" led to "Böcklin's Roman villa,"[113] which apparently referred to one of the artist's most famous paintings, his "Villa by the Sea." This was the first important work of Arnold Böcklin's highly productive stay in Rome from 1862 to 1866. According to the art historian Fritz von Ostini, the artist's intent in this work was "to invest the magnificent, melancholy landscape with a feeling of mourning *[Trauer]* on the part of the last descendants of a famous race."[114] This image, then, was a fitting one for the other current of feeling present in Freud's attitude toward his father, the feeling of reverence and melancholy appropriate to the period of mourning, and altogether at odds with the feelings implicit in the seduction theory. Freud's associations to the dream images diverged along the lines of his conflicted view

[112] Freud, *Origins,* p. 194.
[113] Ibid.
[114] Fritz von Ostini, *Böcklin* (Bielefeld and Leipzig: Velhagen and Klasing, 1909), p. 50.

of his father, and in *The Interpretation of Dreams* he analyzed the Villa Secerno dream in conjunction with the quite similar dream he had at the time of his father's funeral—the dream of closing the eyes. It also expressed his conflicted feelings about his father, in the form of alternate word choices with contrasting lines of associations.[115]

Although Freud's antagonism toward his father was transferred to Fliess in the Villa Secerno dream, the dream associations provide evidence that Freud simultaneously saw Fliess as a brother figure, thereby recapitulating the psychic confusion of his childhood when father and brother figures converged in his mind. The dream, with its associations involving traveling in Italy with Fliess, belongs with the Rome dreams inspired by Freud's Hannibal phantasy. His associations with the words "Villa Secerno" led him to thoughts of "our talks of travel; Secerno sounds Neapolitan-Sicilian rather like Salerno." Freud observed that this connection pointed to Fliess's promise of a meeting "on Italian soil."[116] These comments associated Fliess with Hannibal and the brother band, for in the Italian phase of his campaign against Rome, Hannibal was aided by his brother, Hasdrubal, and the area of the Campagna near Salerno was the site of one of his most important victories. The efforts of the brothers to wreak vengeance on Rome constituted a basic element in the dream's allusions to travel in Italy and complemented the theme of irritation with the father appropriate to the Hannibal phantasy.

Freud's analysis of the dream as elaborated in his letter to Fliess also reveals a conflict in his feelings about his friend. After describing the dream and indicating that it directly concerned Fliess, Freud included in the long paragraph entitled "motivation" various references to the role of the father in his seduction theory, as well as repeated criticisms of Fliess. Freud scholars have long argued that when he began his self-analysis, Freud cast Fliess in the role of a "transference figure," and this dream analysis suggests that Fliess occupied that position as early as April 27, 1897. Heinz Kohut has provided a valuable complement to this traditional view. He notes the advantage to Freud of choosing as the focal point of the transference a man such as Fliess "with whom he was not in direct contact most of the time, i.e., the behind-the-couch distance and thus invisibility of the ordinary analyst was here replaced by the distance between Vienna and Berlin which likewise kept the

[115] Freud, *Interpretation, S.E.,* IV:317–18.
[116] Freud, *Origins,* pp. 194–95.

disturbing reality input at a minimum." In pointing to the singular nature of Freud's self-analytic experience, however, Kohut gives the creative aspect of the transference to Fliess more weight than the therapeutic dimension, arguing that the primary significance the "imago of Fliess" had for Freud was in providing "narcissistic support with regard to the creative (nontherapeutic) aspects of his analysis."[117] Kohut's view supplements rather than contradicts the traditional position, since Freud's self-analysis was both a therapeutic and a creative undertaking, and his image of Fliess included not only elements of the father figure but also elements of the brother figure to whom Freud inevitably turned in search of reinforcement for his own creative drives. The Villa Secerno Dream reveals that in Freud's dream life Fliess could simultaneously play the role of father and brother.

After concluding his preliminary analysis of the dream with the observation that it concerned talks of travel and Fliess's promise of a meeting on Italian soil, Freud continued the letter the next evening (April 29). He began by saying that he had realized the "complete interpretation" when a stroke of luck that morning "brought confirmation of paternal aetiology."[118] From this point until he concluded the letter with a triumphant "Quod Erat Demonstrandum" he never again explicitly mentioned the dream, Fliess, himself, or any of the specific subjects discussed earlier. The entire continuation of the letter was devoted to recounting the case history of his latest patient, a young woman suffering from "a quite ordinary hysteria." Clearly Freud believed that the young woman's case illuminated the basic meaning of his own dream so obviously that no explicit connecting commentary was needed to suggest the "complete interpretation" to Fliess. The woman's case paralleled Freud's dream in two important ways: both revolved around the subject of traveling and both focused on the psychological significance of fathers and brothers. According to Freud, the woman's brother had gone insane, and the insomnia that constituted her "chief symptom" dated "from the time she heard the carriage driving away from the house taking him to the asylum." He reported that since that time she had been desperately frightened "of carriage drives and worried that an accident was going to happen."[119] The emotional significance of traveling in a carriage

[117] Heinz Kohut, "Creativeness, Charisma, Group Psychology: Reflections on the Self-Analysis of Freud," in Gedo and Pollock, *Fusion*, pp. 393, 399. For the traditional view of Fliess as "transference figure," see Ernst Kris's introduction to Freud, *Origins*, p. 34n., also p. 43.

[118] Freud, *Origins*, p. 195; retranslated from Freud, *Anfängen*, p. 207.

[119] Freud, *Origins*, pp. 196, 195.

for this woman closely resembled Freud's own travel anxiety.[120] Having just traveled to and from Nürnberg by train, Freud would have experienced this anxiety once again, and it is quite possible that he may have discussed it with Fliess when they met. He explicitly referred to it in an October 3, 1897 letter to Fliess where he wrote, "My anxiety over travel you have seen yourself in full bloom."[121]

The other point of connection involved the role of the father. Freud's patient, in discussing her case, at first expressed reluctance about mentioning the names of the people with whom she had had early sexual encounters. When Freud explained that it was essential to be specific, she approached the subject slowly and indirectly. He urged her to "speak plainly," and told her that in his analyses he found that it was "the closest relatives, fathers or brothers, who are the guilty men." When she replied, that it did not involve her brother he concluded, "So it was your father, then." Once this had been said, she went on to discuss specific sexual activities in which she and her father took part when she was between the ages of eight and twelve. As Freud observed in summing up her case, he found it easy to convince her that "worse things must have happened to her in her infancy."[122] In this case, then, Freud thought he had found strong support for his seduction theory, and this belief led to his triumphant concluding Q.E.D.

Freud brought up the young woman's case to explain his own dream, which he understood when the case brought "confirmation of paternal aetiology." The original English edition of the letters to Fliess renders this phrase as "confirmation of my theory of paternal aetiology," but there is no basis for the mention of theory in the German original, and the effect of this inaccuracy is to shift attention from Freud's personal situation to his theory. Undoubtedly, Freud had his theory very much in mind throughout the letter, but the error in translation obscures that fact that he also had in mind something much more specific and personal. Since the Villa Secerno dream involved the travel anxiety he shared with his hysterical patient, the question of the origin of hysterical symptoms in himself must also have concerned him greatly. The statement that the complete interpretation of the dream came to him when the case "brought confirmation of paternal aetiology" should be read in this light. Freud was referring not only to his theory

[120] Ibid., pp. 214, 219.
[121] Ibid., p. 219.
[122] Ibid., p. 195.

but even more specifically and immediately to the role of Jakob Freud in his own development of hysterical symptoms.

Freud's Villa Secerno dream reveals the conflicting pressures working on his thoughts and feelings in the days following his return from Nürnberg. The dream's immediate, precipitating cause was his frustration at not being able to communicate to Fliess the flood of ideas resulting from this inner turmoil, and as soon as he was able to have his friend as his "audience" once again, Freud poured out his thoughts to him. In May he wrote Fliess four important letters, three of which were accompanied by drafts of extensive notes. These notes and letters communicated some of Freud's most basic ideas on the nature of hysteria as well as his decision to begin writing his book on dreams. They also contained the first hints of his discovery of the Oedipus complex, the discovery that finally brought clarity to his theoretical structure by unifying his explanation of both normal and abnormal mental activity in a single framework.

That Freud, having just returned from a city renowned for its medieval architecture, entitled his notes "The Architecture of Hysteria" suggests the close relationship between his ideas and the emotional issues associated with his travels. In the letter of May 2 he wrote that he had arrived at "a sure notion of the structure of hysteria. Everything points to the reproduction of scenes which in some cases can be arrived at directly and in others only by way of projected phantasies *[immer über vorlegte Phantasien]*. The phantasies . . . are defensive structures *[Schutzbauten]*."[123] The conception of hysterical phantasies and symptoms as defensive structures was fundamental not only to Freud's theory of hysteria, but also to his understanding of mental life generally. The idea of defense was closely related to the concepts of repression, censorship, and the functioning of the super ego as formulated in his mature thought. In the notes accompanying this letter, he went on to refer to phantasies as "psychical outworks" *(Vorbauten)* which served to block access "to these memories [of primal scenes],"[124] and these references to *Schutzbauten* and *Vorbauten* are but two of many indications that he saw a parallel between hysterical defense and the medieval fortifications of Nürnberg. Further evidence is provided by the diagram accompanying the second installment of his draft notes on the "Architecture of Hysteria," which Freud mailed to Fliess on May 25. This diagram (see Figure 3), which explained

[123] Ibid., p. 196; Freud, *Anfängen*, p. 208.
[124] Freud, *Origins*, p. 197; Freud, *Anfängen*, p. 210.

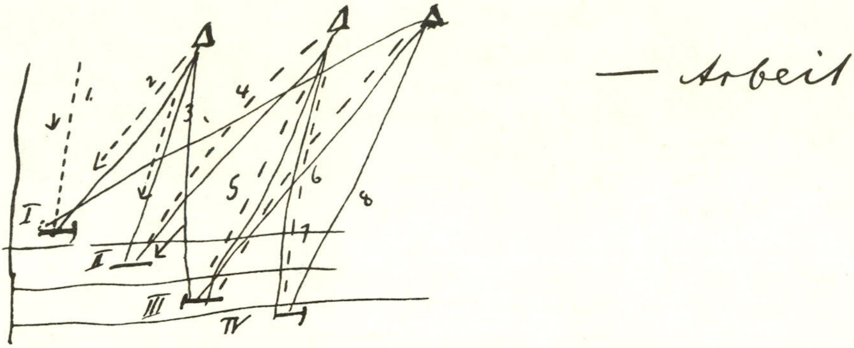

Figure 3. Diagram in Freud's "Architecture of Hysteria" notes. All the dotted lines, arrows, and figures are in red in the original, as well as the word *Arbeit* (Work) and the line beside it. From Sigmund Freud, *Aus den Anfängen der Psychoanalyse.* By permission of Sigmund Freud Copyrights Ltd., Colchester, England.

his theory of the structure of hysteria and the way analysis might free patients from this disorder, bears a striking resemblance to the towers of Nürnberg. Its solid lines form three pyramidal spires representing phantasies, and these spires echo the pyramidal shape of the roofs atop the Nürnberg fortifications (see Figure 4). Moreover, in Freud's diagram, each spire is topped by a small triangle, representing a hysterical symptom, and these too have an analogue, for various pictures of medieval Nürnberg shows that the towers of the fortress *(Burg),* which Freud visited,[125] and the other towers related to the city's defenses were surmounted by small weather vanes in the shape of flags.

The most practical of the arts, architecture expresses the fundamental realities of the culture and time to which it belongs, and approaching Freud's architectural image of hysteria from a point of view which takes into consideration the social and political realities that found expression in Nürnberg's medieval towers shows that the image goes to the very heart of his ideas. These elaborate defensive fortifications reflected the intense political struggle which characterized the city's medieval history; Gerald Strauss, in his history of Nürnberg, describes the way the contest between the city's ruling lord, the Burggraf, and the increasingly powerful middle class was translated into architectural form. In 1377 the citizenry erected a tall tower on the eastern wall of the city to spy on the activities going on in the Burggraf's fortress. The descen-

[125] This is evident from his letter to Fliess of April 14, 1898: Freud, *Origins,* pp. 251–52.

Figure 4. Medieval Nürnberg, from the south. By permission of the Deutscher Verein für Kunstwissenschaft.

dants of the Burggraf responded in kind, and in the fifteenth century his fortress "was equipped with a peaked roof and wooden balconies" which allowed his men to keep watch on the city "while the city's men on their lookout were watching the Burggraf."[126] These are the peaked roofs that resemble the spires of Freud's diagram, and in his analogy the hysterical phantasy was like one of these towers: a static defensive structure arising out of a dynamic power struggle. When he visited Nürnberg, Freud's interests as a traveler centered on the historical,[127] and, moreover, the Nürnberg towers grew directly out of the kind of struggle between aristocracy and populace which had so strongly engaged his youthful political interests. In the romantic radicalism of his adolescence, his sympathies always aligned him with the people and the ideal of freedom, and in such works as *The Robbers* he learned to see a parallel between political and psychic polarizations. Furthermore, his knowledge of Charcot and Bourneville had deeply reinforced his association of hysteria with what he saw as the politically and psychologically polarized middle ages. The political and social history expressed in the architecture of Nürnberg thus fell into a pattern of political and psychological correlations deeply engrained in Freud's way of thinking.

When Freud sent Fliess the first installment of his "Architecture of Hysteria" notes on May 2, he spoke in his accompanying letter of the "big advance in insight" it represented. He was referring not to the concept of defense *per se,* a concept used extensively two years earlier in the *Studies on Hysteria,* but rather to his deepened understanding of the dynamic structure of hysterical defense. Up to this time the only dynamic element in Freud's seduction theory involved the repressive mechanism at work in blocking memories of childhood sexual traumas and in converting their energy into hysterical symptoms. By focusing on sexual traumas, this theory had the effect of sharply separating the personal history and the psychic characteristics of the mentally ill from the world of normal mental development, thereby blocking the way to a more general and unified conception of mental activity. While Freud continued to hold to his seduction theory for some time, the letters and drafts of May 1897 point the way toward his later view of mental dynamics, in which normal and abnormal patterns were embraced within a single spectrum. Initially, his new conception developed within the framework of the old. For example, the letter of May 2 referred

[126] Gerald Strauss, *Nuremberg in the Sixteenth Century* (New York: John Wiley, 1966), p. 33.
[127] For Freud's changing travel interests, see Freud, *Origins,* p. 214.

to phantasies arising from primal scenes (involving sexual traumas) and although Freud assured Fliess that "all the material [of the scenes] is of course genuine," he then went on to observe that "the psychic images *[Gebilde]* which in hysteria are subjected to repression are not properly speaking memories, . . . but impulses *[Impulsen]* deriving from the primal scenes."[128] As Ernst Kris noted, this was the essence of the "big advance" to which Freud referred, for at this point "he has nearly discovered the 'id' (the meaning of instinct)."[129] Freud's new insight involved a dynamically balanced explanation of hysterical phantasies and symptoms isolated within the framework of his old theory. He still thought these repressed impulses derived from primal scenes, but he now viewed their motive force in the formation of phantasies as largely independent and capable of interacting directly with the repressive mechanism.

Taken as a whole, the changes in Freud's theoretical conception of hysteria reflect a much more central and prominent emphasis on the role of emotional impulses, and this crucially important shift occurred at a time when Freud himself was grappling with powerful surges of emotions coming both from within himself and from the outer world in which he lived. The political negotiations over Badeni's new government and the issue of the language ordinances evoked an outpouring of feeling on the part of Austria's Germans, and Freud's dreams, as well as his decision to meet Fliess in Nürnberg, show that at this time he participated emotionally in the general wave of nationalism, despite the fact that earlier he had consciously renounced his youthful commitment to it. The outcome of Badeni's negotiations also testified to the power of emotional impulses. Lueger's triumph resulted from his ability to evoke and channel the potent emotional forces of anti-Semitism, and his success in attracting popular support allowed him to exploit the crisis confronting Badeni in order to win confirmation as mayor of Vienna. The action of the emperor in bowing to the anti-Semites would have been deeply disturbing to Jews in any case, but for Freud the emotional shock waves generated by this event may have been magnified by virtue of their resonance with the inner surges of emotion swirling around the conflicted image of his dead father. Freud's Hannibal phantasy had arisen in response to a similar act of cowardice on the part of his father, and the Villa Secerno dream, which occurred in the wake of Lueger's confirmation, evoked the Hannibal identification to express hostility to Rome (Roman Catholicism), to his father, and to authority generally.

[128] Ibid., p. 196; Freud, *Anfängen,* pp. 208–9.
[129] Freud, *Origins,* p. 197.

The architectural metaphor Freud chose to describe his new insight into the nature of hysteria well expressed the confluence of inner and outer pressures which drove home to him the central importance of emotional impulses. The sociopolitical dynamics that gave rise to Nürnberg's medieval defenses paralleled the struggle between tyranny and populace represented by the Hannibal phantasy and served to express sharply polarized psychic conflict in general. The architecture image derived from Nürnberg's towers summed up a view of hysteria going back at least to Charcot and Bourneville, a view that saw the repressive clerical culture of the middle ages as particularly conducive to hysterical states.

From early in his life, and particularly from his days as a student of Franz Brentano, Freud had learned to look within himself for guidance in seeking to understand psychological phenomena, and the deepened understanding he gained at this time drew on that inner source. The psychic polarization he himself experienced with respect to German nationalism, the split between consciously held values and inner emotional impulses, and also with respect to his father on the issue of the seduction theory (as seen in the Villa Secerno dream) provided valuable if painful insight into the nature of hysterical defense. In the wake of Lueger's confirmation and the triumph of the Catholic clerical forces in Vienna, Freud was moved to affirm even more strongly his adherence to a seduction theory which satisfied his adolescent need to blame his father but failed to provide the theoretical clarity and unity he desired as a scientist. Freud's own defensive reaction to the threats posed by these developments locked him into an intellectual and emotional position that blocked the way to a resolution of his personal and theoretical problems. In the summer of 1897, as he increasingly detected in himself the hysterical symptoms he had long observed in his patients, the very extremity of his dilemma finally helped him find a solution to it. This solution led not only to a greater degree of personal serenity but also to the achievement of a crucial intellectual breakthrough.

5/

The Collapse of the Seduction Theory

Freud's May letters to Fliess hint at the theoretical revolution which was soon to come, with the abandonment of the seduction theory for a conception that saw in the myth of Oedipus a universal archetype. The central importance of this intellectual event lies less in the issue of "seduction" *per se* than in the implied shift in theoretical focus from neurotic abnormality to the general human condition. Freud certainly realized, even after he abandoned the theory, that some cases of hysteria did result from early experiences of real sexual trauma. The important point was his realization that some cases did not, and that they went back instead to childhood phantasy. This realization that repressed phantasy could acquire a driving force strong enough to mold psychic reality, a realization which he experienced directly in his own case, allowed him to unify his exploration of a whole range of phenomena, both normal and abnormal.

Any attempt to explain Freud's advance in insight must consider a complex interplay of internal and external forces.[1] The self-

[1] The cause of Freud's abandonment of the seduction theory has been the subject of intense debate. Jones views it as an intellectual advance and suggests the possibility that Freud's self-analysis was the decisive factor in this occurrence (*Life and Work,* I:265–66). Various analytically inclined scholars have followed this view and elaborated on it; see Schur, *Freud,* pp. 113–14; and Anzieu, *L'auto-analyse de Freud,* I:311–15. Masson (*Assault on Truth,* pp. 105–34) attacks this established view, treating Freud's shift from seduction to phantasy as a mistake motivated by "loss of courage" (p. 134) in the face of professional opposition. For a somewhat similar but much more sophisticated and well-supported view, see Krüll, *Freud und sein Vater,* who also sees Freud's shift as a "step backward" (p. 90) and emphasizes its personal

analysis he began at this time[2] played a key role in this process, and Freud's inner voyage of discovery was closely connected with the work on dreams he began writing in May. Appropriately, the metaphor of the journey appeared frequently in this book which expressed his new insight and recorded the results of his self-exploration.[3] Freud himself observed in it, "It is not surprising that a person undergoing psychoanalytic treatment should often dream of it and be led to give expression in his dreams to the many thoughts and expectations to which the treatment gives rise. The imagery most frequently chosen to represent it is that of a journey."[4] The theme of the journey resonated through Freud's life and background from early childhood to maturity, from the biblical theme of the wandering of the Jews, to the early wanderings of his own family, to the travel neurosis which became a focus of his self-analysis. Furthermore, his actual journey to Italy in the summer of 1897 played a direct role in the events leading to the overthrow of the seduction theory by taking him back in time to reexperience and reevaluate a central event of his youth.

Freud's journey south and back in time had a close literary precedent in one of his favorite works. In Goethe's *Faust* the hero undertook a similar journey, and Thomas Mann has drawn attention to Freud's symbolic identification with the Faust of Part Two. In his lecture "Freud and the Future," he observed, "Freud once called his theory of dreams 'a bit of scientific new-found land won from superstition and mysticism' . . . 'Where id was shall be ego,' he epigrammatically says. And he calls analysis a cultural labor comparable to the draining of the Zuider Zee. Almost in the end the traits of the venerable man merge into the lineaments of the

---

importance as a "creative solution" to his ambivalent feelings for his father (p. 88). Richard Karpe, "Freud's Reaction to His Father's Death," *Bulletin of the Philadelphia Association for Psychoanalysis,* 6 (1956), connects the reversal with Freud's mourning for his father but sees it as an intellectual advance. Since there is no reason to assume that creative or scientific insight must be free of personal motivation to be in some sense true or useful, I have come to the view that Freud's theoretical shift did represent an advance while also involving compelling personal motives. Although I accept the view that this advance emerged from his self-analysis, my position departs from previous treatments in emphasizing the role of political forces in this process. Previous scholars have not considered the important fact that Freud says he realized the meaning of his Hannibal phantasy while on his trip to Italy (in the summer of 1897), and I believe that in conjunction with his mourning, this key self-analytic success brought about the collapse of the seduction theory immediately after his return from that trip.

[2] Schur, *Freud,* pp. 72–73, 112–13.

[3] Leonard Shengold, "The Metaphor of the Journey in *The Interpretation of Dreams,*" in Kanzer and Glenn, *Freud,* p. 51.

[4] Freud, *Interpretation, S.E.,* v:410.

grey-haired Faust."[5] Near the end of Goethe's drama, the aged Faust turned his eyes to the sea as he contemplated his last great enterprise, the draining of the Zuider Zee:

> There wave on wave, by hidden power heaved,
> Reigns and recedes, and nothing is achieved.
> This thing can sadden me to desperation,
> Wild elements in aimless perturbation!
> To soar beyond itself aspired my soul:
> Here would I strive, and this would I control.[6]

Faust's efforts to harness the power of the sea and reclaim the land along the Dutch coast ran parallel to his efforts to win control at last over the emotional forces which had for so long ruled his life. Certainly in this sense Freud could well take Faust as a model.

In Part One of Goethe's drama, the scholar Faust had first turned his attention to the fascinating inner world of feeling in a spirit of scientific observation born of deep personal frustration, believing that if the correct formula could be found nature would at last reveal its hidden essence. The imagery of Freud's May 1897 letters points up the importance of the parallel drawn by Mann, for it shows that at this much earlier turning point in his life Freud also took Faust as his guide. In these letters Freud portrayed himself in an essentially observant attitude, watching the surging waves of emotion within himself and waiting for them to reveal their hidden nature, an attitude similar to what Franz Brentano had called inner perception. In the letter of May 16, he referred to the "seething ferment" he felt inside himself as he waited "for the next surge forward." On May 25, he sent Fliess more notes on hysteria and commented: "The enclosed comes of a surge of guesses." Finally, on May 31, in the most obviously Goethean image of all, he sent more notes and referred to them as a few "fragments thrown up on the beach by the last surge." This reference pulls together the Faustian wave imagery with an allusion to Fliess's previously stated hope that Freud "might find a skull on the Lido to enlighten [him] as Goethe once did."[7] Finding the skull had enabled Goethe to make one of his most important scientific discoveries, and Freud had similar hopes.

One of the notes on hysteria contained in Freud's May 31 letter again involved Goethe. In his first attempt at applying psychoan-

[5] Mann, *Essays*, p. 324.

[6] J. W. Goethe, *Faust, Part Two*, trans. Philip Wayne (Baltimore: Penguin, 1961), p. 221.

[7] Freud, *Origins*, pp. 200, 202, 206, 220.

alytic theory to a literary work, Freud put forth the suggestion that the "mechanism of creative writing is the same as that of hysterical phantasies" and went on to illustrate his point with a discussion of Goethe's youthful novel *Werther.*[8] Freud's thoughts about Goethe, as evidenced in both the Faustian imagery of his letters and the subject matter of this note, provide an important clue to the workings of the creative forces within him as he entered the period when he was simultaneously engaged in carrying out his self-analysis and writing *The Interpretation of Dreams.* Both consciously and unconsciously, Freud found that Goethe and Faust provided crucial guidance for the emotional and intellectual journey on which he was preparing to embark in May 1897.

The importance of this guidance on an unconscious level can be seen in Freud's Hella dream, a dream recounted to Fliess in the same May 31 letter. Freud's account, which revolved around his daughter Mathilde, was brief. He wrote that a short time before he had dreamt of "feeling over-affectionately toward Mathilde, but her name was 'Hella,' and then I saw the word 'Hella' in heavy type before me." According to Freud the dream had two immediate sources, one personal and the other political. He indicated that Hella was the name of one of his nieces "whose photograph we have been sent. Mathilde may have been called Hella because she has been weeping so bitterly recently over the Greek defeats. She has a passion for the mythology of ancient Hellas and naturally regards all Hellenes as heroes." Freud linked the dream's basic meaning to his work on hysteria and his efforts to confirm his theory that paternal "seduction" was the origin of neurotic disorder. He argued that the dream fulfilled a wish "to pin down a father as the originator of neurosis and put an end to my persistent doubts."[9] As Didier Anzieu observes in discussing Freud's interpretation of this dream, "That is to take one's wishes for reality!" He goes on to point out that Freud had blocked out the obvious conclusion that "if it is the wish and not the act which is the source of disorder then his whole theory would have to be changed."[10] At this point Freud was not yet emotionally or intellectually prepared to grasp consciously the deeper Oedipal meaning of this dream in terms of either his theory or his own feelings toward his daughter, but the allusions provided in the dream's day residue reveal how he was beginning to move toward such an understanding.

[8] Ibid., p. 208.
[9] Ibid., p. 206.
[10] Anzieu, I:300.

Freud's reference to Mathilde's tears over the recent Greek defeats provides the most important clue to the deeper levels of meaning in the dream. It also makes it possible to date the dream somewhat more precisely. Freud had mentioned Mathilde's sympathy for the Greeks in his May 16 letter to Fliess, referring to her passion for mythology, and the bitter tears she had wept so recently when the Greeks "suffered such heavy blows at the hands of the Turks."[11] The heavy type in which Freud saw the word "Hella" in his dream echoes the fact that Greece had recently been in the headlines. War had broken out between Greece and Turkey in late April 1897, and by May 7 the Greeks had suffered serious reverses. Since the fighting was over in mid-May, it seems probable that the dream occurred sometime in the second or third week of that month. The crucial battle of the war, in which the Greeks suffered the defeat which ended the conflict, was fought in the rich and important plain of Thessaly near the city of Pharsalos. As the *Neue Freie Presse* pointed out in its detailed coverage of the fighting, Pharsalos was a "historically famous, blood-drenched battlefield" where earlier the Romans had defeated the Macedonians and "Caesar had destroyed the more powerful army of his rival Pompey."[12] In this same context Pharsalos was also a deeply significant symbol in *Faust.* In Part Two of the drama, Faust went back in time to ancient Greece, where he relived in his own experience the history of Western civilization from its most primitive beginnings to modern times, and this temporal, spatial, and spiritual journey began near Pharsalos.

As Faust and his companions approached the battlefield from afar, Homunculus described their destination. At the mention of the famous name Pharsalos, Mephisto interrupted impatiently to forestall a political discussion:

> No more! That privilege I gladly waive
> Of hearing about tyrant versus slave. . . .
> They fight they say, dear freedom's cause to save
> But seen more clearly, slave is fighting slave![13]

In the next scene Erichtho described the Pharsalian fields where the group arrived: "Here of the blossom time of greatness Pompey dreamed. There, for the tremulous, tell-tale balance Caesar

[11] Freud, *Origins,* p. 201.
[12] *Neue Freie Presse,* May 9, 1897, p. 25.
[13] *Faust, Part Two,* p. 104.

watched." Symbolically, the site marked the place where the political freedom of the ancient world gave way to the rule of tyrants:

> For every man who has not wit
> To rule his inner self will be most apt to rule
> His neighbor's will, according to his own proud whim . . .
> Yet here a great example in the fight was proved,
> How force against a force more puissant makes a stand,
> How freedom's fair and thousand-flowered wreath is rent,
> And the stiff laurel coiled to bind the victor's brow.[14]

In this way Goethe suggested the same all-important issue conveyed by the wave imagery later in Part Two, the issue of achieving true freedom or autonomy through control of one's passionate inner drives. For Faust this task was embodied in his quest for Helen of Troy, the archetypal representative of Greek beauty symbolizing the balance, restraint, and proportion that Goethe and the other great German classicists saw as the essence of Greek art. Helen's virtues complemented the vigorous dynamism of Faust's passionate striving, and the drama pointed toward their union as a symbol of the synthesis between control and passion essential to personal fulfillment and cultural greatness. Faust had first glimpsed Helen briefly in the opening scenes of Part One, but was diverted by his involvement with Gretchen. When he set out to find Helen in Part Two, his first attempt took him to the mysterious realm of the mothers, a realm entered by means of a magic key able to grow in size. Faust succeeded in returning from the realm of the mothers with the shade of Helen (and also Paris), but when he attempted to grasp her the experience ended in tragedy. The illusion exploded, leaving him unconscious. To have a successful reunion with her, Faust had to go back in time to ancient Greece, to the childhood of Western culture, so that he could experience Helen's beauty directly, as a living reality rather than as a lifeless memory. This was the ultimate purpose of the journey which began near Pharsalos. In Freud's dream, then, Hella was Helen of Troy and he was Faust preparing to return by means of self-analysis to his own childhood in order to discover how to impose balance and control on his disordered passions.

If the classical imagery of Freud's Hella dream is juxtaposed with the medieval Gothic images associated with his trip to Nürnberg

[14] Ibid., pp. 106–7.

and his "Architecture of Hysteria" diagram, an even fuller set of correspondences with Faust appears. To succeed in his quest for spiritual wholeness, Faust had to abandon the emotionally tense Gothic north, where spirit and senses struggled for dominance, and journey south to the classical lands, where sin and the devil were out of place and feeling coexisted in balanced harmony with spirit. Because Freud described his new understanding of hysterical disorders in Gothic imagery, it was appropriate that the alternate, well-balanced, ideal should be associated with classical images. This was clearly the sort of contrast he saw between his own personality and that of his friend Fliess. Having begun to realize that he himself exhibited the symptoms of a hysterical travel neurosis and having cast Fliess in the role of transference figure as he began his self-analytic treatment of the disorder, Freud saw in his friend the classical virtues he himself lacked. For example, when Fliess expressed a lack of enthusiasm for Venice after his April visit, Freud wrote back on May 2 that while he did not agree he could understand the criticism in view of "the harmony and proportion in the austere constructions of your mental processes."[15] This description conjured up the image of a classic Greek temple, and in letters written several months later, he developed a similar point by contrasting his own erratic moods and the way they affected his handwriting with Fliess's healthy stability. After referring in his letters of July 7 and August 14 to his inability to write, he observed in a letter of August 18 that his handwriting had improved and noted approvingly that Fliess's writing never varied. In the same letter Freud discussed his prospective trip to Italy, and in outlining his itinerary spoke of the way his travel interests were beginning to move toward those of Fliess. "I begin to see your point of view, which looks, not for what is of cultural-historical interest, but for absolute beauty clothed in forms and ideas and in fundamentally pleasing sensations of space and color. At Nürnberg I was still far from seeing it."[16] Here again Fliess's tastes were associated with the classical ideal of beauty toward which Freud aspired to move in contrast to his earlier interest in Nürnberg's medieval defenses. Like Faust, Freud had to abandon the Gothic north for the classical south in order to achieve psychic wholeness, and like Faust in pursuit of Helen, Freud too went in search of "absolute beauty."

[15] Freud, *Origins*, p. 197.
[16] Ibid., pp. 212, 214.

Scholars have long appreciated the importance of Freud's travels to his intellectual work,[17] a psychological connection illustrated by the close relationship between his April visit to Nürnberg and his May "Architecture of Hysteria" notes. Even more important, however, was his subsequent trip to Italy, for it was on this journey that he made the crucial breakthroughs which prepared the way for achieving intellectual coherence in his work and emotional coherence in his life. The shift of interest in what he saw while traveling mentioned in his August 18 letter pointed the way to these advances. Nürnberg's architecture exemplified a history of deep sociopolitical conflict, which Freud's diagram analogously related to the profound psychic divisions characteristic of hysteria. This was a "historical" approach in that the origins of psychic disorder were attributed to specific traumatic incidents in the patient's early personal history. The essence of Freud's intellectual breakthrough involved a movement from the historical conception of hysterical aetiology represented by the seduction theory to a conception which assumed that hysteria was an extreme example of an essentially universal and timeless struggle between sexual instinct and the forces of repression, a conception for which Freud found a classical model in the myth of Oedipus. In Freud's theory as in his actual travels, the movement was from the Gothic north to the classical south.

Seen in the light of the various allusions to Goethe's *Faust,* Freud's new travel interests suggest a shift in the deep inner conflict he experienced throughout most of the period of mourning following his father's death. The political crisis had pushed him toward rebellion by reawakening his adolescent radicalism, while his hopes for academic promotion and his respect for his dead father had revived his childhood Joseph phantasy and the wish to accommodate to authority. In this psychic conflict Fliess's influence seems to have been aligned with the pacific Joseph configuration. In his May 16 letter to Fliess, Freud explained that as an alternative to the uncertainty of his work on hysteria, he had "felt impelled to start writing about dreams, with which I feel on firm ground, and which you feel I ought to write about in any case." This work, he indicated, had been interrupted because he had to prepare an abstract of his publications as part of the process involved in his professorial

[17] See Ernest Jones, "Freud's Early Travels," *International Journal of Psycho-Analysis,* 35, pt. 2 (1954):81–84; John E. Gedo, "Freud's Self-Analysis and His Scientific Ideas," *American Imago,* 25, no. 2 (1968):99–118; and Schorske, "Psycho-archeology," pp. 52–67.

promotion, and a vote on the promotion was imminent. "Now I have finished and can think about dreams again."[18] In comparison with the frustration, doubt, and conflict associated with his work on hysteria, the subject of dream interpretation offered Freud a sense of stability and calm in a time of turmoil. He had established a solid intellectual foundation for this work some two years earlier with his discovery that dreams were wish-fulfillments, and on an emotional level the subject called up the hopes for success and happiness associated with the Joseph identification of his childhood. As the uncle dream of early 1897 shows, Freud's hopes for academic promotion had the power to activate the expectations tied to the Joseph story with its message of success within the system. The letter of May 16, where he interpolated the hopeful news about his promotion into his remarks about turning to the subject of dreams, betrays the same associative pattern. This pattern and the classical imagery which Freud associated with Fliess suggest that in the paternal dimension of his role as transference figure, Fliess embodied the qualities of balance, restraint, and stability characteristic of Joseph.[19] In adopting Fliess's classical point of view and deciding to look for absolute beauty on his travels, Freud revealed the increasing influence exercised by this element of his divided psyche.

Freud's actual trip to Italy testifies to the continuing intensity of his inner conflict, for even though he set out consciously in search of absolute beauty, his route was unconsciously determined by his deep fascination with military history. He outlined his specific itinerary in his August 18 letter to Fliess, in which he indicated that the idea of visiting Naples had been dropped in favor of a route "via San Gimignano, Siena, Perugia, Assisi, Ancona."[20] These cities had relatively little to offer the tourist in search of classical beauty. San Gimignano was known as the "city of the beautiful towers" because it was one of the few Italian cities which had preserved its medieval defensive structures almost intact. Moreover, in traveling in the area of Siena and Perugia, Freud went near Lake Trasimene, the site of Hannibal's most famous victory over the Romans, and it was shortly thereafter that he realized that on this journey he had quite literally been following in Hannibal's

[18] Freud, *Origins,* pp. 200–201.

[19] In fact Fliess's scientific work was at times extravagantly speculative—hardly a model of balance and restraint—but in this phase of their relationship Freud seems to have been blind to this flaw.

[20] Freud, *Origins,* p. 214.

footsteps. The realization led to the first important success of his self-analysis, and he described it in detail in *The Interpretation of Dreams:*

> It was on my last journey to Italy, which among other places, took me past Lake Trasimene, that finally—after having seen the Tiber and sadly turned back when I was only fifty miles from Rome—I discovered the way in which my longing for the eternal city had been reinforced by impressions from my youth. I was in the act of making a plan to by-pass Rome next year and travel to Naples, when a sentence occurred to me which I must have read in one of our classical authors: "Which of the two, it may be debated, walked up and down his study with greater impatience after he had formed his plan of going to Rome—Winckelmann, the Vice-Principal, or Hannibal, the Commander-in-Chief?" I had actually been following in Hannibal's footsteps. Like him, I had been fated not to see Rome; and he too had moved into the Campagna when everyone had expected him in Rome.[21]

Freud went on to explain that he had identified closely with the Carthaginian general in his later school days, for the Carthaginians, like the Jews, were a Semitic people, and their long struggle with Rome symbolized to Freud "the conflict between the tenacity of Jewry and the organization of the Catholic church." The longing to visit Rome which had manifested itself so powerfully in the series of Rome dreams early in 1897, and which now revealed itself to have been an underlying determinant of his Italian journey, thus had the character of a defiant, Hannibal-like, reaction to the rising intensity of anti-Semitic pressure. As Freud observed, "the increasing importance of the effects of the anti-Semitic movement upon our emotional life helped to fix the thoughts and feelings of those early days."[22] Indeed he discovered, with this self-analytic breakthrough, that he was literally "driven" by the emotional power of this adolescent phantasy.

Freud accounted for the power of this feeling by relating the memory which surfaced when he realized he was actually following in Hannibal's footsteps: "At that point I was brought up against the event in my youth whose power was still being shown in all these emotions and dreams."[23] He then related the story that gave rise to his Hannibal phantasy, the story of how when he was a boy of ten or twelve his father had told him of the incident in which

[21] Freud, *Interpretation, S.E.,* IV:196.
[22] Ibid.
[23] Ibid., p. 197.

a Christian had knocked his fur cap into the mud and shouted "Jew! get off the pavement!" Having exalted his father to the status of the biblical Jacob in childhood phantasy, Freud was crushed by his father's unheroic response—simply walking out into the street to pick up his hat. From that point on he had felt a phantasy identification with the heroic Hannibal.

Although the kind of disillusionment Freud experienced in this incident is in many ways typical of the onset of adolescence, the long persistence of an adolescent emotional pattern and the driving power that the phantasy continued to display in his adult life indicate that his disillusionment was deeply significant and constituted a substantial barrier to the normal process of maturation. Having lost faith in the example of manhood presented by his father, Freud had no adequate model to follow and had difficulty completing the process of growing up. His various close male friendships, all ending in disillusion, constituted unsuccessful attempts to find this essential missing example, and his attitude toward his father settled into an ambivalent mixture of appropriate filial piety with a hostile unconscious feeling that his father was an ineffectual failure. His father's death had further intensified this ambivalence. In remembering the incident that gave rise to his Hannibal phantasy, Freud made an important advance in his efforts at resolving his conflicted attitude: having brought the memory to consciousness, he could examine it in the light of real-life experiences rather than continuing on an unconscious level to measure it against the impossibly heroic standards of adolescent phantasy. As Martin Bergmann observes, "It should be recognized that within the framework of organized Jewish life the behavior of Freud's father was anything but undignified. A Jew was expected to be able to control his anger, not to be provoked; his feelings of inner dignity were sustained by a belief in his own spiritual superiority which a ruffian and 'Goy' can in no way touch."[24] Viewed in this light, Jakob's response was a sensible example of pragmatic restraint and emotional self-control, virtues that Freud had come to admire in Fliess and miss in himself. The conscious recall and reevaluation of this adolescent incident made possible a diminishing of its emotional power, which had highly beneficial consequences for both Freud's emotional life and his intellectual work.

Certain clues suggest how and why he succeeded in remembering it. The death of his father had left Freud in a psychologically vulnerable state at just the time when the political situation called

[24] Bergmann, "Moses," pp. 11–12.

up in his mind memories and feelings of adolescent political radicalism. The disastrous conclusion of Badeni's cabinet negotiations with the promulgation of the language ordinances and the emperor's confirmation of Lueger represented a major triumph of anti-Semitic and anti-German forces, and Freud's dream of a street corner in Rome testifies to his unconscious sympathy for the German cause. Furthermore, the confirmation of Lueger had deep symbolic significance. As Freud observed in interpreting one of his 1898 dreams, "A Prince is known as the father of his country,"[25] a particularly apt expression in the case of Austria-Hungary, for it was a patriarchal, dynastic state held together by loyalty to Franz Josef and the Habsburg family. Freud's observation shows that in the emotional world expressed in his dreams he saw the emperor as a father figure. That being so, Franz Josef's action in confirming Lueger represented a striking reenactment of the incident in which his own father had seemed to bow to anti-Semitic pressure. Moreover, the fact that this event occurred immediately before Passover could only have deepened its emotional significance. Considered in this context, the powerful revival of Freud's Hannibal phantasy in the period from April through September has the character of a full-scale response to this 1897 reenactment of the original incident. This interpretation of events is supported by the fact that Freud formulated his plan for the Italian trip at his Nürnberg meeting with Fliess only days after this momentous political event had occurred.[26]

In accounting for the fact that Freud suddenly became conscious of the reenactment while on his trip to Italy, one must balance a consideration of the external and internal factors at work in the situation. Freud's actions and thoughts were not politically determined in any narrow sense. The political shock waves that buffeted him in the spring and summer of 1897 could affect him powerfully because they resonated so profoundly with the phantasies of his inner world. The relationship between such unconscious phantasies and the emergence of scientific insight in Freud's thinking has been analyzed by Mark Kanzer in connection with another of Freud's self-analytic experiences involving travel, his 1904 trip to Athens. "Interrelationships between the emergence of repressed fantasies and the formation of scientific ideas are repeatedly demonstrated," Kanzer notes. He goes on to point out the conditions favoring the sudden emergence of these insights: "The usual equi-

[25] Freud, *Interpretation, S.E.*, IV:217.
[26] Freud, *Origins*, pp. 194–95.

librium within Freud could be shifted by three interrelated mechanisms. 1) Travel which changed the outer scene; 2) Self-analysis which changed the inner scene; 3) Creative thoughts which combined inner and outer worlds into new designs."[27] All three factors applied to the breakthrough Freud achieved with the reemergence of his repressed Hannibal phantasy.

Freud's own description of this experience illuminates the forces at work in it. It occurred in connection with a quotation from "one of our classical authors" which he suddenly remembered: "Which of the two . . . walked up and down his study with the greater impatience after he had formed his plan of going to Rome—Winckelmann, the Vice-Principal, or Hannibal, the Commander-in-Chief?" Carl Schorske offers an important insight into the nature of the alternatives posed by this quotation, the same alternatives that surface so often in the imagery of Freud's dreams and letters during this period. Noting that in his explanation of the event Freud unhesitatingly identified himself with Hannibal rather than Winckelmann, Schorske observes, "Here Freud conceals an important truth from us, if not from himself. . . . The Rome of his mature dreams and longings is clearly a love object. It is not Hannibal's Rome but that of Johann Joachim Winckelmann, the great eighteenth-century archeologist and art historian. He ardently loved Rome as the mother of European culture. A Protestant, Winckelmann overcame his scruples and embraced Catholicism in order to enter Rome and pursue his passion for classical antiquity as a papal librarian."[28] The choice was the same as that in the Hella dream, where the movement was from vain military conflict to a loving search for timeless classical beauty. Moreover, just as the Hella dream, through its allusion to Faust's journey to ancient Greece in search of Helen, pointed to Freud's prospective return to his early life by means of self-analysis, so in the surfacing of his adolescent memory the figure of Winckelmann had a similar significance. Freud associated archaeological imagery with psychoanalysis throughout his life, and by means of his work as an archaeologist Winckelmann, like Faust, had been able to return to the ancient world and bring back a measure of its beauty and wisdom to his own time, for his writings played an important role in the revival of classical tastes in the late eighteenth century.

Freud indicated that the quotation offering a choice between Hannibal or Winckelmann occurred to him while he "was in the

[27] Kanzer, "Sigmund and Alexander Freud," pp. 352–53.
[28] Schorske, *Vienna*, p. 192.

act of making a plan to by-pass Rome next year and travel to Naples," for Hannibal too "had moved into the Campagna when everyone had expected him in Rome." Here again, Freud's published analysis of the experience neglected the significance of Winckelmann, for he too had "moved into the Campagna," but for a quite different purpose. Winckelmann's most important work was done in connection with the newly rediscovered cities of Pompeii and Herculaneum, both located in the Campagna not far from Naples. Hannibal or Winckelmann? The choice posed in the quotation was the choice confronting Freud in his real life, and however much he may have emphasized the figure of Hannibal as an illustration of the childhood sources of dreams, it was Winckelmann who pointed the way to the future.

By the time he set out on his trip to Italy, Freud was fully engaged in his self-analysis[29] and, as has been seen, that trip was intertwined in the closest way with the psychic return to childhood symbolized in the Hella dream by Faust's return to ancient Greece. In his interpretation of that dream, Freud had continued to adhere to the assumption of paternal guilt implicit in his seduction theory despite the fact that the dream spoke a different message. On an unconscious level, his dream pointed him away from a history of conflict toward an erotic quest for the balance and beauty of the classical world, but the continuing power of his Hannibal fixation prevented him from drawing that conclusion. On a conscious level, however, he had already begun to move in that direction in his description of what he would look for on his trip to Italy. Having, in the course of his self-analysis, cast Fliess in the role of a surrogate father, he now imitated him in looking not for what was of cultural-historical interest but for "absolute beauty," just as he had followed his advice in deciding to write on dreams. In these ways, the beginning stage of Freud's self-analysis, with the increased influence accorded to Fliess as paternal (classical) model, reinforced that element of Freud's psyche which offered an alternative to the violent political defiance of Hannibal. This alternative pointed toward the rational scientific approach Freud had first associated with Joseph, the dream interpreter, who accepted authority and worked skillfully from within to achieve success, as Winckelmann also had done.

Hannibal or Winckelmann? The choice occurred to Freud at just that point where his actual travels intersected with the psychic journey forecast in the Hella dream. It was after he had gone past the site of Hannibal's great victory near Lake Trasimene, had "seen

[29] Schur, *Freud,* pp. 112–13.

the Tiber and sadly turned back . . . only fifty miles from Rome." At this point, he considered the possibility of a future trip to the Campagna, where both Hannibal and Winckelmann had gone before. This thought in itself concealed the psychic alternatives confronting him, and when he remembered the quotation from the classical author it triggered the conscious surfacing of the Hannibal memory.

In remembering the incident on which the Hannibal phantasy rested, Freud achieved the first great success of his self-analysis, and by demonstrating the driving power of phantasy, that breakthrough had dramatic intellectual and emotional consequences. As soon as he got back to Vienna, he wrote Fliess a letter (September 21, 1897) announcing in joyous tones what ought to have been the most discouraging sort of news. He wrote that he had returned feeling "refreshed, cheerful, impoverished and without work. . . . Let me tell you straight away the great secret which has been slowly dawning on me in recent months. I no longer believe in my neurotica." He then enumerated the reasons why he had finally come to reject the seduction theory, the theory that constituted the whole foundation of his attempt at understanding hysteria. First, there was his continuing failure ever to bring an analysis to a successful conclusion. Moreover, in view of the unexpected frequency of hysteria and the surprising fact that "perverse acts by the father" were always suggested as the cause, he found it hard to believe "that perverted acts against children were so general." The third consideration involved the realization that within the unconscious there was no "indication of reality" making it "impossible to distinguish between truth and emotionally-charged fiction." Finally, Freud cited the consideration that, even in the most far-reaching states of psychotic delirium, the memory of the traumatic incident did not break through.[30] It would be a mistake to underestimate the real importance of these various conscious doubts that had accumulated in his mind regarding his theory—but none of them was new, and he could have drawn up the same list in May. The timing of Freud's renunciation of his theory and the feelings associated with its rejection testify strongly to the unconscious motivating forces lying behind this crucial intellectual advance.

It is clear from his letter that Freud felt elated at the theory's collapse. As he observed after enumerating the doubts which led to its abandonment: "Were I depressed, jaded, unclear in mind,

[30] Freud, *Origins*, pp. 215–16.

such doubts might be taken for signs of weakness. But . . . I am in just the opposite state." He went on, "It is curious that I feel not in the least disgraced. . . . I have a feeling more of triumph than of defeat (which cannot be right)."[31] It *was* right as far as Freud's personal situation was concerned, however, for his abandonment of the seduction theory represented the outcome of a crucial psychological triumph over himself and the removal of an intellectual and emotional barrier of major proportions. Once he had consciously regained the memory of the adolescent incident on which his Hannibal phantasy rested, that memory began to lose some of the driving force it had possessed in its repressed state, and hence much of the deep need to blame the father implicit in that incident began to dissipate. When it lost this vital source of unconscious emotional support, Freud's seduction theory, in which "the *father,* not excluding my own, had to be accused of being perverse," became vulnerable to the conscious reservations he had developed, and it was abandoned.[32]

Freud had a directly personal reason to feel elated: if the collapse of the seduction theory cleared fathers in general of responsibility for the neuroses of their children, it also removed his suspicions that his own father was to blame for his neurosis. In a subsequent letter to Fliess, he explicitly discussed this possibility and rejected it, writing that in his own case, his father "played no active role," although he realized that he had "projected on to him an analogy from myself."[33] Freud's September 21 letter announcing the abandonment of his seduction theory was written two days before the end of the eleven-month period of mourning traditional in Jewish families. He thus had good cause to feel pleased, for before the mourning period was over he had begun to make substantial progress in clarifying his feelings toward his father.[34]

Further evidence of Freud's emotional breakthrough in dealing with the conflicted issue of anti-Semitism and his father is provided by his decision to join B'nai B'rith immediately after his return from Italy. This organization, which had been founded in New York for the purpose of helping German-Jewish immigrants orient themselves to their new culture, later spread to Europe where its growth received a powerful impetus from the increase of anti-Semitism.[35] Freud's later statements about his membership as well

[31] Ibid., p. 217.

[32] Freud, *Complete Letters,* p. 264. In *Origins* this passage from the September 21, 1897 letter was censored to omit the reference to his own father.

[33] Freud, *Origins,* p. 219.

[34] Karpe, pp. 25–29.

[35] Klein, *Jewish Origins of the Psychoanalytic Movement,* p. 75.

as the timing of his decision to join suggest that anti-Semitic hostility figured in his specific case. In a 1935 letter to his lodge brothers, he recalled, "I soon became one of you, enjoyed your sympathy and—surrounded by extreme hostility—almost never failed to go to the place where I was certain to find friends." As Dennis Klein argues, this comment suggests that he "sought refuge specifically from anti-Semitic ostracism."[36] Even more suggestive is the timing of his decision. Although approached to join the organization in 1895, he did not do so until September 29, 1897,[37] less than two weeks after his return from Italy. Not only did membership in the B'nai B'rith offer a more sensible answer to anti-Semitic prejudice than the vain emotional heroics of the Hannibal phantasy, but joining it also represented a direct act of reconciliation with the memory of his father: he renounced his unjust adolescent criticism by choosing the same sort of restrained and dignified response to anti-Semitism that Jakob Freud had chosen. In so doing he reaffirmed the values of enlightened humanitarianism in which his father had believed while bringing himself back into closer contact with the traditions of his forefathers.

With the collapse of his seduction theory, Freud redirected the focus of his self-analysis from his previous fixation on psychic conflict involving the father to the theme of erotic attraction to the mother.[38] This theme had manifested itself unconsciously in the imagery of the Hella dream and in the alternative of Winckelmann rather than Hannibal. In his analysis of the dream, however, Freud had seen only a confirmation of the antipaternal seduction theory, and in his analysis of the quotation, only a reenactment of the antipaternal Hannibal phantasy. After his return from a brief visit with Fliess in Berlin, hurriedly scheduled to discuss the new intellectual situation in which he found himself, Freud entered a period of dramatic advances in his self-analysis as well as in his development of a new theoretical framework, and during this period mother figures dominated his thoughts almost as thoroughly as father figures had done previously. Despite his doubts about the seduction theory, Freud's lack of any alternative momentarily brought him back to it from time to time, as in his letter of October 3, where he discussed the results of his most recent dream analysis. But now

[36] Ibid., p. 72.

[37] Ibid., pp. 72, 96.

[38] See Jim Swan, "*Mater* and Nannie: Freud's Two Mothers and the Discovery of the Oedipus Complex," *American Imago* 31 (Spring 1974):1–64; and Kenneth A. Grigg, "All Roads Lead to Rome: The Role of the Nursemaid in Freud's Dreams," *Journal of the American Psychoanalytic Association* 21 (1973):108–26.

his suspicions were focused on the family maid who had taken care of him as a child in Freiburg. He wrote, "my 'primary originator' [of neurosis] was an ugly, elderly, but clever woman who told me a great deal about God and hell."[39] He then went on to say that later when he was about two or two-and-a-half years old "libido toward *matrem* was aroused;" and he indicated that this occurred on the journey involved in the move from Leipzig to Vienna, when "we spent a night together and I must have had the opportunity of seeing her *nudam*."[40] In his conscious acknowledgment of his early sexual attraction to his mother, Freud's use of Latin has significance. He expressed his deeply embedded reservations about confronting such an idea by wrapping his mother's nudity in the solemn purity of this classical language.

The family maid received much less ceremonious consideration, but Freud's dreams and the mixture of memories and phantasies he retrieved through them placed her in a much more central role than his mother. In his letter of October 3 he observed that if he succeeded in resolving his hysteria, he would owe it to "the memory of the old woman who provided me at such an early age with the means for living and surviving." In a continuation of the letter written the next day, Freud recounted a dream that occurred during the intervening night, a dream that revealed still more about the woman. He reported that "she was my instructress in sexual matters"—possibly a reference to the sexual excitation she may have caused in washing him, but at this point Freud seems to have assumed that some kind of "seductive" intent was also involved.[41] This dream also suggested that she had gotten young Sigmund to steal ten Kreuzer coins and give them to her.

At this point Freud still had no firm basis for distinguishing in his analytic work between phantasies and real memories, and at the end of the letter he raised this problem, noting that "a severe critic might say that all this was a phantasy projected into the past instead of being determined by the past." He believed, however, that these were real memories, and to test his belief he decided to ask his mother if she remembered the maid who had cared for him. In response she described a shrewd old woman who had frequently taken him to church; and she went on to reveal what lay behind Freud's memory that the maid had gotten him to steal

[39] Freud, *Origins*, p. 219; two later passages from the letters of Dec. 12 and Dec. 22, 1897 show that Freud was still considering the possible validity of the seduction theory at that time (*Complete Letters*, pp. 286, 288–89).

[40] Freud, *Origins*, p. 219.

[41] Freud, *Origins*, pp. 219–220.

for her.[42] His mother told him that at the time she was confined to bed because of Anna's birth, the woman had taken advantage of the situation "and all the shiny Kreuzers and Zehners and toys that had been given you were found to be among her things." His brother Philipp, she said, had personally summoned the police and the woman had received ten months in jail. Freud took his mother's testimony as confirmation that through his dream analysis he had regained an accurate memory from his earliest years, even though he realized it could also be argued that he might have learned about the woman's theft later in his childhood and simply forgotten about it until it reappeared in his dream. Freud admitted that indeed this must have been the case but put forward as additional evidence for the reality of this early memory another mental fragment that occurred to him in connection with it. He theorized that with the sudden disappearance of a woman who meant so much to him "some impression of the event must have been left inside me. Where was it now?"[43] At that point he recalled the scene—which had been recurring to him for many years without his understanding it—in which he was crying bitterly because his mother was gone and demanding that his brother Philipp open a cupboard because he suspected she was inside. He now understood that the scene expressed his fear that his mother had suffered the same fate as the maid. He also realized that the fact that he turned to his brother Philipp in the screen memory indicated that he knew about "his part in my nurse's disappearance."[44] Freud later came to believe that this scene, like most such early memories reconstructed through analysis, was a screen memory put together from a series of emotionally related memories scattered over time, but at this point he took its emergence as proof that his memories of the maid were real.

Freud's letters also mentioned several other early memories which recurred to him during this analytic breakthrough of late September and early October. In his letter of October 3, after discussing the memories of the maid and of his mother, he recalled his feeling of guilt about the death of his young brother Julius, and his memories of his "companion in crime," his nephew John. His early relationships with these two, Freud concluded, had "determined, not only the neurotic side of all my friendships, but also their depth. My anxiety over travel you have seen yourself. . . ."[45]

[42] Ibid., p. 221.
[43] Ibid., pp. 221–22.
[44] Ibid., p. 223.
[45] Ibid., p. 219.

Freud's reference to his travel anxiety came at the end of the whole list of early associations he had recalled, including his memory of the maid and of seeing his mother nude on the train, and Max Schur has argued that all of them are closely related to the screen memory involving the maid's disappearance, which Freud understood several days later, after he asked his mother about the old woman. Schur argues:

> The affect which comes through most prominently in these reconstructions is the desperate fear of losing the mother. . . . Thus the disappearance of the "nurse" . . . and some very short separations from his mother were condensed in these memories. These events, moreover, occurred against the background of the appearance and disappearance of his brother and the appearance of his sister Anna. . . . We must remember that only a few months after these appearances and disappearances Freud's father and immediate family left Freiberg. . . . At the same time the families of Emanuel and Philipp moved to Manchester, England; thus Freud's playmates as well as his home and the meadows and woods of the rural scene also disappeared. All these "disappearances" were probably condensed in this screen memory.[46]

It should also be added that these reconstructions showed a strong sense of guilt. Freud discussed this feeling explicitly in connection with John and with the death of his brother Julius; the dream fragments involving the maid also suggest pervasive feelings of guilt.

The pattern of strong desire associated with negative consequences and guilt was also linked to the one other reconstruction of his early childhood that Freud mentioned in his October 15 letter to Fliess. In his conversation with his mother about the maid, he had also asked her about a doctor he remembered from their time in Freiberg. Freud wrote that he "had a dream full of animosity about him," and in analyzing the dream his associations led him to connect the doctor with his former history teacher, although he failed to understand why, since he had gotten along well with the teacher. When his mother revealed that the doctor had only one eye, he realized the reason for the association: his history teacher had suffered from the same disability.[47] The one-eyed doctor was connected with a frightening experience from his childhood which Freud recounted in connection with a much later dream: "I had climbed up on to a stool in the store-closet to get

[46] Schur, *Freud,* p. 124.
[47] Freud, *Origins,* p. 222.

something nice that was lying on a cupboard *[Kasten]* or table. The stool had tipped over and its corner had struck me behind my lower jaw; I might easily, I reflected, have knocked out all my teeth. The recollection was accompanied by an admonitory thought: 'that serves you right'.[48] This accident had been serious enough to require the attention of the one-eyed doctor, who stitched up the wound. Here again as in the screen memory of his mother in the cupboard, something good had been *eingekastelt,* and the child's desire to have it led only to sorrow and guilt.

The themes of forbidden desire and guilt haunted the dream of the one-eyed doctor just as they did the screen memory, and Freud's search for the source of this guilt led him in early October to a conclusion which pointed toward a new understanding of human nature. Since Freud's father suffered from unilateral glaucoma and appeared in other dreams in association with one-eyed figures,[49] there can be little doubt that he lay behind the figure of the one-eyed doctor and that the hostility directed at the doctor actually involved him. Taken together with the maternal reference involved in the child's experience of coming to grief while trying to get something nice from the *Kasten,* this dream, it can be seen, alluded to both desire for the mother and antipathy toward the father, the two sources of Oedipus' guilt. The dream and its analysis provided the introduction for Freud's first statement of the Oedipal theory, for after having reported to Fliess what he had learned from his mother about the one-eyed doctor and the family maid he went on to suggest the central importance of the myth of Oedipus to his new self-understanding. Summing up the results of his analytic work, he observed that he had drawn from it, "one idea of general value. . . . I have found love of the mother and jealousy of the father in my own case too, and now believe it to be a general phenomenon of early childhood. . . . If that is the case, the gripping power of *Oedipus Rex* . . . becomes intelligible. . . . Every member of the audience was once a budding Oedipus in phantasy."[50] Here at the bottom layer of his psychic dig, Freud's search for the sexual basis of hysteria revealed not fact but phantasy, not history but myth, and as in the case of Oedipus, his unexpected discovery implied that he himself was the guilty party.

In May, Freud's Hella dream had prefigured the route of his analytic return to earliest childhood by alluding to Faust's journey back to the mythic realm of ancient Greece, and the imagery of

[48] Freud, *Interpretation, S.E.,* V:560.
[49] Ibid., IV:216.
[50] Freud, *Origins,* p. 223.

Freud's October letters suggests that in the period following his theoretical breakthrough Faust continued to be his guide but that now it was the aged Faust who, like Oedipus, was blinded at the moment of his deepest self-knowledge. Near the end of the drama when Faust confronted the ghostly figure of *Sorge* (care or anxiety), following his unwitting crime against Baucis and Philamon, he renounced any external aid and relied solely on his own inner strength. This final struggle, which represented his achievement of inner autonomy and freedom, was balanced by the loss of his vision, for in the course of the struggle *Sorge* put out his eyes. Despite this tragic loss, it was a moment of triumph for Faust, and he could declare, "Deep falls the night in gloom precipitate; What then? Clear light within my mind shines still." In the following scene Faust had his final vision: "Such busy, teeming throngs I long to see, / Standing on freedom's soil, a people free."[51] This soil—to be won from the sea along the Dutch coast—symbolized the eternal need of human beings to win their freedom anew by learning to channel their inner passions toward a fruitful goal. This was the vision to which Thomas Mann pointed in mentioning Freud's comparison of analysis to the draining of the Zuider Zee, and despite its far-reaching social and political implications, Faust's vision, as well as Freud's, was clearly and specifically detached from the particular outer reality of his time. It was a timeless and eternal vision realizable only through inner conquest of oneself.

Carl Schorske has observed that one "peculiarity of Freud's treatment of Oedipus related to the problem of neutralizing politics. Freud pays no attention to the fact that Oedipus was king. . . . Not so for the Greeks. Sophocles' *Oedipus Rex* is unthinkable except as *res publica,* with its regal hero motivated by political obligation: to remove the plague from Thebes."[52] Freud's sense of political obligation had crystallized in his Hannibal phantasy, and only a month before his discovery of the Oedipus complex, the conscious realization that he was retracing Hannibal's footsteps had vividly shown him that political passions had the power to determine his actions regardless of his conscious intent. Freud responded to this demonstrated infringement of his freedom just as the blinded Faust did after the tragedy of Baucis and Philomen had shown him the vanity of his attempts at social reform; he became blind to the outer world of society and politics in order to see more clearly the vision of freedom opened up through his new understanding of the inner man.

[51] *Faust, Part Two,* pp. 267, 269.
[52] Schorske, *Vienna,* p. 199.

The letters Freud wrote to Fliess in the weeks following his first statement of the Oedipal theory betray an attitude of inner concentration reminiscent of the blinded Faust. On October 27 he wrote that he had nothing to report about himself except what involved his analysis: "I am living only for 'inner' work."[53] In his next letter, written four days later, he spoke of the way his moods "often completely hide reality." In the same letter he wrote, "My own analysis is going on, and it remains my chief interest. Everything is still dark . . . but at the same time I have a reassuring feeling that one has only to put one's hand in one's store-cupboard to be able to extract . . . what one needs."[54] For Freud as for Faust, there was darkness without but light within. The October 27 letter also contained implicit and explicit allusions to Goethe's drama. In an image reminiscent of Faust's journey through time in Part Two, Freud said of his analysis, "It gets hold of me and hauls me through the past in rapid association of ideas."[55] He went on to quote from the dedication of Goethe's *Faust:*

> And many well loved spirits rise
> Like an ancient half remembered myth
> First love and friendship come to view.[56]

Freud's blindness to reality was in part a temporary and natural manifestation of the intensity of his analytic work, but a dream of the same period shows that his analytic breakthrough produced an enduring determination to turn a blind eye to politics. The dream of Dr. Lecher reveals what was to be an ongoing counterpolitical stance expressing Freud's determination to reduce politics to an epiphenomenon of human psychological nature and to employ psychoanalytic insight as a tool for depriving a hysterical political world of its hold on his emotions. Both his account and his analysis of the Dr. Lecher dream were quite brief: "I saw in the window of a book-shop a new volume in one of the series of monographs . . . on great artists, on world history, on famous cities, etc. *The new series was called 'Famous Speakers' or 'Speeches' and its first volume bore the name of Dr. Lecher.*" In his analysis Freud wrote that "it seemed to me improbable that I should be concerned in my dreams with the fame of Dr. Lecher, the non-stop speaker of the German obstructionists in Parliament. The position *[Sachverhalt]* was that

[53] Freud, *Origins,* p. 225.
[54] Ibid., p. 227.
[55] Ibid., p. 225.
[56] Freud, *Anfängen,* p. 240; my translation.

a few days earlier I had taken on some new patients for psychological treatment and was now obliged to talk for ten or eleven hours every day. So it was I myself who was a non-stop speaker."[57] Since Dr. Otto Lecher delivered his famous speech on October 28–29, 1897, Freud's dream must have occurred after that date, most probably on or about the 29th or 30th. This dating is supported by a passage from his October 31 letter to Fliess, which mentioned the new patients: "As I have time on my hands I have decided to take on two cases without fee. That, including my own, makes three analyses which bring in nothing."[58] In *The Interpretation of Dreams,* Freud used this dream as an example of the inevitable egoism of dreams in the section immediately following his discussion of the Oedipal theory, so it occupied the same position in his theoretical exposition that it did in the actual chronological development of his thought.

Dr. Lecher's speech came at a crucial moment in an unfolding German-Czech crisis that threatened Austria with revolution more seriously than at any time since 1848. Through most of the summer Freud's absence from Vienna—first his vacation with his family in Aussee and then his trip to Italy—had taken him away from the growing political turmoil, but during that time the German opposition to the Badeni language ordinances had steadily mounted in intensity. The bitterness of the political conflict found expression in a duel fought on September 15, a few days after Freud's return from Italy, between the minister-president, Count Badeni, and Karl Hermann Wolf, a leader of the most radical German nationalist group in parliament. Badeni had agreed to the duel and simultaneously offered his resignation to the emperor in the apparent hope that if the resignation were accepted under such circumstances it would offer a graceful and honorable way out of the crisis, but the emperor responded to the mounting calls for the minister's dismissal by refusing the resignation and expressing his deepest sympathy when Badeni was wounded.[59] In the parliamentary arena, the opposition of the German parties manifested itself in their efforts to obstruct the conduct of business and thereby force Badeni to terms. The tactic was effective because the government faced an urgent deadline on legislation of fundamental importance to

[57] Freud, *Interpretation, S.E.,* IV:268, 269. The published English translation, "German Nationalist obstructionists," is an error which falsely suggests that Lecher was a member of the Pan-German party.

[58] Freud, *Origins,* p. 227.

[59] Friedrich Kornauth, "Graf Badeni als Ministerpresident" (Diss., University of Vienna, 1949), pp. 93–94.

the Empire. The Ausgleich between Austria and Hungary, the treaty governing the full range of commercial and economic relations between the two halves of the Empire, expired in 1897, and it was essential to complete passage of the renegotiated treaty through the Austrian Reichsrath by December 1, the deadline set by the Hungarians. Lecher's speech aimed to thwart the government's efforts to secure passage of this legislation.

In Freud's dream, the book he saw bearing Lecher's name was entitled *Famous Speakers* or *Speeches,* and this element of the dream image involved no exaggeration. Dr. Lecher's speech won him international attention and at least a measure of fame, since it inspired two important thinkers to mention him in their work. One of the thinkers was Freud—although his laconic reference does scant justice to the heroic proportions of Dr. Lecher's speech, and the other was Mark Twain, who was in Austria closely observing political events, and who made the speech the dramatic centerpiece of his essay "Stirring Times in Austria." The contrast between Twain's enthusiastic sixteen-page account of the speech and the highly reserved fourteen lines Freud devoted to both the dream and its analysis is striking, for in most respects including their politics, the tastes and temperaments of these two men were closely aligned. When asked later in his life to list "ten good books," Freud included a work by Mark Twain,[60] and when Twain delivered a reading from his works during his stay in Vienna, Freud attended and reported to Fliess that he had greatly enjoyed hearing "our old friend, Mark Twain, in person."[61] If Twain was sufficiently moved by Lecher's speech to describe it as an "important spiritual accomplishment,"[62] why did Freud so lightly dismiss the possibility that he too might have been sympathetic to Lecher? A close examination of Twain's account reveals a multitude of factors that suggest why Freud might have identified with Dr. Lecher, and once the nature of this identification is understood it will be seen that Freud's analysis of the dream gives evidence of his new attitude toward politics.

Mark Twain began his account with a graphic portrayal of the conflict-ridden Austrian parliament. He described the clamor which greeted the announcement by the chair that "Dr. Lecher has the floor . . . Yells from the Left, counter yells from the Right,

[60] Jones, III:422.

[61] Freud, *Origins,* p. 245. Freud and Twain also had a close friend in common, Friedrich Eckstein; see Eckstein, *"Alte unnennbare Tage!"* pp. 274–81.

[62] Karl Stiehl, "Mark Twain in der Wiener Presse zur Zeit seines Aufenthaltes in Wien 1897–1899" (Diss., University of Vienna, 1953), p. 32.

explosions of yells from all sides at once, and all the air sawed and pawed and cloven by a writhing confusion of gesturing arms and hands." The bearing of Twain's hero stood in sharp contrast to this seething cauldron of emotion: "Out of the midst of this thunder and turmoil and tempest rose Dr. Lecher, serene and collected, and the providential length of him enabled his head to show out above it. He began his twelve-hour speech. At any rate, his lips could be seen to move and that was evidence."[63] Although Lecher opposed the government, the forces of the opposition were badly split, with each faction hoping to gain public support and attention by outdoing the others in inflicting delays and setbacks on the government. For this reason Lecher, who was a representative of the Liberal center, found himself opposed both by the conservative forces in control of the chair and the more radical Pan-German nationalists led by Wolf, the anti-Semitic demagogue who had recently fought the duel with Badeni. Wolf repeatedly attempted to interrupt Lecher and gain recognition for a motion he wished to introduce.[64] Failing in the effort, he began hurling insults to which, according to Mark Twain, the chair "blandly answered that Dr. Lecher had the floor. Which was true, and he was speaking, too, calmly, earnestly, and argumentatively; and the official stenographers had left their places and were at his elbows taking down his words, he leaning and orating into their ears—a most curious and interesting scene."[65] In spite of the taunting of Wolf's followers, Lecher steadfastly refused to descend to their level and held his ground against their effort to usurp the floor.

But although the presiding officer repeatedly supported Lecher against attempts to interrupt him, the chair was by no means favorably disposed toward him. He had been recognized because the rules required that a certain number of opposition speakers be heard before a vote could be called, and it was the government's intention to hear him out, quickly call a vote, and then refer the legislation to committee, all in one sitting: "But into the government's calculations," Twain noted, "had not entered the possibility of a single-barreled speech which should occupy the entire time limit of the sitting, and also get itself delivered in spite of all the noise."[66] Ordinarily the government could expect to defeat such a filibuster because the rules of the Austrian parliament were strict

[63] Mark Twain, "Stirring Times in Austria," *The Writings of Mark Twain,* 22 (New York: Harper, 1929), 209.
[64] Ibid., p. 210.
[65] Ibid., p. 211.
[66] Ibid., p. 217.

in demanding that speeches be relevant to the subject under debate. As Twain explained, "In the English House an obstructionist has held the floor with Bible-readings and other outside matters; but Dr. Lecher could not have that restful and recuperative privilege—he must confine himself strictly to the subject before the House. More than once, when the President could not hear him because of the general tumult, he sent persons to listen and report as to whether the orator was speaking to the subject or not."[67] So in addition to fending off interruptions from the more radical nationalists such as Wolf, Lecher also had to be constantly on guard lest the chair try to withdraw the floor on the grounds that he was not speaking to the subject.

The real triumph of Lecher's speech lay not so much in the fact that it was in Twain's words, "the longest flow of unbroken talk that ever came out of one mouth since the world began," as in the fact that the entire twelve-hour oration was all strictly to the point.[68] Moreover, as Twain observed, "The subject was a peculiarly difficult one, and it would have troubled any other deputy to stick to it three hours without exhausting his ammunition, because it required a vast and intimate knowledge . . . of the commercial, railroading, financial and international banking relations between two great sovereignties, Hungary and the Empire." However, as president of the board of trade in his native city of Brünn (in Moravia), Lecher had the necessary information at his disposal. "His speech was not formally prepared," Twain wrote. "He had a few notes jotted down for his guidance; he had his facts in his head; his heart was in his work; and for twelve hours he stood there, undisturbed by the clamour around him, and with grace and ease and confidence poured out the riches of his mind, in closely reasoned arguments, clothed in eloquent and faultless phrasing."[69] Gradually as the night wore on and Lecher continued to hold forth with undiminished vigor and clarity, even members of the government majority began to be moved by admiration of his unprecedented performance. "When Dr. Lecher had been speaking eight hours he was still compactly surrounded by friends who would not leave him and by foes (of all parties) who *could* not; and all hung enchanted and wondering upon his words, and all testified their admiration with constant and cordial outbursts of applause. Surely this was a triumph without precedent in history."[70] So having

[67] Ibid.
[68] Ibid., p. 206.
[69] Ibid., pp. 217, 218.
[70] Ibid., p. 220.

persevered through the attempts of the impassioned radicals to interrupt his delivery and having outwitted the chair through extraordinary intelligence, endurance, and lucidity, Lecher finally found himself in a position where even his enemies were willing to acknowledge the magnitude of his accomplishment.

Although Twain's narrative vividly conveys his unabashed enthusiasm for Lecher's performance, the evidence indicates that his account was accurate and his reaction typical of that segment of the political spectrum to which Freud belonged. The paper Freud read, the *Neue Freie Presse,* reviewed and quoted extensively from Twain's essay after it was published in *Harper's* in early 1898, and the review praised the careful accuracy of his report as well as his thorough understanding of the political situation.[71] The liberal historian Richard Charmatz also noted that this event "created a great sensation not only because of the endurance of the speaker, but also because of the profound content and strict objectivity of his speech." He added that on October 31 when Lecher returned to Brünn, the city he represented, twenty thousand people met him at the train station and welcomed him "like a military commander who has emerged victorious from a difficult battle."[72] By all accounts, then, Lecher's speech made him an overnight sensation, and among members of the political and social circles to which Freud belonged it aroused particularly intense admiration.

In Freud's dream, a number of surface factors stand out as conducive to a close identification with this famous speaker. Lecher had gained the widespread fame and admiration for which Freud longed, and he had won it in a heroic manner reminiscent of Freud's adolescent phantasies of military glory. Lecher, like Freud, was a member of the liberal German middle class; he represented a city in Moravia not far from the village where Freud was born, and he spoke on behalf of a political cause with which Freud sympathized—at least in his dream life. Moreover, Lecher possessed a range of character traits ideally suited to arouse Freud's admiration. He was serene and untroubled in the face of the violent emotional storm raging around him; he was a man of masterful intellect who displayed a comprehensive understanding of the difficult subject under discussion; he responded like a gentleman to Wolf's insults; he was a polished and eloquent orator. All in all, it is difficult to imagine a politician who could more fully have represented the range of personal values and political views that Freud admired.

[71] *Neue Freie Presse,* Feb. 24, 1898.
[72] Charmatz, *Österreichs innere Geschichte,* II:114.

Nonetheless, Freud's interpretation of the dream brushed aside any possibility that political sympathies could have brought about his identification with Lecher and pointed rather to professional activities as the real subject of the underlying dream thoughts, an interpretation that would be plausible were it not so one-sided. Focusing simply on the extraordinary length of Lecher's speech, he noted that he had very recently taken on some new patients and was obliged to be "a non-stop speaker," talking for ten or eleven hours every day. Initially, Freud's interpretation seems odd; and there is no reason to believe that he was then a more active or talkative analyst than later. But in one of the new cases he was both analyst and patient, and was thus obliged to do a double dose of "talking." In the letter to Fliess which coincided with this dream (October 31), and which mentioned that he had taken on two new cases without fee, Freud added, "That, including my own, makes three analyses which bring in nothing. My own analysis is going on, and it remains my chief interest."[73] This comment shows that Freud included his self-analysis among the new cases and, if one considers the egoistic nature of dreams as well as the fact that he describes it as his "chief interest," it seems evident that it was primarily his own analysis which had made him a non-stop speaker. Indeed his letters to Fliess show that during the preceding weeks he had been in a state of almost non-stop analysis, as each night's dreams produced new material from his early life and then led into the next night's dreams.[74] So like Lecher's, his speech went on through the night.

Considering Freud's own interpretation in conjunction with the dream's political allusions makes possible a much more comprehensive understanding of the dream. Because Lecher's filibuster aimed at thwarting the government's attempt to stifle discussion of the Ausgleich, Freud's identification with him aligned psychoanalysis with freedom of speech, thereby recapitulating an associative pattern which appeared often in his images and dream life. Moreover, the political context of the speech had several similarities to Freud's conception of hysteria. Lecher spoke at a time of intense political polarization when all effective communication between a repressive government and a highly emotional popular opposition had ceased and parliament had lapsed into a state of paralysis. The chaotic parliamentary scene paralleled the inner chaos of hysterical disorder which Freud saw as resulting from an ummediated psychic

[73] Freud, *Origins,* p. 227.
[74] Ibid., pp. 218–19, 221, 225, 227.

conflict between the forces of repression and libidinal desire. Lecher's extraordinary accomplishment lay in the fact that in the world of politics he had momentarily bridged this yawning chasm, for his speech effectively translated the passionate desires of the opposition into the kinds of rational, factual arguments that the government had at least to listen to if not respect. Through a masterful and determined exercise of his basic parliamentary right to freedom of speech, he had warded off the distractions of the emotional hotheads such as Wolf and, by sticking strictly to the subject, prevented the government's ally in the chair from breaking off his speech. What Lecher accomplished in parliament closely resembled what Freud aimed at achieving through analysis, where speech provided the medium for translating repressed emotional desires into consciously understood needs.

Another detail of the dream's political allusions also tied in closely with Freud's self-analysis. As Mark Twain noted in his account of the speech, the tremendous amount of noise generated by the obstructionists actually prevented Lecher from being heard much of the time and made it necessary for the official stenographers to move from their places so that he could deliver his oration directly into their ears. So Lecher's speech reached its audience first through the written rather than the spoken word—also the case with Freud's self-analysis, in contrast to the analyses of his patients. Even though Freud frequently referred to Fliess as his audience or his public, he had to be content with sending off the results of his self-analysis to Fliess in the form of letters. Moreover, Freud always felt great frustration when he thought his "audience" was not paying close enough attention,[75] and he found himself in this situation at the time of the Dr. Lecher dream. On October 15 he had revealed to Fliess the results of his most far-reaching attempts at reconstructing the key events of his early emotional development and had concluded his letter by elaborating the various elements of the Oedipal theory, the theory which was to provide a new foundation for his thought and which more than any other single idea was to make him world famous. His eagerness for a response is seen in the first sentence of his next letter (October 27), which began with the comment that he was unable "to 'wait' for your answer," and went on to speculate in a joking manner about the reasons for Fliess's silence.[76] Shortly thereafter, Freud received a letter from his friend to which he responded on October 31, but that letter

[75] See ibid., p. 194.
[76] Ibid., p. 225.

still contained no reaction to the all-important analysis of the Oedipus myth. Finally, on November 5, Freud began his letter by referring to his need for encouragement; several paragraphs later he observed that Fliess had said nothing in response to his new idea and asked him specifically for his reaction to the "interpretation of *Oedipus Rex* and *Hamlet.* As I have not said anything about it to anyone else, because I can imagine the hostile reception it would get, I should be glad to have some short comment on it from you."[77] Like Lecher, Freud had to contend with an unresponsive audience as he began to develop his masterful analysis of the basic problems disturbing the "psychic polity."

The dream of Dr. Lecher fulfilled a wish to overcome all these frustrating obstacles standing in the way of success and fame. Despite almost insurmountable difficulties, Lecher had persisted in his speech with such skill that eventually even his enemies began to listen and react with favor. Freud had displayed a similar tenacity through much of his early career, persisting in the exploration of subjects such as hypnosis, male hysteria, and dream interpretation, subjects that much of the Viennese medical establishment regarded with suspicion. As he indicated in his letter to Fliess, he expected a similarly hostile reaction to his Oedipal theory. Through his identification with Lecher, Freud's dream thoughts suggested that fame and acceptance would be the reward for enduring the unresponsiveness of his "audience" and the hostile criticism of his enemies. In the dream image he saw Dr. Lecher's oration transformed into a book, and since he identified himself with the non-stop speaker, the book was also his book. *The Interpretation of Dreams*—begun several months earlier—contained the results of Freud's self-analysis, so it was his own non-stop speaking, which was being turned into a book, and as subsequent history has shown the wish that the book might bring him fame was fulfilled.

Freud's dream of Dr. Lecher was the first of his political dreams to which he gave an openly counterpolitical interpretation. Earlier in the year, his uncle dream and the dream of a street corner in Rome had betrayed his emotional engagement in the political events going on around him, and Freud had so indicated in his analyses. In his interpretation of the Dr. Lecher dream, however, he relied on the parallel between politics and psychoanalysis while denying that he could have been concerned with Lecher's political fame. The psychological developments associated with Freud's summer trip to Italy set in motion forces that substantially altered his

[77] Ibid., p. 229.

emotional relationship to the political world in which he lived, and his counterpolitical interpretation reveals one of the most important intellectual repercussions of his self-analytic breakthrough. In his Hannibal phantasy Freud had symbolically taken up the struggle against Rome abandoned by his father and projected into it the full force of adolescent anger and disappointment which his father's apparent cowardice seemed to justify. Paradoxically, the phantasy expressed both a filial obligation to fulfill the political promise his father had seen in him and a directly antagonistic desire to triumph over his father; and this ambivalence characterized Freud's attitude toward authority and his father through much of his adult life. With his father's death, the frustrations of his hope for promotion, and the deterioration of the political situation, this inner conflict greatly intensified. Its power can be seen in the itinerary of the Italian journey, which he suddenly realized was a retracing of Hannibal's footsteps. Simultaneously with this realization, Freud brought to consciousness the choice that expressed this ambivalence, the choice between defiant Hannibal, heroic but unsuccessful, and the man who compromised with Rome to achieve brilliant intellectual success, Winckelmann.

Freud's actions show that his choice was for Winckelmann and the classical balance of ancient Greece rather than the continued political antagonism and strife symbolized by Rome and medieval Catholicism. Within a month of his return from the summer voyage of self-discovery, Freud accomplished two fundamentally important, interrelated tasks. In his scientific work he revolutionized his theoretical assumptions by discarding the seduction hypothesis and moving toward a unified conception of neurotic and normal development based on the workings of the Oedipus complex. Simultaneously, in his personal life, his self-analysis broke through the emotional barriers represented by his adolescent fixation on political struggle in the image of Hannibal and penetrated much more deeply into the apolitical world of early childhood. Within this context, the new counterpolitical thrust of Freud's dream interpretation becomes intelligible. Having discovered that he was literally driven by political frustration, Freud set about trying to free himself from the neurotic compulsions associated with the world of politics, and his newly deepened understanding of the human psyche provided him with the necessary resources for this task. Having moved toward an exoneration of "the father," emotionally by recalling the story of the anti-Semitic incident and intellectually by abandoning the seduction theory, Freud now came to regard political reality *per se* as his real antagonist. Politics had raised and then dashed his father's hopes just as thoroughly as it had his own, and as a result of his Italian journey he realized that the answer to this frustration lay in the direction pursued by Winckelmann, the scientist, rather than Hannibal, the warrior. Freud would conquer his political frustrations through scientific understanding rather than continued combat. His interpretation of the Dr. Lecher dream evidenced this new-found determination. Political feelings were dismissed as insignificant in themselves and reduced to the deeper meaning represented by his analytic work. Freud's interpretation represented a wish-fulfillment no less than the dream itself—the wish to free himself from the power of politics.

6/

The Psychic Polity

The analytic breakthrough Freud achieved in the summer and fall of 1897 led him to reconsider his most basic theoretical assumptions and substantially altered the internal balance of emotional forces manifested in his dream life. It also brought him to the point where he could begin work in earnest on *The Interpretation of Dreams.* Even after the fall of 1897, when Freud first suggested the story of Oedipus as a timeless model of human nature, he continued to grope for an adequate theoretical structure and sometimes returned in his uncertainty to the seduction theory. Through his writing of *The Interpretation of Dreams,* however, he was gradually able to develop a theoretical framework that allowed him to explain the nature of dreams and neurotic symptoms as well as a variety of other psychological phenomena such as jokes, slips of the tongue, and lapses of memory.

In his search for theoretical clarity, as in his parallel and closely related search for emotional stability, Freud worked primarily through the analysis of his own dreams. His early philosophical and psychological training with Brentano, as well as his reading of Feuerbach, had taught him the value of seeking to understand psychological phenomena through the comparative study of inner perception and outer observation. This technique proved particularly fruitful during the period of his self-analysis when his own highly political dreams suggested a close parallel between the inner world of feeling and the outer sociopolitical realm, where nationalistic passions raged out of control. Freud drew on that parallel in formulating his theory, and in an expanded concept of censorship as the agency controlling wishes he found the clarity and balance he was seeking. At the same time, in giving a political dimension to his scientific work on dreams, he provided a therapeutic outlet for his frustrated political drives. From late 1897 through the first half of 1898 Freud poured his thoughts and feelings into what he later called "the finest—and probably the only lasting—discovery that I have made,"[1] and when his work finally ground to a temporary halt in the summer of 1898 he had brought the first scientific treatment of dream interpretation the greater part of the way to completion.

While Freud wrote, the political world around him moved closer to revolution than at any previous moment in his life. Although he had abandoned any sympathy for radical politics long before, Freud's deep emotional investment in politics allowed these stirring events to play an important role in the formulation of his own revolutionary theory of dreams. They were dramatic times by any standard. The climax of the crisis enveloping the Badeni government came in late November, and as Mark Twain said, "It takes its imposing place among the world's unforgettable things. I think that in my lifetime I have not twice seen abiding history made before my eyes, but I know that I have seen it once."[2] After Lecher's epic speech, the German opposition continued to use the rules of the house to obstruct consideration of the Ausgleich, and the government failed to recover the parliamentary initiative to secure its passage. Finally, in a desperate gamble, the government resorted to repressive force. On November 25, with the house in such a state of deafening chaos, that he was heard only by those immediately surrounding him, one of the conservative leaders, Count Franz Falkenhayn, read a motion calling for far-reaching changes in the rules of the house, changes that would allow the government to use force, if necessary to bring order.[3] The presiding officer immediately put the motion to a vote, calling for all those in favor to stand. As Twain described the situation, "The House was already standing up; had been standing for an hour; and before a third of it had found out what the President had been saying, he had proclaimed the adoption of the motion! And only a few heard that. In fact, when that House is legislating you can't tell it from an artillery practice."[4] Although the opposition objected to the legality of this maneuver, the government held its ground and employed the new law to expel those members of parliament who continued to protest.

[1] Freud, *Origins,* p. 281.
[2] Twain, "Stirring Times in Austria," p. 242.
[3] Charmatz, *Österreichs innere Geschichte,* II:116.
[4] Twain, p. 238.

The next escalation in the conflict came when the Social Democrats, who had hitherto stood aloof from both sides, expressed their outrage at the *Lex Falkenhayn* by physically seizing control of the rostrum and expelling the presiding officers. The government responded by calling in armed police to restore the ousted officials. With this stroke the government lost all. On November 26 Vienna witnessed massive demonstrations in front of the city hall, the parliament and the Ministry of the Interior, and these initial demonstrations, led mainly by students and intellectuals, were repeated with growing support from workers the following day. Richard Charmatz described the situation on Sunday, November 28: "Vienna had the appearance of a city in which an insurrection might break out at any moment. The Ring Streets overflowed with people who appeared ready for the worst. From thousands of throats roared out the cry 'Down with Badeni.' "[5] By this time the Badeni government had in fact already fallen. The previous evening the emperor had called in his minister to ask for his resignation, and in order to calm the masses the news was announced later on Sunday in special editions of the *Weiner Zeitung.*

While the Viennese greeted the news of Badeni's fall with joy, the inhabitants of Prague reacted with outrage. Mark Twain wrote that "there were three or four days of furious rioting in Prague; . . . the Jews and Germans were harried and plundered, and their houses destroyed; in other Bohemian towns there was rioting—in some cases the Germans being the rioters, in others the Czechs—and in all cases the Jew had to roast, no matter which side he was on."[6] Freud referred to these Prague riots in a letter to Fliess written on December 3, when martial law had finally restored a measure of order, and his comment provides evidence of a new dimension in his reaction to political danger. Noting that he had recently come to a standstill in his analytic work, Freud observed that unlike other forms of work this kind could not be forced. "I have to wait until things move inside me and I experience them. . . . You must know that the events in Prague *[die Ereignisse in Prague]* have proven me right."[7] His point in mentioning the "events in Prague" had to do with the attitude of inner perception he had just described: he felt that these events had justified him in paying close attention to the voice of his unconscious and following its lead. He went on to explain what he meant by relating his earlier dream of a street corner in Rome, the dream that

[5] Charmatz, II:117.
[6] Twain, p. 243.
[7] Freud, *Origins,* p. 236; retranslated from Freud, *Anfängen,* p. 251.

reflected a wish to substitute a trip to Rome for the planned trip to Prague. This dream had expressed his nationalist sentiments as well as fears for his safety in Prague, but in fact, no significant anti-German reaction occurred at that time. However, with the anti-German and anti-Semitic outbursts that followed the fall of Badeni eight months later, the fears expressed in the dream seemed to be confirmed. Freud thus felt justified in claiming that the Prague riots had proven him right.

In Freud's letter, political events assumed significance as evidence for the truth of his inner perception, a reflection of the new attitude toward politics emerging from his analytic and intellectual breakthrough of summer and fall. As Max Schur observed of this period, "He now knew that he had solved one of the great riddles of nature. With this conviction he also achieved an inner independence."[8] This attitude of inner independence can be seen not only in Freud's relationship with Fliess (Schur's point), but also in his increasingly conscious understanding of the hold politics and religion had on his emotions. Having returned from the realm of the mothers with the Oedipal key to sexuality, he now set about using his theory to explain the religious and political issues that had become so closely intertwined with sexuality in his own psycho-intellectual development. In his next letter to Fliess (December 12), he applied his theory to religious myth in a passage that strongly echoed the outlook of Feuerbach: "The dim inner perception of one's own psychical apparatus stimulates illusions, which are naturally projected outwards, and characteristically into the future and a world beyond. Immortality, retribution, the world after death, are all reflections of our inner psyche . . . psycho-mythology."[9] The explicit application of the theory to politics did not come until some months later, but even in the December 3 letter, he pointed up the Oedipal origins of his own political passions by indicating their relationship to his Hannibal phantasy. After recounting the street corner dream, he expressed his belief that his wish to go to Rome was "deeply neurotic" and connected it with his adolescent admiration "of the Semitic Hannibal." As he went on to observe, "in fact this year I have no more reached Rome than he did from Lake Trasimene."[10] Here, for the first time, Freud revealed to Fliess the central discovery of this Italian journey, the discovery that his political desire to vanquish Rome rested on his Hannibal

[8] Schur, *Freud*, p. 139.
[9] Freud, *Origins*, p. 237.
[10] Ibid., p. 236.

phantasy and that it had literally driven him to retrace his hero's footsteps.

Freud could expect that in explaining to Fliess, his surrogate analyst, the neurotic origins of his political drives he would begin to dissipate their emotional power by opening them to rational analysis. This expectation constituted a basic assumption of his analytic technique, and the conclusion that he was here applying it to himself is supported by comparison of the letter with a passage from the work which he explicitly described as a piece of his self-analysis: *The Interpretation of Dreams.* Here in Chapter V, "Material and Sources of Dreams," he followed exactly the same line of thought—first discussing the street corner dream and then turning immediately to his Hannibal fixation.[11] Freud's letter as well as his book reflects his effort to consolidate on an emotional level what he had gained intellectually in his analytic breakthrough. Having realized that his "neurotic" political feelings drew much of their strength from his ambivalent attitude toward his father, Freud now had to learn to neutralize his political feelings as part of his more mature understanding and acceptance of his father's unheroic response to anti-Semitism. In the December 3 letter to Fliess, he relieved the emotional pressure aroused by the anti-Semitic riots in Prague by offering his friend a scientific explanation of his powerful political drives. Political passion would yield to scientific discovery.

The process of transforming political frustration into scientific success influenced Freud's most fundamental theoretical formulations in his work on *The Interpretation of Dreams,* and to understand how and why this happened it is necessary to bear in mind the complex changes set in motion by the first successes of his self-analysis. The most fundamental change involved Freud's attitude toward his father. By recalling the experience of adolescent disillusionment underlying his Hannibal phantasy, Freud prepared the way for a more dispassionate and adult view of his father's conduct. Jakob Freud had in fact behaved with dignity and self-control toward the anti-Semite, so once the unrealistic adolescent expectations fell away, so too did one of the chief obstacles to Freud's ability to identify with his father and to be more comfortable with the view of himself as a father.

At the same time, Freud embarked on a collision course in his friendship with Fliess.[12] Particularly from the time of their April

[11] Freud, *Interpretation, S.E.,* IV:195–96.
[12] Schur, *Freud,* pp. 115–52.

1897 meeting, strong transference elements had developed on Freud's part, elements involving both father and brother figures. For example, the balance and restraint Freud repeatedly attributed to his friend seems in fact quite uncharacteristic of Fliess's wildly speculative theories and can be more plausibly understood as an unconscious preparation for Freud's reevaluation of these qualities in his father. Evidence of Freud's diminishing regard for Fliess and his ideas can be seen near the end of Freud's November 14 letter, the letter which elaborated for the first time his theory on the development of the libido. He declared that he had decided to abandon the notion of regarding repression as a feminine factor and libido as a masculine one.[13] With this decision Freud took an important step away from the bisexual hypothesis that had previously tied his theoretical speculations to Fliess's. Even though Freud subsequently reaffirmed his belief in the centrality of bisexuality, he continued to move away from it in his work.

The incipient conflict between the two friends surfaced as a result of their December meeting in Breslau. At this meeting Freud declined to accept Fliess's extension of the bisexual hypothesis into a theory of universal bilaterality, a theory that argued for the existence of a masculine right side and a feminine left side in all human beings. In his letter of December 29, Freud noted their disagreement with apparent regret and observed that they had not differed on such an issue for a long time. In the following letter he tried to temper Fliess's strong reaction to this open skepticism. "It interests me," he wrote on January 4, "that you should take it so amiss that I am still unable to accept your interpretation of left-handedness."[14] He then went on to explain his doubts in the most conciliatory way possible, even suggesting vaguely toward the end of the letter that unconscious motives might account, after all, for his reservations. The letter leaves little doubt that he had begun to hide from Fliess and perhaps from himself the true depth of his skepticism for the purpose of preserving their friendship.

The increasing ambivalence of Freud's feelings for Fliess represents but one of the significant changes which his psychoanalytic breakthrough wrought in his inner emotional constellation, and these changes also manifested themselves in his dream life. The close interrelationship between personal, political, and intellectual issues in Freud's mind during this important period emerges strikingly in his "my son the Myops" dream. In seeking to date this

[13] Freud, *Origins,* p. 234.
[14] Ibid., pp. 241, 242.

dream, both Alexander Grinstein and Didier Anzieu concluded that it must have occurred not long after Freud's discussion of bilaterality with Fliess at Breslau, since that issue figured prominently in the dream.[15] Another detail of the manifest content makes it possible to be somewhat more precise: the dream must have occurred on or about January 5, 1898, since Freud linked it to a performance he had seen of Theodor Herzl's play *The New Ghetto,* which opened on that date.[16] A newly available passage from Freud's letters to Fliess shows that he attended on opening night in the company of Fliess's Viennese in-laws. On January 4, 1898, he wrote, "On Wednesday we shall go with your entire family (Bondy, Rie) to a Jewish play by Herzl, in the Carl Theater—a first night, which has already played a role in my dreams." This final comment is somewhat puzzling since Freud clearly indicated that he had the Myops dream after he saw the play; either he had more than one dream about the play, or he perhaps read it or read about it before seeing it. In the letter to Fliess, Freud went on in the next paragraph to mention a theme relating both to the play and to the Myops dream: "Recently in a daytime fantasy . . . I hurled these words at his excellency, the minister of education: 'You cannot frighten me. I know that I shall still be a university lecturer when you have long ceased to be called minister.' "[17] The issue of anti-Semitism raised by the play directly activated Freud's long-smoldering antagonism at the delay in his promotion to the rank of professor.

Freud's account of the dream indicated that it had three parts. The first scene was a brief fragment in which a Professor M., a man on the staff of the university, said to him, *"My son, the Myops,"* and the second scene involved "a dialogue made up of short remarks and rejoinders"[18] which Freud did not report. He described the third segment in full detail:

> *On account of certain events which had occurred in the city of Rome, it had become necessary to remove the children to safety, and this was done. The scene was then in front of a gateway, double portals in the ancient style (the 'Porta Romana' at Siena, as I was aware during the dream itself). I was sitting on the edge of a fountain and was greatly depressed and almost in tears. A female figure—an attendant or nun—brought two boys out and handed them over to their father, who was not myself. The elder of the two*

[15] Grinstein, *Freud's Dreams,* pp. 326–27; Anzieu, *L'auto-analyse de Freud,* I:343.
[16] *Neue Freie Presse,* Jan. 5, 1898, p. 13.
[17] Freud, *Complete Letters,* p. 293.
[18] Freud, *Interpretation, S.E.,* IV:269.

was clearly my eldest son; I did not see the other one's face. The woman who brought out the boy asked him to kiss her good-bye. She was noticeable for having a red nose. The boy refused to kiss her, but, holding out his hand in farewell, said 'AUF GESERES' *to her, and then* 'AUF UNGESERES' *to the two of us (or to one of us). I had a notion that this last phrase denoted a preference.*[19]

Freud's first associations to the dream linked it to his central political concern: the rising power of anti-Semitism. He noted that it arose from thoughts provoked by *The New Ghetto* and added that among the relevant dream thoughts were "The Jewish problem, concern about the future of one's children, to whom one cannot give a country of their own, concern about educating them in such a way that they can move freely across frontiers. . . ."[20] Nonetheless, Freud gave a counterpolitical thrust to his interpretation at the very outset by an important omission, discussed by Peter Loewenberg in his analysis of this dream.[21] Freud neglected to say that Theodor Herzl was the author of the play, and his first comment on the dream suggests that the omission may have been intentional. Herzl wrote *The New Ghetto* in 1894 during his pre-Zionist period, and the play expressed a strong plea for reconciliation between Jews and Gentiles. By 1898, however, Herzl had become a *cause célèbre* in Jewish circles with his publication of *The Jewish State* (1896), the first work to develop his Zionist vision. As Loewenberg shows, Freud's initial associations to this dream suggest that he was aware of Herzl's Zionist position and did not share it. Not only did he leave out Herzl's name, but he also expressed concern for his children "to whom one cannot give a country of their own," an assertion that directly dismissed Herzl's new cause. As in his analysis of the Dr. Lecher dream, Freud's interpretation led away from politics and toward scientific concerns.

The New Ghetto provided Freud's dream thoughts with abundant material for the expression of his personal concerns. Set in Vienna in 1893, this powerful play depicted the problems confronted by Jews caught between the beliefs and customs of their traditional culture and those of the rapidly changing business and social world around them. The hero, Jakob Samuel, displayed a deep sense of integrity and compassion in his dealings both with his fellow Jews and with Gentiles. In striving to overcome the tradition of isolation

[19] Ibid., V:441–42. I have retranslated "Tore" as "portals."

[20] Ibid., p. 442.

[21] Peter Loewenberg, "A Hidden Zionist Theme in Freud's My Son, the Myops Dream," *Journal of the History of Ideas,* 31 (Jan.-March 1970):130–31.

represented by the ghetto, he came to realize that it had been replaced by a "new ghetto" with walls made up of the continuing web of habits and attitudes developed by Jews during their long oppression. Jakob's frustration reached a climax when his closest friend, a Christian named Franz Wurzlechner, turned away from him out of concern that in the prevailing anti-Semitic climate his chances for a political career might be hurt by their friendship. Arguing that Jews could not be blamed for continuing to follow instincts ingrained in them over the centuries, Jakob pointed to one of their acquaintances whom Wurzlechner had found particularly offensive, and declared that he had become "what the fate of his ancestors made him. It is not his fault . . . Morality comes in at a later point: namely with consciousness! With the overcoming of instincts. . . . First you kept us in slavery for a thousand years—then from one day to the next we are supposed to develop inner freedom!"[22] In the course of this drama Jakob's own quest for freedom came to be symbolized by the fate of Moses of Mainz, a fourteenth-century Jew whose story was recounted by one of the characters. One night while pursuing his studies, this young man heard cries for help coming from outside the walls of the ghetto and, ignoring warnings of danger, went to offer help and was brutally murdered. Jakob affirmed the story of Moses of Mainz as preferable to the continued isolation of the ghetto and finally came to suffer a similar fate when he died defending his honor in a duel with an anti-Semite who had insulted him. As he lay dying, he thanked Franz Wurzlechner, who had returned to stand by him, and delivered a plea for reconciliation. With his final words he reaffirmed his quest for freedom from the new inner ghetto by declaring, "Dear Franz . . . Tell the Rabbi: like Moses of Mainz!"[23]

The problem of anti-Semitism around which Herzl's play revolved carried over directly into Freud's dream as a major cause of anxiety and sorrow. The scene began with allusions to the kind of anti-Semitic threat Freud always associated with Roman Catholicism: *"On account of certain events which had occurred in the city of Rome, it had become necessary to remove the children to safety, and this was done."* The dream thoughts then carried him to Siena where, near the Porta Romana, he sat down on the edge of a fountain feeling *"greatly depressed and almost in tears."* Freud's associations to the dream show that the Siena references also alluded to prejudice against Jews. Near the Porta Romana in Siena he had earlier seen

[22] Theodor Herzl, *Das Neue Ghetto* (Vienna and Berlin: R. Löwit, 1920), p. 48.
[23] Herzl, p. 116.

an insane asylum, and this detail led him to recall that "shortly before I had the dream I had heard that a man of the same religious persuasion as myself had been obliged to resign the position which he had painfully achieved in a State asylum." Furthermore, he recognized in the mention of the fountain and his tears a reference to the Psalm containing the line *"By the waters of Babylon we sat down and wept"*[24]—again an allusion to the long history of Jewish persecution. The dream thoughts also referred to the escape from oppression represented by the flight out of Egypt. Tracing out the associations to the curious words spoken by his eldest son at the conclusion of the dream, Freud realized that *Geseres* and *Ungeseres* alluded to *gesäuert* and *ungesäuert,* meaning "leavened" and "unleavened," words which recalled the fact that "in their flight out of Egypt the Children of Israel had not time to allow their dough to rise."[25] In this way, the dream wish answered anti-Semitic oppression with the promise of escape and freedom.

Further reassurances were offered by elements of the dream scene that Freud left uninterpreted, elements involving his father. Herzl's play must have struck a particularly deep chord in Freud's psyche with its characterization of the hero Jakob Samuel, who displayed all the virtues young Sigmund had seen in his father Jakob without any of the failings which later gave rise to his Hannibal phantasy. Jakob Samuel responded heroically to the anti-Semitic challenge, defending his honor in a duel and sacrificing his life for his ideals, and in the underlying dream thoughts this highly positive father image was echoed by references to the Joseph story. Freud dreamed that a female figure *"brought two boys out and handed them over to their father, who is not myself. The elder of the two was clearly my eldest . . . ,"* an apparent absurdity that mirrored the end of the Joseph story, where the same thing took place (Genesis 48). As Jacob saw death approaching, Joseph was told to bring forth his two sons, Manasseh and Ephraim, so that they might be blessed. When they were brought, Jacob adopted both of them as his own sons, and in preparing to confer his blessing, he placed his right hand on the younger son, Ephraim, and the left one on Manasseh. Knowing that the old man's eyesight was failing, Joseph objected, "Not so, my father: for this is the first born," to which Jacob replied, "I know it, my son." In his dream Freud played the role of Joseph as he observed his sons being handed over to their new father, Jacob. The next words of the dream scene, "the elder

[24] Freud, *Interpretation, S.E.,* V:442.
[25] Ibid., p. 443.

of the two was clearly my eldest *[mein Ältester],*"[26] recalled Joseph's objection almost exactly.

The subject of Jacob's poor vision also linked the Bible story and Freud's dream, in which the theme of failing eyesight was suggested by the word "Myops" (myopic). After pointing out the dream's reference to the Exodus, Freud recalled the meeting with Fliess at which they discussed the significance of bilateral symmetry. On this occasion his friend had begun a sentence by saying "If we had an eye in the middle of our foreheads like a Cyclops . . ." and Freud recognized that these words provided the basis for the neologism "Myops." He also recalled a situation involving the eyesight of Professor M.'s son, who was referred to in the dream's opening fragment. While still in school, M.'s son had contracted a disease affecting one of his eyes, and after it had cleared up the other eye became infected, causing his mother to send for the doctor in a state of high anxiety. Annoyed at being needlessly inconvenienced, the doctor had accused her of making an unnecessary "*Geseres*"—Yiddish slang for weeping and wailing—and assured her that "if *one* side has got well, so will the *other.*"[27] This association brought Freud to the central point of his interpretation, which linked the themes of myopia and bilaterality. Noting that his own son had recently received as a gift the desk at which Professor M.'s son had studied, a desk designed to protect its user from becoming short-sighted or one-sided, Freud was able to explain the dream's puzzling conclusion. In turning to one side to say "*Auf Geseres*" and to the other to say "*Auf Ungeseres,*" his son was guarding himself against one-sidedness by "*acting with due attention to bilateral symmetry!*"[28] Freud carried his interpretation no further, but the allusion to the Joseph story deepens the significance of the relationship between myopia and bilateral symmetry. Since Joseph was well aware that in the previous generation his grandfather Isaac's failing eyes had allowed Jacob to steal the blessing from his brother Esau, he was particularly concerned about Jacob's poor vision and took great care to avoid a mistake. Genesis 48:13 reported that he took "Ephraim in his right hand toward Israel's left hand, and Manasseh in his left hand toward Israel's right hand, and brought them near unto him." So Joseph too acted with due attention to bilateral symmetry as he went through the ritual bestowal of the blessing. Here again the dream offered reassurances about the welfare of Freud's sons.

[26] *G.W.,* II:370.
[27] Freud, *Interpretation, S.E.,* V:443; see also Bergmann, "Moses," p. 13.
[28] Freud, *Interpretation, S.E.,* V:444.

In a number of respects Freud's "my son the Myops" dream is strikingly similar to the dream of his uncle with the yellow beard, which had occurred a year earlier. Then too, anti-Semitic discrimination provided the impulse leading to the dream's formation—Freud had just received news which led him to believe that his promotion to professor was likely to be blocked on those grounds, and as his January 4, 1898 letter to Fliess reveals, he was concerned with the same problem at the time of the Myops dream. In both dreams the threat to his career ambitions called forth as a response the reassuring Joseph identification of his youth. Furthermore, the wish for academic promotion underlying the uncle dream also figured in the Myops dream. In his very brief analysis of the dream's opening fragment, Freud reported, "So far as the dream's latent content was concerned, Professor M. and his son were men of straw—a mere screen for me and my eldest son"[29]—an identification with a university professor, reflecting his continuing desire for promotion. Finally, the two dreams paralleled each other in alluding to the biblical theme of brother rivalry over the benefits of the paternal blessing.

There were also significant differences between the two dreams. The most important of these involved the issue of fatherhood, and here the contrast offers evidence of Freud's psychoanalytic progress. The Myops dream stands apart from all his previous published dreams, for in it Freud appeared for the first time with his sons in his role as father, a role he played with increasing frequency in the subsequent dreams of 1898 and 1899. I believe that this striking fact—like his decision to join B'nai B'rith three months earlier—shows that Freud's success in understanding the tie between anti-Semitism and his ambivalent feelings toward his father had begun to diminish that ambivalence and allow him to feel much more at home in a fatherly role. In the dream his fears revolved around the safety of his children, and his interpretation of the dream pointed in the same direction. Furthermore, the underlying allusions to the Joseph story reinforced this point, for they centered on the part of the story in which Joseph first appeared as a father with his sons—immediately after which Jacob died and was given a magnificent funeral by Joseph. The dream's allusions thus reflected Freud's desire to lay the memory of his father to rest and to take on the role of father in his own right.

Freud's newly reinforced sense of himself as a father also produced changes in his relationship with Fliess, and these came to

[29] Ibid., IV:269.

the surface in the emphasis on bilateral symmetry in his interpretation. The importance of this issue to Freud's analysis of the Myops dream can be understood only against the background of his long history of brother relationships. The adolescent rebelliousness that Freud retained well into middle age pushed him toward intellectual collaboration with brother figures who shared his rebel stance, and these ties of loyalty—rooted in homoerotic feelings—vied with strong feelings of competition and rivalry. Freud later discussed his relationship with Fliess in letters to his friend Sandor Ferenczi, and in an unpublished letter of October 17, 1910, he expressed his pleasure over "the resultant greater independence that comes from having overcome my homosexuality."[30] The opportunity for intellectual collaboration with Fliess had centered on the issue of bisexuality, which seemed to offer a bridge between Fliess's biology and Freud's psychology. However, as Freud's progress in his self-analysis allowed him to assume a more paternal role, he became less dependent on his friendship with Fliess for support. Emotional and intellectual changes ran parallel: as the latent homosexual tie to Fliess began to lose some of its intensity Freud began to withdraw from the intellectual commitment to bisexuality. Didier Anzieu, in his analysis of the Myops dream, also notes the close link between Freud's intellectual and emotional involvement in this issue: "Freud's at once enthusiastic and reticent interest vis-à-vis the notion of bisexuality is thus in direct rapport with a type of homosexual 'transference effect.' "[31] When Fliess reacted strongly to Freud's new assertiveness in criticizing bilaterality, Freud perceived the threat to the cherished relationship and moved instinctively to save it. Just as his letter of January 4 attempted to explain and smooth over their difference of opinion, so his interpretation of the Myops dream paid due respect to bilateral symmetry. This mood of reconciliation also ran through the Myops dream's associations, for at the conclusion of *The New Ghetto* Jakob Samuel and his friend Franz were reunited after their quarrel, and Joseph had been reunited with his brothers by the time Jacob conferred his blessing. Still, the Bible story's strong emphasis on the continuing issue of priority among the brothers also has an analogue in the fact that Freud later advanced the erroneous claim that he rather than Fliess had first suggested the idea of bisexuality. This issue connects with Anzieu's argument that when, in the dream analysis, Freud confused the Nürnberg and Breslau conversations on the

[30] Quoted in Masson, *Assault on Truth*, p. 208.
[31] Anzieu, I:345.

subject of bisexuality, it "seems to announce his later cryptomnesia and the quarrel over priority which will develop between them."[32] The Myops dream thus suggests that even though Freud had made important progress in resolving his ambivalence toward his father, his brotherly ties remained deeply conflicted.

The changed relationship of political, professional, and personal concerns reflected in Freud's interpretation of the Myops as opposed to the uncle dream points up his continuing efforts to deprive politics of its hold on his feelings. His analysis of the earlier dream began with his desire for professional success and finally revealed a political wish to become a minister, whereas the Myops dream, although inspired by the political problem of anti-Semitism, led him back to the current intellectual concern of his professional and personal life, the issue of bilateral symmetry. This interpretive motion from politics to scientific theory also appeared in the way Freud treated the issue of freedom in the Myops dream. In response to the threat of anti-Semitism the dream thoughts first evoked the image of Joseph, the Jew who overcame prejudice to become prime minister of Egypt, and then, directly following the narrative line of the Bible story, alluded to the quest for freedom from oppression represented by the flight of the Children of Israel out of Egypt. Freud's first associations to the dream alluded to this flight from political oppression when he mentioned the "tangle of thoughts" provoked by Herzl's play: "The Jewish problem, concern about the future of one's children . . . concern about educating them in such a way that they can move *freely* across frontiers" [emphasis mine—W. McG.]. His interpretation clearly equated his own children with the Children of Israel, but the basic thrust of his analysis followed that of Herzl's play in emphasizing the quest for freedom primarily as a task carried out within each individual. In *The New Ghetto,* when Jakob Samuel quarreled with his friend Franz, the focus of his concern was the need for time to develop "inner freedom,"[33] and as Alexander Grinstein observed of Freud's dream, his thoughts about his children "were combined with other thoughts dealing with *freedom* for himself as well: his longing for intellectual freedom."[34] Thus, even though the highly political Moses of the Bible may underlie the dream's allusions to the Exodus, Freud's own interpretation more closely echoed the dying words with which Jakob Samuel expressed his desire for freedom from the inner

[32] Ibid.
[33] Herzl, p. 48.
[34] Grinstein, p. 332.

psychic bonds of the new ghetto: "Tell the Rabbi: like Moses of Mainz!"

The counterpolitical stance revealed in Freud's interpretation of the Myops dream made sense in at least two different ways, both important for understanding the place of politics in his creative work. On the level of theory, Freud must have believed that when his analysis of his Hannibal phantasy revealed the very personal roots of political passion in himself he had made a discovery of general validity. Living at a time when public political passion had reached a crescendo of intensity, Freud took his personal discovery as a key to understanding the outer disorder that threatened so many of his hopes. When he employed the stories of Oedipus and Hamlet to illustrate his newly realized truth, he chose, in both cases, highly political works to which he gave interpretations that rendered politics incidental to inner psychological reality. Moreover, the intellectual tradition of Enlightenment thought which had shaped Freud's early values and education taught him to see a close correlation between the hierarchy of society and politics on the one hand and that of the psyche on the other. So it was only logical that his analyses of the dreams that occurred after his analytic breakthrough tended to move from the political to the personal; the latter sphere of life now appeared to him to be the more fundamental. Furthermore, since Freud recognized his Hannibal fixation as a neurotic symptom, his experience with his patients would have made him assume that one way to improve his own emotional condition was to find an appropriate vehicle for expressing the original conflict on which the neurosis rested. His many political dreams of this period provided only a symptomatic outlet for the feelings bound up in his neurotic complex, but by attempting in his interpretations to expose and explain rationally the personal dimension of these feelings, he could expect their intensity to diminish as the complex gradually dissolved.

Freud's writing of *The Interpretation of Dreams* provided yet another, ultimately much more important, arena for resolving his conflicted feelings. By advancing his revolutionary theory of dreams, Freud could relive his conflicts in a way that was much more conducive to success than playing them out in real-life experiences. He began writing the dream book with what is now Chapter II, "The Method of Interpreting Dreams," and an examination of its opening pages reveals the rebel stance so familiar to his dreams and phantasies. His words rang with defiance of the scientific establishment as he declared, "With my presumption that dreams can be interpreted I enter immediately into opposition to the ruling theory of dreams." Freud then turned from scientific authority to popular wisdom in search of support for his view: "Lay opinion has taken a different attitude throughout the ages. . . . It seems to assume that . . . every dream has a meaning, though a hidden one, that dreams are designed to take the place of some other process of thought, and that we have only to undo the substitution correctly in order to arrive at this hidden meaning."[35] While accepting the popular view that dreams could be interpreted, he rejected various interpretive techniques that had been used through the ages on the grounds that they could not meet the necessary standards for "a scientific treatment of the subject." Having delineated the gulf between scientific authority and the popular viewpoint, Freud went on to advance a middle position. He stated his conviction that "here once more we have one of those not infrequent cases in which an ancient and jealously held popular belief seems to be nearer the truth than the judgment of the prevalent science of today. I must affirm that dreams really have a meaning and that a scientific procedure for interpreting them is possible."[36] So here again, as in the Myops dream, the presentation emphasized conflict within a framework of reconciliation.

The combative stance Freud assumed in presenting his theory of dreams reflects his long-standing identification with the minority position—as a Jew among Catholics, as a republican in a monarchy, as an advocate of hypnotism in a skeptical scientific community. From his university years onward, the opposition to authority that had earlier found a political focus came increasingly to be displaced into his scientific work, but in writing his dream book Freud turned back to politics to find a model for explaining scientifically the conflict inherent in mental activity. This undoing of the displacement is apparent in his newly generalized assumption that one of the two basic forces shaping mental activity involved a process of censorship carried out by an agency similar to that of a censor in the political world. Freud had first employed the term "censorship" in describing hysterical phenomena some two years earlier in *Studies on Hysteria,* and he subsequently used it in the same context in a paper written in early 1896.[37] After that it did not reappear in his professional writings or his letters until the end of 1897. Then, in the course of his work on *The Interpretation of Dreams* the issue of

[35] Freud, *Interpretation, S.E.,* IV:96; the first passage is retranslated from the German.

[36] Ibid., pp. 99, 100.

[37] Freud, *Studies on Hysteria, S.E.,* II:269, 282; Freud, "Further Remarks on the Neuro-Psychoses of Defence," *S.E.,* III:182–83, 185.

censorship became centrally important not only to his theory but also to his personal and professional life.

When Freud returned to this concept in his December 22, 1897 letter to Fliess, it had much the same restricted sense as in his earlier usage, but the context tied it closely to the role of language in the dynamics of psychic interaction. He wrote that he was becoming convinced that "in obsessional neuroses the *verbal idea,* and not the concept dependent on it, is the point at which the repressed break through." After providing various examples of the way ambiguous words served as contact points between conscious and unconscious mental processes, he asked Fliess if he had ever seen a foreign newspaper which had "passed the censorship at the Russian frontier? Words, sentences and whole paragraphs are blacked out, with the result that the remainder is unintelligible." The seemingly senseless deliria which occurred in psychoses, Freud observed, resulted from the imposition of a "Russian censorship."[38] This reference is useful in attempting to date the emergence of Freud's conception of dream censorship, for his subsequent comments on the progress of his dream book indicate that from this narrow, specifically hysterical usage of the term he soon moved to a more general and elaborate conception. Freud later observed that "the kernel of my theory of dreams lies in my derivation of dream distortion from the censorship,"[39] and this development had occurred by April 15, 1898, when he sent Fliess the manuscript of the chapter containing what he called "the professor-dream"[40] (later referred to as the dream of his uncle with the yellow beard), for it was the analysis of this dream that brought the concept of censorship into a central position in Freud's understanding of the dream processes. Moreover, the records of Freud's B'nai B'rith chapter indicate that he addressed its members twice on the subject of dream interpretation during December 1897,[41] so it seems likely that he was at work on the subject of dream theory at the time he made his comment on Russian censorship. The available evidence thus points to the period around and immediately after December 1897 as the time when he began to extend application of the censorship concept from neurotic and psychotic phenomena to the more general sphere of dream activity.

Freud's theory of dream censorship recapitulated in microcosm the basic structure and dynamics of the political world in which

[38] Freud, *Origins,* pp. 239, 240.
[39] Freud, *Interpretation, S.E.,* IV:308.
[40] Freud, *Origins,* p. 248.
[41] Klein, *Jewish Origins of the Psychoanalytic Movement,* pp. 156–57.

he lived. His method of argument and his examples suggest that in the formation of his theory, as in his dreams, the motion was from the political to the psychological. Having advanced the initial argument that every dream was the fulfillment of a wish, Freud had to deal first with the obvious problem posed by nightmares or anxiety dreams. If dreams expressed wishes, why were they so often confused or terrifying? He set out to answer this question by distinguishing between the manifest or surface content of the dream and its latent meaning. He argued that this latent dream content involved the expression of a wish which became distorted and unrecognizable in the confused manifest content. "Let us describe this . . . as 'the phenomenon of distortion in dreams.' Thus our second problem is: what is the origin of dream-distortion?"[42] To provide a solution Freud undertook a detailed analysis of his uncle dream, the dream in which his wish to become a professor caused him to malign his academic colleagues by accusing one of being a simpleton and the other a thief. Freud noted that a strong feeling of affection for his friend R., a striking element of the dream's manifest content, served to disguise the accusation of stupidity implicit in the latent dream material.

This clearly purposeful distortion led him to seek parallels in the world of social and political relationships, where he found particularly close similarities in the problems political censorship posed to writers. "A similar difficulty confronts the political writer who has disagreeable truths to tell to those in authority. If he presents them undisguised, the authorities will suppress his words." Still, the writer was not without resources in attempting to surmount this difficulty. Long experience of living with censorship in the theater and the press had taught all educated Viennese to read between the lines in search of a writer's true meaning. Likewise, an author learned to veil his message so as to elude the censor but still reach his audience. As Freud observed:

> A writer must beware of the censorship, and on its account he must soften and distort the expression of his opinion. According to the strength and sensitiveness of the censorship he finds himself compelled either merely to refrain from certain forms of attack, or to speak in allusions in place of direct references. . . . The stricter the censorship, the more far-reaching will be the disguise and the more ingenious too may be the means employed for putting the reader on the scent of the true meaning.[43]

[42] Freud, *Interpretation, S.E.,* IV:136.
[43] Ibid., p. 142.

Here Freud reached the crux of his argument, and in the passage which follows he clearly revealed an underlying belief that the forces at work within the human psyche and those that shaped social and political reality were not only similar but in fact identical. He wrote, "The fact that the phenomena of censorship and of dream-distortion correspond down to their smallest details justifies us in presuming that they are similarly determined. We may therefore suppose that dreams are given their shape in individual human beings by the operation of two psychical forces (or we may describe them as currents or systems)."[44] From this assumption emerged the basic structure of Freud's dream theory, with its conflict between the dream wish, which he saw as equivalent to popular opinion, and its opponent, the censorial agency, which held the power over admission to consciousness and corresponded to repressive political authority. At the key point in the presentation of his case Freud employed a method of argument (essentially he used an argument drawn from analogy) which indicated his belief that he had discovered a fundamental—almost Platonic—correspondence between the nature of the individual and the nature of the state. Furthermore, as in Plato's *Republic,* it was the political world that suggested the structure and dynamics of the individual psyche rather than the reverse.

As he delineated the basic elements of his psychic polity, Freud turned repeatedly to the political world for examples and parallels. He specifically noted that "if this picture of the two psychical agencies and their relation to consciousness is accepted, there is a complete analogy in political life," and the example he chose pointed directly to the political crisis he had just lived through. He wrote, "I transpose myself *[Ich versetze mich]* into the life of a state in which a struggle is in process between a ruler who is jealous of his power and an alert public opinion. The people are in revolt against an unpopular official and demand his dismissal."[45] This example paralleled the near revolutionary political situation threatening the Badeni government during its final days, and since it is possible to date the development of Freud's idea of a dream censor to the months immediately following the climax of this crisis, the example and the other political references in his theory suggest that his intellectual work received an impetus from these political events not unlike that imparted in the spring of 1897 by the onset of the Badeni language crisis.

[44] Ibid., pp. 143–44.
[45] Ibid., pp. 144–45; the second passage is retranslated from the German.

There was, however, an important difference in the way the two situations affected Freud and his work. In the spring of 1897 he had not yet come to understand the complex origins of his deeply conflicted political feelings, and the events of that time cast his inner emotional turmoil into bold relief. Lueger's confirmation and the promulgation of the language ordinances aroused not only the powerful feelings associated with Freud's sense of Jewish identity but also—paradoxically—those directly opposing feelings tied to his desire for assimilation into German culture. In the wake of these events, Freud referred in his letters to the seething ferment within himself while in his theoretical work he moved toward a greater appreciation of the central position of emotional impulses in mental life. By the end of the year his analysis of his Hannibal phantasy had brought him a much deeper awareness of his acute sensitivity to politics. Subsequently, when the fall of Badeni produced the violent anti-Semitic and anti-German outbursts in Prague, Freud may have experienced many of the same feelings that had been aroused earlier in the year but, as his letter of December 5 shows, his response now was to consolidate his conscious understanding of these feelings by telling Fliess about his street corner dream and his Hannibal phantasy rather than simply reliving them.[46] Concurrently, in his work on dreams, he turned to a description of the repressive mental agency responsible for admitting ideas to consciousness, the censor. The repressive nature of political authority had been on display in the fall of 1897—not only in parliament with the *Lex Falkenhayn* but also in the daily press, where censorship increased. At the height of the crisis the censor confiscated two editions of Freud's paper, the august *Neue Freie Presse*, and the vigorous but capricious censorship during this period attracted the attention of Mark Twain, who gave the subject prominent attention in his account of these stirring times.[47] Freud did the same in his dream book, where the censor became a factor of importance equal to the dream wish in the formation of the dream.

Freud's Myops dream of early 1898 appears to reflect his movement toward this "two-sided" theoretical structure. At the heart of his interpretation of it, Freud argued that the scene involving his eldest son (Martin) reflected a wish that the boy avoid one-sidedness, either physical or intellectual: "After the child had turned to *one side* to say farewell words, he turned to the *other side* to say the contrary, as though to restore the balance." Freud's emphasis

[46] Freud, *Origins*, p. 266.
[47] Twain, pp. 200–201.

on the role of the censor in his theory also had the effect of restoring the balance—in this case to his psychological system, and his dream expressed the desire for bilateral symmetry on this level as well. In the dream the boy turned first to the woman with the red nose whom Freud linked to the family nurse and to Catholicism. Both these themes suggest memories of his own Catholic nursemaid, the woman who played the role of censor in his childhood and also in other of his dreams. Then, in the dream, the boy turned toward Freud to utter the words *"Auf Ungeseres,"* a detail that points toward the theme of freedom from oppression. The dream created a balance between authority and freedom exactly parallel to the balance in his theory between the authority of the censor to control what was admitted to consciousness and the freedom of the dream wish to find expression. Furthermore, this interpretation fits in with a concern Freud expressed about the possible one-sidedness of his eldest son. Martin showed a great interest in poetry, and in a later dream Freud revealed a fear that this gift of poetic inspiration might lead him to grief. He feared that poets might be more likely than others to come to grief over women, that is, as a result of their sexual impulses.[48] So the idea of redressing Martin's one-sidedness also pointed toward a greater emphasis on controlling these impulses—the role of the censor.

Having arrived at the theoretical conclusion that normal, well-balanced mental life necessarily involved the censorship of certain unconscious wishes, Freud still faced the problem of restoring a balance within himself, for his dream life reveals that he continued to suffer from the emotional power of what might best be called his political complex, that web of thoughts and feelings typified by his Hannibal phantasy. To achieve its resolution required not only an understanding of its origins in his early ambivalence toward his father and his brothers but also a determined effort to put those feelings to rest. The deepened sense of himself as a father apparent in the Myops dream suggests his progress in understanding and resolving the paternal dimension of the problem, but the political feelings which had developed out of this early ambivalence remained to be dealt with directly. Freud either had to find an acceptable outlet for his buried political loyalties or he had to reinforce their suppression. The evidence indicates that he pursued both alternatives in the course of his self-analysis.

With respect to his early passion for German nationalism Freud chose suppression; he decided to censor any expression of German

[48] Grinstein, pp. 223–28.

nationalist feelings. Evidence of this adaptive strategy can be seen in his letter to Fliess of March 10, 1898. Here he remarked that his university lecture course was "particularly lively this year" and added that in spite of the involuntary interruption which occurred when the university was closed he continued lecturing "over a mug of beer and with cigars,"[49] a reference to political events in the aftermath of the Badeni crisis, when conflict between Czechs and Germans continued to rage. To calm the tense situation in Prague, the government had ordered the German nationalist fraternities not to display their colors in that city, and in response to this infringement of their traditional rights the students called on January 31, 1898, for a strike by all of Austria's German-speaking students. On February 3, lectures were suspended at the University of Vienna, and soon thereafter it was closed for the remaining weeks of the winter semester.[50] Freud's decision to continue lecturing despite the suspension represented an act of defiance toward the German nationalist cause, a stubborn assertion that scientific learning would not yield to political passion.

During the first half of 1898 when the preliminary draft of the dream book was taking shape, Freud's own dreams continued to reflect the complex interplay between his inner psychological constellation, the external pressures of political and professional concerns, and the development of his theoretical understanding of dreams. His dream of the botanical monograph, which occurred on or about March 10,[51] offers particularly valuable insight into the psychological background against which the dream book came into being. Freud included this passage in his account of the dream scene: "*I had written a monograph on a certain plant. The book lay before me and I was at the moment turning over a folded coloured plate. Bound up in each copy there was a dried specimen of the plant, as though it had been taken from a herbarium.*"[52] As his own extensive analysis showed, the dream alluded in a variety of ways to the frustration of his desire for professional success. The allusion to the botanical monograph recalled his earlier work on cocaine and the thwarting of the youthful hope that it would bring him widespread scientific recognition. On that occasion Karl Koller had become famous instead of Freud because he had taken the trouble to carry out the experiments necessary to demonstrate the drug's anesthetic

[49] Freud, *Origins*, p. 247.

[50] Charmatz, II:124; Sutter, *Badenischen Sprachverordnungen*, II:252.

[51] This date is based on Freud's letter to Fliess of March 10, 1898, and a connecting comment in his discussion of the dream; see Freud, *Origins*, p. 246n1.

[52] Freud, *Interpretation*, *S.E.*, IV:169.

properties. In his analysis Freud associated the dream with one of his phantasies, in which he imagined that if he ever got glaucoma he would go to Berlin to be operated on incognito in the house of his friend Fliess. The unknown surgeon "would boast once again of how easily such operations could be performed since the introduction of cocaine; and I should not give the slightest hint that I myself had had a hand in the discovery." This phantasy then led Freud to a significant memory: "Shortly after Koller's discovery, my father had in fact been attacked by glaucoma; my friend Dr. Königstein, the ophthalmic surgeon, had operated on him; while Dr. Koller had been in charge of the cocaine anaesthesia and had commented on the fact that this case had brought together all of the three men who had had a share in the introduction of cocaine."[53] In Freud's phantasy he took his father's place in the incident, an expression on a familial level of one of the motivating wishes of the dream. Freud's memories of Karl Koller aroused intense feelings of competition and brother rivalry, and in the phantasy he gained success in this competition by taking his father's place.

Although these associations echoed the theme of brother rivalry for priority which ran through the biblical allusions of the Myops dream, the dream of the botanical monograph also expressed the positive dimension of Freud's brother relationships. The first lines of the dream scene reveal a close identification with Fliess. The day before the dream Freud had received a letter from his Berlin friend in which he said, "I am very much occupied with your dream-book. *I see it lying finished before me and I see myself turning over its pages.*" Freud's dream scene directly realized the situation described in Fliess's comment, so he had put himself in his friend's place. As Freud observed in his analysis, "How much I envied him his gift as a seer! If only *I* could have seen it lying finished before me!"[54] The dream not only expressed the wish that he might finish his book and thereby win the fame and recognition he had so long desired, but also revealed the close tie between Freud's psychological involvement with brother figures and the mixed emotions aroused by his scientific work. His work on dreams, like that on cocaine, involved a highly controversial topic that offered the prospect of either fame or notoriety depending on its reception in the scientific community. As he had done from adolescence on, Freud looked

[53] Ibid., pp. 170, 171.
[54] Ibid., p. 172.

to brother figures for models and for support when embarking on a radical or dangerous course, and the dream expressed this need.[55]

Freud took the dream's message to heart, for in his next letter to Fliess (March 15) he asked his friend to read the first draft of what he had just written about dreams. This marked the beginning of Fliess's role as first critic of the dream book. Freud sent him what was then intended to be the second chapter, covering material later expanded into Chapters II, III and IV in the published version. He also said that the first chapter, dealing with the literature on the subject, had not been written and went on to outline his plan for the remainder of the book: "3. Dream Material; 4. Typical Dreams; 5. The Psychical Process in Dreaming; 6. Dreams and the Neuroses."[56] Fliess responded with the hoped-for encouragement. In his letter of March 24, Freud wrote, "your judgment of my dream manuscript made it a good day for me," and in expressing the hope that they would soon meet to discuss it, he urged Fliess not to "refuse the duties attached to being my first reader and supreme arbiter."[57] Although Fliess did not refuse, Freud was disappointed in his hope for an early opportunity to discuss his manuscript with his friend in person. Illness forced Fliess to cancel their plans for an Easter meeting, and Freud decided to take a vacation trip to the Adriatic with his brother Alexander instead.

The theme of brother rivalry reappeared frequently in Freud's dreams during the spring of 1898, and its increasing prominence in his dream life parallels the intensifying emotional conflict involving the role of brother relationships in his creative activity. The highly controversial nature both of his own research and of Fliess's recalled his adolescent phantasies of belonging to a band of genius rebels, but Freud's own desire for the highest prize of creative genius and for priority among the brothers cultivated a spirit of rivalry at odds with his feelings of loyalty and affection. In sending his friend the manuscript of the dream book Freud was offering to share with him the rewards of revolutionary scientific discovery, but making Fliess the "supreme arbiter" of the manuscript also invited him to express doubts and reservations and thereby expressed the deep ambivalence which continued to characterize their relationship. This inner conflict emerged prominently

[55] Freud's emotional needs as revealed in this dream would seem to support Kohut's theory of a creativity transference involving Fliess (Kohut, "Creativeness, Charisma," pp. 403–5).

[56] Freud, *Origins*, p. 248.

[57] Ibid., p. 249.

in three dreams of April and May 1898: the dreams of Goethe's attack on Herr M.; of dishonesty; and of the castle by the sea. The theme running through all three was fear of attack, a fear that found expression in three different areas of life: professional, personal, and political respectively.

The dream of Goethe's attack on Herr M. occurred soon after April 27,[58] and its precipitating cause involved an unpleasant situation which confronted Freud immediately after he returned from his visit to the Adriatic. At that time he discovered that a medical journal with which he was associated had published a devastating review of Fliess's latest book, and Freud felt obliged to lodge a strong protest with the editor, who was also a close friend. In the dream itself Freud found: *"One of my acquaintances, Herr M., had been attacked in an essay with an unjustifiable degree of violence, as we all thought—by no less a person than Goethe. Herr M. was naturally crushed by the attack. . . . Incidentally, the attack was contained in Goethe's well-known essay on 'Nature'."* These pieces of the dream scene clearly reflected the critic's attack on Fliess—as Freud indicated in his own analysis—but as he went on to point out, since all dreams were prompted by egoistic motives, the dream actually expressed a fear that he himself would come under similar attack. "I could say to myself: 'The kind of criticism that has been applied to your friend will be applied to you.' " Freud thus found that in the dream he had put himself in his friend's place, and while this substitution expressed a fear that his work on dreams might come under attack in the scientific community, it also offered certain reassurances. As he noted, "There was a very clear reminder in the dream that *'mea res agitur'* [these things concerned me], in the allusion to Goethe's short but exquisitely written essay."[59] It recalled Freud's decision in his last year of high school to pursue a career in science rather than radical politics, a decision which avoided the dangers of political involvement in favor of detached scientific inquiry. Moreover, it alluded quite specifically to the situation that had caused him to hear the reading of Goethe's essay and thus precipitated his change in plans, his agreement to review Carl Brühl's lecture for his friend Heinrich Braun. Here too, as in the dream, he had literally taken his friend's place. The identification with his much admired adolescent comrade offered reassurance, but the allusion to the career change suggests that the dream also expressed a directly contradictory desire: to avoid the dangers of

[58] Grinstein, pp. 245, 247–48.
[59] Freud, *Interpretation, S.E.,* v:439, 441.

scientific radicalism by abandoning the brother band. This conclusion fits with that reached by Alexander Grinstein, who argues that the dream shows "the emergence of Freud's aggression against his friend Fliess."[60] The dream expressed both sides of the conflicted attitude that Freud's brother relationships always involved.

In Freud's dream of dishonesty, which occurred soon after the dream of Goethe and Herr M.,[61] the primary theme was the fear of being examined and accused of dishonesty. He wrote that *"I knew in the dream that something had been missed and that the examination was due to a suspicion that I had appropriated the missing article."* In the dream Freud first found that he was declared innocent and told he could go, only to discover that he could not find his hat *"and could not go after all."* In his analysis he observed, "My not being able to find my hat meant accordingly: 'After all you're *not* an honest man'." He went on to say that the sensation of inhibition of movement which characterized the end of the dream represented a *"conflict of will,"* but he did not explain how it related to the subject of dishonesty.[62] The theme of dishonesty, however, did pertain directly to the book Freud was writing at the time, because most of the evidence on which *The Interpretation of Dreams* rested was drawn from his own inner life, and in presenting it he was forced to censor and distort highly personal material. If, like so many of Freud's dreams from this period, this one involved his work on the dream book, the issue of dishonesty may have alluded to this question of censoring personal information. Freud also discussed the dream phenomenon of inhibition of motion in connection with exhibitionist dreams, where he argued: "It serves admirably in dreams to represent a conflict in the will or a negative. The unconscious purpose requires the exhibiting to proceed; the censorship demands that it shall be stopped."[63] The use of Freud's own dreams to illustrate his theory of dreams forced him to bare his soul to the public, and this "exhibitionism" could well have fostered a conflict of will on both the conscious and unconscious levels.

The conflict characterizing Freud's brother relationships again figured in the dream of dishonesty. One of the associations Freud mentioned in connection with it involved a line from Schiller's play *Fiesco:* "The Moor has done his duty; the Moor *can go,*" and he went on to note that when he was born he had such a profusion

[60] Grinstein, p. 266.
[61] Freud provides this information in *Interpretation, S.E.*, IV:337n.
[62] Ibid., pp. 336, 337.
[63] Ibid., p. 246.

of black hair that his mother declared that he was "a little Moor."[64] These allusions recall Freud's adolescent identification with Karl Moor, and in fact many of the themes of *Fiesco* strongly echoed those of *The Robbers.* In both the action centered on ill-fated rebellion against unjust authority; like Karl Moor, Fiesco paid with his life for his ambitious challenge to the existing political order. He met his death at the hands of Verrina, a fellow conspirator, who declared "We loved each other fraternally"[65] as he tried to persuade Fiesco not to assume the dictatorial authority of the overthrown duke of Genoa. Failing in this, he pushed Fiesco into the sea where he drowned. These associations to the dream point both to the deep conflict over priority within the brother band and to fears aroused by the idea of challenging authority. In the dream scene, Freud wrote, he entered a hall with *"hellish instruments of punishment. Stretched out on one apparatus I saw one of my colleagues, who had every reason to take some notice of me; but he paid no attention. I was then told I could go."*[66] Freud's dream wish transferred the punishment for the assault on authority to his colleague while exonerating himself, but at the same time his guilt at forsaking the brother band surfaced in the dream's concluding conflict over whether or not he could go after all.

Freud had a third dream of attack only a short time later, for, as Leslie Adams demonstrated in his masterful analysis, the dream of the castle by the sea must have occurred on the night of May 10–11, 1898.[67] Because this long and complex dream has received considerable attention in the literature on Freud's dreams, it will suffice here to concentrate on its close relationship to the surrounding dreams and to Freud's conflicted brother relationships. In this dream Freud's fear of attack took an openly military form, and he found himself in a castle by the sea serving as second in command to the Governor, a Herr P. Fearing assault from enemy warships, Herr P. gave him instructions on what to do and prepared to leave, but Freud held him back to ask some questions. Herr P. then fell down dead and as Freud observed in the dream, *"No doubt I had put an unnecessary strain upon him with my questions. After his death, which made no further impression on me, I wondered whether his widow would remain in the castle . . . and whether I should take over command of the castle as being next in order of rank."*[68] In a later

[64] Ibid., p. 337.
[65] Grinstein, p. 274.
[66] Freud, *Interpretation, S.E.,* IV:336.
[67] Adams, "A New Look at Freud's Dream," p. 382.
[68] Freud, *Interpretation, S.E.,* V:463–64.

segment of the dream, Freud reported, "*Then my brother was standing beside me and we were both looking out of the window at the canal. At the sight of one ship we were frightened and cried out: 'Here comes the warship!'* " Freud's analysis of the dream pointed to its "allusions to the *maritime war* between America and Spain and to anxieties to which it had given rise about the fate of my relatives in America,"[69] and Adams has gone a good deal further in showing just how much of the detailed material in the dream pertained to this conflict.[70] The relatives in question were Freud's sister Anna and her husband, Eli Bernays, who was the brother of Freud's wife. They lived in New York City, which, it was feared at the time of the dream, might come under attack from a Spanish fleet that had recently set sail from the Azores. Adams has demonstrated conclusively that the surface content of the dream was drawn in large part from what Freud read about the war in the *Neue Freie Presse* of May 10, 1898. On that day the paper published its first reports of the battle of Manila, in which Admiral Dewey inflicted a devastating defeat on the Spanish forces in the Philippines. Adams has argued that Freud's dream involved an identification with this heroic military figure.

Adams did not attempt to relate this dream to Freud's recurrent phantasies of military glory, but it clearly fits into the pattern of his Hannibal phantasy, with Roman Catholic Spain representing Rome and Admiral Dewey, the defender of democratic America, representing Hannibal challenging Rome's authority. The challenge to authority also appeared directly in the dream: Freud's questioning of Herr P., his immediate superior, caused him to fall down dead. Freud's own desire to become an authority likewise found expression: "*I wondered . . . whether I should take over command of the castle as being the next in order of rank.*" But such a commanding position, however desirable, implied certain dangers, which found repeated expression in Freud's dreams of spring and summer 1898. In this dream he and his brother were frightened at the sight of one of the warships, and the dream as a whole created "a tense and sinister impression."[71] Moreover, Freud interpreted elements of the dream as expressing fears of his premature death, and as in the earlier dream of dishonesty and the subsequent Hollthurn dream, allusions to Schiller were associated with the subjects of death and danger. But there were also elements which seem to reflect the progress of Freud's self-analysis in resolving his fears about assuming an

[69] Ibid., p. 464.
[70] Adams, pp. 383–84.
[71] Freud, *Interpretation, S.E.,* V:464.

authoritative fatherly position. Since this was the first of Freud's published dreams in which his younger brother appeared directly, it resembles the Myops dream of January 1898, where his sons first appeared, in pointing to Freud's gradual resolution of these fears. Freud still needed the support of his brother band to undertake the assault on Roman authority, but in turning to his much younger brother Alexander (whose name, it will be remembered, he himself had chosen to recall the military genius of Alexander the Great) he found an ally who clearly stood in a subordinate position to himself.

Another element of the dream scene which seems to bear on Freud's self-analysis involves his reaction to the death of Herr P. which, he said, *"made no further impression on me."* As Adams showed, this was an allusion to Admiral Dewey's unemotional behavior during the battle of Manila, when he coolly ordered a halt to the attack precisely at 7:00 A.M. in order to have breakfast served to his crew. The *Neue Freie Presse* report played up this and other examples of Dewey's imperturbability.[72] Freud's similar behavior in the dream suggests his wish to master his own feelings over the death of his father and attain the kind of emotional balance and restraint which were attributed to Dewey and which he attributed both to Fliess and to his father.

In many of its details, Freud's dream of the castle by the sea drew on his various trips to Italy, including his most recent vacation in Istria with his brother, and this source related closely to the dream's allusions to Hannibal and the brother band. The year before, in April 1897 when he met with Fliess in Nürnberg, Freud's Hannibal phantasy had been so powerfully activated that he formulated plans for the Italian journey which followed the path of Hannibal's campaign. The fact that in May of that year he experienced an intense period of creative activity suggests a crucial link between his rebellious phantasy and the creative energies mobilized in his scientific work. In the spring of 1898, however, Freud had to forgo his usual meeting with Fliess, and the political world provided no energizing impulse comparable to that imparted to him the year before by the crisis involving Lueger's confirmation and the promulgation of the Badeni language ordinances. On May 1, 1898, he sent Fliess a preliminary draft of Chapter II of his dream book and complained that he regarded it as dull and lifeless. He added, "I wish a powerful stimulus of some kind were present. . . . So far I have hardly got to the stage of feeling tired this

[72] Adams, p. 383.

year."[73] Freud's dreams of April and May suggest that his drive to challenge authority was being increasingly undercut by doubt and fear as well as by a growing sense of rivalry for priority within the brother band. As he began to resolve his ambivalent feelings toward his deceased father, brother rivalry came increasingly to the fore in his emotional life, and his work on the dream book languished until after he was able to make progress in resolving that problem.

Even though Freud's self-analysis had advanced his understanding of the hold politics had on his emotions, there was no diminution in the frequency with which political themes appeared in his dreams over this period. Indeed, in the summer of 1898 Freud had three openly political dreams, which expressed his earlier political radicalism with unprecedented clarity: the dream of the stately house, the Hollthurn dream and the revolutionary dream. While the timing may seem paradoxical, it is not inconsistent with the evidence that his emotional relationship with the political world had begun to change: the unambiguously political character of these dreams suggests that his political impulses fell victim less often to the unconscious process of censorship. In fact, Freud's treatment of the first of these dreams, the dream of the stately house, suggests that in his efforts to come to terms with his political past he had succeeded in partially changing antipolitical censorship from an unconscious process to a conscious decision. Taken together, these political dreams provide a clear view of the way he succeeded in transforming political frustration into psychoanalytic insight.

Freud's dream of the stately house occurred in June 1898, while he was immersed in work on the dream book manuscript, and it reflects the problem of privacy posed by using intimate themes and materials as evidence for his theories. The month before, Freud had sent Fliess a part of the manuscript with the understanding that he would criticize it and suggest what, if anything, should be eliminated to avoid possible embarrassment. Fliess responded by suggesting that Freud leave out one particularly important and elaborate dream. Then on June 9 Freud wrote back:

> Warm thanks for your criticism. You have taken on a thankless task. I must acknowledge that I need your critical advice because in this case I myself have lost the modesty which an author must have. So the dream is damned. But now that the sentence has been imposed I must shed a tear for it and confess that I am sorry and that I can

[73] Freud, *Origins*, p. 254.

> hope to find no better substitute. You must know—a beautiful dream and no indiscretions—they don't go together. At least write and tell me what theme you regarded as offensive and where you fear the attack of the wicked critics—whether it is my anxiety, or Martha, or my financial miseries or my lack of a fatherland *[Vaterlandlosigkeit]*—so that I can leave it out of the substitute dream *[Ersatztraum]*, for I can order up such dreams at will.[74]

Although we do not have Fliess's answer to this very interesting request, Max Schur concluded from a reference in Freud's next letter that the deletion was motivated by a political theme. On June 20, 1898, Freud wrote, "The mourning for the lost dream goes on. As if out of spite I at last had a substitute dream in which a house built out of stone collapsed ('We had built a stately house' *[Wir hatten gebauet ein staatliches Haus]*) and which thus, because of this allusion, could not be used."[75]

The reason Freud could not use this dream either was because "We had built a stately house" was the first line of a well-known German nationalist student song, and as such it directly recalled his involvement with the radical German nationalist Leseverein der deutschen Studenten Wiens, to which he had belonged from 1873 to 1878. When the government moved in December 1878 to dissolve this society, the members met the next day near the university and joined in singing "We Had Built a Stately House" as an act of defiance in the face of repression. The relevance of this allusion can be understood in the context of the political situation prevailing at the time of the dream. In the continuing conflict between Czechs and Germans over the language ordinances, the attempts of the new Austrian minister president, Count Franz Thun, to arrive at a compromise acceptable to both parties seemed increasingly doomed to failure. The German parties of the Austrian parliament regarded Thun's position as overly sympathetic to the Czechs, and they therefore decided to resume the obstructionist tactic of using parliamentary devices to bring the conduct of legislative business to a halt. Even though broadly supportive of the German cause, the *Neue Freie Presse,* the chief organ of Austrian liberalism, viewed this development with alarm, and on June 1 its lead story opened a lengthy analysis of the parliamentary situation with the ominous words, "A desperately ill parliament gathers together today. . . ." The obstructionism of the German parties

[74] Quoted in Max Schur, "Weitere Tagesreste zum Traummuster," *Der unbekannte Freud,* ed. Jürgen vom Scheidt (Munich: Kindler Verlag, 1974), p. 137.
[75] Ibid., p. 138.

had proved effective in bringing down the Badeni government the year before, and Count Thun reacted harshly when its resumption signaled the failure of his attempted compromise. After the fruitless session of June 7, which was followed by a short recess, he impetuously decided to adjourn parliament indefinitely before it could meet again, as it was scheduled to do on June 14. By this act, which became known on June 13, he not only expressed his contempt for parliament but also left it with a record of total paralysis and failure. These events strongly suggest that in Freud's dream the stately house was the house of parliament, and this interpretation is supported by a peculiarity evident in Freud's association to the dream: in referring to the song, he spelled stately "st*aat*liches" rather than "st*att*liches," the former conveying the idea of a house of state rather than a stately house. The collapse of the house thus symbolized both the dissolution of parliament and more generally the failure of democratic hopes for parliamentary government.

Freud's lifelong involvement with the values of liberal culture would not have allowed him to harbor a wish for parliamentary failure or defeat, so what is the meaning of the collapse depicted so vividly in the dream scene? Here, the words and the history of the nationalist song suggest a plausible answer. It was written in 1819 by August von Binzer, who was at the time a university student and a member of the Deutsche Burschenschaft, a nationalistic fraternity devoted to the ideals of German unity and democratic freedom.[76] During the years immediately following the final defeat of Napoleon, Metternich presided over the conservative restoration aimed at eliminating any further possibility of revolutionary outbreaks. One particular area of problems for him involved the perpetuation of liberal, democratic and nationalist ideals among the German student fraternities, and his concern was heightened when these groups came together to hold the Wartburg festival in October 1817. The festival commemorated the beginning of the Protestant Reformation as well as the Battle of the Nations at Leipzig, the battle that wrested control of Germany from Napoleon. To the students each of these historical events symbolized an important political principle: Luther's reformation stood for the rebirth of freedom of thought from the tyranny of Catholic dogma; the Battle of Leipzig symbolized the possibility of a liberated and

[76] Kurt Stephenson, "Charakterköpfe der Studentenmusik," *Darstellungen und Quellen zur Geschichte der deutschen Einheitsbewegung im neunzehnten and zwanzigsten Jahrhundert,* ed. Kurt Stephenson, Alexander Scharff, Wolfgang Klötzer (Heidelberg: C. Winter, 1965), 6:26.

united German nation. To express this ideal of national unity and provide a means for the achievement of both liberal and nationalist goals, the various fraternities agreed that henceforth they would all merge into one unified group, the Deutsche Burschenschaft. Subsequently, when more radical students resorted to political violence and murdered August von Kotzebue, Metternich seized the opportunity to persuade the leaders of the other German states to take strongly repressive measures. Meeting in Karlsbad in 1819, they agreed on a series of decrees which included the dissolution of the Deutsche Burschenschaft and the institution of newspaper censorship.[77]

It was in reaction to the promulgation of these Karlsbad decrees that von Binzer wrote his song, and its words expressed continued faith in his political ideals despite these acts of repression:

> We had built a stately house, and in it put our trust in God through tempest, storm, and dread.
>
> We lived so true, so united, so free; to the wicked it was terrible that we were so true.
>
> They lied, they deceived and betrayed, they slandered and cursed the young green seed.
>
> What God put inside us—the world has scorned; even among the good the unity caused distrust.
>
> They call it a crime, they are much deceived; the form can be broken but never the love.
>
> The frame has been shattered from without; and that for which one strove is empty talk and show.
>
> The band has been cut; it was black, red, and gold, and God has allowed it; who knows his will?
>
> The house may collapse—what does it matter? The spirit lives in us all, and our fortress is our God.[78]

With its final allusion to Luther's hymn "A Mighty Fortress Is Our God," the song recalled the response of Lutheran Pietism to the

[77] Bruno Gebhardt, *Handbuch der deutschen Geschichte* (Stuttgart: Union Verlag, 1960), 3:102–3.

[78] Stephenson, 6:40–41, gives the German text of the song.

problem of worldly oppression, a response that looked to the inner spiritual realm as a sanctuary from the world's evil and the source of future renewal.[79] The last verse held out the hope that even though political authority had shattered the outer structure of the stately house, its spirit would live on within each individual. Von Binzer reinforced the final message by returning to the Wartburg, where he wrote his song in the visitor's book and added the words, "Be consoled! The Lord's day must come! For now, hold right firmly together even without our fraternity." Then at the final meeting of the Burschenschaft before the decree was put into effect, he addressed the student members and led them in singing his song.[80] It is important to note that the scene in Freud's dream depicting the collapsing house alluded specifically to this final verse with its message of inner renewal—conveying Freud's dream wish to rebuild within what had been lost without.

The Leseverein der deutschen Studenten Wiens had recapitulated the unifying mission of von Binzer's Deutsche Burschenschaft as well as carrying on its devotion to German unity and democratic reform. When the government moved to dissolve the Leseverein in 1878, von Binzer's song served as the perfect symbol for the students' defiance of the government's attempts to stifle the expression of their political feelings. The theme of censorship thus appears in both layers of historical events, those of 1819 and those of 1878, and it also figured in the basic context of the dream. As Freud's letters indicate, this dream was an *Ersatztraum,* a substitute dream for one that Fliess had recommended censoring, and it in turn was eliminated by Freud's own censorship on the same political grounds. Both content and context of Freud's dream of the stately house reflect the close relationship between politics, the psychological changes associated with his self-analysis and the development of his dream theory. As Freud came to terms with his political complex and the memory of his father, he also came to terms with the principle of authority within the psyche. All around him he could see the dangers of the powerful emotions aroused by Austria's nationality conflict, and at the same time he could feel them within himself even though he had consciously repudiated any loyalty to the German nationalist cause in the 1880s. By 1898 Freud had made a conscious decision to reaffirm his Jewishness in the face of the rising tide of anti-Semitic agitation, and for this reason too it

[79] Ibid., p. 27.
[80] Kurt Stephenson, "August Daniel von Binzer," in *Darstellungen und Quellen,* 5:142.

was appropriate that the German nationalist dream of the stately house be censored from his dream book.

Freud was determined to free himself from the power of his political past, and he did so by suppressing the German nationalist component while sublimating the democratic liberal elements into his book. It was to the inner world of the psyche that he turned in the face of deep political disillusionment. If his youthful hope of controlling the political forces of the outer world had failed, he could still hope to teach others how better to control the closely analogous forces of the human mind, how to reconcile inner freedom with inner authority.

One of the clearest illustrations of this movement from politics to the world within is a dream Freud had during a train ride on the night of July 18–19, 1898, the Hollthurn dream.[81] He was traveling under very uncomfortable conditions, for even though he had a first-class ticket the train was crowded, and he was forced to share a compartment with a rather disagreeable old couple who were determined to keep all the windows closed despite the hot weather. According to Freud's description, the pair "appeared to be very aristocratic," and he observed that experience had taught him that "conduct of this ruthless and overbearing kind is characteristic of people who are travelling on a free or half-price ticket [i.e., one obtained on the basis of privileged position]."[82] Such proved to be the case with this couple, and Freud thus felt justified in seeing their conduct and manner as stemming from the sort of assumption of aristocratic privilege that always caused him to bridle in anger. In the opening scene of his dream he took revenge on his traveling companions in a way which he "had to leave almost uninterpreted on account of its gross indecency,"[83] and in subsequent elements of the dream his anger assumed a political character. He dreamed that he was in the train at "*the spot at which valiant men had fought in vain against the superior power of the ruler of their country—yes, the Counter-Reformation in Austria.*" His resentment at the aristocratic presumption of the old couple thus aroused his associations with the brave Protestants of the sixteenth and seventeenth centuries, who had fought against the allied powers of the Austrian emperor and the Roman Catholic Church. The next passage alluded to the possible rewards of such heroic conduct. First he saw a "*small museum, in which the relics or belongings of these men were preserved,*" thus indicating that their struggle had earned

[81] On this date see Anzieu, 1:427.
[82] Freud, *Interpretation, S.E.*, v:456–57.
[83] Ibid., p. 519.

them a place in history. At this point in the dream he wanted to get out of the train but hesitated to do so. The other reward this portion of the dream held out to Freud the heroic rebel was sexual. He looked out of the train and saw *"women with fruit on the platform. They were crouching on the ground and holding up their baskets invitingly.—I hesitated because I was not sure whether there was time."* Freud's hesitation in accepting the fruits of boldness apparently masked a fear of what might follow such a course of action, for later in his analysis of the dream he mentioned a memory from his early childhood when "driven by sexual curiosity" he "had forced his way into his parents' bedroom and been turned out of it by his father's orders."[84] In this first half of the Hollthurn dream, then, political rebellion was closely associated with sexual rebellion and both were undercut by hesitation over their possible consequences.

The second half of the dream proposed escape as the solution to the conflict raised by his rebellious impulses. The dreamer found that he was *"suddenly in another compartment. . . . I was surprised by this, but I reflected that* I MIGHT HAVE CHANGED CARRIAGES WHILE I WAS IN A SLEEPING STATE. *There were several people, including an English brother and sister."* The analysis showed that various elements of the dream went back to Freud's memories of his 1875 trip to England; it seems highly likely that his nephew John and his niece Pauline lay behind the English brother and sister whom he substituted for the disagreeable Austrians. In place of the dangerous elements of rebellion and possible retribution represented in the first half of the dream, Freud's dream thoughts now offered the rewards of scholarly and scientific success. Whereas the first scene had shown him the relics of the valiant but defeated heroes of the Austrian Counter-Reformation, the second alluded to the books of great thinkers, Adam Smith's *The Wealth of Nations* and James Clerk-Maxwell's *Matter and Motion,* as well as an unnamed book by Schiller. In the dream Freud noted, *"It seemed that the books were sometimes mine."*[85] Furthermore, whereas the first half of the dream had offered blatant but threatening sexuality, the second half alluded to Freud's scholarly work on sexuality in an innocent and confirmatory sense,[86] by recalling an English grammatical error he had made on his trip to England. While he was standing on the seashore holding a starfish, a little girl had come up to him and asked, "Is

[84] Ibid., pp. 455, 459.
[85] Ibid., pp. 455–56.
[86] It should be recalled that Freud had chosen the scientific study of sexuality over direct expression of sexual feelings at various times in his life, including the trip to England.

it alive?" Freud replied, "Yes, . . . he is alive," and then corrected himself, "It is alive." His analysis showed that this "served as the most innocent possible example of my using a word indicating gender or sex in the wrong place—of my bringing in sex (the word 'he') where it did not belong." Thus did Freud's unconscious seek to defend him and refute the critics of his sexual theories. In the dream, when he corrected an analogous grammatical mistake in his conversation with the English pair, the brother commented to the sister, *"Yes, . . . he said that right,"*[87] thus providing the kind of confirmation that Freud always looked for from the various nephew John figures who supported his explorations into the realm of sexuality.

The contrast between the two halves of the Hollthurn dream is striking. When Freud changed compartments in the middle of it he escaped a conflict-ridden Austrian world dominated by parallel thoughts of vain political revolt against a superior Catholic emperor and equally vain sexual revolt of child against father, dream thoughts inhibited on both levels by hesitation over their consequences. The compartment he entered revealed an English world in which he was socially accepted and his revolutionary sexual theories brought fame without guilt. Under these circumstances the means of passage from the first world to the second is of great significance, and Freud illuminates this point with particular clarity. In the dream he felt surprised that he was in a different compartment but then reflected that "I MIGHT HAVE CHANGED CARRIAGES WHILE I WAS IN A SLEEPING STATE." In his analysis Freud recognized this as an allusion to the mental problems of one of his patients, a man who had phantasies that he might kill people while sleepwalking. Freud had virtually cured the man and several weeks earlier had accompanied him on a pleasant overnight railroad journey to visit the man's relatives in the country. Freud drew an important conclusion from his identification with this man. "I knew that the root of his illness had been hostile impulses against his father, dating from his childhood and involving a sexual situation. In so far, therefore, as I was identifying myself with him, I was seeking to confess something analogous."[88] Since the patient's cure involved bringing to consciousness and verbalizing his repressed hostility toward his dead father, Freud could presumably expect an analogous benefit in making his own confession. In identifying himself with his cured patient Freud was actually applying his own psychoanalytic tech-

[87] Freud, *Interpretation, S.E.,* v:519–20.
[88] Ibid., p. 458.

nique to himself in the dream in order to dissipate the guilt aroused by the rebellious feelings toward his emperor and his father in the first half of it.

The references to Schiller and more specifically the identification of Freud's books with those of the poet ("It seemed that the books were sometimes mine") further support the idea that his dream was transforming frustrated political freedom into psychological freedom. Austrian liberals had long revered Schiller as the greatest German freedom poet, and in one of the early additions to his *Interpretation of Dreams* Freud quoted Schiller to support the concept of *free* association—the "relaxation of the watch upon the gates of Reason" that allowed unconscious ideas "to emerge 'of their own free will'."[89] This portion of the dream thus offers a valuable insight into the relationship between Freud's theories and the societal pressures of his time. The uncongenial sociopolitical reality confronting him in his day-to-day life aroused conflicting emotions of revolt and guilt that powerfully reinforced his tendency to turn inward in search of the psychological secrets that would free him from this conflict. In the Hollthurn dream Freud's own psychoanalytic method provided the all-important key to an escape from the Austrian world of political and social discontent into a harmonious English world of intellectual progress and social concord.

On a night in late July 1898,[90] not long after having that dream, Freud had another, remarkably similar one which illuminates even more clearly the intimate relationship between his psychology and the politics of his time. Like the Hollthurn dream, Freud's revolutionary dream—as he called it—occurred while he was on an

[89] Ibid., IV:102–3. For the significance of Schiller to Viennese liberals see Richard Charmatz, "Wiens Schillerfeier im Jahre 1859," *Neue Bahnen,* 5 (1905):238–41.

[90] It was probably the night of July 23–24. In the prologue to the dream, Freud says he had left in the evening for his summer holiday at Aussee, and in his letter to Fliess of July 7, 1898, he writes, "I am not going to Aussee yet" (*Complete Letters,* p. 319). Jones (*Life and Work,* I:301) writes that Freud met Fliess in or near Aussee in July 1898, and Freud's letter to Fliess of July 30, which was written from Aussee, says that it was "less than a week" since they had seen each other (*Complete Letters,* p. 320). This would point to a meeting shortly after July 23 and a departure from Vienna on about that date. The *Ischler Fremden-Liste* of July 25 indicates that Count Thun was registered at a hotel in Ischl, whereas the previous issue, that of July 23, does not list him. So he must have arrived for his consultation with the emperor on July 23, 24 or 25, and he would have left Vienna on July 22, 23 or 24. Freud writes in his prologue to the dream that it was raining the evening that he and Count Thun left Vienna, and since the meteorological records indicate that July 23 was the only one of these days on which it rained in Vienna, this is the probable date of Freud's departure (*Jahrbücher der K. K. Central-Anstalt fur Meteorologische und Erdmagnetismus,* Jahrgang 1898 [Vienna: Wilhelm Braumüller, 1900], p. A-67). I am indebted to Peter Swales for suggesting this date and providing the information about the weather and the date of Thun's visit to Ischl.

overnight train ride and was provoked by irritation at aristocratic privilege. In this case the person involved was no less a figure than Count Thun, the minister-president of Austria. While waiting to catch the train for Aussee to join his family for his summer vacation, Freud had observed Count Thun's departure for Ischl, where he was going to confer with the emperor. According to Freud, "The ticket inspector at the gate had not recognized him and had tried to take his ticket, but he waved the man aside with a curt motion of his hand and without giving any explanation." This example of aristocratic presumption aroused all the fighting instincts of Freud's Hannibal phantasy, and he soon found that "all kinds of insolent and revolutionary ideas were going through my head."[91]

The rebellious mood continued into the dream. In his analysis Freud noted, "The dream as a whole gives one the impression of being in the nature of a phantasy in which the dreamer was carried back to the Revolutionary year 1848."[92] It contained four scenes. In the first, which was by far the most revolutionary, Freud condensed a half-century of political frustration for middle-class German liberals. The dream began with *"A crowd of people, a meeting of students—A count (Thun or Taaffe) was speaking. He was challenged to say something about the Germans, and declared with a contemptuous gesture that their favorite flower was colt's foot, and put some sort of dilapidated leaf . . . into his buttonhole. I fired up . . . though I was surprised at my taking such an attitude."*[93] In his analysis of the dream Freud recalled Adolf Fischhof, the liberal student leader of the 1848 revolution, and this first scene bore a striking resemblance to the events of March 13, 1848. On that day there was a mass meeting of students in the Aula of the university, and after shouting down demands for moderation they marched to the Landhaus, where the estates were in session. Here for the first time Fischhof addressed the crowd and brought them together in demanding a free press, free speech, trial by jury, and the other freedoms basic to political liberalism. From that point on he played a crucial role in the unsuccessful attempt to establish a liberal framework for Austrian political life.[94] Since he, like Freud, was a Jew from Moravia who entered the medical profession and served as a doctor in the Vienna General Hospital, Freud could easily identify with

[91] Freud, *Interpretation, S.E.,* IV:209.
[92] Ibid., p. 211.
[93] Ibid., pp. 209–10.
[94] Richard Charmatz, *Adolf Fischhof. Das Lebensbild eines österreichischen Politikers* (Stuttgart and Berlin: J.G. Cotta Nachfolger, 1910), pp. 5–89.

him and in doing so give expression to the revolutionary feelings aroused in him by the evening's events.

The dream also drew upon some of Freud's own memories of belonging to the brother band of student rebels. The two socialists who were brothers-in-law, Heinrich Braun and Viktor Adler, both figured in his analysis of the first scene. Certain of its elements, he indicated, recalled his Gymnasium days, when he and Braun had joined with some of their schoolmates in a conspiracy against their unpopular and tyrannical German-language teacher.[95] Freud associated his "firing up" in opposition to the speaker in the dream with memories of his encounter with an older student (clearly Viktor Adler) in the German nationalist reading society during the mid-1870s. In this encounter, Adler's suggestion that Freud, despite his radicalism, would follow the path of the prodigal son in eventually returning to his father's house, caused Freud to respond with an insulting remark. "There was a general uproar," he recalled, "and I was called upon from many sides to withdraw my remarks, but I refused to do so."[96] He traced another element of the first scene back to an anti-Semitic incident that had occurred in December 1883, when he was on a train trip to Leipzig, an incident in which he had valiantly held his ground in the face of insults and superior strength.[97] By alluding to these various instances in which he had stood up to his opponents despite their superior positions, his dream attempted to satisfy the rebellious feelings excited by the examples of aristocratic presumption he had witnessed. As in the Hollthurn dream, Freud's first response was to express the antagonism embodied in his Hannibal phantasy.

The two dreams were also parallel in that his defiant reaction was undercut by doubt and guilt. In the revolutionary dream he was surprised at his passionate German nationalist reaction to Count Thun's anti-German gesture, and this surprise, as well as other elements of the dream, accurately reflected the conflict between these rebellious dream impulses and the attitude of Freud's waking consciousness, represented in the dream by the force of the dream censorship. As he surveyed the Viennese political scene of 1898, Freud had good reason to feel the deepest sort of inner conflict. A few weeks earlier Count Thun's efforts at resolving the violent

[95] See above Chap. 2, p. 82. In his analysis Freud masked the identity of both Braun and Adler, but in each case he offered clues. Adler's identity was long ago discerned by James Strachey (Freud, *Interpretation, S.E.*, IV:213n).

[96] Freud, *Interpretation, S.E.*, IV:213.

[97] Ibid., p. 212; Freud, *Letters*, pp. 77–80.

language conflict had collapsed, and Thun had expressed his anger at the Germans and his frustration with parliamentary obstruction by contemptuously closing the parliament, a useless action which greatly damaged his own political position.[98] According to Josef Baernreither, a member of Thun's cabinet, this sort of conduct was typical of Thun and had played a role in his failure, for the negotiations were undercut by "his own autocratic manner which is repugnant to the free and independent manner and style of the Germans."[99] The response to Count Thun's contemptuous anti-German gesture in Freud's dream accurately reflected the attitude of the German parties; in the dream's first scene he faithfully reenacted this political crisis, taking the German part. In reality, however, Freud could feel even less sympathy for the German obstructionists led by Georg von Schönerer than for Count Thun. It was after Schönerer and his student supporters had led the way in launching the anti-Semitic movement in Austria in the early 1880s that Freud had consciously repudiated the nationalist cause. Nonetheless, in discussing his political position in his Paris letter of February 2, 1886, Freud indicated that despite this conscious change of views his inner feelings continued to be moved by the German cause,[100] and this conflict reemerged in the opening scene of the revolutionary dream in the form of surprise, doubt, and guilt.

These crosscurrents of surprise and guilt were expressed in a variety of allusions which associated the rebellious politics of the brother band with images of fratricidal conflict. By stressing the conflict within the band and his resentment at the older brother figures who led it, Freud could provide himself with justifications for his abandonment of the brotherhood. In the dream his aggressive response was incited by the count's putting a leaf in his buttonhole, and his analysis traced this gesture to a scene from Shakespeare, in which the beginning of the Wars of the Roses was symbolized by the two sides' taking up the red and white roses as emblems. From there Freud's associations led him to the red and white carnations which symbolized the opposing socialist and anti-Semitic forces in Vienna. Freud realized, moreover, that other

[98] Joseph Maria Baernreither, *Der Verfall des Habsburgerreiches und die Deutschen*, ed. Oscar Mitis (Vienna: A. Holzhausens Nachfolger, 1939), pp. 68–69. Schorske, *Vienna*, pp. 193–98, also discusses Freud's revolutionary dream at length and develops the complex political background in detail.

[99] Baernreither, p. 51.

[100] Freud, *Letters*, p. 203.

elements of the scene alluded to Emile Zola's novels *Germinal* and *La terre,* works in which the themes of political and sexual rebellion against authority were linked to each other and associated with fratricidal conflict.[101] Indeed, the very way that the dream called up Freud's own history of German nationalist student activism suggested the fratricidal theme: the figures associated with Count Thun were Freud's aristocratic co-conspirator from the Gymnasium incident and Viktor Adler from the nationalist reading society. In reacting against them in the dream, Freud emphasized the antagonistic side always present in his brother relationships, and thereby pointed toward his own break with the brother band, symbolized in the quarrel with Adler. The dream's allusion to Adler's remark that Freud was like the prodigal son called up the parable's reference to conflict between brothers as well as the comforting thought that Freud would be rewarded for returning to his father's house rather than punished for his disobedience. Thus, as in the Hollthurn dream, the first scene of Freud's revolutionary dream was dominated by violent conflict. The political reality of his time placed him in an impossible dilemma—his liberal sentiments were outraged by the autocratic style of government, and his impulse to rebellion was undercut by knowledge of the fratricidal consequences of revolt. Just as the liberal middle had dropped out of Austrian political reality, so too had it disappeared from the dream world which that reality called up in Freud.

The second segment of the revolutionary dream also paralleled the Hollthurn dream: revolt was replaced by flight. The dreamer found himself in the Aula, the great ceremonial hall of the university: "*The entrances were cordoned off and we had to escape.*" The dreamer next passed through a series of beautiful government rooms and eventually reached "*a corridor, in which a housekeeper was sitting, an elderly stout woman. I avoided speaking to her, but she evidently thought I had a right to pass.*"[102] This reference alluded to the idea of passing the censorship. As in the Hollthurn dream, Freud's flight was from the frustrations of political failure to the rewards of scientific success, and once again the escape was made possible by his own psychological theories, in this case his understanding of the mechanism of dream censorship. The crucial link between the political activity of the first scene and the scientific accomplishments of the later ones was a passage in the second scene in which Freud

[101] Freud, *Interpretation, S.E.,* IV:213; Grinstein, pp. 11–24.
[102] Freud, *Interpretation, S.E.,* IV:210.

was actually dreaming about the theory of dreams. In his analysis of this scene, he wrote that he was unable to deal with it in detail "out of consideration for the censorship," and a sentence later he added, "*I should not be justified in passing* the censorship at this point, even though the greater part of the story was told me by a Hofrat [imperial counselor]."[103] Word games constituted one of Freud's favorite amusements and in these sentences he was indulging in this pastime, for it was ambiguous whether he was referring here to the censorship he was applying to his book or to the dream censorship that might block his rebellious dream thoughts.[104]

In the dream's first scene the issues of freedom of speech and the press had been alluded to in a revolutionary context not only on the political level, through Adolf Fischhof and the radical student movement, but also on the personal level in the quarrel with Adler, where Freud refused to withdraw (and thus censor) his insulting remarks despite the demands of the crowd. In the second scene Freud escaped such direct confrontation between freedom of expression and censorial authority by outwitting the censorship rather than rebelliously rejecting it. The lady with the lamp thought that the dreamer was "*justified in passing*" and later the dreamer felt "*very cunning in thus avoiding inspection at the end.*"[105] Referring to the second scene with its allusions to the processes of dream censorship, Freud wrote, "In this boastful dream I was evidently proud of having discovered those processes,"[106] and as he later showed, this boastful mood was necessitated by the threatening nature of the conflicts in the first scene. In effect Freud was boasting that his discovery had freed him from the tyranny of confrontation politics, from the fruitless dialectic of revolt and guilt to which his own psychological nature and Austrian political reality had condemned him. In the second scene, having renounced the open defiance of the brother band, Freud followed a course which acknowledged the formal authority of the censor while allowing his revolutionary thoughts to escape without significant alteration. By transposing the conflict from the world of politics to the world of the human psyche Freud could achieve the kind of middle

[103] Ibid., p. 214.

[104] In a 1910 article Herbert Silberer pointed out that an understanding of this scene depends on the parallel between psychological censorship within the dream and book censorship in the analysis, a view Freud indirectly acknowledged as correct in subsequent editions of *The Interpretation of Dreams:* Silberer, "Phantasie und Mythos," *Jahrbuch für Psychoanalytische und Psychopathologische Forschungen*, 2 (1910):554–56.

[105] Freud, *Interpretation, S.E.*, IV:210, 214; retranslated from the German.

[106] Ibid., p. 215n.

position that had become impossible in Viennese politics and in so doing transform himself from victim into master.

In the third scene of the revolutionary dream, the dreamer's flight continued: *"It was as though the second problem was to get out of the town, just as the first one had been to get out of the house."* The next lines involved a tangle of absurdities concerning a coach ride, and in the analysis Freud's associations led him to connect the coachman with Count Thun and his own younger brother, Alexander.[107] Freud regarded his analysis of this segment of the dream as particularly significant. In a letter accompanying the manuscript which he sent to Fliess, he referred to it as the climax of his achievements in dream interpretation.[108] In the final published version he presented this passage from the revolutionary dream as the "solution to the mystery" and flatly declared, "We are now to discover the significance of absurdity in dreams and the motives which lead to its being admitted or even created."[109] Absurdity, he argued, represented an unconscious train of thought involving criticism or ridicule—in this case directed both at Count Thun and Freud's brother. More specifically, the absurdities here concerned two related riddles that Freud had tried vainly to solve while visiting the house of the lady alluded to in the form of the censor in the second scene. Their solution involved the words "ancestors" and "descendants," and the dream thoughts that Freud proudly untangled from the absurdities imposed by the censorship were saying, "It is absurd to be proud of one's ancestry; it is better to be an ancestor oneself."[110] On one level the first half of this statement, with its attack on aristocratic presumption and its implicit slander of Freud's father, represented a continuation of the rebellious, antiauthoritarian thoughts of the first scene, but on another level the dream thoughts were resolving these impulses by reassuring Freud that his lack of ancestors was an insignificant problem. "It is better to be an ancestor," to be a great and famous scientist whose descendants would be proud of him. Once again the dream managed to dissolve political frustration and conflict with the solvent of scientific success. It is important to note that this is one of the few places where Freud clearly and completely stated the latent dream thoughts underlying the manifest content of his dreams, and as such it can be seen as a triumph of free speech over the power of censorial authority in its most extreme form. Here at

[107] Ibid., IV:210; V:432.
[108] Freud, *Origins,* p. 299.
[109] Freud, *Interpretation, S.E.,* V:433.
[110] Ibid., p. 434.

last he could take on as scientist the role of liberator denied him by political reality. His pride in solving the central riddle of absurdity in dreams can thus be seen as part of his sense of triumph.

At this point in the dream the Roman context of Freud's Hannibal complex seems particularly relevant to his conception of the censor. In ancient Rome the censor was responsible for drawing up the lists of those to be admitted to the Senate, the forum of the fathers, and in addition he acted as an overseer of public morality. He could, for example, assign citizens to the *aerarii,* which subjected them to a special tax as a mark of disgrace for criminal or immoral acts. An allusion to this ancient practice came in the second scene of the dream; Freud noted that the public rooms referred to public women, "*ärarische Frauenzimmer,*" a term recalling the ancient Roman custom and also conveying the contemporary meaning, "woman of the street." The wide range of activities Freud ascribed to the dream censor in governing the entry of thoughts into consciousness as well as repressing immoral impulses had precedents in the history of censorship from ancient Rome to turn-of-the-century Austria.

The fourth and final scene of the revolutionary dream brought to completion the process through which Freud dissolved history and politics into psychology. In this scene all references to brothers or brother substitutes disappeared and Freud found himself alone at the train station with a partially blind old man whom his analysis connected both with his father and with Count Thun. The scene was filled with allusions to Freud's own psychological discoveries, and these discoveries placed him in a position of authority over the feeble old man. In his analysis Freud collapsed the entire range of allusions to social and political rebellion in the dream as a whole into the basic psychological relationship with his father. He argued that "the whole rebellious content of the dream, with its *lèse majesté* and its derision of the higher authorities, went back to rebellion against my father. A Prince is known as father of his country; the father is the oldest, first, and for children the only authority, and from his autocratic power the other social authorities have developed."[111] Carl Schorske notes that "in this passage Freud adumbrates his mature political theory, the central principle of which is that all politics is reducible to the primal conflict between father and son. . . . Patricide replaces regicide; psychoanalysis overcomes history. Politics is neutralized by a counterpolitical psychology."[112]

[111] Ibid., IV:217.
[112] Schorske, *Vienna,* p. 197.

In this final scene Freud celebrated in his dream world the victory over politics that the reality of Viennese life had denied him, for as scientist and professional he could boast of having finally mastered the political forces that originally gave rise to his Hannibal phantasy.

7/

Brothers and Sisters

During the final year of his work on the Dream Book, Freud accomplished another crucial piece of self-analysis and once again employed it to fill out his developing theory of dreams. The year before in August 1897, the breakthrough he achieved in understanding his ambivalent feelings toward his father had been followed by a revolution in his thought as the seduction theory gave way to the myth of Oedipus. In the fall of 1898 Freud made a somewhat similar, though more partial, advance in understanding his emotionally tangled brother relationships. In so doing he also came to understand how screen memories developed as well as how the dream work translated underlying dream thoughts into manifest content. In both cases he discovered that language played a significant role, a discovery which provided an important missing link in his theoretical structure. As Freud's own dreams reveal, the personal and theoretical advances that allowed him to complete *The Interpretation of Dreams* also brought him a greater measure of emotional maturity and self-assurance. His dreams and his work on his book show that the biblical themes that shaped his childhood interests returned at this supreme moment of accomplishment to offer the paternal example of Moses as a guiding image for his future work as leader of the psychoanalytic movement.

A trail of flowers led Freud to his new discoveries. His revolutionary dream of July 1898 contained a veritable bouquet of politically and sexually significant flower symbolism. In its first scene, when Count Thun was addressing the meeting, he said with a gesture of contempt that the Germans favourite flower was colt's foot, and put "some sort of dilapidated leaf . . . into his buttonhole." Freud's analysis connected this leaf with the Shakespeare play that depicts the beginning of the Wars of the Roses and moved on to white and red carnations—in Vienna emblems respectively of the anti-Semitic Christian Social movement and the Jewish-led Social Democrats.[1] The flowers directly recalled Freud's earlier involvement in radical politics, and they also alluded to a real political event that had occurred two months earlier. On June 7, at what proved to be the last meeting of the Reichsrath's twenty-fourth session, a deputy had passed out blue cornflowers (bachelor's buttons) to all the Pan-German members of the house as part of a protest against the government's action in suppression of German nationalist agitation in Graz.[2] Rather than face Parliamentary examination on this issue, Count Thun then dissolved the session, so this contemptuous gesture and the flower symbolism had been associated in recent history, just as they were in Freud's dream.

The flower symbolism of the revolutionary dream reveals a direct link between Freud's political sentiments and the homoerotic feelings involved in his brother relationships. In his analysis, Freud associated the flowers with the theme of political conflict through allusions to his own past involvement with Viktor Adler, the leader of the Social Democrats, and with Alder's brother-in-law, Heinrich Braun, whose political and sexual vigor led Freud to connect him here with Henry VIII of England.[3] Allusions to Braun can be seen in references to two different flowers that figured in this dream. His name (Braun means brown) appeared as the color of the flowers in scene three, where Freud found himself on a local train with "*a peculiar plaited, long-shaped object*" in his buttonhole. He indicated that the object had "*violet brown violets*" on it, and in his associations he described the object as a *Mädchenfänger* (girl catcher). He connected the color of these flowers with a color in the second scene: the government rooms had "*furniture upholstered in a colour between brown and violet.*"[4] Like Heinrich Braun, the color brown in the dream was associated both with sexual prowess (the girl catcher) and with political power (the furniture in the government rooms). The other flower alluding to Braun in the associations to the revolutionary dream was the dandelion (*Löwenzahn*)—lion's tooth—in German, as mentioned earlier. The play on words contained in

[1] Freud, *Interpretation, S.E.*, IV:212.

[2] Sutter, *Badenischen Sprachverordnungen*, II:367–71. This ties into the reference to Graz in the dream (Freud, *Interpretation, S.E.*, IV:210, 215).

[3] Freud, *Interpretation, S.E.*, IV:212.

[4] Ibid., pp. 210, 215–16.

this allusion can be understood in the light of Freud's own revealing description of his adolescent friendship with Braun: "I compared him secretly with a young lion."[5]

The image of the young lion gains particular significance in view of the discovery made by Herbert Lehmann that one of the dreams Freud discussed in the *The Interpretation of Dreams* and attributed to an unnamed physician, a dream involving a yellow lion, was actually one of his own.[6] Freud wrote, "This lion out of his dreams made its appearance one day in bodily form, as a china ornament that had long disappeared. The young man then learnt from his mother that this object had been his favorite toy during his early childhood."[7] This yellow lion further illuminates the meaning of the dandelions in the revolutionary dream. Through a chain of associations, Freud linked the flower in the dream scene to the dandelions gathered by a child in Emile Zola's novel *Germinal.* Zola, like Heinrich Braun, held both political and sexual significance for Freud, and the novel explored in detail both the revolutionary politics and the unrestrained sexuality of the working class. Moreover, Zola's actions in the Dreyfus affair exemplified the highest ideals of political courage and self-sacrifice in the face of virulent anti-Semitism. Freud's dream associations alluded to a passage in *Germinal* in which Jeanlin, the ten-year-old son of a miner, was sent out to gather dandelions for a salad, a task he fulfilled in the company of the neighbor's daughter and another boy. Afterward Jeanlin and the girl engaged in sexual play while the friend looked on. "She was his little wife and together in holes and corners they used to try out the love-making that they saw and heard at home."[8]

Freud hid the fact that the dream of the yellow lion was his own, just as he masked his identity in the screen memory of the yellow flowers, because both alluded to Braun's role in an essentially bisexual phantasy which had played a central role in his emotional life. His interpretation of the screen memory involving his nephew and niece, which was strikingly similar to the scene in *Germinal,* emphasizes the parallel to Zola's story: "Taking flowers away from a girl means to deflower her." The bisexual or homoerotic components of the screen memory were suggested more indirectly,

[5] Freud, *Letters,* p. 379.

[6] Herbert Lehmann, "Two Dreams and a Childhood Memory of Freud," *Journal of the American Psychoanalytic Association,* 14 (April 1966):388–405.

[7] Freud, *Interpretation, S.E.,* IV:190.

[8] Grinstein, *Freud's Dreams,* p. 112; Emile Zola, *Germinal,* trans. L. W. Tancock (Harmondsworth: Penguin, 1971), p. 127.

however. In his conversation with the fictional patient he asked, "For instance, your boy cousin helping you to rob the little girl of her flowers—can you make any sense of the idea of being helped in deflowering someone?"[9] The fictional patient could not, but Ernest Jones regarded this phantasy as a "sign that Freud's sexual constitution was not exclusively masculine after all, to 'hunt in couples' means sharing one's gratification with someone of one's own sex."[10] In the essay, Freud turned immediately from the unanswered question to another example concerning two boys engaged in sexual play with each other, an example in which almost the same words recurred. It involved a memory of "his being helped to do it by someone."[11] The screen memory of the dandelions expressed Freud's need to bolster his own incomplete sense of masculinity by exploring sexuality with the aid of a virile friend, a need which had led to a life history of sexually charged brother relationships with men such as the "young lion," Heinrich Braun.

As yet, the exact date at which Freud accomplished the piece of self-analysis involving the screen memory of the yellow flowers has not been determined, but the evidence of his dreams and recently published passages from his letters to Fliess point to an emerging concern with the screen memory's underlying themes over the second half of 1898 and a realization of its meaning toward the end of December. In his letter of January 3, 1899, he wrote that following his late December meeting with Fliess he had "suddenly glimpsed several things. . . . In the first place, a small bit of my self-analysis . . . has confirmed that fantasies are products of later periods and are projected back . . . into early childhood."[12] This comment, which various scholars have taken as a reference to his screen memory of the yellow flowers,[13] echoes a passage in Freud's July 7, 1898 letter to Fliess, where he observed that in the formation of phantasies "a new experience is in fantasy projected back into the past so that the new persons become aligned with the old ones, who become their prototypes. The mirror image of the present is seen in a fantasied past."[14] The conception of phantasy underlying Freud's understanding of screen memories was

[9] Freud, "Screen Memories," *S.E.*, III:316.
[10] Jones, *Life and Work,* I:11.
[11] Freud, "Screen Memories," *S.E.*, III:319.
[12] Freud, *Complete Letters,* p. 338. The first part of this passage was omitted in *Origins.*
[13] Freud, *Origins,* p. 271n; Anzieu, *L'auto-analyse de Freud,* II:525–26.
[14] Freud, *Complete Letters,* p. 320. The last part of this passage was omitted in *Origins.*

clearly articulated as early as July, and there are many thematic links between the revolutionary dream of late July and the sexual configuration of the screen memory. Even if Freud was not yet conscious of the screen memory's emotional message when he had the dream, it seems evident that it was at least exerting an unconscious influence on his dream images at that time.

In Freud's dream life the theme of the brother and sister became particularly prominent during the summer and fall of 1898. The theme's emergence seems closely related to the process of retrieving the screen memory of the yellow flowers and it may also be related to Freud's feelings about his sister-in-law, Minna Bernays, who lived with his family, shared in his intellectual work, and (in contrast to his wife) frequently accompanied him on his vacations.[15] The brother and sister theme appeared, in the Hollthurn and revolutionary dreams of mid-summer 1898, in the dream of the three Fates, which probably occurred that September or October, and in the *Non vixit* dream of late October.[16] It surfaced with particular clarity in the Hollthurn dream of July, where the English brother and

[15] Peter Swales indicates that Freud called Minna "Schwester" (sister) rather than "Schwägerin" (sister-in-law), which might tie into the brother-sister theme in his dream life. Swales has argued that Freud not only felt a strong attraction for Minna but that he actually had an affair with her: Swales, "Freud, Minna Bernays and the Conquest of Rome." Evidence that there was such an affair also comes from Carl Jung, who discussed it in an interview with John Billinsky. Referring to a 1907 visit to Vienna, Jung declared: "Soon I met Freud's wife's younger sister. She was very good-looking and she not only knew enough about psychoanalysis but also about everything that Freud was doing. When, a few days later, I was visiting Freud's laboratory, Freud's sister-in-law asked me if she could talk with me. She was very much bothered by her relationship with Freud and felt guilty about it. From her I learned that Freud was in love with her and that their relationship was indeed very intimate. It was a shocking discovery to me, and even now I can recall the agony I felt at the time.

"Two years later Freud and I were invited to Clark University in Worcester, and we were together every day for some seven weeks. From the very beginning of our trip we started to analyze each other's dreams. Freud had some dreams that bothered him very much. The dreams were about the triangle—Freud, his wife, and wife's younger sister. Freud had no idea that I knew about the triangle and his intimate relationship with his sister-in-law. And so, when Freud told me about the dream in which his wife and her sister played important parts, I asked Freud to tell me some of his personal associations with the dream. He looked at me with bitterness and said, 'I could tell you more, but I cannot risk my authority' ": John M. Billinsky, "Jung and Freud (The End of a Romance)," *Andover Newton Quarterly,* 10 (Nov. 1969): 42. Various Freud scholars have discounted Jung's testimony as biased, but the question of the affair remains open. The prominence of the brother-sister theme in Freud's dreams strongly suggests that he was at least very much attracted to Minna.

[16] On this theme in the revolutionary dream, see Grinstein, p. 129; on the date of the three Fates dream and the role of this theme in it, see Grinstein, pp. 161, 167–68, 174, 183, 189; see Schur, *Freud,* p. 160, for the date of *Non vixit,* and pp. 158–64 for the brother-sister theme in it.

sister were substituted for the disagreeable Austrians with whom Freud was traveling, and the wishes underlying this dream are directly relevant to the important dreams of the fall. In the Hollthurn dream, Freud's own psychoanalytic technique allowed him to escape the conflicts (political and sexual) of the Austrian half of the dream and reach the peaceful English compartment containing the congenial brother and sister. This friendly English world symbolized the security Freud saw as an alternative to the aggressive world associated with sex, politics, and professional ambition, and this alternative figured prominently in Freud's own interpretation of the screen memory. In it, Freud and his nephew first "deflowered" Pauline by taking away her bouquet and then discarded the flowers in favor of the bread offered by the peasant woman. In the essay, Freud as fictional patient observed that much later when he was a university student he had visited these relatives in their now distant homeland and that the visit had contributed to the phantasy expressed in the screen memory, for at the time his father and half-brother together planned to have him "exchange the abstruse subject of my studies for one of more practical value, settle down, after my studies were completed, in the place where my uncle [half-brother] lived, and marry my cousin [niece]." In his role as analyst Freud then commented on this phantasy of marrying his niece: "Throwing away the flowers in exchange for bread strikes me as not a bad disguise for the scheme your father had for you: you were to give up your unpractical ideals and take on a 'bread-and-butter' occupation."[17] The screen memory wish for security in place of exploring taboo sexuality emerged in the Hollthurn dream as well as in those of the fall, and these dreams were linked by other major themes in addition to that of the brother and sister. For example, it is particularly significant that the most important and thoroughly analyzed of the fall dreams, the *Non vixit* dream, contained allusions to Schiller just as the Hollthurn dream did. Moreover, in both (as in the intervening revolutionary dream) Freud's own psychoanalytic theory figured prominently in the subject matter of the manifest content.

Since Freud himself subjected the *Non vixit* dream to an unusually thorough and penetrating analysis, Freud scholars have been able to develop a much more complete understanding of it than has been possible for most of his other dreams. The interpretations advanced by Schur, Grinstein, and Anzieu all illuminate important dimensions of its meaning. Schur's determination that the dream

[17] Freud, "Screen Memories," *S.E.*, III:314, 315.

must have occurred within a few days of October 28[18] places it in the same period as the dream of the three Fates. This latter dream, *Non vixit,* and a psychological slip (involving the name Mosen) that occurred at this time reveal similar themes and associations, and examining *Non vixit* in the context of these recurrent patterns helps to fill out an understanding of the dream and its bearing on the screen memory phantasy.

Freud gave the following account of the dream, which he used to explain the meaning of speeches in dreams.

> *I had gone to Brücke's laboratory at night, and, in response to a gentle knock on the door, I opened it to* (the late) *Professor Fleischl, who came in with a number of strangers and, after exchanging a few words, sat down at his table.* This was followed by a second dream. *My friend, Fl.* [Fliess] *had come to Vienna unobtrusively in July. I met him in the street in conversation with my* (deceased) *friend P., and went with them to some place where they sat opposite each other as though they were at a small table. I sat in front at its narrow end. Fl. spoke about his sister and said that in three quarters of an hour she was dead, and added some such words as 'that was the threshold'. As P. failed to understand him, Fl. turned to me and asked me how much I had told P. about his affairs. Whereupon, overcome by strange emotions, I tried to explain to Fl. that P. (could not understand anything at all, of course, because he) was not alive. But what I actually said—and I myself noticed the mistake—was,* 'NON VIXIT.' *I then gave P. a piercing look. Under my gaze he turned pale; his form grew indistinct and his eyes a sickly blue—and finally he melted away. I was highly delighted at this and I now realized that Ernst Fleischl, too, had been no more than an apparition, a 'revenant'* ['ghost'—literally, 'one who returns']; *and it seemed to me quite possible that people of that kind only existed as long as one liked and could be got rid of if someone else wished it.*[19]

Freud's analysis of the early parts of the dream indicated that it revolved around individuals with whom he had stood in a collegial or brotherly relationship at different times in his career. In addition to Fliess, the dominant brother figure at the time of the dream, it also involved or alluded to Ernst Fleischl von Marxow, Joseph Paneth, and Josef Breuer, all closely associated with Freud during the time he was working in Brücke's laboratory. Freud saw that various elements of the dream pointed to the keen competitive feelings he and other members of this brother band had had in their desire to obtain a permanent position in the great man's laboratory.[20]

[18] Schur, *Freud,* p. 160.
[19] Freud, *Interpretation, S.E.,* v:421.
[20] Ibid., p. 484.

The desire for professional success expressed in this part of the dream had as its corollary on the personal level the desire to triumph over the brothers in succeeding to the father's position. On this level of meaning Max Schur's interpretation is particularly valuable. Schur argues that *Non vixit* occurred almost exactly two years after the death of Freud's father and that it was an anniversary dream, expressing the wishes and fears appropriate to the death of a father.[21] He also shows convincingly that the dream signaled a deepening of the crisis developing in Freud's personal relationship with Fliess. In the *Non vixit* dream the problem posed by the intensity of Freud's desire to overcome the brothers and take the father's place found a dream solution that pointed the way toward the answer he subsequently found in real life.

One of the reassurances the *Non vixit* dream offered to the fears aroused by the problem of succession can be seen in its many allusions to Freud's phantasy identification with Joseph. Josef was the first name of Freud's friend P. (Paneth), who appeared directly in the dream, and of another former friend, Breuer, who was alluded to in the dream associations.[22] Moreover, Freud indicated that the words which provided the dream's central puzzle, the words "Non vixit," were taken from the inscription on the base of a statue honoring Kaiser Josef II, the enlightened emperor whose political values Freud greatly admired. Freud also noted that Kaiser Josef Strasse figured in his associations to the dream.[23] Moreover, an important detail of the dream's manifest content alluded directly to the Joseph story. In the dream Freud said that "*Fl. turned to me and asked me how much I had told P. about his affairs*," and in his analysis he recognized this question as an allusion to both recent and much earlier events in his life. One of the motivating factors in the dream was his concern for Fliess, who had recently undergone a serious operation. In connection with initially unfavorable reports about the outcome, Freud said that he was "given a warning not to discuss the matter with anyone. I had felt offended by this because it implied an unnecessary distrust of my discretion." He found this reproach particularly annoying, he admitted, because events from an earlier time in his life seemed to give it some justification. During the period when he was working in Brücke's laboratory he had "caused trouble between two friends . . . by quite unnecessarily telling one of them . . . what the other had said about him. . . . One of the two friends concerned was

[21] Schur, *Freud*, pp. 154, 160–61.
[22] Freud, *Interpretation, S.E.*, V:482.
[23] Ibid., pp. 422–23.

Professor Fleischl; I may describe the other by his first name of 'Josef'. . . ."[24] The biblical Joseph was also a "bearer of tales" who caused trouble for his brothers by reporting their activities to their father, a practice which had intensified their dislike of him. The frequency of these allusions led Freud to make a guarded admission that he did in fact identify with the biblical Joseph. In a footnote to the dream he observed, "It will be noticed that the name Josef plays a great part in my dreams. . . . My own ego finds it very easy to hide itself behind people of that name, since Joseph was the name of a man famous in the Bible as an interpreter of dreams."[25] In its allusions to Joseph, the *Non vixit* dream offered Freud reassurance that he was his father's favorite son and would triumph over his brothers in the contest to secure the father's blessing.

As Schur has demonstrated, the problems involved in Freud's relationship with Fliess lay at the heart of the *Non vixit* dream, and the hostile side of Freud's ambivalent feelings toward his friend expressed itself with unprecedented intensity. In earlier dreams this ambivalence had found an outlet in critical or negative dream thoughts, but in *Non vixit* the dream wish directed at Fliess implied his death or annihilation.[26] In analyzing his competitive feelings toward various deceased members of the academic brotherhood, Freud revealed the following dream thoughts: "It's quite true that no one's irreplaceable. How many people I've followed to the grave already! But I'm still alive. I've survived them all; I'm left in possession of the field." As he went on to observe, the fact that these thoughts occurred immediately after Fliess's operation "at a moment at which I was afraid I might not find my friend [Fl.] alive if I made the journey to him, could only be construed as meaning that I was delighted because I had once more survived someone, because it was *he* and not I who had died, because I was left in possession of the field."[27] In explaining the source of these deeply hostile feelings, Freud pointed to the same early childhood relationship with his nephew John which figured in the screen memory of the yellow flowers: "My warm friendships as well as my enmities with contemporaries went back to my relations in childhood with a nephew who was a year my senior. . . . All my friends have in a certain sense been re-incarnations of this first

[24] Ibid., pp. 481, 482.
[25] Ibid., p. 484n.
[26] Schur, *Freud,* p. 168.
[27] Freud, *Interpretation, S.E.,* V:485.

figure; . . . they have been *revenants.*"[28] While there is no reason to doubt Freud's contention about the origins of his ambivalence, Schur has argued convincingly that the intensity of his hostility also directly reflected the contemporary conflict in his relationship with Fliess.[29] As Freud gradually overcame his fears and doubts about assuming a paternal role, it would be natural that his sense of competition within the brother band for the father's position would intensify.

In the manifest content of the *Non vixit* dream Freud did directly assume the father's role in one passage: *"I then gave P. a piercing look. Under my gaze he turned pale; his form grew indistinct and his eyes a sickly blue—and finally he melted away."* Freud said in his analysis that this scene was copied from an experience that occurred while he was working in Brücke's Institute. One morning when he arrived late to open the laboratory he found Brücke himself, waiting to be let in. "His words were brief and to the point. But it was not they that mattered. What overwhelmed me were the terrible blue eyes with which he looked at me and by which I was reduced to nothing—just as P. was in the dream, where, to my relief, the roles were reversed."[30] In this reversal of roles Freud not only escaped the punishment of the annihilating gaze; he also took Brücke's place in the incident, thereby assuming the paternal position.

In his analysis of the *Non vixit* dream Freud established the link between his contemporary feelings of rivalry and his early childhood relationship with his nephew through associations tied to this annihilating gaze. He indicated that he was punishing P. for his own ambitious desires: "As he had deserved well of science I built him a memorial, but as he was guilty of an evil wish . . . I annihilated him." Freud then recognized that the structure, cadence, and meaning of this sentence imitated that of "Brutus' speech of self-justification in Shakespeare's *Julius Caesar,* 'As Caesar loved me, I weep for him . . . as he was valiant, I honour him; but as he was ambitious, I slew him'."[31] By means of this associative link, Freud realized that he "had been playing the part of Brutus in the dream," a realization that had the greatest significance for his understanding of its underlying meaning. It is also important in revealing the intellectual origins of Freud's psychoanalytic theory. Once he rec-

[28] Ibid., p. 483.
[29] Schur, *Freud,* p. 167.
[30] Freud, *Interpretation, S.E.,* v:422.
[31] Ibid., p. 423.

ognized the dream allusion to Brutus, Freud could follow the dream thoughts back to his childhood experiences. He wrote, "I really did once play the part of Brutus. I once acted in the scene between Brutus and Caesar from Schiller. . . . I was fourteen years old at the time and was acting with a nephew who was a year my senior. He had come to us on a visit from England; and he, too, was a *revenant,* for it was the playmate of my earliest years who had returned in him."[32] In the context of the dream, then, the revenant theme echoed the psychoanalytic insight that this early relationship continued to exercise emotional power over the events of Freud's adult life.

As both Grinstein and Schur have demonstrated, the dream's allusions to *The Robbers* give important clues to its meaning.[33] Neither scholar, however, has fully explored the political significance of these allusions or their relevance to the development of Freud's psychoanalytic theory. The dialogue between Brutus and Caesar in "the Roman song"—the scene Freud and his nephew acted—occurred when the shades of the two Romans encountered each other in Hades, so in a certain sense they too were revenants. Whereas Brutus, like Karl Moor, represented the ideal of freedom, Caesar stood for the principle of authority and power, and presented himself as father of his country unjustly slain by his son, Brutus. Both Grinstein and Schur have rightly emphasized the Oedipal significance of the dream allusions to this scene, but this emphasis should be balanced by an appreciation of the brother conflict that provides its context. In the drama, the Brutus/Caesar scene epitomized the conflict between freedom and authority which was the play's central theme, but Karl Moor's antagonist was his brother, Franz, rather than his father. Where Karl Moor's unrestrained exercise of freedom initially threatened to degenerate into license, his brother's thirst for power and authority led to political tyranny. Only at the conclusion of the play did Karl Moor achieve a synthesis of freedom and authority that pointed the way to genuine freedom. The emphasis on father/son conflict in "the Roman song" and on brother conflict in the play as a whole might be seen as a confusing element in Schiller's drama, but if so it was a confusion which perfectly fitted the problems inherent in what Freud called his "family complex." As he indicated in his analysis of the screen memory of his mother locked in the cabinet, as a young child he had identified his half-brother Philipp, rather than his father, as

[32] Ibid., p. 424. See Chap. 2, pp. 66–73.
[33] Grinstein, pp. 297–305; Schur, *Freud,* pp. 165–66.

his chief Oedipal rival, and this confusion of brother and father continued to manifest itself in various dreams and psychological slips during his adult life. The brother figures Fleischl, Paneth, and Breuer who appeared in the *Non vixit* dream also had a paternal dimension in that they all provided financial support to help Freud pursue his scientific career, something his own father did not have the resources to do.[34] Here, as in Freud's adolescence, the brothers compensated for the father's inadequacy.

Freud's realization that he way playing the role of Brutus in the dream also illuminates the meaning of its remarkable conclusion. After P. melted away under Freud's annihilating gaze, he realized that "*Ernst Fleischl, too, had been no more than an appartition, a 'revenant'; and it seemed to me quite possible that people of that kind only existed as long as one liked and could be got rid of if someone else wished it.*" Here, as in the Hollthurn and revolutionary dreams, it seems evident that Freud was dreaming about his own psychoanalytic technique. His work with hysterical patients taught him that people could indeed be haunted by ghosts or revenants from their emotional pasts and that it was possible to exorcise such ghosts. In playing the role of Brutus in the dream, he was doing just that to himself, and in this dream allusion he once again aligned the concept of freedom with the concept of psychoanalysis. The political freedom which Brutus and Karl Moor asserted against the power of the tyrants Caesar and Franz became translated in Freud's dream into psychoanalytic freedom from the tyranny of the passions associated with his brother relationships. In his analysis he referred to his nephew as his tyrant, and in the dream Freud, as Brutus, slew the revenant of this tyrant. He had used exactly the same imagery and allusions in referring to the power his passions exercised over him in an earlier letter to Fliess (April 27, 1895): he wrote that he had to have "a consuming passion—in Schiller's words a tyrant."[35] In this way the dream wish expressed Freud's desire to gain greater autonomy by freeing himself from his emotional dependence on Fliess.

The *Non vixit* dream also suggested another way out of the emotional problems posed by the existence of psychological revenants. In the dream and its associations, Freud's analysis revealed that name coincidences played a large role—the two Ernsts, the various Josefs, the similarity of Fleischl and Fliess—and this feature ties the dream to the dream of the three Fates, which also occurred

[34] Schur, *Freud,* p. 157; Jones, 1:60–61.
[35] Freud, *Origins,* p. 119.

during this period. Freud's analysis of the latter dream revealed allusions to some of the same academic colleagues who figured in *Non vixit* (Ernst Fleischl, Ernst Brücke), and he found that he was misusing or playing with the names. The three Fates dream translated the name of another colleague, Knödel, into its literal meaning: "dumpling." It also made use of the similarity between Fleischl and *Fleisch* (meat). As Freud observed, even the "honored name of Brücke [bridge]" fell prey to this "need to set up forced connections."[36] This kind of literal interpretation of names and words by the dream work is a common characteristic of all dreams, and Freud's dreams seem particularly given to it. In the *Non vixit* dream, however, the significance of names was much more central. Freud developed this point in connection with the dream's allusions to Fliess, whose wife had given birth to a daughter a short time before: "I was aware of how deeply he had mourned the sister he had so early lost and I wrote and told him I was sure he would transfer the love he felt for her on to the child, and that the baby girl would allow him at last to forget his irreparable loss."[37] Fliess had, in fact, named his new daughter Pauline after his dead sister, and in a letter of October 9, 1898, Freud had written: "Note how soon Paulinechen will reveal herself to you as the reincarnation of your sister."[38] As Schur quite rightly observed, "Here is the revenant theme of the non vixit dream!"[39] That Pauline was also the name of Freud's niece, the sister of his nephew John, served to emphasize further Fliess's role as a revenant of the childhood playmate around whom Freud's screen memory of the yellow flowers formed. But the birth of Fliess's daughter and Freud's comment about it also illustrated how becoming a father could lessen the disturbing emotional power of such revenants. Freud observed that considering the various name coincidences in the dream led him to think of his own children and the names he had chosen for them: "I had insisted on their names being chosen, not according to the fashion of the moment, but in memory of people I have been fond of. Their names made the children into *revenants.* And after all, I reflected, was not having children our only path to immortality?"[40] Freud had named one of his sons Oliver after Oliver Cromwell, whose revolutionary politics he admired, and his other two sons Jean Martin and Ernst, after his two great teachers, Charcot and

[36] Freud, *Interpretation, S.E.,* IV:206.
[37] Ibid., V:486.
[38] Quoted in Schur, *Freud,* p. 158.
[39] Ibid.
[40] Freud, *Interpretation, S.E.,* V:487.

Brücke. His daughters were named Mathilde after Breuer's wife; Sophie after the niece of Freud's religious teacher, Samuel Hammerschlag, and Anna after Hammerschlag's daughter.[41]

Although this use of names to pass on to others the emotional legacies of the revenants might seem a somewhat magical or at least quite limited solution to emotional problems, the allusions to Freud's brother relatonships were also linked to a wish for escape from the emotional tyranny exerted by his homoerotic feelings. In his analysis of the dream Freud noted that when he learned of the birth of Fliess's daughter, "It gave me great *satisfaction* when I heard that the baby was to be called 'Pauline'," and this feeling of satisfaction formed a link to the final part of the dream scene.[42] In it, after expressing his realization that the various brother figures were revenants and that "*people of that kind only existed as long as one liked and could be got rid of if someone else wished it,*" Freud noted "the great satisfaction it gave me."[43] The feeling of satisfaction emerged from the psychoanalytic insight that it was indeed possible to transfer strong feelings from one individual to another and that it was also possible to redirect the aim of these feelings. Freud's attraction to various male friends could be overcome by transforming it into intellectually productive labor. The names in the *Non vixit* dream all involved men with whom Freud was closely involved in his scientific work, and Joseph, the name that occurred most frequently, was the name of the man with whom Freud coauthored his *Studies on Hysteria.* Freud clearly entertained the possibility of a similar outlet for the powerful feelings involved in his troubled relationship with Fliess. In a letter written to him three years later when the friendship was coming to an end, he discussed this possibility quite openly in terms of his brother relationships:

> As far as Breuer is concerned, you are certainly quite right in calling him *the* brother. However, I do not share your contempt for friendship between men, probably because I am to a high degree a party to it. As you well know, in my life a woman has never been a substitute for a comrade, a friend. If Breuer's masculine inclination were not so odd, so faint-hearted, so contradictory, as is everything emotional in him, he would be a beautiful example of the kinds of achievements to which the androphile current in men can be sublimated.[44]

[41] Clark, *Freud,* p. 111.
[42] Freud, *Interpretation, S.E.,* v:486.
[43] Ibid., pp. 421–22.
[44] Quoted in Schur, *Freud,* pp. 216–17.

In the same letter Freud suggested the possibility that he and Fliess might collaborate on a biological-psychological study of human bisexuality.[45] Fliess had become the focus of Freud's own bisexual feelings, and through the theme of name coincidences, with its associated idea of redirecting emotions, the dream suggested the possibility that psychoanaylsis could open the way to freedom from the tyranny of the revenants.

The *Non vixit* theme of naming the children also expressed a desire for a more basic solution to Freud's emotional difficulties, namely the wish to take on a more paternal role. Since Freud was already the father of six children, this wish must be understood primarily on a symbolic level: what he saw as his own father's inadequacies seems to have blocked his desire to see himself as a father. In the *Non vixit* dream, the Brücke identification, the annihilation of the brother revenants, and the theme of naming the children all pointed toward a desire to succeed to the father's position. But in contrast to such previous dreams as that of the castle by the sea, the desire in *Non vixit* was not hedged in by doubts. This greater certainty suggests that Freud's continuing self-analysis was leading him to a more advanced level of emotional maturity, and his progress seems related to his retrieval of the psychic material analyzed in the screen memory of the yellow flowers. Both the screen memory and the *Non vixit* dream recalled memories of his childhood friendship with John and Pauline Freud, memories underlying the brother and sister theme that appeared so frequently in his dream life over this period.[46] Moreover, Freud's self-analytic success in understanding the meaning of his screen memory was followed by a shift in the subject matter of his dreams: the political and sexual themes associated with his involvement in the brother band, the themes which appeared so frequently in the 1898 dreams, did not figure prominently in any of those we know to have occurred in 1899. In place of the brother themes, these later dreams far more frequently involved Freud's children, a change that suggests his development of a more paternal self-image.

The theme of name coincidences and playing with names so prominent in the *Non vixit* dream and the dream of the three Fates was also important in the earlier revolutionary dream (Count Thun-Nicht Thun, *Giraffe-Affe, Adler,* and so on).[47] The emergence of this theme thus coincided with Freud's first breakthrough in un-

[45] Ibid., p. 217.

[46] See Grinstein, pp. 169, 189, 193; Freud, *Interpretation, S.E.,* IV:231.

[47] Freud, *Interpretation, S.E.,* IV:209, 213–14. Freud explains these puns in his analysis of the dream.

derstanding another category of psychic phenomena involving names and words: the occurrence of slips and lapses of memory which he examined in his *Psychopathology of Everyday Life.* Freud announced his first success in understanding these slips of memory in a letter to Fliess of August 26, 1898, and the second in a letter of September 22, 1898. The latter example, involving the name of the Italian painter Luca Signorelli, became the subject of a detailed analysis in his *Psychopathology,* but Freud never published his analysis of the slip about which he first wrote to Fliess, even though he said in his letter that he was able to resolve its meaning completely. He had forgotten, he reported, "the name of the poet who wrote *Andreas Hofer* ("*Zu Mantua in Banden . . .*"). I felt it must be something ending in *au*—Lindau, Feldau, or the like. Actually of course, the poet's name was Julius Mosen; the "Julius" had not slipped my memory." Although Freud did not reveal the results of his analysis to Fliess, he did provide an outline of how the memory slip had functioned. He wrote that he had been able to determine that certain associations with the name Mosen had caused him to repress it, that material from his early childhood was involved in the repression; and that the names which he thought of in place of the correct one "arose, just like a symptom, from both groups of material." He also observed that although his analysis had completely resolved the meaning of the slip, "I cannot make it public any more than my big dream"[48]—the dream Fliess had objected to earlier in the year, for which Freud had then provided as an equally unsatisfactory substitute, the dream of the stately house.

Although Freud's censorship of the Mosen slip makes a full understanding of it difficult, the name Julius provides a starting point for unraveling its meaning. Julius was the name of Freud's brother who had died in infancy and who, according to an 1897 letter to Fliess, had been greeted with ill feelings and infantile jealousy. Freud also said that Julius' death left him with a sense of guilt and that this brother, along with his nephew, provided the bases for the neurotic side of his friendships as well as their depth.[49] This comment linking Julius to Freud's deeply conflicted brother relationships reveals a connection between the Mosen slip and the *Non vixit* dream, where the name Julius referred to the tyrant Julius Caesar, whom Freud, as Brutus, also greeted with ill wishes.[50] The *Non vixit* dream alluded to Freud's adolescent Schiller phantasy,

[48] Freud, *Origins,* pp. 261–62.
[49] Ibid., p. 219.
[50] On the Brutus theme in the dream of the three Fates, see Grinstein, p. 172.

and it seems likely that a similar allusion lay behind his inability to remember the name Mosen—a name quite similar to Moser, one of the most important characters in *The Robbers.* It was Pastor Moser who represented the voice of conscience in the play and who, at its climax, revealed to Franz Moor the meaning of the terrifying nightmare he had had. Driven almost to insanity, Franz asked Moser to tell him what were the worst possible sins a man could commit. Moser replied that there were two: "Parricide the one is called, fratricide the other—"[51] In the negative form of his adolescent phantasy Freud sometimes cast himself as the ugly Franz to Heinrich Braun's Karl,[52] and a similar impulse of self-doubt may have been at work in the Mosen slip. The death of Julius had left Freud with guilty feelings about his own fratricidal impulses, and he sought to repress them by blotting out the name Mosen, which was so reminiscent of Moser, the voice of conscience.

Freud connected his feelings about Julius with the mixed emotions involved in his relationship with nephew John and indicated that these early childhood experiences eventually led to the political outlook expressed in the Brutus-Caesar dialogue enacted when John visited him in Vienna. Both the father-son conflict and the conflict between brothers around which Schiller's play revolved tied into the central political theme of freedom versus tyranny, and analogous conflicts in Freud's own familial relationships infused his similar political outlook with deep personal significance. This connection seems to have been at work in the Mosen slip, for the text of the poem "Andreas Hofer," which Freud mentioned in his associations to the memory lapse, centered around this political theme. Freud wrote the letter to Fliess mentioning the Mosen slip immediately after returning from a trip which took him through the Tyrol, and Andreas Hofer, the hero of the Tyrol, was just the sort of figure to excite Freud's admiration. Against overwhelming military odds, he had for a time successfully resisted Napoleon's effort to detach the Tyrol from the German empire and incorporate it into his own imperial system. Eventually Hofer was captured by Napoleon's forces and taken to Mantua in northern Italy, where he was executed. Mosen's poem celebrated Hofer's heroic behavior during his final days. After the first two verses described his being taken to Mantua in chains, the third revealed his proud and defiant attitude. When he saw his fellow soldiers behind bars, he declared, "God be with you, and with the betrayed German Empire, and

[51] Schiller, p. 197.
[52] See above, Chap. 3, p. 80.

with the land of Tyrol!" The next verses referred to "Andreas, free even in chains," refusing his captors' demand that he kneel down, and declaring that he would die standing upright. In the final verse the corporal unbound his hands, and Andreas Hofer prayed for the last time before telling the firing squad to aim carefully.[53] In Freud's associations to his memory lapse, as in so many of his 1898 dreams, the concept of an inner freedom invulnerable to the bondage of the outer world emerged as a central element. This was the same concept of freedom which appeared in the only association to the dream of the stately house, the student song by August von Binzer, and since that unpublished dream was an *Ersatztraum* for the censored "big dream" to which Freud compared the Mosen slip, it seems quite possible that all three were tied together by a common political thread. A further political connection is suggested by the fact that Mosen was a member of the Jena Burschenschaft.[54]

That the memory lapse was linked to the theme of freedom versus tyranny also tends to support those who have argued that it may involve an allusion to Moses.[55] In the poem "Andreas Hofer," the concept of inner freedom was closely tied to religious feeling, and, it will be recalled, the Philippson Bible's commentary followed the German Pietist and idealist traditions in emphasizing that the freedom from bondage celebrated at Passover pointed toward this inner freedom of will. This concept of freedom also involved the idea of self-imposed law, for Philippson argued that the Passover rules involved "an inner necessity" rather than an arbitrary form, and Moses as the Israelites' supreme law-giver represented the loftiest realization of freedom through law.

The same idea of achieving freedom through self-imposed law appeared in the revolutionary dream, where a compromise emerged between the need for freedom of expression and the need for self-censorship. It again figured prominently in the associations to the *Non vixit* dream, for the same conception was developed in *The Robbers:* though in the early parts of the play, freedom was used to mean unrestrained license, at its conclusion, Karl Moor declared: "Oh, fool that I was to suppose that I could make the world a fairer place through terror and uphold the cause of justice through lawlessness." He then decided to turn himself in to the authorities to show that he believed in "the powers above" and that he was

[53] Julius Mosen, *Sämtliche Werke* (Leipzig: W. Friedrich, 1880), 6:99–100.
[54] Mosen, p. 325.
[55] Robert, *From Oedipus to Moses,* p. 202; Anzieu, II:469.

"dying for justice of my own free will *[mit Willen].*"[56] The idea of freedom represented by Andreas Hofer in Mosen's poem, by Moses in Philippson's commentary, and by Pastor Moser in Schiller's drama all point to the concept of psychoanlytic freedom so central to the *Non vixit* dream.

The allusion to Moses in the Mosen slip also echoed another theme of the revolutionary and *Non vixit* dreams, that of becoming a father. Because Moses plays an essentially paternal role in the Bible, an identification with him in the memory lapse would fit with the desire to assume a fatherly role evidenced in these two dreams. In the revolutionary dream, Freud deciphered one key element of the latent dream thoughts as saying, "It is absurd to be proud of one's ancestry; it is better to be an ancestor oneself," and in the *Non vixit* dream he overcame the brothers in succeeding to the father's position. The personal, familial dimension of the slip and the dreams parallels the intellectual dimension bound up with the idea of freedom under law, for a mature conception of fatherhood implied both freedom of action and responsibility.

The Mosen slip also fits into a pattern of biblical allusions which ran through Freud's dreams, a pattern particularly important for understanding the final phase of his work on the dream book. Here a comparison of the *Non vixit* dream with the Myops dream of early 1898 is instructive. The themes of the Myops dream foreshadowed those of *Non vixit* in several important ways. The Myops dream was the first published dream in which Freud's children appeared directly; with the *Non vixit* dream, and those that followed it, the theme of the children became a recurrent element. The Myops dream alluded to the part of the Bible dealing with Joseph's triumph over his brothers in succeeding to the father's position, just as did the *Non vixit* dream. Problems in the relationship with Fliess played a major role in fostering both. With all these points of similarity, however, there were also important contrasts, most significantly in the themes involving Fliess and freedom. In the Myops dream the thrust of the underlying dream thoughts pointed toward reconciliation with Fliess, whereas in *Non vixit* they pointed toward a final break. Paralleling this difference, the theme of freedom appeared only peripherally in Myops where in *Non vixit* it occupied a central position. The juxtaposition lends further credence to the possibility suggested by analysis of the *Non vixit* dream that as Freud's self-analysis began to establish contact with the early childhood phase of his ambivalent brother relationships,

[56] Schiller, p. 159. This echoes Pastor Moser's belief in an "inner tribunal."

the phase in which the screen memory of the yellow flowers was rooted, it increasingly fostered in him the wish for freedom from the emotional tyranny of the brother band.

The various pieces of evidence bearing on Freud's self-analytic progress during the second half of 1898 indicate a breakthrough in understanding the childhood origins of his feelings of sibling rivalry, the feelings which had helped shape the intellectual interests of that later period in his childhood when the Bible stories of Joseph and Moses in the land of Egypt had gripped his imagination. It was appropriate then, that in completing the dream book, the record of his self-analysis, he should be guided by metaphors rooted in his early Egyptian stage of his development when the question of Jewish self-identity in a foreign culture had found intellectual expression and satisfying resolution. Problems concerning Freud's Jewish self-image had been a central factor in his adolescent disillusionment, and the resulting ambivalence involved his Jewish identity as well as his father. Even though he defiantly rejected the apparent political cowardice of his father in the face of anti-Semitism, he also went beyond his father's assimilationist position in espousing a radical German nationalism. His self-analysis pushed toward a resolution of this ambivalence. In the late summer of 1897, after unraveling his Hannibal fixation, one of his first actions was to formalize his membership in the B'nai B'rith society. A year later when the brother dimension of the father-brother complex began to yield to his self-analysis, this development occurred in a context of enhanced Jewish self-consciousness as seen in the way the dream and memory lapse imagery of this period associated his theory with Jewish tradition. Comparison of the Mosen slip with the Myops and *Non vixit* dreams points to the Jewish biblical roots of the basic Freudian concept of psychoanalytic freedom, and the *Non vixit* theme of naming the children also fits in closely with Jewish tradition. In the dream and its analysis, the naming of children became not only a means of securing freedom from the emotional ghosts of deceased friends, colleagues and relatives, but also a path to immortality.

Freud's success in analyzing his screen memory also had important implications for his understanding of dreams. His work on *The Interpretation of Dreams* had come to a stop in June 1898, when he reported to Fliess that he was "stuck over the relationship between the two systems of thinking,"[57] the relationship between the latent and manifest content of dreams that he eventually resolved in his

[57] Freud, *Origins*, p. 255.

chapter on dream work. He remained stuck through the summer, normally his most productive time, and into the fall, telling Fliess in a letter of October 23 that his work on the book had come to a complete halt and that "the gap in the psychology, and the other gap left by the thoroughly analyzed example" remained obstacles he could not overcome.[58] It was only in January 1899 that his work on dreams once again began to move foward. In the January 3 letter to Fliess, where he mentioned the piece of self-analysis which revealed that screen memories were later phantasies projected back into childhood, he also observed that he had "found out how it happens, again by verbal association." In response to the key question of what had actually happened in early childhood, Freud now answered, "Nothing, but the germ of a sexual impulse was there." He promised to explain the matter at greater length when they met at Easter, but when he continued the letter the next day he disclosed his realization that "the dream pattern is capable of universal application, and that the key to hysteria really lies in dreams. I understand now why . . . I was unable to finish the dream book."[59] These comments represent Freud's final farewell to the seduction theory, which he had continued to toy with even after the September 1897 letter that announced his abandonment of it.

Freud's success in analyzing the screen memory of the yellow flowers carried his self-analysis back to the early stages of his childhood development, and in deepening his understanding of how phantasies worked it also provided the missing link necessary to the completion of the dream book. Moreover, it seems evident that Freud used his writing of these final parts of the book as a vehicle for his further psychoanalytic maturation. This likelihood is suggested by a remarkable letter he sent to Fliess on May 28, 1899. After mentioning that he had sent off the piece on screen memories to a publisher in Jena, he went on to announce that the dream book had "suddenly taken shape." He observed that none of his other works was "so completely my own as this; it is my own dung-heap, my own seedling and a *nova species mihi* (sic!) [a new species of myself (yes!)]."[60] Then, near the end of the letter he illuminated this emerging self-transformation by means of one of his archaeological allusions. He wrote that he had enjoyed reading the account Heinrich Schliemann, the man who discovered the ruins of Troy, gave of his childhood in his book *Ilios.* "The man found happiness

[58] Ibid., p. 269.
[59] Ibid., pp. 270–71.
[60] Ibid., p. 281.

in finding Priam's treasure, because happiness comes only from fulfillment of a childhood wish. This reminds me that I shall not be able to go to Italy this year. Better luck next time."[61] Having recently come to a deeper understanding of his own childhood desires, Freud could appreciate the autobiographical insight that Schliemann offered into the driving power of childhood phantasies.

Schliemann devoted the first few pages of his *Ilios* to showing how his desire to excavate Troy and more generally "how the work of my later life [have] been the natural consequences of the impressions I received in my earliest childhood."[62] The myths and stories associated with the town of Neu Buchow, where he was born, fired his childhood imagination. There were stories of buried treasures, and the boy wondered why when his father complained of money problems, he didn't simply dig up the treasure and become rich. The father also communicated to his son his deep interest in the events of the Trojan War. Young Heinrich grieved over the total destruction of Troy and was overjoyed to find in a book he received as a Christmas present during his eighth year, "an engraving representing Troy in flames, with its huge walls and Scaean gate, from which Aeneas is escaping, carrying his father, Anchises, on his back and holding his son, Ascanius, by the hand." Believing that the artist must have seen Troy to be able to depict it, the boy challenged his father's contention that no trace of the city remained: "He maintained the contrary, whilst I remained firm in my opinion, and at last we both agreed that I should one day excavate Troy." To Freud the story would have provided a perfect example of the way the Oedipal strivings of childhood could become linked with a powerful mythic image and thereby impel an adult to great accomplishments.

Indeed, Freud had experienced something quite similar in his own childhood. Like Schliemann, he too, when he was about eight, received a book which fired his imagination, and what Freud wrote of that book, the Philippson Bible, was strikingly similar to what Schliemann said of his childhood experiences: "My deep engrossment in the Bible story . . . had, as I recognized much later, an enduring effect upon the direction of my interest."[63] Freud's childhood dream of the bird-beaked figures with its Egyptian surface images drawn from the Philippson Bible and its underlying phantasy identification with Joseph, the supremely successful son, reveals the

[61] Ibid., p. 282.

[62] Heinrich Schliemann, *Ilios: The City and Country of the Trojans* (New York: Harper, 1881), pp. 1–3.

[63] Freud, *Autobiographical Study, S.E.,* xx:8.

same ingredients of myth and Oedipal striving which impelled Schliemann to success. Moreover, Freud could feel, at the moment he wrote the letter to Fliess, that like Schliemann he had realized at least part of his childhood phantasy. By then he knew with certainty that he had unlocked the secret to interpreting dreams. The letter spoke of the dream book as the "finest—and probably the only lasting discovery that I have made," and with this accomplishment he could indeed see himself as a modern-day Joseph.[64]

In the same letter he also wrote of it as representing a "new species of myself," thus pointing toward the successful completion of his self-analysis, and the evidence of his inner life suggests that Freud's image of Moses played a role in shaping this analytic self-transformation. Just as in his earliest readings he had gone on from the story of Joseph the successful son to that of Moses the powerful father, so in his self-analysis he pushed forward his own emotional development from discontented son to successful father. Freud's disillusioned feeling that his father had not lived up to the standard of Moses as a defender of his people led to the generation of his Hannibal phantasy; the dream book offers evidence that as this phantasy yielded to self-analytic insight and Freud seemed to become more comfortable in a paternal role himself, the story of Moses took on increasing symbolic importance as an expression of his inner desires. This evidence indicates a close link between Moses and Rome in Freud's unconscious thought processes. In his analysis of one of the undated Rome dreams he wrote that "the theme of 'the promised land seen from afar' was obvious in it," and in the Myops dream of early 1898 an identification with Moses played an important role as a response to threatening events *"which had occurred in the city of Rome."*[65] Both of these dreams involving Rome were also Moses dreams. Freud alluded to his Rome fixation immediately after citing Schliemann as an example of the principle that happiness came from the fulfillment of childhood wishes: he went on to say that this reminded him that he would "not be able to go to Italy this year. Better luck next time." One of Freud's unrealized childhood wishes was to play a heroic role in overthrowing the oppressors of his people, and in the Bible it was Moses who accomplished this task. In the development of Freud's inner mythology, the image of Moses underlay his adolescent desire to play Hannibal against the power of Rome, and Freud's comment in the letter alluded to this wish. As Schliemann pursued his

[64] Freud, *Origins,* p. 281.
[65] Freud, *Interpretation, S.E.,* IV:194; V:441–43.

childhood dream by following his discovery of Troy with his spectacular excavations at Mycenae, so Freud would add the accomplishments of Moses to those of Joseph.

A dream Freud had in the summer of 1899, as well as the pattern that emerged from the final stage of work on the dream book, indicates the importance of the Moses image to his new view of himself. This dream, the dream of dissecting his own pelvis must have occurred around June because in his analysis of it he stated that the self-dissection referred to the self-analysis he had incorporated in the dream book and to the painful feelings connected with the idea of publishing it. For this reason, he said, he had "delayed publication of the prepared *[bereitliegenden]* manuscript for more than a year."[66] This remark indicates that the delay involved the problem of censorship and points to his decision in June 1898 to eliminate a particularly important dream because of the personal embarrassment it might cause. The difficulty had brought work on the book to a halt, and it was to this year's delay that Freud referred in his analysis of the dissection dream.

In the dissection dream, Freud saw himself dissecting his own pelvis and legs, and then, *"I was once more in possession of my legs and was making my way through the town."*[67] Feeling tired, he then took a cab which drove through the front gate *[Haustor]* of a house, down a passage, and out into the open. He then found himself on a journey with an Alpine guide, who helped carry him and his belongings through a variety of exotic changing scenes. At the end of the journey he entered a small wooden house with an open window in the far wall. *"There the guide set me down and laid two wooden boards, which were standing ready, upon the window-sill, so as to bridge the chasm which had to be crossed over from the window."* At this point Freud became frightened because of the condition of his legs, but then the situation changed somewhat. *"I saw two grown-up men lying on wooden benches that were along the walls of the hut, and what seemed to be two children sleeping beside them. It was as though what was going to make the crossing possible was not the boards but the children."* As Freud indicated in his analysis of the dream, the various journeys in it were metaphors for the psychoanalytic explorations involved in his self-analysis. One of the dream's inciting causes was the annoyance he felt at being reminded by one of his patients that he still had not completed the dream book. The patient had asked him to recommend something to read. When

[66] *G.S.*, II:404.
[67] Freud, *Interpretation, S.E.*, V:452.

he suggested a "strange" novel by Rider Haggard involving the themes of "the eternal feminine" and the "immortality of our emotions," she interrupted his description to say that she meant one of his own works. Freud replied that his own "immortal works" had not yet been written.[68] This train of thought aroused anxieties about the possibility that he might not live to complete his work, fears that figured prominently in the dream.

Of the various scholarly analyses devoted to this long, complex, and important dream, Alexander Grinstein's is the most extensive and illuminating, but neither Grinstein nor any other scholar has noticed the allusions to Moses both in the dream and in Freud's discussion of it. Although Strachey's English translation somewhat obscures it, Freud's own analysis of the dream's conclusion recalls the image of Moses being denied entry into the promised land. Freud indicated that the idea being expressed at the end of the dream was that "perhaps the children will attain [*erreichen*—reach] what has been denied *[versagt]* to the father." At a later point in his discussion he repeated this idea in even more suggestive language: "I would have to leave it to the children to arrive at the goal *[ans Ziel]* of the hard journey *[in der schwierigen Wanderung]*."[69] Here the dream alluded to that part of the Moses story reported in *Numbers* 14 and 20. In chapter 14, the Bible told how God punished the Israelites for their lack of faith that he would indeed deliver the promised land to them despite the strong fortifications which their spies had discovered as they drew near it. Angered by their weakness, God appeared to them and said that, except for Joshua and Caleb, who remained true to him, all the adults, all of those over twenty, would wander in the desert where they would die and their bodies would rot. Only then would Joshua and Caleb lead their children into the promised land. Chapter 20 told how a similar fate befell Moses, the greatest of all Jews. Again, in an effort to convince his doubting people, God had told Moses that he would provide them with much-needed water if Moses would lead them before a rock and speak to it until it produced water. Always a man of high spirits, Moses was carried away and spoke harshly to the people before striking the rock twice with his rod. With the second stroke the rock did indeed astonish the people by producing water, but God was displeased with Moses for not following his instructions exactly. As punishment, God told Moses and Aaron that they would not lead the Israelites into the promised land.

[68] Ibid., p. 453.
[69] *G.S.*, II:385, 404.

As well as the idea of the children reaching the goal denied to the fathers, several other elements of the dissection dream tied it to this episode. First there is the theme of "passing over." In punishing Moses for his hot temper, God allowed him to see the promised land from afar, but told him, "you shall not pass over into it *[dahin hinübergehen]*."[70] Freud in the dream feared the passage *(Übergang)* over the abyss, just as in the Bible the Israelites feared to pass over into the promised land in the face of possible death. Another point of connection involved the number two. Freud indicated that the wooden boards were drawn from Rider Haggard's novel *She* but, as Grinstein notes, in that novel only a single wooden board is used to bridge the chasm.[71] The fact that there were two in the dream pointed to the Bible story where God spared two adults, Joshua and Caleb, to lead the children of Israel over into the promised land. In the dream, there were two adults and two children. They represented the bridge from the past to the future. Most important of all, however, the dream and the biblical episode were linked in their underlying meaning. The dream arose in answer to Freud's fears that he would not complete his "immortal work," *The Interpretation of Dreams,* and the biblical passage explained why Moses failed to complete his great work. The Philippson Bible interpreted the story in just this way. Philippson's commentary emphasized that the incident showed that Moses and Aaron "should not complete their great work" because they were temperamentally unsuited to the task. In large part Moses' inability to master his feelings was responsible for this failure. Philippson explained that the incident showed that he lacked the essential "elevation above human events and the passions of the moment."[72] At the time of the dream an exactly similar problem confronted Freud: as he said in his analysis of the dream, it was his inability to master the painful feelings associated with publishing the results of his self-analysis which held him back from completing it. He noted that in the dream he felt no gruesome feeling about his self-dissection and argued that this reflected the wish "that I might get over this inhibiting feeling."[73] So the dream reassured Freud in his doubts about his work, not only by suggesting that he could overcome the problems blocking its completion, but also through the identification with Moses, whose greatness was assured and whose work was completed by his children.

[70] Philippson, p. 993.
[71] Grinstein, pp. 400, 414.
[72] Philippson, pp. 773, 774.
[73] *G.S.*, II:404.

In the dream, the work Freud wanted to complete was his psychoanalytic work, so the idea that his children might have to complete it for him carries important implications. Although his daughter Anna did indeed carry on his work, he presumably did not have this in mind in 1899, when she was three years old. So in the dream the children actually represented his followers, and the underlying wish pointed toward his founding of the psychoanalytic movement. Freud hoped to secure intellectual followers to spread the understanding and practice of psychoanalysis, and the image of Moses was extremely appropriate to such an enterprise.[74] Freud used it specifically with reference to himself and his movement ten years later in a letter to Jung. He wrote, "If I am Moses, then you are Joshua and will take possession of the promised land of psychiatry, which I shall only be able to glimpse from afar."[75]

In addition to the wish to be Moses revealed in the dissection dream, there is other evidence that Freud acted out the role of Moses during the summer of 1899. A pattern emerges if the final segments of the dream book manuscript he wrote during that summer are considered in a block. When his work on the book came to a halt in mid-1898, it lacked the initial chapter discussing the literature on the subject, an important part of the dream work chapter, and most of the final chapter.[76] In the first segment Freud wrote in the summer of 1899, he presented the world of the authorities against which he would take his stand; in the second, he mounted his strongest challenge to their position; and in the last, he laid down the fundamental principles which would guide those who followed his new movement. Such a pattern may have appeared more than once in the heroic literature of which Freud was fond, but in terms of his intellectual development it was first and foremost the pattern of the Moses story.

Freud's comments to Fliess on the first chapter reveal the emotional underpinnings of this intellectual exercise. His attitude toward the existing literature was one of contempt and disdain. On May 28, 1899, he wrote that it seemed as if the gods had created the existing literature on the subject to discourage new contributions

[74] As Klein (*Jewish Origins of the Psychoanalytic Movement,* chap. 3) has shown, Freud took the first steps toward the establishment of an intellectual forum for the discussion of psychoanalytic theory during the period from 1897 to 1901, and he did so in the specifically Jewish context of the B'nai B'rith chapter, which he joined in 1897. His activities in B'nai B'rith anticipated the 1902 formation of the Wednesday discussion group that became the nucleus of the psychoanalytic movement.

[75] Freud and Jung, *The Freud/Jung Letters:* pp. 196–97; cited in Klein, p. 94.

[76] Freud, *Origins,* pp. 269, 281, 287, 288, 292.

to it. "The first time I tackled it I got stuck, but this time I shall work my way through it; there is nothing that matters in it anyway."[77] In his letter of June 9 his comment was more openly antagonistic: he observed that the work of some of the previous contributors to the literature made him wish that he "had never had anything to do with it. One of them is named Spitta (spit). . . ."[78] Freud's urge to spit in the face of authority can again be seen in the letter of July 17 where he reported that the first chapter of his book was in proof and that he would be taking the "Lasalle" [*sic*] with him on his vacation. Then a few sentences later he mentioned the introductory quotation he had chosen for the book: "*Flectere si nequeo superos, Acheronta movebo* [If I cannot bend the higher powers, I shall stir up the underworld]."[79] Carl Schorske has convincingly analyzed the connection between the Latin quotation and the reference to Lassalle in conjunction with Freud's Autodidasker dream. He points out that the quotation was from Virgil's *Aeneid* and that the words "are spoken by Juno, divine defender of the Semitic Dido, against Aeneas, founder of Rome." The same words graced the title page of a work by Ferdinand Lassalle, the former leader of the German socialists, and this work, *The Italian War and the Task of Prussia,* developed a strongly anti-Habsburg, revolutionary theme.[80] The allusive undercurrents of Freud's letter pointed back through the various stages in the development of his antiauthoritarian stance. From the progress report on Chapter I with its discussion of the scholarly authorities whose position he would overturn, to the mention of Lassalle who sought to range the popular forces of German and Italian nationalism against Habsburg authority, to the Latin quotation evoking the Carthaginian challenge to Rome, and finally to the underlying theme of this challenge, the resistance of the Jews to the persecution by their oppressors, the letter was laden with antiauthoritarian feeling.

Freud's final comment on Chapter I came in his letter of August 6, where he responded to Fliess's negative reaction to it. He expressed his own dislike of it but added that to avoid putting "a weapon in the hands of the 'learned,' we must put up with it somewhere." Then, using a metaphor based on Dante's *Divine Comedy,* he observed that the book was organized "on the model

[77] Ibid., p. 281.
[78] Ibid., p. 282.
[79] Ibid., p. 286.
[80] Schorske, *Vienna,* pp. 200–201.

of an imaginary walk. First comes the dark wood of the authorities (who cannot see the trees). . . ."[81] Freud clearly enjoyed sharing with his fellow rebel, Fliess, the hostility he felt toward the learned authorities.

The part of the dream work chapter that constituted his main attack against them had to be rewritten in the summer of 1899 because of the decision made a year earlier to censor the thoroughly analyzed dream to which Fliess objected. Freud referred to this in his letter of August 1, 1899: "The gap made by the big dream which you took out is to be filled by a small collection of dreams (innocent and absurd dreams, calculations and speeches in dreams, affects in dreams)."[82] He subsequently altered the order of discussion, but the description clearly corresponds to the material covered in sections F, G, and H of the dream work chapter. Although the contents of the eliminated "big dream" are unknown, the motives for its elimination were, as I noted, probably political, and in the *Ersatztraum* which might have replaced it, the dream of the stately house, the theme of freedom of expression versus the restrictions of the authorities was strongly articulated. The same theme played out on various levels dominated the segment of Chapter VI which Freud wrote to replace the "big dream."

The issue of freedom of expression versus the censorial function had direct relevance to the problem Freud confronted in completing this part of the dream book, where his purpose was to show the interplay of the factors he had discovered to be at work in the formation of dreams.[83] To show that these factors (condensation, displacement, representability, and secondary revision) gave dreams their characteristic form required detailed analysis of his own dreams, but he feared that any disclosure of their deepest meaning could bring great personal embarrassment. Freud could and did solve this part of his problem by carefully selecting certain themes for thorough examination while avoiding the full-scale analysis he had attempted in the censored "big dream." His solution, however, worked against the self-analytic function of his writing for, as he had discovered, the resolution of his emotional problems depended on a controlled expression of the antiauthoritarian sexual and political impulses from which they sprang. Freud resolved the dilemma by giving vent to these impulses in the way he presented his argument while revealing their origin piecemeal in the subject matter of the various dreams he used as evidence. The self-reve-

[81] Freud, *Origins*, p. 290.
[82] Ibid., p. 288.
[83] Freud, *Interpretation*, *S.E.*, V:405.

lation was there, but in a fragmentary form that obscured its overall coherence from all but the psychoanalytically informed.

The centerpiece of Freud's "collection of dreams" was formed by the section on absurdity, in which he celebrated his triumph over the scholarly authorities he was challenging. When he had finished writing it, he sent the proofs to Fliess and declared exultantly that this installment contained the "climax of my achievements in dream interpretation. . . . Absurdity in dreams!"[84] In the introductory paragraph of this section Freud carefully delineated the position he would challenge by noting that "the absurdity of dreams has provided those who deny the value of dreams with one of their principal arguments in favour of regarding them as the meaningless product of a reduced and fragmentary mental activity." After referring to this established position as "the ruling theory of dreams" and explaining how a particular absurd dream would be interpreted under it, he went on to advance his own psychoanalytic interpretation. Only in a casual aside did Freud hint at the Oedipal analogue to the attack on authority he mounted here: he wrote, "I shall begin by giving a few examples in which the absurdity is only an apparent one and disappears as soon as the meaning of the dream is more closely examined. Here are two or three dreams which deal (by chance, as it may seem at first sight) with the dreamer's dead father."[85]

Freud then took up the revolutionary dream once again to bring to a point his explanation of the meaning of absurdity in dreams. He showed that the latent dream thought that "ran as follows: 'It is absurd to be proud of one's ancestry; it is better to be an ancestor oneself'," indicated that absurdity sprang from a train of thought involving criticism or ridicule. Freud could then drive home his argument that it was no coincidence that so many of his examples of absurdity in dreams related to a dead father. "The authority wielded by a father provokes criticism from his children at an early age, and the severity of the demands he makes upon them leads them, for their own relief, to keep their eyes open to any weakness of their father's; but the filial piety called up in our minds by the figure of a father, particularly after his death, tightens the censorship which prohibits any such criticism from being consciously expressed."[86] Absurdity thus involved an attack on authority, and in the dreams Freud then presented from his collection various authority figures became the object of his criticism. In the town

[84] Freud, *Origins,* p. 299.
[85] Freud, *Interpretation, S.E.,* v:426–27.
[86] Ibid., pp. 434, 435.

council dream, it was two men of great intellectual importance to him, Josef Breuer and Theodor Meynert, against whom his rebellious feelings were directed. In the Goethe and Herr M. dream, it was the intellectual authority of Fliess that was called into question. But in his treatment of all these dreams Freud honored the need for censorship either by disguising the individuals involved or by obscuring the true point of his criticism.

The Myops dream provided the final example in Freud's discussion of absurdity, and here he aligned its political content with the political allusions of his theory. He focused attention on an absurd verbal form, "auf geseres," which in the dream was directed at "an attendant or nun" who accompanied his two sons. This was one of Freud's Rome dreams and since the word "geseres" had negative associations[87] and was directed at a nun, the example of absurdity involved a criticism of Roman Catholic authority, his most fundamental political foe. Freud then summed up his discussion of absurdity by drawing a parallel with the most famous of Shakespeare's political plays, *Hamlet.* "The Prince in the play, who had to disguise himself as a madman, was behaving just as dreams do in reality; so that we can say of dreams what Hamlet said of himself, concealing the true circumstances under a cloak of wit and unintelligibility: 'I am but mad north-north-west: when the wind is southerly I know a hawk from a hand-saw!' "[88] In the Myops dream, the theme of freedom versus Catholic oppression was directly expressed,[89] and Freud's explanation of absurdity in his book also struck a blow for freedom by making it possible for the rebellious dream thoughts to be understood despite the efforts of dream censorship to render them absurd. With his solution to the problem of absurdity, Freud had plumbed the deepest secrets of dreams. In the remaining sections of his "small collection," he filled out in detail the way the dynamic interaction of wish and censorship worked within the constraints of condensation, displacement, representability, and secondary revision to produce the manifest dream content from the latent dream wish.

As Freud revealed in the January 3, 1899 letter that presaged his completion of the dream book, it was his insight into the nature of screen memory phantasies which provided the missing link nec-

[87] Bergmann ("Moses," p. 13) points out that "the Hebrew word 'gezerot' is specifically used to denote anti-Jewish laws," but it is uncertain whether or not Freud knew of this meaning.

[88] Freud, *Interpretation, S.E.*, v:444.

[89] See above, Chap. 6, pp. 243–44, and Bergmann, p. 13.

essary to complete his dream theory. This analytic success allowed him to finish the chapter on the dream work and the final psychological chapter during the following summer. His insight involved the realization that in the unconscious a screen memory phantasy worked both backward and forward in time, recasting old memories in the service of the phantasy's forward-driving force, a process in which language played a central role. As he had observed in the January 3 letter it happened "by verbal association."[90] What Freud had in mind connected with a point he made in the dream work section on considerations of representability where he observed: "There is no need to be astonished by the part played by words in dream-formation. Words, since they are the nodal points of numerous ideas, may be regarded as predestined to ambiguity; and the neuroses (e.g., in framing obsessions and phobias), no less than dreams, make unashamed use of the advantages thus offered by words for purposes of condensation and disguise."[91] As he explained more exactly in a later addition to the dream book, if the meaning of a word or expression was "an ambiguous one, the dream-work may exploit the fact by using the ambiguity as a switch-point: where one of the meanings of the word is present in the dream-thoughts the other one can be introduced into the manifest dream."[92] In dealing with such verbal ambiguity from the point of view of those trying to understand dreams, Freud offered this reassurance: "In spite of all this ambiguity, it is fair to say that the productions of the dream-work, which, it must be remembered, *are not made with the intention of being understood,* present no greater difficulties to their translators than do the ancient hieroglyphic scripts to those who seek to read them."[93] Dream interpretation was thus a matter of translation, and although this passage came from a 1909 addition, both the conception of interpretation as translation and the comparison of dream language with Egyptian hieroglyphics were strongly emphasized in the original dream work chapter completed in late 1899.

In the introduction to that chapter Freud observed that the latent dream thoughts and the manifest dream content were "presented to us like two versions of the same subject-matter in two different languages. Or, more properly, the dream-content seems like a transcript of the dream-thoughts into another mode of expression,

[90] Freud, *Origins,* p. 271.
[91] Freud, *Interpretation, S.E.,* v:340–41.
[92] Ibid., p. 410. This passage was added in 1914.
[93] Ibid., p. 341.

whose characters and syntactic laws it is our business to discover by comparing the original and the translation."[94] This task, as Freud described it, recalled the discovery and deciphering of the Rosetta stone, which also involved a parallel text in different languages, one of them Egyptian hieroglyphics. Freud was implicitly comparing this archaeological discovery, which unlocked the ancient history of mankind, with his psychological discovery, which illuminated the primal past of the individual, and his image recalled his own childhood: the Rosetta stone was discovered by Napoleon's forces during their Egyptian campaign, and as Shengold and Kanzer have demonstrated, Freud's admiration for Napoleon was closely tied to his Joseph identification.[95] The allusions drew together two of Freud's childhood impulses: the wish for the glory of conquest associated with Napoleon and the desire to gain scientific success by translating the hidden meaning of dreams, as Joseph had done. The phrases in which he went on to describe the language of the dream content continued to play on the Egyptian allusion: "The dream-thoughts are immediately comprehensible, as soon as we have learnt them. The dream-content, on the other hand, is expressed as it were in a pictographic script. . . . If we attempted to read these characters according to their pictorial value instead of according to their symbolic relation, we should clearly be led into error."[96] Translation thus worked in two directions. As Freud noted, the dream work "carries out no other function than the translation of dream-thoughts in accordance with the four conditions to which it is subject";[97] and translation was the task Freud as a scholar pursued in unlocking the secrets of dreams.

Freud's role as translator of this primal pictographic language recalled the first book he ever read, the Bible, and the part of the dream book he completed at this time included his Egyptian dream, the childhood dream which drew its imagery from Philippson's illustrations. Philippson too had had the task of translating an ancient text into understandable modern language and, either consciously or unconsciously, Freud seems to have imitated him in writing the concluding pieces of *The Interpretation of Dreams,* the book which was to be the Bible of the psychoanalytic movement. He alluded to this resemblance in his book's final chapter, "The Psychology of the Dream Processes," where he discussed the im-

[94] Ibid., IV:277.

[95] Shengold, "Freud and Joseph," pp. 77–84; Kanzer, "Sigmund and Alexander Freud," pp. 267–81.

[96] Freud, *Interpretation, S.E.,* IV:277.

[97] Ibid., V:445.

portance of seemingly trivial details in interpreting dreams: "We have attached no less importance in interpreting dreams to every shade of the form of words in which they were laid before us. And even when it happened that the text of the dream as we had it was meaningless or inadequate . . . we have taken this defect into account as well. In short, we have treated as Holy Writ *(einen heiligen Text)* what previous writers have regarded as an arbitrary improvisation."[98] Moreover, as in the Philippson Bible, the primal text Freud presented for translation in his dream book was visually different from the text of his translation and commentary. Throughout his book, Freud had the manifest content of the dreams as well as the fragments of the manifest content involved in dream associations printed in the German equivalent of italics, in which emphasis was achieved through a wide spacing of individual letters. Freud's Holy Writ, the dream texts, thus stood out distinctly, even as did the Hebrew of Philippson's Bible.

The letters Freud wrote to Fliess from his vacation retreat in Berchtesgaden while he was working on these final segments also suggest that at this time his thoughts and feelings were drawn back to the land of Egypt he had first encountered in Philippson's Bible. For example, in his letter of August 1, 1899, he alluded to his collection of Greek and Egyptian antiquities in connection with his progress on the manuscript: "My grubby old gods . . . take part in the work as paper-weights." In an August 6 letter he reported that in a recent excursion to Salzburg he had "picked up a few old Egyptian things. Those things cheer me and remind me of distant times and countries." On August 27, when he had finished the dream work sections and was preparing to start the final chapter, he exuberantly proposed that he and Fliess spend next Easter in Rome if he had "not been locked up, lynched or boycotted on account of the Egyptian dream book. I have looked forward to it for so long."[99] At the moment when he could anticipate the early completion of his *magnum opus,* Freud longed to fulfill the desire of his Hannibal phantasy in at last reaching Rome.

The Egyptian allusions that surrounded Freud's work on the final segments of the dream book provided an appropriate context for the Moses image which hovered before him in his final self-transformation. The most important sense in which Freud acted out the role of Moses in completing *The Interpretation of Dreams* involved the nature and purpose of its concluding chapter. This

[98] Ibid., pp. 513–14.
[99] Freud, *Origins,* pp. 288, 291, 294.

chapter afforded him the opportunity to develop a systematic set of principles to guide the psychoanalytic movement that he already envisioned coming into being as a result of his work, and here he recapitulated the role of Moses as lawgiver to his recently liberated people. For example, early on in the chapter, in discussing interruptions of psychoanalytic work, Freud observed, "Psychoanalysis is justly suspicious. One of its rules is that *whatever interrupts the progress of analytic work is a resistance.*"[100] As with his dream passages, Freud had this principle and the others which followed printed with emphasis, so that they stood out from the text. These emphasized passages, concerning psychoanalysis, dream interpretation, the neuroses, and related subjects, represented the major conclusions of his work and thus deserved emphasis on that basis alone, but they also established a set of guiding principles for those who would come after him. At the time he wrote the concluding chapter, Freud had for followers a few close medical colleagues and some members of the local B'nai B'rith lodge, but in this chapter he sought to guide those who might be persuaded by his work. In the first section he raised "a number of further, somewhat disconnected points on the subject of interpreting dreams, which may perhaps help to give readers their bearings should they feel inclined to check my statements by subsequent work on their own dreams."[101] He then observed, "No one should expect that an interpretation of his dreams will fall effortlessly into his lap. Practice is needed. . . . It is . . . difficult to get hold of 'involuntary ideas.' Anyone who seeks to do so must familiarize himself with the expectations raised in the present volume and must in accordance with the rules laid down in it, endeavour during the work to refrain from any criticism, any *parti pris,* and any emotional or intellectual bias."[102] The work of free association so fundamental to dream analysis and psychoanalysis demanded a considerable amount of self-discipline on the part of the interpreter. Here too Freud recapitulated Moses in offering his followers freedom through self-imposed law, and he achieved a similar synthesis in himself by bringing the dream book containing his self-analysis to a conclusion.

Not long after the book's publication, Freud was finally able to realize his phantasy of going to Rome, and it was on that 1901 trip that he first saw the statue of Moses by Michelangelo to which he later devoted an analytic essay. Freud mentioned seeing the statue in a postcard to Martha, which also indicated that he had

[100] Freud, *Interpretation, S.E.,* v:517.
[101] Ibid., p. 522.
[102] *G.S.,* II:444.

"suddenly understood" it,[103] and he published his 1914 essay on Michelangelo's sculptural masterpiece anonymously—presumably because it was so self-revelatory. In it he mentioned his repeated visits to see the statue and declared, "no piece of statuary has ever made a stronger impression on me than this."[104] Freud's essay said more about himself than about Michelangelo's work of art. "I can recollect my own disillusionment," he observed, "when, during my first visits to San Pietro in Vincoli, I used to sit down in front of the statue in expectation that I should now see how it would start up on its raised foot, dash the Tables of the Law to the ground and let fly its wrath." As he continued to observe the statue, Freud had to revise the emotional expectations associated with it: "the stone image became more and more transfixed, an almost oppressively solemn calm emanated from it, and I was obliged to realize that something was represented here that could stay without change; that this Moses would remain sitting like this in his wrath for ever."[105] Freud's analysis of the statue revolved around the issues which had been important to him in his disillusionment with his father, a disillusionment rooted in the feeling that, unlike Moses, Jakob Freud had not reacted angrily to the enemies of his people; his coming to see the statue as portraying emotional self-control reflected his changed interpretation of his father's conduct. His interpretation also reflected his view of himself as Moses in a way that echoed the self-dissection dream of summer 1899, in which one of his underlying wishes was that in gaining greater control over his emotions he might overcome his inhibitions about completing and publishing his book. The theme of imposing emotional control was central in Freud's interpretation of the statue: "The lines of the face reflect the feelings which have won the ascendancy [the imposed calm]; the middle of the figure shows the traces of suppressed movement; and the foot still retains the attitude of the projected action. It is as though the controlling influence had proceeded downwards from above." Controlling or channeling unruly emotions was essential to success; he observed of Moses, "He remembered his mission and for its sake renounced an indulgence of his feelings"[106]—exactly describing the wish for himself that underlay the self-dissection dream. That dream expressed the hope that his painful self-examination might prepare him to lead his children, his psychoanalytic followers, from psychic oppression to

[103] Jones, II:365.
[104] Freud, "The Moses of Michelangelo," *S.E.*, XIII:213.
[105] Ibid., pp. 220–21.
[106] Ibid., p. 230.

the promised land of freedom. In the dream, as in writing the final sections of his dream book, he played out the role of Moses so appropriate to the movement he hoped to launch, and years later, in 1914, and later still, at the end of his life when he wrote *Moses and Monotheism,* he continued to see himself as Moses. The biblical stories Freud wove into his phantasy life provided a guiding influence from childhood through the time of his greatest discoveries and beyond, to the flight to England and freedom which marked his final years.

Conclusion: Fathers and Sons

Freud was not alone in his dream of becoming a Moses, for in certain ways the times called for such dreams. Hanns Sachs, for example, has pointed out that Bismarck had a Moses dream in 1863 when he was planning his strategy for the unification of Germany,[1] and an even more obvious instance of a historically significant phantasy identification with Moses can be found in Freud's Viennese contemporary Theodor Herzl. As the founder of the Zionist movement Herzl recapitulated the work of Moses in liberating the Jews from bondage and leading them back to the promised land. In his biography of Herzl, Amos Elon writes that shortly before his death Herzl reported to a friend a dream that he had at the age of twelve. He said that the "King-Messiah" had appeared, "and carried me off on wings of heaven. On one of the iridescent clouds we met . . . Moses. (His features resembled those of Michelangelo's statue. As a child I loved . . . this marble portrait.) The Messiah called out to Moses. '*For this child I have prayed!*' To me he said, 'Go and announce to the Jews that I shall soon come and perform great and wondrous deeds for my people and for all mankind'!"[2]

That Freud saw Herzl as a modern-day Moses seems evident from his Myops dream and Peter Loewenberg's analysis of it,[3] and Freud apparently had another, undatable dream of Herzl. Leo Goldhammer reports that in a lecture delivered around 1905 or 1907 Freud gave the following account of one of his own dreams: "Herzl appeared to me, a majestic figure with a pale, darkly toned

[1] Quoted in Freud, *Interpretation, S.E.*, v:378–81.
[2] Amos Elon, *Herzl* (New York: Holt, Rinehart, & Winston, 1975), p. 16.
[3] See Loewenberg, "A Hidden Zionist Theme."

face adorned by a raven-black beard and with infinitely sad eyes. This apparition forced me to do something at once to clarify to myself what I must do should the Jewish people be saved. These words surprised me by their fierce logic and intense accompanying feeling."[4] Here Freud's own Moses phantasy merged with his view of Herzl as Moses. The element of surprise in the dream seems appropriate in the light of Freud's ambivalent feelings about assimilation and Zionism.

These dream allusions anticipated a remarkable discussion Freud had with Herzl's son Hans. In a 1913 interview, nine years after the death of Theodor Herzl, Freud supported Hans Herzl's own arguments against participating in the Eleventh Zionist Congress and went on to caution him more generally against following in his father's footsteps. Freud told him: "Your ambitions are poisoning your life. You should finally bury your father within your soul, which is still carrying him alive." He then went on to describe the elder Herzl in a way which illuminates Freud's own complex views on the interrelationship between phantasy, reality, and the world of politics. "Your father is one of those people who have turned dreams into reality. This is a very rare and dangerous breed. It includes the Garibaldis, . . . the Herzls . . . I would simply call them the sharpest opponents of my scientific work." Although Freud's own attitude toward Moses always had a positive character, his view of Herzl as Moses seems strikingly negative, and this contrast reflected the different ways he and Herzl approached the world of phantasy. What Freud meant in calling the men of this rare breed opponents was that they did the mirror opposite of what he did: "It is my modest profession to simplify dreams, to make them clear and ordinary. They on the contrary, confuse the issue, turn it upside down, command the world while they themselves remain on the other side of the psychic mirror. It is a group specializing in the realization of dreams. I deal in psychoanalysis; they deal in psychosynthesis."[5] Here Freud revealed his awareness of Herzl as a practitioner of the "new-key politics" which characterized *fin-de-siècle* Vienna.

In his insighful study of this new antiliberal political style, Carl Schorske characterizes it as "the politics of phantasy."[6] Citing the

[4] Leo Goldhammer, "Theodor Herzl und Sigmund Freud: Traeume," *Theodor Herzl Jahrbuch,* ed. Tulo Nussenblatt (Vienna: Victor Glanz, 1937), pp. 266–68; cited in Avner Falk, "Freud and Herzl," *Midstream,* 23 (Jan. 1977):3.

[5] Jacob Weinshal, *Hans Herzl* (Tel Aviv: Hazzon, 1945), pp. 116–30; cited in Falk, p. 19.

[6] Schorske, *Vienna,* p. 134.

poet Hugo von Hofmannsthal's observation: "Politics is magic. He who knows how to summon the forces from the deep, him will they follow,"[7] Schorske analyzes the political artistry of Georg von Schönerer, Karl Lueger, and Theodor Herzl. He argues that they attracted their mass followings "by composing ideological collages—collages made of fragments of modernity, glimpses of futurity, and resurrected remnants of a half-forgotten past. In liberal eyes, these ideological mosaics were mystifying and repulsive, confounding the 'above' and the 'below,' the 'forward' with the 'backward.' "[8] Freud's comments to Hans Herzl reveal that he saw the new politics of his time in just this light.

Theodor Herzl himself possessed a clear grasp of the relevance of phantasy to the new mass politics of his day. Like Freud he had participated in the German nationalist student movements of the 1870s and 1880s and had appreciated the emotional power of the artistic political style they introduced. In a diary entry of June 3, 1895, he observed "Believe me, the politics of an entire people . . . can only be made with imponderables which shimmer high in the air. Do you know how the German empire was made? Out of dreams, songs, phantasies, and black-red-gold ribbons—and in short time. Bismarck only shook down the fruit of the tree which the masters of phantasy had planted."[9] In describing these politicians of "psychosynthesis" as a "dangerous breed" Freud did not exaggerate. During his youth he had experienced the destruction of his liberal democratic hopes at the hands of Lueger, Schönerer, and their like; in his old age he would witness the triumph of his fellow Austrian Adolf Hitler, who carefully studied the artistic, psychological politics of Lueger, Schönerer, and Viktor Adler in fashioning his own terrifyingly successful brand of psychopolitics.[10]

Freud's further comments to Hans Herzl have a dramatic quality which can be appreciated only in light of the bitter disillusionment of his own early political dreams. In referring to the politicians of psychosynthesis he declared: "They are robbers in the underground of the unconscious world. . . . Stay away from them, young man. . . . Stay away even if one of them was your father . . . perhaps because of that."[11] Freud's image reveals the dramatic transformation wrought in his political sentiments over the course of his

[7] Ibid.
[8] Ibid., p. 120.
[9] Theodor Herzl, *Tagebücher, 1895–1904* (Berlin: Jüdischer Verlag, 1922), 1:32.
[10] Adolf Hitler, *Mein Kampf,* trans. Ralph Manheim (Boston: Houghton Mifflin, 1943), pp. 41–43, 97–100, 125, 472–75.
[11] Falk, p. 19.

life. In *The Robbers,* which epitomized his radical adolescent political impulses, the robber band was tied by allusion to the demonic psychic underworld of both genius and madness. The play's political tyrant was punished for his evil attempts at psychological manipulation by being himself overwhelmed by madness and destruction; in real life, however, Freud had seen psychopoliticians achieve great success. It was in this sense too that he called such men 'the sharpest opponents of my scientific work." While turning away from the political direction of Schiller's play, Freud had remained true to its central message of freedom. In his allusions to the play in the analysis of his *Non vixit* dream Freud acted the role of Brutus, defender of republican liberty, against the tyranny of Caesar, and the dream associations trace the intellectual paths he followed in transforming this *sturm und drang* freedom into a scientifically grounded concept of psychoanalytic freedom.

Freud's observations about his relationship to the psychopoliticians were both historically acute and prescient of the ominous future. Whereas he as analyst attempted to win a measure of freedom from the driving forces of mental life, they aimed to "command the world while they themselves remain on the other side of the psychic mirror." The most dangerous of the breed certainly understood this technique well and discussed it clearly in *Mein Kampf.* After explaining how important to the success of a political speech it was to give it in an appropriate hall, and at night rather than during the day, Hitler chose a Wagnerian example to convey the essence of his phantasy-oriented politics: "Thus, a performance of *Parsifal* in Bayreuth will always have a different effect than anywhere else in the world. The mysterious magic of the house on the Festspielhügel in the old city of the margraves cannot be replaced or even compensated for by externals. In all these cases we have to do with an encroachment upon man's freedom of will."[12] Hitler, Herzl, Schönerer, Adler, and the other new-key politicians well understood the political implications of Richard Wagner's great masterpieces of psychological manipulation.

The tone of fatherly admonition in Freud's advice to Hans Herzl sprang in part from a feeling of having himself experienced the young man's problem. As Avner Falk observes, "It is clear that Freud is talking about himself no less than about Hans Herzl."[13] Freud too had wanted to see his father as Moses and had suffered from an inability to come to terms with his conflicted feelings

[12] Hitler, p. 474.
[13] Falk, p. 19.

about him. For Freud, however, it was precisely as a political example, as a leader and defender of his people, that his father had failed, whereas Hans Herzl's father had realized the essentials of this heroic standard and thereby set the son an unsurpassable example in the realm of politics. Freud advised Hans Herzl to bury the image of his father in his soul, and in the course of his self-analysis that is just what Freud himself did with the political expectations associated with his dead father. One of the final dreams incorporated in *The Interpretation of Dreams* was Freud's dream of his father on his death-bed like Garibaldi, a dream which must have occurred sometime between October 1898 and the following spring.[14] In the dream Freud found that "*After his death my father played a political part among the Magyars and brought them together politically. . . . I remember how like Garibaldi he looked on his death-bed, and felt glad that that promise had come true.*"[15] In associating his dead father with Garibaldi, whom he specifically included among the dangerous breed that specialized in the realization of dreams, Freud once again gave expression to his counterpolitical stance. As Schorske observes, "The substance of the dream speaks clearly enough: a successful Father Garibaldi-Freud in Hungary made his son's pursuit of politics unnecessary."[16] By burying the ghost of his father's political legacy within himself, Freud aimed to set himself free from a political world which seemed to threaten the very existence of freedom.

The part of Jakob Freud's legacy that lived on most vitally within his son was comprised in the values he had conveyed to the young boy as his first teacher, and in this role he may have more adequately fulfilled the image of Moses. We gain an insight into this dimension of his personality in the gift he presented to his son on Sigmund's thirty-fifth birthday. It was a newly rebound copy of the Philippson Bible Freud had read as a child, and it included a dedication in Hebrew. A. A. Roback gives this translation of Jakob's words: "To my Dear Son, Solomon. It was in the seventh year of your life that the Spirit of God began to stir you and spake to you [thus]: 'Go thou and pore over the book which I wrote, and there will burst open for thee springs of understanding, knowledge and reason. It is indeed the book of books. Sages have delved into it and legislators have derived [from it] knowledge and law.' Thou hast seen the vision of the Almighty. Thou hast listened and ventured and achieved, soaring on the wings of the wind." Jakob Freud had

[14] See Schorske, *Vienna*, p. 198, and Grinstein, *Freud's Dreams*, p. 375.
[15] Freud, *Interpretation*, *S.E.*, V:427–28.
[16] Schorske, *Vienna*, p. 199.

good reason to be proud of his son's education, firmly founded on the reading of Philippson's Bible, and by the time he wrote these words (May 6, 1891) he also had good reason to be proud of his son's professional and scientific accomplishments. He could scarcely guess at that time how far his son would go, but his gift expressed his deep love and confidence: "For long the book had been lying about like broken tablets in a closet of mine. And as you were completing your thirty-fifth year, I put on it a new leather cover and I called out: 'Spring up, o well; sing ye unto it.' And I am presenting it to you as a keepsake and a token of love. From your father who has an undying love for you. Jacob the son of Solomon Freud. . . .[17] Jakob Freud chose the gift and words of dedication to impress on his son the continuing importance of the religious tradition in which he had been raised. Once beyond his youth, Sigmund Freud seems to have been tempted by religious belief only rarely—as under the magnetic influence of Franz Brentano. Nonetheless, he retained a deep fascination with the inner world of feeling explored within his religious tradition, and the intellectual history of his development shows how his early interest in religious psychology exercised a powerful influence on the development of psychoanalysis.

Toward the end of his dedication, Jakob Freud employed a Mosaic image: "broken tablets" recalled the occasion when Moses broke the tablets of the law in outrage at his people's lack of faith. The dedication suggests that the gift was meant to make whole the broken parts of the book in order to restore their educational function, and in this aim Jakob Freud represented the opposite of the angry Moses the young Freud had wanted his father to be. However, for the "new species of himself"[18] Freud hoped would emerge from his self-analysis, this image of the self-controlled father Moses, who renounced his feelings for the sake of his mission, was very important. Freud's *Non vixit* and self-dissection dreams as well as his interpretation of Michelangelo's Moses show that he wished to foster this quality in himself. In overcoming the phantasy image he had projected onto his father, Freud was able to develop a more real identification with him.

Freud's advice to Hans Herzl strongly emphasized the dangers of phantasy and the importance of coming to terms with reality. As he put it in the interview: "To use the metaphor of your own dream, you must stop your dangerous trips across the enchanted

[17] Abraham Aaron Roback, *Freudiana* (Cambridge, Mass.: Sci-Art, 1957), p. 92.
[18] Freud, *Origins*, p. 281.

bridge. Put your two feet firmly on solid ground."[19] In Freud's Vienna the worlds of phantasy and reality had become perhaps too closely intermingled—at least for his taste. Certainly a part of his professional work involved reducing the fantastic to the real in order to make life more bearable. Nonetheless, Freud appreciated the role of phantasy in artistic and intellectual creativity, and his own life provides a vivid example of the importance of phantasy to greatness. His phantasy identifications did help to point him toward the goal of high achievement in a way that was similar to what Nietzsche described as self-overcoming. In his early (1874) book *Schopenhauer as Educator,* Nietzsche argued that "culture is the child of every individual's self-knowledge and inadequacy. Everyone who possesses culture is, in fact, saying: "I see something higher and more human than myself above me. Help me, all of you to reach it.' "[20] Nietzsche believed that it was through the cultivation of inspiring "images of man" that an individual "gains that desire to look beyond the self and seek with all its might a higher self which is hidden there. Only he who has given his heart to some great man receives the *'first consecration of culture'.*"[21] Nietzsche's examples indicate that he had in mind a process of conscious phantasy identification: "There are three images of man which our modern times have erected one after another, and from the contemplation of which mortals will presumably, for a long time to come, derive the incentive to transfigure their own lives. There are the Rousseauian man, Goethian man, and Schopenhauerian man."[22]

It was Schopenhauer who provided Nietzsche's own guiding image of man, and in his title *Schopenhauer als Erzieher,* the word *Erzieher* conveys the idea of a person who rears someone, rather than simply an educator. Nietzsche's description of his own attitude toward Schopenhauer confirms the parental dimension of his psychological-philosophical concept. Commending Schopenhauer's disdain for rhetoric, he observed: "Schopenhauer speaks to himself, and if one wants to imagine a listener, let him think of a son whom his father is instructing. It is sincere, firm, good-natured speaking, before a listener who listens with love. . . . His power and well-being envelop us from the first sound of his voice." Nietzsche stressed his own need to move beyond a mere admiration for Schopenhauer's ideas:

[19] Falk, p. 19.

[20] Friedrich Nietzsche, *Schopenhauer as Educator,* trans. J. W. Hillesheim and M. R. Simpson (Chicago: Regnery, 1965), p. 61.

[21] Ibid., pp. 40, 61.

[22] Ibid., p. 40.

"It is true that I only found a book, and that was a great lack. And thus I made all the more effort to see beyond the book and to picture the man whose great testament I had to read, the man who promised to make only those his heirs who wished to be and were capable of being more than just his readers: namely, his sons and pupils."[23] Nietzsche's words reveal the way his conscious phantasy identification took the place of a deficient real identification with his father. It seems likely that Nietzsche's ideal image of Schopenhauer drew much of its power from that presumably unconscious source, for the elder Nietzsche died when his son was still a boy.

Nietzsche's concept of self-overcoming gave these conscious-unconscious phantasy identifications a central role in the process of creating culture, and even at the time of his interview with Hans Herzl Freud probably regarded the matter in a similar light. In part his emphasis on reality rather than phantasy had to do with his professional perspective and in part with his age and the issue of age. Nietzsche wrote *Schopenhauer as Educator* as a man of thirty, and he directed it at an audience still younger than himself. Phantasy served an essential role to the young as Freud well understood. He also appreciated its creative role in adult life, but the powerful persistence of phantasy drives into adulthood posed a basic dilemma with regard to the relationship of the individual to the world around him. Should the individual seek a greater measure of psychological peace and comfort by bringing his phantasies down to reality or should he give his creative dreams and ambitions free rein at the expense of his ordinary life? It was, as he observed later, a choice between the life and the work. Freud's own development shows his oscillation between these alternatives, and in his self-analysis he attempted to achieve a compromise solution. In the last of his 1910 Clark University lectures he broached this problem, noting the way people "find reality unsatisfying quite generally, and for that reason entertain a life of phantasy in which we like to make up for the insufficiencies of reality by the production of wish-fulfillments. These phantasies include a great deal of the true constitutional essence of the subject's personality as well as of those impulses which are repressed where reality is concerned." For Freud the key to a solution lay in bringing the phantasy wish to consciousness. As he observed in his Clark lecture: "our experiences have taught us with certainty . . . that the mental and somatic power of a wishful impulse, when once its repression has failed, is far stronger

[23] Ibid., pp. 13, 17.

if it is unconscious than if it is conscious." Becoming conscious of such wishes opened up the possibility of freedom in a previously deterministic situation. It gave the individual the ability to choose. "What, then," he went on, "becomes of the unconscious wishes which have been set free by psycho-analysis? Along what paths do we succeed in making them harmless to the subject's life?" He then outlined the alternatives of continued suppression, the sublimation of creative work, and a greater degree of direct libidinal satisfaction.[24] There is evidence that Freud's self-analysis allowed him to profit from all three of these alternatives in his own life.

In his own creative work Freud could take satisfaction that his discovery of psychoanalysis, a process so closely interwoven with the violent political history of his time, had won for himself and for other human beings a measure of freedom from the despotism of the disordered passions. In a brief phonograph recording made shortly before his death, he concluded a thumbnail sketch of his life by noting that as a consequence of the German invasion of Austria he had come to England "where I hope to end my life in freedom." From the bright hopes of a youthful education steeped in the values and culture of the late German Enlightenment to the increasing gloom and darkness of an old age that witnessed the politics of phantasy triumphant, Freud held on tenaciously to this ideal of freedom. It was the guiding star of both his life and his work.

[24] Sigmund Freud, "Five Lectures on Psycho-Analysis," *S.E.*, XI:50, 53–54.

Bibliography

Adams, Leslie. "A New Look at Freud's Dream: 'The Breakfast Ship.' " *American Journal of Psychiatry,* 110, no. 5 (1953):381–84.

Amacher, Peter. "Freud's Neurological Education and Its Influence on Psychoanalytic Theory." *Psychological Issues,* 4, no. 4, monograph 16. New York: International Universities Press, 1965.

Anzieu, Didier. *L'auto-analyse de Freud et la découverte de la psychanalyse.* 2 vols. Paris: Presses Universitaires de France, 1975.

Baernreither, Joseph Maria. *Der Verfall des Habsburgerreiches und die Deutschen.* Ed. Oscar Mitis. Vienna: A. Holzhausens Nachfolger, 1939.

Barclay, James R. "Franz Brentano and Sigmund Freud." *Journal of Existentialism,* 5 (1964):1–36.

Bergmann, Martin S. "Moses and the Evolution of Freud's Jewish Identity." *The Israel Annals of Psychiatry and Related Disciplines* 14 (March 1976):3–26.

Bernfeld, Siegfried. "Freud's Scientific Beginnings." *American Imago,* 6 (1949):163–96.

———. "Sigmund Freud, M.D., 1882–1885." *The International Journal of Psychoanalysis* 32 (1951):204–17.

Bettelheim, Bruno. *The Uses of Enchantment: The Meaning and Importance of Fairy Tales.* New York: Vintage, 1977.

Billinsky, John M. "Jung and Freud (The End of a Romance)." *Andover Newton Quarterly,* 10 (Nov. 1969):39–43.

Blumenthal, Ralph. "Freud: Secret Documents Reveal Years of Strife." *The New York Times,* June 24, 1984. C1–5.

Braun-Vogelstein, Julie. *Heinrich Braun.* Stuttgart: Deutsche Verlag, 1967.

Brentano, Franz. *Psychology from an Empirical Standpoint.* Trans. A. C. Rancurello, D. B. Terrell, and L. L. McAllister. New York: Humanities Press, 1973.

Breuer, Josef, and Sigmund Freud. *Studies on Hysteria. The Standard Edition of the Complete Psychological Works of Sigmund Freud.* 24 vols. Trans. and ed. James Strachey with Anna Freud, Alix Strachey, and Alan Tyson.

London: The Hogarth Press and the Institute of Psycho-Analysis, 1953–74. II.

Burschell, Friedrich. *Schiller.* Reinbek bei Hamburg: Rowohlt, 1968.

Buxbaum, Edith. "Freud's Dream Interpretation in the Light of His Letters to Fliess." *Bulletin of the Menninger Clinic,* 15, no. 6 (1951):197–212.

Charmatz, Richard. *Adolf Fischhof. Das Lebensbild eines österreichischen Politikers.* Stuttgart and Berlin: J. G. Cotta Nachfolger, 1910.

———. *Österreichs innere Geschichte von 1848 bis 1907.* 2 vols. Leipzig: B. G. Teubner, 1909.

———. "Wiens Schillerfeier im Jahre 1859." *Neue Bahnen,* 5 (1905):238–41.

Clark, Ronald W. *Freud: The Man and the Cause.* New York: Random House, 1980.

Decker, Hannah S. *Freud in Germany: Revolution and Reaction in Science, 1893–1907.* New York: International Universities Press, 1977.

Dorer, Maria. *Historische Grundlagen der Psychoanalyse.* Leipzig: Felix Meiner, 1932.

Eckstein, Friedrich. *'Alte unnennbare Tage!' Erinnerungen aus siebzig Lehr und Wanderjahren.* Vienna: H. Reichner, 1936.

Eissler, K. R. "Creativity and Adolescence: The Effect of Trauma on Freud's Adolescence." *The Psychoanalytic Study of the Child.* Ed. Ruth S. Eissler et al. Vol. 33. New Haven: Yale University Press, 1978:461–517.

———. *Goethe: A Psychoanalytic Study.* Detroit: Wayne State University Press, 1963.

———. *Sigmund Freud und die Wiener Universität.* Bern: Verlag Hans Huber, 1966.

Ellenberger, Henri F. *The Discovery of the Unconscious: The History and Evolution of Dynamic Psychiatry.* New York: Basic Books, 1970.

Elon, Amos. *Herzl.* New York: Holt, Rinehart, & Winston, 1975.

Erikson, Erik H. *Childhood and Society.* New York: Norton, 1963.

———. *Insight and Responsibility.* New York: Norton, 1964.

Falk, Avner. "Freud and Herzl." *Midstream,* 23 (Jan. 1977):3–24.

Feuerbach, Ludwig. *Sämtliche Werke.* 13 vols. Ed. W. Bolin and F. Jodl. Stuttgart: Frommann Verlag, 1960–67.

———. *Das Wesen des Christenthums.* Leipzig: n.p., 1841.

Franz, Georg. *Liberalismus, Die deutschliberale Bewegung in der habsburgischen Monarchie.* Munich: G. W. D. Callwey, 1955.

Freud, Ernst L. "Jugendbriefe Sigmund Freuds." *Neue Rundschau,* 80 (1969):678–93.

Freud, Sigmund. *On Aphasia: A Critical Study.* New York: International Universities Press, 1953.

———. *Aus den Anfängen der Psychoanalyse, Briefe an Wilhelm Fliess, Abhandlungen und Notizen aus den Jahren 1887–1902.* Introduction by Ernst Kris. Ed. Marie Bonaparte, Anna Freud, and Ernst Kris. London: Imago, 1950.

———. *An Autobiographical Study. The Standard Edition of the Complete Psychological Works of Sigmund Freud.* 24 vols. Trans. and ed. James Strachey with Anna Freud, Alix Strachey, and Alan Tyson. London: The Hogarth Press and the Institute of Psycho-Analysis, 1953–74. XX:3–74.

——. "A Case of Successful Treatment by Hypnotism." *Standard Edition.* I:115–28.

——. "Charcot." *Standard Edition.* III:11–23.

——. *Cocaine Papers.* Ed. Robert Byck. New York: Stonehill, 1974.

——. *The Complete Letters of Sigmund Freud to Wilhelm Fliess, 1887–1904.* Trans. and ed. Jeffrey Moussaieff Masson. Cambridge: The Belknap Press of Harvard University Press, 1985.

——. "Contribution to a Questionnaire on Reading." *Standard Edition.* IX:245–47.

——. "Creative Writers and Day-Dreaming." *Standard Edition.* IX:141–53.

——. "A Disturbance of Memory on the Acropolis." *Standard Edition.* XXII:239–48.

——. "Extracts from Freud's Footnotes to His Translation of Charcot's Tuesday Lectures." *Standard Edition.* I:137–43.

——. "Five Lectures on Psycho-Analysis," *Standard Edition.* XI:7–55.

——. "Further Remarks on the Neuro-Psychoses of Defence." *Standard Edition.* III:162–85.

——. "On the History of the Psycho-Analytic Movement." *Standard Edition.* XIV:7–66.

——. "Hysteria." *Standard Edition.* I:39–59.

——. *The Interpretation of Dreams. Standard Edition.* IV and V.

——. *Introductory Lectures on Psychoanalysis. Standard Edition.* XV and XVI.

——. *The Letters of Sigmund Freud.* Ed. Ernst L. Freud, trans. Tania and James Stern. New York: McGraw-Hill, 1964.

——. "The Moses of Michelangelo." *Standard Edition.* XIII:211–36.

——. "Obituary of Professor S. Hammerschlag." *Standard Edition.* IX:255–56.

——. *The Origins of Psycho-Analysis, Letters to Wilhelm Fliess, Drafts and Notes: 1887–1902.* Ed. Maria Bonaparte, Anna Freud, Ernst Kris, trans. Eric Mosbacher and James Strachey. New York: Basic Books, 1954.

——. "Preface to the Translation of Bernheim's Suggestion." *Standard Edition.* I:75–85.

——. *The Psychopathology of Everyday Life. Standard Edition.* VI.

——. "Report on My Studies in Paris and Berlin." *Standard Edition.* I:5–15.

——. "Screen Memories." *Standard Edition.* III:303–22.

——. "Sketches for the 'Preliminary Communication' of 1893." *Standard Edition.* I:147–54.

——. *Die Traumdeutung. Gesammelte Schriften.* Vol. 2. Leipzig: Internationaler Psychoanalytischen Verlag, 1925.

Freud, Sigmund, and Karl Abraham. *A Psycho-Analytic Dialogue, The Letters of Sigmund Freud and Karl Abraham, 1907–1926.* Ed. Hilda C. Abraham and Ernst L. Freud, trans. Bernard Marsh and Hilda C. Abraham. New York: Basic Books, 1965.

Freud, Sigmund, and Carl Jung. *The Freud/Jung Letters: The Correspondence between Sigmund Freud and C. G. Jung.* Ed. William McGuire, trans. Ralph Manheim and R. F. C. Hull. Princeton: Princeton University Press, 1974.

Gebhardt, Bruno. *Handbuch der deutschen Geschichte.* 4 vols. Stuttgart: Union Verlag, 1956–60.

Gedo, John E. "Freud's Self-Analysis and His Scientific Ideas," *American Imago,* 25, no. 2 (1968):99–118.

Gedo, John E., and George H. Pollock, eds. *Freud: The Fusion of Science and Humanism, The Intellectual History of Psychoanalysis. Psychological Issues,* 9, nos. 2/3 monograph 34/35. New York: International Universities Press, 1976.

Gedo, John E., and Ernest S. Wolff. "The Ich. Letters." In Gedo and Pollock, 71–86.

Gicklhorn, Josef, and Renée Gicklhorn. *Sigmund Freuds akademische Laufbahn.* Vienna: Urban & Schwarzenberg, 1960.

Gicklhorn, Renée. "Eine Episode aus S. Freuds Mittelschulzeit." *Unsere Heimat,* 36 (1965):18–24.

Goethe, J. W. *Faust.* Trans. Philip Wayne. Baltimore: Penguin, 1961.

Goldstein, Jan. "The Hysterical Diagnosis and the Politics of Anticlericalism in Late Nineteenth-Century France." *Journal of Modern History,* 54 (June 1982):209–39.

Grigg, Kenneth A. "All Roads Lead to Rome: The Role of the Nursemaid in Freud's Dreams." *Journal of the American Psychoanalytic Association,* 21 (1973):108–26.

Grinstein, Alexander. *On Sigmund Freud's Dreams.* 2d ed. Detroit: Wayne State University Press, 1980.

Guillain, Georges. *J.-M. Charcot, 1825–1893: His Life—His Work.* Ed. and trans. Pearce Bailey. New York: Paul B. Hoeber, 1959.

Hammerschlag, Samuel. "Das Programm der Israel. Religionsschule in Wien." *Bericht der Religionsschule der Israelitischen Cultusgemeinde in Wien über die Schuljahre 1868 und 1869.* Vienna: Jacob Scholssberg, 1869.

Herzl, Theodor. *Das Neue Ghetto.* Vienna and Berlin: R. Löwit, 1920.

——. *Tagebücher, 1895–1904.* 3 vols. Berlin: Jüdischer Verlag, 1921–23.

Jahrbücher der K. K. Central-Anstalt für Meteorologie und Erdmagnetismus. Jahrgang 1898. Vienna, Wilhelm Braumüller, 1900.

Jahresberichte des Leopoldstädter Communal-Realgymnasiums in Wien. Ed. Alois Pokorny. Vienna: Gerold, 1866.

Jahresbericht des Lesevereines der deutschen Studenten Wiens über das IV. Vereinsjahr 1874–75. Vienna: Leseverein d.d.S., 1875.

Janz, Curt Paul. *Friedrich Nietzsche: Biographie.* 3 vols. Munich: Carl Hanser, 1978.

Jerusalem, Wilhelm. *Gedanken und Denker, Gesammelt Aufsätze.* Vienna: Wilhelm Braumüller, 1905.

Jones, Ernest. "Freud's Early Travels." *International Journal of Psycho-Analysis,* 35, pt. 2 (1954):81–84.

——. *The Life and Work of Sigmund Freud.* 3 vols. New York: Basic Books, 1953–57.

Kanzer, Mark. "Sigmund and Alexander Freud on the Acropolis." In Kanzer and Glenn, 259–84.

Kanzer, Mark, and Jules Glenn, ed. *Freud and His Self-Analysis.* New York: Jason Aronson, 1979.

Karpe, Richard. "Freud's Reaction to His Father's Death." *Bulletin of the Philadelphia Association for Psychoanalysis,* 6 (1956):25–29.

Klein, Dennis B. *Jewish Origins of the Psychoanalytic Movement.* New York: Praeger, 1981.

Kohut, Heinz. "Creativeness, Charisma, Group Psychology: Reflections on the Self-Analysis of Freud." In Gedo and Pollock, 379–425.

Kornauth, Friedrich. "Graf Badeni als Ministerpresident." Diss., University of Vienna, 1949.

Krüll, Marianne. *Freud und sein Vater, Die Entstehung der Psychoanalyse und Freuds ungelöste Vaterverbingung.* Munich: C. H. Beck, 1979.

Lehmann, Herbert. "Two Dreams and a Childhood Memory of Freud." *Journal of the American Psychoanalytic Association* 14 (April 1966):388–405.

Lesky, Erna. *The Vienna Medical School.* Trans. L. Williams and I. S. Levij. Baltimore: The Johns Hopkins University Press, 1976.

Lipiner, Siegfried. "Zwei Schriften von Rokitansky." *Deutsche Zeitung,* July 27, 1881:1–2.

Loewenberg, Peter. "A Hidden Zionist Theme in Freud's My Son, the Myops Dream." *Journal of the History of Ideas,* 31 (Jan.-Mar. 1970):129–32.

Mann, Thomas. *Essays.* Trans. H. T. Lowe-Porter. New York: Vintage Books, 1958.

Masson, Jeffrey Moussaieff. *The Assault on Truth: Freud's Suppression of the Seduction Theory.* New York: Farrar, Straus, & Giroux, 1983.

McGrath, William J. *Dionysian Art and Populist Politics in Austria.* New Haven: Yale University Press, 1974.

Meynert, Dora Stockert. *Theodor Meynert und seine Zeit.* Vienna: Österreichischer Bundesverlag, 1930.

Meynert, Theodor. *Psychiatry: A Clinical Treatise on Diseases of the Fore-Brain Based upon a Study of Its Structure, Functions and Nutrition.* Trans. B. Sachs. New York: Putnam, 1885.

———. *Sammlung von Populär–Wissenschaftlichen Vorträgen über den Bau und die Leistungen des Gehirns.* Vienna: Braumüller, 1892.

Mischler, Ernst, and Josef Ulbrich. *Österreichisches Staatswörterbuch Handbuch des gesammten öffentlichen Rechtes.* 3 vols. Vienna: Alfred Hölder, 1895.

Müller, Friedrich, and Gerold Valentin. *Deutsche Dichtung.* Paderborn: Verlag Ferdinand Schöningh, 1958.

Ostini, Fritz von. *Böcklin.* Bielefeld and Leipzig: Velhagen and Klasing, 1909.

Owen, Alan R. G. *Hysteria, Hypnosis and Healing: The Work of J.-M. Charcot.* London: Dobson; New York: Garret Publications, 1971.

Philippson, Johanna. "The Philippsons, a German-Jewish Family." *Publications of the Leo Baeck Institute.* Vol. 7 (London: 1962):95–118.

Philippson, Ludwig, ed. *Die Israelitische Bibel.* 4 vols. Leipzig: Baumgärtners Buchhandlung, 1858.

Rawidowicz, Simon. *Ludwig Feuerbachs Philosophie: Ursprung und Schicksal.* Berlin: Walter De Gruyter, 1964.

Ricoeur, Paul. *Freud and Philosophy.* Trans. Denis Savage. New Haven: Yale University Press, 1970.

Rieff, Philip. *Freud: The Mind of the Moralist.* New York: Viking Press, 1959.

Roback, Abraham Aaron. *Freudiana.* Cambridge, Mass.: Sci-Art, 1957.

Robert, Marthe. *From Oedipus to Moses: Freud's Jewish Identity.* Trans. Ralph Manheim. Garden City, N.Y.: Anchor Press, Doubleday, 1976.

Rosenberg, Samuel. *Why Freud Fainted.* Indianapolis/New York: Bobbs-Merrill, 1978.

Rosenfeld, Eva M. "Dreams and Vision: Some Remarks on Freud's Egyptian Bird Dream." *International Journal of Psychoanalysis,* 37 (1956):97–105.

Sajner, Josef. "Sigmund Freuds Beziehungen zu seinem Geburtsort Freiberg (Pribor) und zu Mähren." *Clio Medica,* 3 (1968):167–80.

Schiller, Friedrich. *The Robbers.* Trans. R. J. Lamport. New York: Penguin, 1979.

Schliemann, Heinrich. *Ilios: The City and Country of the Trojans.* New York: Harper, 1881.

Schönau, Walter. *Sigmund Freuds Prosa: Literarische Elemente seines Stils.* Stuttgart: Metzler, 1968.

Schopenhauer, Arthur. *Parerga and Parlipomena.* Trans. E. F. J. Payne. 2 vols. Oxford: Clarendon Press, 1974.

———. *Sämtliche Werke.* Ed. Paul Deussen. 15 vols. Munich: R. Pier, 1911–33.

———. *The World as Will and Representation.* Trans. by E. F. J. Payne. 2 vols. New York: Dover, 1969.

Schorske, Carl. *Fin-de-siècle Vienna.* New York: Knopf, 1980.

———. "Freud: The Psycho-archeology of Civilizations." *Proceedings of the Massachusetts Historical Society,* 92 (1980):52–67.

Schur, Max. *Freud: Living and Dying.* New York: International Universities Press, 1972.

———. "Some Additional 'Day Residues' of the Specimen Dream of Psychoanalysis." In Kanzer and Glenn, 87–116.

———. "Weitere Tagesreste zum Traummuster." *Der unbekannte Freud.* Ed. Jürgen vom Scheidt. Munich: Kinder Verlag, 1974:116–49.

Shengold, Leonard. "Freud and Joseph." In Kanzer and Glenn, 67–86.

———. "The Metaphor of the Journey in *The Interpretation of Dreams.*" In Kanzer and Glenn, 51–65.

Silberer, Herbert. "Phantasie und Mythos." *Jahrbuch für Psychoanalytische und Psychopathologische Forschungen* 2 (1910):541–622.

Silverman, Barry. "Freud's Psychology and Its Organic Foundation: Sexuality and Mind-Body Interactions." *Psychoanalytic Review,* 72 (Summer 1985):203–28.

Silverman, Debora Leah. "Nature, Nobility and Neurology: The Ideological Origins of 'Art Nouveau' in France, 1889–1900." Ph.D. diss., Princeton University, 1983.

Stanescu, Heinz. "Ein Gelegenheitsgedicht des jungen Sigmund Freud—Hochzeitscarmen," *Deutsch für Ausländer.* Ed. Hermann Kessler. Königswinter: Verlag für Sprachmethodik, 1967, 13–18.

———. "Unbekannte Briefe des jungen Sigmund Freud an einen rumänischen Freund," *Neue Literatur, Zeitschrift des Schriftstellerverbandes des R.V.R.*, 16 (June 1965):123–29.

———. "Young Freud's Letters to his Rumanian Friend, Silberstein." *The Israel Annals of Psychiatry and Related Disciplines,* 9 (Dec. 1971):195–209.

Stephenson, Kurt. "August Daniel von Binzer." *Darstellungen und Quellen zur Geschichte der deutschen Einheitsbewegung im neunzehnten und zwanzigsten Jahrhundert.* Ed. Kurt Stephenson, Alexander Scharff, and Wolfgang Klötzer. Vol. 5. Heidelberg: C. Winter, 1965.

———. "Charakterköpfe der Studentenmusik." *Darstellungen und Quellen zur Geschichte der deutschen Einheitsbewegung im neunzehnten und zwanzigsten Jahrhundert.* Ed. Kurt Stephenson, Alexander Scharff, and Wolfgang Klötzer. Vol. 6. Heidelberg: C. Winter, 1965.

Stewart, Larry. "Freud before Oedipus." *Journal of the History of Biology,* 9 (Fall 1976):215–28.

Stiehl, Karl. "Mark Twain in der Wiener Presse zur Zeit seines Aufenthaltes in Wien 1897–1899." Diss., University of Vienna, 1953.

Stoeffler, F. Ernest. *German Pietism during the Eighteenth Century.* Leiden: Brill, 1973.

Sulloway, Frank. *Freud, Biologist of the Mind.* New York: Basic Books, 1979.

Sutter, Berthold. *Die Badenischen Sprachverordnungen von 1897.* 2 vols. Graz-Cologne: Verlag Hermann Böhlaus, 1960.

Swales, Peter. "Freud, Johann Weier, and the Status of Seduction: The Role of the Witch in the Conception of Fantasy." Privately published by the author, 1982.

———. "Freud, Minna Bernays and the Conquest of Rome." *New American Review,* 1 (Spring/Summer 1982):1–23.

Swan, Jim. "*Mater* and Nannie: Freud's Two Mothers and the Discovery of the Oedipus Complex." *American Imago,* 31 (Spring 1974):1–64.

Tennyson, A. B. *Sartor Called Resartus.* Princeton: Princeton University Press, 1965.

Trosman, Harry. "The Cryptomnesic Fragment in the Discovery of Free Association." In Gedo and Pollock, 229–53.

Trosman, Harry, and Roger Dennis Simmons. "The Freud Library." *Journal of the American Psychoanalytic Association,* 21 (1973):646–87.

Twain, Mark. "Stirring Times in Austria." *The Writings of Mark Twain.* Vol. 22. New York: Harper, 1929.

Volkelt, Johannes. *Kants kategorischer Imperativ und die Gegenwart.* Vienna: Leseverein d.d.s., 1875.

Wartofsky, Marx W. *Feuerbach.* Cambridge: Cambridge University Press, 1977.

Wittels, Fritz. *Freud and His Time.* New York: Grosset & Dunlap, 1931.

Index

nalys
s are st
ng and i
f the cu
ortant re
and in his

J. McGrat
of Roches
n the Unive
uthor of *Dio*
Austria.

icanc
sial. M
e first
hoana
erest

istor
is P
Be
opulis